English

Writing and Skills

CORONADO
FIRST COURSE

Critical Readers and Contributors

The authors and the publisher wish to thank the following people, who helped to evaluate and to prepare materials for this series:

Charles L. Allen, Baltimore Public Schools, Baltimore, Maryland
Kiyoko B. Bernard, Huntington Beach High School, Huntington Beach, California
Sally Borengasser, Rogers, Arkansas
Deborah Bull, New York City, New York
Joan Colby, Chicago, Illinois
Phyllis Goldenberg, North Miami Beach, Florida
Beverly Graves, Worthington High School, Worthington, Ohio
Pamela Hannon, Kirk Middle School, Cleveland, Ohio
Lawana Indermill, San Diego State University, San Diego, California
Carol Kuykendall, Houston Public Schools, Houston, Texas
Wayne Larkin, Roosevelt Junior High School, Blaine, Minnesota
Nancy MacKnight, University of Maine, Orono, Maine
Catherine McCough, Huntington Beach Union School District, California
Kathleen McKee, Coronado High School, Coronado, California
Lawrence Milne, Ocean View High School, Long Beach, California
Al Muller, East Carolina University, Greenville, North Carolina
Dorothy Muller, East Carolina University, Greenville, North Carolina
Arlene Mulligan, Stanley Junior High School, San Diego, California
John Nixon, Santa Ana Junior College, Santa Ana, California
Jesse Perry, San Diego City Schools, California
Christine Rice, Huntington Beach Union School District, Huntington Beach, California
Linda C. Scott, Poway Unified High School District, Poway, California
Jo Ann Seiple, University of North Carolina at Wilmington, Wilmington, North Carolina
Joan Yesner, Brookline, Massachusetts
Seymour Yesner, Brookline Education Center, Massachusetts
Arlie Zolynas, San Diego State University, San Diego, California

Classroom Testing

The authors and the publisher also wish to thank the following teachers, who participated in the classroom testing of materials from this series:

David Foote, Evanston High School East, Evanston, Illinois
Theresa Hall, Nokomis Junior High School, Minneapolis, Minnesota
Carrie E. Hampton, Sumter High School, Sumter, South Carolina
Pamela Hannon, Proviso High School East, Maywood, Illinois
Wayne Larkin, Roosevelt Junior High School, Blaine, Minnesota
Grady Locklear, Sumter High School, Sumter, South Carolina
William Montgomery, Hillcrest High School, Jamaica, New York
Josephine H. Price, Sumter High School, Sumter, South Carolina
Barbara Stilp, North High School, Minneapolis, Minnesota
Joseph Thomas, Weymouth North High School, East Weymouth, Massachusetts
Travis Weldon, Sumter High School, Sumter, South Carolina

Teachers of the Huntington Beach Union High School Writing Program

Cassandra C. Allsop	Carol Kasser	Catherine G. McCough
Eric V. Emery	Patricia Kelly	Cathleen C. Redman
Michael Frym	Stephanie Martone	Christine Rice
Barbara Goldfein	Lawrence Milne	Michael D. Sloan
Joanne Haukland	Richard H. Morley	S. Oliver Smith
Don Hohl	John S. Nixon	Glenda Watson
Sandra Johnson		

Dorothy Augustine, District Consultant in Writing

English

Writing and Skills

W. Ross Winterowd
Patricia Y. Murray

 **CORONADO PUBLISHERS**

San Diego   Chicago   Orlando   Dallas

The Series:

English: Writing and Skills, First Course

English: Writing and Skills, Second Course

English: Writing and Skills, Third Course

English, Writing and Skills, Fourth Course

English: Writing and Skills, Fifth Course

English: Writing and Skills, Complete Course

A test booklet and teacher's manual are available for each title.

W. ROSS WINTEROWD is the Bruce R. McElderry Professor of English at the University of Southern California. Since 1975, Dr. Winterowd has traveled widely as a writing consultant for numerous schools in North America.

PATRICIA Y. MURRAY is Director of Composition at DePaul University in Chicago. Dr. Murray taught junior and senior high school English in the Los Angeles city schools. She is also a consultant in curriculum development and teacher training.

Printed in the United States of America

ISBN 0-15-717000-4

Table of Contents

1   *Writing*

7   Persuasive Writing

8   Writing Poems and Stories

9   *Writing Friendly Letters*

10   *Writing Social and Business Letters*

2   *Grammar and Usage*

19 Interjections

20 Sentence Structure

3 Mechanics

21 Punctuation

22   *Capitalization*

4   *Language Resources*

23   *Vocabulary and Spelling*

24   *Changes in Language*

25 Library Skills

26 Reference Works

27   *Speaking and Listening Skills*

1
Writing

1 The Writing Process

From Ideas to Words

As a teenager Langston Hughes was already writing the poetry that would one day make him a famous man. In the following selection Charlemae Rollins describes how the young poet began to write one of his best-known poems.

Model: *From Ideas to Words*

As you read, notice how ideas came to Langston Hughes and how he responded to them.

The teen-ager gazed idly through the grimy window as the train rolled across the Illinois prairies. All at once the sound of the wheels changed. The windows joggled and clattered in rhythm with the whine of the rails beneath the train. The young man sat up straighter and looked more closely at the scene outside. Instead of houses and fences, trees and telephone poles, he saw metal girders black against the sunset sky. The train was on a bridge—a railway bridge—and below the moving train flowed a vast wash of muddy water stretching to the western horizon.

"The Mississippi River. It's the ol' Mississip'," he murmured. He had read about it in his geography books. He had even crossed it several times where it was narrower and less conspicuous. He knew it, too, from his histories. Not only was this river a part of the history of the country, but it was also part of his own life and the lives of his people. It was the same river down which Abraham Lincoln had traveled to New Orleans, where he had seen the slave markets that changed his life and his point of view. Here it was, the great river at last, sneaking up on the young man just when he was feeling low.

Words jumped into his head. He listened to the words that almost spoke aloud to him. Another poem. A poem to keep him company and drive away the homesick feelings on this long journey. He reached·into his pocket for pencil and paper. All he found was the stump of a pencil and an envelope.

He began writing the words that sang themselves into his brain—"I've known rivers. . . ."

Indeed, he had known rivers, some intimately, some not so well, but he had known and felt them in his imagination. He had read about them, heard about them, studied about them, not only in textbooks and novels, but also in the tales told him by the old folks among his people.

He thought of the Ohio, which Eliza crossed to escape the bloodhounds in *Uncle Tom's Cabin;* the Nile, where the Egyptian princess found the baby Moses, who was to become the leader and emancipator of his people; the Euphrates, where a dark-skinned people watched the stars and invented a way to keep exact records by their light; and the Congo, flowing through the green jungles of Africa and into his memory and his blood. He wrote the words as they rushed into his mind:[1]

> I've known rivers:
> I've known rivers ancient as the world and older than
> the flow of human blood in human veins.

An *emancipator* is a person responsible for freeing other people.

---

[1]From *Black Troubadour: Langston Hughes,* by Charlemae H. Rollins. Copyright 1970 by Charlemae H. Rollins. Published by Rand McNally. Reprinted by permission of J. W. Rollins, Jr.

My soul has grown deep like the rivers.
I bathed in the Euphrates when dawns were young.
I built my hut near the Congo and it lulled me to sleep.
I looked upon the Nile and raised the pyramids above it.
I heard the singing of the Mississippi when Abe Lincoln
went down to New Orleans, and I've seen its muddy
bosom turn all golden in the sunset.
I've known rivers:
Ancient, dusky rivers.
My soul has grown deep like the rivers.[2]

Think and Discuss

1. Where was Langston Hughes when he got the first idea for his poem?

2. From what sources did Hughes get other ideas for his poem? For example, he remembered things he had read in textbooks. What other sources of information did he remember?

3. How did Hughes record his ideas?

Langston Hughes' poem, like all writing, is the product of the *writing process:* the process of turning ideas into words on paper. A student writing a note to a friend, a reporter writing an article, a senator writing a speech, and a poet writing a poem all use variations of the writing process.

This book divides the writing process into three stages: *prewriting, writing,* and *postwriting.* In the sections that follow, you will learn about and practice these stages.

Writing Practice 1: *From Ideas to Words*

Langston Hughes had a special feeling for the Mississippi River. To him, the river represented much of his people's history. Think of a place or object for which you have a special feeling. Perhaps the place or object represents your family background or the area where you live. Copy the first line of Langston Hughes' poem. Replace the word *rivers* with your place or object: "I've known *mountains*"; "I've known *city streets*." Then in your own words, continue describing your feelings about the place or object as Langston Hughes did in his poem.

---

[2]"The Negro Speaks of Rivers" by Langston Hughes. Copyright 1926 by Alfred A. Knopf, Inc. and renewed 1954 by Langston Hughes. Reprinted from *Selected Poems of Langston Hughes* by Langston Hughes. By permission of Alfred A. Knopf, Inc.

Prewriting

Prewriting is the exciting first stage of the writing process: gears move, wheels spin, thoughts connect, sparks fly. Any activity that gets your brain moving on a writing task is prewriting. A student writer described a common prewriting experience: "My mind is totally baffled, then something triggers a good idea. It feels great!"

How does prewriting help? Let's take a possible assignment: writing about an early childhood experience. Your teacher gives you time to discuss memories of kindergarten with other classmates. As you talk, the rust crumbles off your memory, and you recall cutting out pictures, drawing monsters, and playing on the jungle gym. A flood of memories rushes to your brain as you talk and listen. That's one kind of prewriting activity. It gets you started thinking.

Writing

Writing is the stage in which you form your ideas into sentences and paragraphs. Sometimes you don't know exactly what you want to say until you begin writing sentences and paragraphs. You discover your thoughts as you write. When this happens, prewriting and writing are the same. Good writers are not afraid to start without knowing exactly what they will say. They know that they can always change what they write.

Postwriting

The third stage of the writing process, *postwriting*, involves making changes in your writing. Postwriting involves *revising* (improving the content and organization of your writing) and *proofreading* (correcting errors in spelling, grammar, usage, and mechanics). Postwriting also includes sharing your writing with others.

Prewriting to Find Ideas

Many prewriting techniques can help you discover ideas for writing. In this section you will practice three basic prewriting techniques: brainstorming, clustering, and free writing.

Brainstorming

To *brainstorm* is to let your thoughts roam freely over a subject. Although brainstorming can be done alone, it works best with a small group. The first step is to concentrate on a subject—perhaps a word, a poem, a picture—for about three to five minutes. Then let your mind explore the subject without trying to force your thoughts in any one direction.

If you brainstorm in a group, say each thought aloud as it comes to you. Your thoughts will help other members of the group think of ideas; in turn, their ideas will help you. One person in the group can write down the ideas.

The purpose of brainstorming is to gather as many ideas as possible on a subject. Do not stop to decide whether or not ideas are "good." You can go over the list later and choose the ideas that are most helpful.

Model: Brainstorming

One seventh-grade class brainstormed on the subject *school lockers*. Notice that their ideas are written as words, phrases, or sentences.

School Lockers

pictures
avalanches
stickers
messy and crowded
They need repair.
dented
unsafe
need to be redesigned
books
gross smells
gym clothes
locker numbers
old sandwiches
ants
assignments and papers
trash
socks
money
locker partner

The above list shows how brainstorming works. One person thought of a description of a locker: *messy and crowded*. Other students contributed related ideas: *they need repair, dented, unsafe, need to be redesigned*. These thoughts could lead to several possible writing subjects, such as *why our school lockers are in bad repair* or *the ideal locker design*.

After you have decided on a subject, you can often gather more information by brainstorming again. Then look at your list. You may want to combine, delete, or add ideas.

Writing Practice 2: *Brainstorming an Invention*

Brainstorm on an idea of your own or one of the following five topics to come up with a new invention.

1. new rainwear

2. an ideal supermarket

3. transportation of the future

4. twenty-first century music equipment

5. new alarm clock

Clustering

Sometimes your mind works as though you had an electric current running through it. You think of one idea, and that idea sparks a related idea from somewhere in your mind. By drawing circles and lines around words on a piece of paper, you can use the connections your mind makes to help you discover ideas for writing. This prewriting method is called *clustering*.

Think of a word or phrase that interests you. Write this word or phrase on a sheet of paper and draw a circle around it:

Now let your mind wander over your subject, just as you did when brainstorming. As you think of related ideas, write them around your subject. The following example shows how to do this:

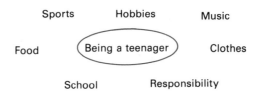

Draw circles around the related ideas and attach them to the first subject with lines.

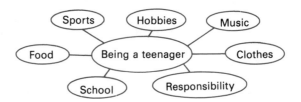

Now let your thoughts wander over the related subjects. As your mind makes connections between these ideas and new ones, continue to write down the ideas and circle them. Connect circles that are related to each other. The following example shows how your paper might look after several minutes of making connections:

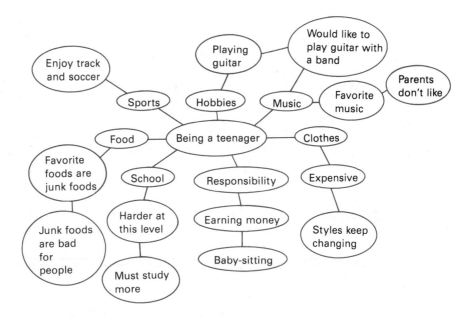

In these connections the writer can find several ideas for a paper. One is the increased responsibility that being a teenager brings. Other ideas are junk foods and why they are harmful, and why certain music seems to appeal especially to teenagers.

Writing Practice 3: *Clustering*

In the center of a piece of paper, write one of the following subjects or make one up. Draw a circle around it. Let your mind wander freely over the subject. As you get new ideas, write them around the center and circle them. Draw lines from your subject to each new idea and continue to make connections.

1. Science fiction
2. Monsters
3. Earning money
4. Weekends
5. Growing up

Next, read over the cluster you have made. On a sheet of paper, list three ideas from your cluster that you could use as subjects for writing.

Free Writing

One of the best ways to find ideas for writing is to free write. To do this, set a time limit of approximately five minutes. Write continuously, without worrying about correctness and without reading your words, until the time period ends. The first time you try this, you may be surprised at how often you have the urge to correct errors or to evaluate your writing before the end of the time period. But every time your pen or pencil stops, your flow of ideas stops, too. Free writing can help you produce new ideas and original phrases.

At the end of the time limit, read your free writing. Underline the good ideas and original phrases that you find. Later, during the next stage of the writing process, you can form that material into sentences and paragraphs.

Model: Free Writing

Read the free writing that Anna did about the time she borrowed her older sister's ten-speed bicycle. Notice which words and phrases she underlined later to use in writing.

> I begged to ride my sister's ten-speed, she said sure, as long as you don't go down the hill. As I went riding around there was a burning feeling inside of me that I wanted to go down that hill. I checked around. My sister was playing with her friends. Watching me, too far away to catch me. I made my break. I could barely reach the pedals, but I built up as much speed as I could. My sister came running after me, screaming. My plan was to go down to the bottom of the hill,

stop, and come back up. There was only one problem with this plan I couldn't work the brakes. I went flying down the hill at speeds our car had never gone. Wind blowing through my hair so fast I thought I'd be bald by the time I hit the bottom I WAS SCARED!

The bottom of the hill finally came, I hit a dirt mound, and flew about twenty feet.

Even though Anna's free writing contains grammatical errors, it also shows vivid, original use of language. The parts Anna underlined will help make her writing lively.

Writing Practice 4: *Free Writing*

Free write about an experience that made an impression on you when you were younger. Your teacher will tell you when to start writing and when to stop. Write steadily, without worrying about errors and without reading what you have written. If you get stuck, repeat the last word you wrote until a new idea comes along. After your teacher tells you to stop writing, read your work and underline the parts you like best. Save your work for a later assignment.

Prewriting for Greater Depth

Finding a subject is the first step in prewriting. The next step is to gather details about your subject. Two other prewriting methods, *questioning* and *changing viewpoints*, can help you explore subjects in depth.

The Six Basic Questions

Using a set of basic questions can help you discover information on a subject.

The six basic questions are *who? what? where? when? why?* **and** *how?*

Suppose you have thought about the subject *A frightening experience*. The following are questions about the experience:

1. *Who* was involved in the experience?

2. *What* happened?

3. *Where* did the experience happen?

4.   *When* did the experience happen?

5.   *Why* did the experience happen?

6.   *How* did the experience make you feel?

Answering the questions gave one student the following information about a frightening experience:

1.   The experience involved me and the two-year-old boy I was baby-sitting.

2.   I took the little boy, Juan, to the park. He was playing in the sandbox, and I was reading my library book. I got so involved in my book that I forgot to check on Juan. When I remembered to look up, the little boy was gone. I looked all around the sandbox, but couldn't find him. I ran across the park and found him standing at the edge of the busy street.

3.   The experience happened in our neighborhood park.

4.   The experience happened last Saturday afternoon.

5.   This experience happened because I was not being very responsible.

6.   When I first missed Juan, I was just a little worried. I thought he might have gone over to the swings. But when I couldn't find him there, I was terrified. All the things that could have happened to him went through my mind. Later I felt ashamed for not taking better care of Juan after his parents had trusted me.

You should answer the six basic questions with as many details as possible, just as the student did when thinking about the frightening experience. The answers to questions 2 and 6 are the longest because the writer's purpose is to tell the story of a personal experience.

Writing Practice 5: *The Six Basic Questions*

Select one of the subjects listed below or make up one of your own. On a sheet of paper, write down the *who? what? where? when? why?* and *how?* questions to ask yourself about your subject. Then write detailed answers to your questions.

1. A happy experience

2. An unusual experience

3. A family celebration

4. A person whom you admire

5. An experience with a pet

6. An exciting experience

7. A funny experience

8. An experience that helped you grow up

9. An interesting experience of a friend or relative

10. A place where you like to go

Purpose

An important part of prewriting is deciding on a purpose for writing.

The purpose of writing helps direct the questions that you ask about a subject. For example, the picture on page 14 shows Georgia O'Keeffe, a famous American painter. One purpose for writing about Georgia O'Keeffe might be to *tell the story* of her life and her painting. Another purpose might be to *describe* the artist as she appears in the picture. The following list is a set of questions for gathering details about Georgia O'Keeffe's life and work:

Purpose: To Tell Georgia O'Keeffe's Life Story

1. *Who* is Georgia O'Keeffe?

2. *When* was she born?

3. *Where* was she born?

4. *When* did she first begin to paint?

5. *What* was her early painting like?

6. *How* did her painting change?

7. *Why* did her painting change?

8. *What* are her most recent paintings like?

9. *Why* is Georgia O'Keeffe famous?

Writing about a person's life and accomplishments calls for many kinds of details. The six basic questions help you gather these details.

Sometimes, however, it is helpful to concentrate on one or two of the six basic questions. For example, the second purpose for writing about Georgia O'Keeffe is to *describe* the artist as she appears in the above picture. The list below is a set of questions which will be helpful in gathering details about the picture of Georgia O'Keeffe:

Purpose: To Describe Georgia O'Keeffe from a Picture

1. *What* does Georgia O'Keeffe's face look like?

2. *What* is the expression on her face?

3. *What* kind of dress is she wearing?

4. *How* is she wearing her hair?

5. *How* is she holding her hands?

6. *What* do her hands look like?

7. *What* is the object above Georgia O'Keeffe?

8. *How* does the object resemble the artist?

9. *What* kind of person does the artist seem to be?

10. *What* could she be thinking?

The questions for describing the picture of Georgia O'Keeffe are mostly *what?* questions. These questions ask for details about the artist's picture.

Another purpose for writing is to *explain how something works*—a bicycle, for example:

1. *How* does the bicycle go forward and backward?

2. *How* do the gears work?

3. *How* does the rider stay balanced on a two-wheeled bicycle?

Supporting an opinion is another purpose for writing. You may feel that teenagers should not be limited in their television viewing time or that they should have an allowance. *Why?* questions ask for details about reasons for an opinion:

1. *Why* should teenagers have unlimited television time?

2. *Why* do parents want to limit television time?

3. *Why* do teachers want to limit television time?

The six basic questions ask for basic information about a subject. The purpose for writing tells you which of the questions to think most about while gathering information. If you write about a complicated subject, such as a person's life, you may need to concentrate on several different kinds of questions. However, when your purpose is to describe, to explain how something works, or to give reasons for an opinion, you can concentrate on one kind of question.

Writing Practice 6: *Purpose*

Select one of the subjects on the next page or make up one of your own. Decide on a purpose for writing about the subject. Write a set of questions that ask for details about the subject. Then write the answers to your questions.

1. How to play backgammon

2. A wet cat

3. The lion at the zoo

4. How to roller skate

5. Your mother, father, or other adult relative

6. A snowball fight

7. A haunted house

8. A nightmare

9. President George Washington

10. The Reverend Martin Luther King, Jr.

Changing Viewpoints

A *viewpoint* is a way of looking at someone or something.

Study the picture below. At first, it may seem that the picture is upside down. You may want to turn the picture so that the trees grow upward instead of downward. Now look at the picture again, this time concentrating on the fish.

From the fish's viewpoint, the picture is not upside down. The fish is in the lake, and trees are reflected in the surface. For most people it is natural to look at the world from their own viewpoints, but one way to gather information for writing is to change viewpoints.

The Sword and the Stone, by T. H. White, is a book about the boyhood of King Arthur. In the book, Merlin the Magician used his magic power to change the young king into different animals. The boy became a fish, a bird, a hedgehog, and several other animals. Through these changes he acquired new viewpoints and learned about the wondrous life around him.

Although people cannot become animals, they can change their viewpoints. A teenager can look at a subject as an adult might. A person of one national origin can try to imagine how a person of a different nationality would think. Even brothers and sisters can try to understand each other's attitudes.

Suppose you decide to write about the rules at your local swimming pool. You feel that they are too strict and give reasons such as the following ones for your opinion:

1. It isn't much fun when we can't play games around the pool.

2. I hate wearing a bathing cap to swim.

3. The lifeguard won't let a person with even a small cut go into the water.

Now take the lifeguard's viewpoint and ask yourself *why*? questions about the rules. These questions give details such as the following ones:

1. The lifeguard is the person responsible for the safety of each person at the pool. Playing games around the pool is dangerous.

2. Long hair clogs the pool filter. Cleaning a filter means extra work for an employee.

3. Germs from even a small cut can spread through the water.

Writing Practice 7: *Changing Viewpoints*

Select one of the subjects on the following page or make up one of your own. Use your imagination to write about the subject from the unusual viewpoint described.

1. A bath, from a cat's viewpoint

2. A houseplant that needs water, from the plant's viewpoint

3. A picnic, from an ant's viewpoint

4. A gym class, from a tennis shoe's viewpoint

5. Running a race, from a horse's viewpoint

6. A fish being caught, from the fish's viewpoint

7. A walk around the neighborhood, from a dog's viewpoint

8. Thanksgiving Day, from a turkey's viewpoint

9. A dark night, from a bat's viewpoint

10. A day at the zoo, from a gorilla's viewpoint

Revising

The word *revise* means to make changes in a piece of writing. Most writers make some revisions while they are writing. For example, suppose you write about your first day of school this year. Early in the entry you write a sentence like this:

I dropped everything on the floor.

After thinking about the sentence, you realize you need details to describe what really happened. Without details, readers cannot share the experience with you, so you cross out the sentence and write a second one, adding details.

~~I dropped everything on the floor.~~

In English class I jumped up to sharpen my pencil, and everything in my lap—papers, pen, books, and my collection of baseball cards—fell noisily to the floor.

Most writers also go over a finished piece of writing for a final revision. It is often the third or fourth revision that makes writing sound simple and direct, as though the words flowed from the writer's pen without effort. Robert Frost's poem "Stopping by Woods on a Snowy Evening" is such a piece of writing.

Model: Revision

Robert Frost said that the first verse of the poem was easy to write, but he made many changes in the last three verses before he was satisfied. The poem on the left is "Stopping by Woods on a Snowy Evening" as you see it printed in books. On the right are the last three verses of the poem in Robert Frost's handwriting, showing some of the changes that he made during the revision.

**Stopping by Woods
on a Snowy Evening**[1]
Whose woods these are I think I know.
His house is in the village, though;
He will not see me stopping here
To watch his woods fill up with snow.

My little horse must think it queer
To stop without a farmhouse near
Between the woods and frozen lake
The darkest evening of the year.

He gives his harness bells a shake
To ask if there is some mistake.
The only other sound's the sweep
Of easy wind and downy flake.

The woods are lovely, dark, and deep,
But I have promises to keep,
And miles to go before I sleep,
And miles to go before I sleep.

Robert Frost

---

[1]"Stopping by Woods on a Snowy Evening" from *The Poetry of Robert Frost* edited by Edward Connery Lathem. Copyright 1923, © 1969 by Holt, Rinehart and Winston. Copyright 1951 by Robert Frost. Reprinted by permission of the Estate of Robert Frost and Holt, Rinehart and Winston, Publishers.

Let's follow a student's story through the postwriting stage. Here Jenny wrote on memories of being five years old.

When I was about 5 years old, every day after school I ate peanut butter and jelly sandwiches, made very soggy by dipping it into milk. When I got bored sometimes I would run around outside and pour salt on snails and watch them bubble up and die. On the weekends my sister and I had picnics on the roof and if anyone walked by we bombed balloons with water on them down on their heads. My favorite game to play was cowboys and indians. One day I spent the weekend at my friends house. I had one problem. It was going to be my mom and dads anniversary on Monday and I wanted to get something very special. But I had no money. I went to a garage sale and I bought a lucky charm for 50 cents. Walking to the car, I was very sad cause I had no presents. I decided to keep my lucky charm in my pocket. Then suddenly sitting in a pool of oil, I saw something gold it was a 14 karate gold bracelet. We stopped at the gas station on our long ride home, and when I opened the door there on the ground was a mans timex watch. I couldn't believe my eyes. I got to terrific presents for 50 cents because of my lucky charm.

For help with her revision, Jenny asked a classmate to read her story. The classmate used a response sheet to comment.

Response Sheet   Writer's Name
                                                    Jenny

1.   List two things you liked about this story.
        I like the story about the lucky charm.
        I like the way you show how amazed you were.

2.   List two things you'd like to see changed
        The begining is fun, but could be cut out.
        Rewrite the lucky charm story to make it clearer.
        One day I spent a weekend ---??

                                                    Sam
                                                    Editor's Name

From the response sheet, Jenny learned that the best part of her story was the part about the lucky charm. She also knows that parts of her story were confusing to her reader. What does Jenny do now? Revise! Here's Jenny's revised story:

When I was 5 I ate peanut butter and jelly sandwiches, poured salt on snails, and dropped water balloons from our roof onto strangers. What I remember the most about being 5 is the day I bought my lucky charm. It was supposed to be a fun weekend for me at Kim's house, but I was worried about what I'd do Monday. Monday was my parents anniversary and I wanted to get them something special. I had no money. On Sunday Kim and I went to a garage sale. I bought a lucky charm, for fifty cents. As I walked to the car I was pleased with my charm, but sad to have no present for my parents. Then I saw, in a pool of oil, a bracelet -- a 14 karat gold bracelet! On my way home from the sale, we stopped at a gas station. I remember that I reached into my pocket to touch my lucky charm. When I opened the door, on the ground was a mans timex watch. I couldn't believe my eyes! I spent 50 cents on a lucky charm and got to terrific presents.

Using a Checklist to Revise

Revision involves improving the content of your writing, as Jenny did after reading her partner's response sheet. A checklist like the one on the next page can help you revise on your own. Jenny used the checklist to make a few further changes in her story. Her revised story is on page 24.

Checklist for Revision

1. Does my writing have a clear focus?

2. Do I need to add more details?

3. Is my writing organized in a way that makes sense?

4. Are there any unnecessary parts I should leave out?

5. Is my writing style appropriate for my purpose and audience?

6. Are my sentences clear and complete?

7. Could I improve my choice of words?

Proofreading

The final step in revising your writing is *proofreading*, which means checking for errors in capitalization, spelling, punctuation, and grammar. The time to proofread is after you have finished revising. The following list covers important points to remember in proofreading. As you proofread, check your work carefully against the list.

Checklist for Proofreading

1. Each sentence begins with a capital letter.

2. Each sentence ends with a period, question mark, or exclamation point.

3. Each word is spelled correctly.

4. All proper nouns and adjectives are capitalized.

5. Word endings such as *-s*, *-ing*, and *-ed* are not omitted.

6. A singular verb is used with each singular subject and a plural verb with each plural subject.

7. The standard form of pronouns is used.

8. The paper is neat.

For Extra Help

For help with any of the areas on the Checklist for Proofreading, see the following chapters:

Capitalization	Chapter 22
Punctuation	Chapter 21
Spelling	Chapter 23
Subject-verb agreement	Chapter 14
Pronoun usage	Chapter 13

After the final revision, Jenny proofread her story and corrected errors. She used the following set of marks to show the needed corrections:

Proofreading Marks

Mark	Meaning	Example
≡	Use a capital letter	mr. Murchison
lc /	Use a lowercase letter	lc in the Doghouse
ℓ	Take it out	I saw ~~saw~~ it.
∧	Add	Where is it?
¶	Indent paragraph	¶ When my friends discouraged
Sp○	Spell correctly	Do you beleive Sp

After revising and proofreading, Jenny has a piece of writing ready to share.

When I was five I ate peanut butter and jelly sandwiches, poured salt on snails, and dropped water balloons from our roof onto strangers. But what I remember most is the day I bought my lucky charm.

It was supposed to be a fun weekend for me at Kim's house, but I was worried about what I'd do on Monday. Monday was my parents' anniversary, and I wanted to get them something special. I had no money. On Sunday, Kim and I went to a garage sale. I bought a lucky charm for fifty cents. As I walked to the car, pleased with my lucky charm but sad to have no present for my parents, I saw, in a pool of oil, a bracelet—a 14-karat gold bracelet!

On the way home from the sale, we stopped at a gas station. I remember that I reached into my pocket to touch my lucky charm. When I opened the car door, there on the ground was a man's Timex watch. It was unbelievable. I spent fifty cents on a lucky charm and got two terrific presents.

Ever since, my parents have called me Lucky Jenny Penny. But Lucky Jenny Penny isn't five any more.

Writing Practice 8: *Revising and Proofreading*

Take the free writing you did for Writing Practice 4 and use it as the basis for a story two or more paragraphs long. After you have written your story, revise it, using the Checklist for Revision on page 22. Finally, proofread your revised story and copy it neatly. Share it with your classmates as your teacher directs.

Sentence Variety:
Joining Sentences

Writing Varied Sentences

The story "The Tiger's Heart" by Jim Kjelgaard is about a man named Pepe who goes into the jungle to kill a tiger. In the following paragraph from the story, Pepe faces the tiger. His only weapon is a large knife called a *machete*. As you read, try to form a mental image of the action.

Model: *Writing Varied Sentences*

The tiger whirled, and hot spittle from his mouth splashed on the back of Pepe's left hand. Holding the machete before him, like a sword, he took a swift backward step. The tiger sprang, launching himself from the ground as though his rear legs were made of powerful steel springs, and coming straight up. His flailing left paw flashed at Pepe. It hooked in his shirt, ripping it away from the arm as though it were paper, and burning talons sank into the flesh. Red blood welled out.[1]

By carefully choosing his words, the writer helps you experience the excitement of the fight. When Jim Kjelgaard writes that the tiger's "rear legs were made of powerful steel springs," you can see the tiger and feel the danger. But there is more to writing than choosing which words to use.

An important part of writing is how a writer puts words together. Jim Kjelgaard knows that how words are put together is important. When he describes the attack of the tiger, the writer arranges his words in the following way:

The tiger sprang, launching himself from the ground as though his rear legs were made of powerful steel springs, and coming straight up.

The flow of words in this sentence helps readers experience the action. Suppose Jim Kjelgaard had used the same words in the following way:

---

[1]Excerpt from "The Tiger's Heart" by Jim Kjelgaard. Reprinted by permission of Esquire Magazine © 1951 by Esquire Publishing Inc.

The tiger sprang. The tiger launched himself from the ground. The tiger's rear legs were made of steel springs. The steel springs were powerful. The tiger came straight up.

The many short sentences do not help the action; instead, they slow it down.

In this part of the book, you will learn about different ways to put sentences together. Knowing different ways of putting sentences together is important for two reasons. First, variety helps make your writing interesting. Second, the way you put sentences together is important to the meaning of what you write.

The method you will use to learn different ways of putting sentences together is called *sentence combining*. Throughout the sentence-combining lessons in this unit, you will find writing assignments to help you practice the skills you learn.

Using Connectors

One way to combine sentences is to join them with words called *connectors*. Certain marks of punctuation can also join sentences. In this lesson you will learn how to join sentences with connectors and punctuation.

Connectors are words that let you join equal parts together. The first connectors you will work with are *and, but, or, for, yet, so,* and *nor*. (More information about connectors, also called *coordinating conjunctions*, is in Chapter 18.)

The examples below show how these combinations work:

Sentences: Jo made the eggs.
Jim fixed the pancakes (*and*)

Combined: Jo made the eggs, *and* Jim fixed the pancakes.

Sentences: JoAnn started to mow the lawn.
The lawnmower broke down before she finished. (*but*)

Combined: JoAnn started to mow the lawn, *but* the lawnmower broke down before she finished.

Sentences: This tree will have to be treated for termites.
I will have to cut it down. (*or*)

Combined: This tree will have to be treated for termites, *or* I will have to cut it down.

The word in parentheses is a *signal*, telling you which word to use to join the sentences. The signals in this lesson are (*and*), (*but*), (*for*), (*or*), (*yet*), (*so*), (*nor*).

The word *nor* is different from other connecting words because it causes a change in word order. Also, since *nor* means *not*, the word *not* in one of the sentences must be removed:

Sentences: I don't want to go to the movies.
I don't want to go to the beach. (*nor*)

Combined: I don't want to go to the movies, *nor do* I want to go to the beach.

Connecting words do more than join sentences; they also add meaning. The following list defines the connecting words:

Word	Meaning
and	plus; in addition
but	on the other hand; an exception; an opposite
for	because; as a result of
or	either one or the other
yet	still; nevertheless; in spite of
so	consequently; as a result; thus
nor	not; not either

When you use a connector to join sentences, think about the meaning the word adds. For example, consider the following sentences:

The small dog kept begging.

I gave him my hamburger.

Which of the following connectors gives the best meaning to the combined sentences?

The dog kept begging, *and* I gave him my hamburger.

The dog kept begging, *but* I gave him my hamburger.

The dog kept begging, *so* I gave him my hamburger.

Using the connector *and* does not show that the dog's begging had anything to do with getting the hamburger. The connector *but* makes it seem the dog got the hamburger in spite of begging. Only the connector *so* shows that the dog's getting the hamburger was a result of its begging.

Exercise 1: Using Connectors

Combine each of the following sets of sentences into one sentence by following the signals. Place a comma before the connector when you join the sentences. Copy each new sentence on a sheet of paper numbered 1–10.

Examples

a. The timekeepers gave the signal.
   The runners were on their way. (*and*)
   The timekeepers gave the signal, and the runners were on their way.

b. I looked high and low.
   I couldn't find my guitar. (*but*)
   I looked high and low, but I couldn't find my guitar.

1. The rains came too early in the summer.
   The raisin crop was ruined. (*so*)

2. Carlos was not admitted to the show.
   He had forgotten to bring his ticket. (*for*)

3. The pioneers who traveled the American prairies suffered from bad weather and poor food.
   They never lost their will to go on. (*yet*)

4. The actors refused to put on the costumes.
   They would not go out on the stage. (*nor*)

5. The flood had reached the steps of the courthouse.
   The citizens decided to head for higher ground. (*so*)

6. You must pay close attention.
   You will not understand this assignment. (*or*)

7. Franklin Delano Roosevelt was elected to a fourth term as President.
   He died before his term was completed. (*but*)

8. Pedro was not allowed to play baseball until his injured elbow healed.
   He was not permitted to continue his karate lessons. (*nor*)

9. The woman was badly injured in a skiing accident.
   She never lost her enthusiasm for the sport. (*yet*)

10. Connie has decided to stay home from school.
    She has not been feeling well for several days. (*for*)

Writing Practice: *Using Connectors*

Reread the story you wrote for Writing Practice 8. Revise it again, using the sentence-combining techniques you have learned in this lesson. Try to vary the length and patterns of your sentences so that your writing is interesting and flows smoothly.

2 The Writer's Notebook

A *Writer's Notebook* is a record of a writer's thoughts and feelings.

A Writer's Notebook is a good way to begin writing because you write about yourself, a subject you know better than any other. You may use your notebook as a way to remember experiences, to find ideas for other kinds of writing, or to explore your thoughts and feelings. Every time you make a notebook entry, you get more of the valuable writing practice that becoming a good writer requires. Entries may be made at any opportune moment.

In this chapter you will learn how to use the Writer's Notebook to develop your writing skills.

Keeping a Writer's Notebook

You can keep your notebook in a spiral binder or on separate sheets of paper in a Manila folder. The form is not as important as what you write. Your teacher will tell you how to organize your notebook.

Each time you write in your notebook, you write an *entry*. Some people write entries every day. As you do the assignments in this chapter, you will write several entries, but you may wish to do more than just those assignments. Remember that this is *your* notebook, and you can write in it as much and as often as you want. Remember that you will be sharing your notebook with your teacher and classmates, so you should not include material that you do not want others to read.

You can make your entries interesting for yourself and your readers by writing about experiences that are important to you. These are not neccessarily events that make headlines; they may stand out only in your own life. In fact, you may be the only one who knows about them. Experiences that are important to you are more likely to be interesting to readers because your strong feelings about them will, naturally, be reflected in your writing.

Recording Experiences

People often take pictures or make tape recordings to help them remember people, places, and events in their lives. With a notebook, you can create a record more valuable than either a picture or a tape. A camera preserves how a subject looks, and a tape recorder captures sound. In your notebook you can do both and more besides. You can use words to capture the thoughts and feelings that gadgets cannot.

When you take a photograph, you must set the focus correctly, or your picture will be blurry. You will not be able to make out details of the person or place, and the picture will not mean much to you later.

Good Writer's Notebook entries also have details.

Entries without details will have little value for you later, and they will not be interesting to your readers. For example, suppose a writer wrote the following notebook entry on May 3:

My friends gave me a surprise birthday party last night.

For some time the writer may remember details about the party, but soon they will begin to fade. By December, when the writer looks back at this entry to remember the experience, the sentence may have the same effect as a blurred photograph. Without details the entry has little interest for readers. The following entry about the same experience would be a better record for the writer and would interest more readers:

Model: *Using Details*

May 3

My friends gave me a surprise birthday party last night. At school yesterday my friend Joan was the only one who mentioned my birthday, and I thought everyone had forgotten. I was really disappointed, but I tried not to show it. To make things even worse, my mother didn't say much about my birthday, either. She just rushed around getting ready for work, as usual. I tried telling myself it wasn't such a big deal. "After all, I'm thirteen now," I thought. But that didn't help much.

The biggest event of the day was stopping by Joan's house on the way home to listen to her new record. Joan walked home with me, and when we opened the door, I didn't know whether to laugh or cry. My mother had come home from work early, and all the friends I thought had deserted me were there. Joan joined them, and they sang "Happy Birthday"—off key, as usual. I turned six shades of red! The gifts were silly and fun. Joan gave me a Fuzzy to put in my room. It's on a stick, and I turn the stick to show how I feel. If I'm upset and twirl the stick hard, Fuzzy's hair sticks out. Mom had my cat poster framed as a special surprise. I'll never forget the trouble everyone took for my birthday. To know my friends really care about me is the greatest gift anyone could ever give me.

Details make writing interesting only when they are included for a reason. The writer of the entry about the birthday party included details that related to feelings about the event. These included such details as how the writer's friends and mother at first ignored the birthday and the writer's later surprise. The writer did not include details about the mother's job or about the new record because these details had nothing to do with the party.

When you write a notebook entry, think about the six basic questions discussed in Chapter 1. Then answer those questions with the details you add to your entry. For example, suppose you want to write about your favorite book.

Your readers might ask questions like these:

1. *Who* are the people in the book? What are they like?

2. *What* exactly happens in the book? What does the title mean?

3. *When* does the story take place? If it takes place in the past or in the future, how are the people and places different from people and places today?

4. *Where* does the story take place? What are the surroundings like? How does the place affect the people?

5. *Why* do you like the book?

6. *How* did the book make you feel when you read it?

On a sheet of paper, write down questions that apply to your entry, and then make notes about the answers. Use the notes to write your entry, but remember that the entry should be more than a list of answers.

Writing Practice 1: *Using Details*

Write one sentence in your notebook about yourself, about another person, or about a place or event. Then add details to make a better record and to make the entry more interesting. Use the six basic questions to help you think of details, but include only details that relate to your subject.

Example

My grandmother is seventy years old.
   She walks five miles every day, goes roller-skating once a week, and can't understand why my friends and I

tire so easily. When my parents were painting our stucco house last year, she was always there to help. Once, when she was painting outside by herself, some people driving by were so impressed with her work that they asked if they could hire her to paint their house. In the summer she is always the first one to go swimming in the lake, long before the water warms up. She believes icy water is good for her circulation. All this she does in the evenings and on weekends because she has a full-time job. She's head gardener at a local nursery.

Using Sense Details

The five human senses are *sight, hearing, touch, taste,* and *smell.*

Using details about the senses helps readers see, hear, touch, taste, and smell what you describe.

In the following sets of sentences, the first sentence only *tells* about a sight, sound, touch, taste, or smell. The second sentence uses sense details to make the experience come alive. What are the words in the second sentence of each set that help you see, hear, feel, taste, or smell what the writer describes?

Sight

Just as we were ready to get rid of it, the tree bloomed.

Just as we were ready to cut it down for firewood, the gnarled, old tree sprouted tiny, bell-shaped blossoms.

Sound

In the middle of the pond, I heard a sound that told me our rubber raft was sinking.

In the middle of the silent pond, I heard a sputter and then a quiet but steady hiss that told me our rubber raft was sinking.

Touch

The best part of summer is walking barefoot on sidewalks and through grass.

The best part of summer is scorching my bare feet on gritty sidewalks and then cooling them off in the feathery softness of wet grass.

Taste

After eating the popcorn, I needed a drink and a napkin.

After eating the salted, buttery popcorn, I needed a cold drink and a napkin.

Smell

When I opened my locker after a three-week absence, it smelled.

When I opened my locker after a three-week absence, it smelled of unwashed tennis shoes and rotting apples.

Writing with sense details helps make your notebook a vivid record of your experiences. For example, think of a time you would like to remember, perhaps a windy Saturday you spent flying a kite. You remember how the red kite *looked* against the blue sky, and you also remember the *sound* of the kite flapping in the wind and the cries of your friends as you raced to keep up with it. You can think how it *felt* when gusts of wind almost jerked the kite from your hand. You also recall the wind and the *taste* of the cinnamon gum you and your friends shared.

Model: Using Sense Details

In the following paragraph from her autobiography *A Scottish Childhood*, Christian Miller describes the old castle where she lived. Notice the details of sight and touch.

> The front door of the castle was so heavy that a child could only just open it. Entering, one found oneself in the front hall, which had been made some three hundred years previously. It was a dark, depressing room, panelled with polished oak and hung with the stuffed heads of stags. The seldom used fireplace was flanked with carved angels, the supporters of our family coat of arms; they were roughly the size of a six-year-old child, and when I was about that age I used to hug them secretly, hoping that they might come to life and play with me, for I was often lonely.[1]

Think and Discuss

1. Christian Miller begins by describing the front door of the castle as "so heavy that a child could only just open it." Which other sentences contain descriptions that relate to touch or texture?

2. Which details in the paragraph relate to sight?

3. Imagine for yourself the front hall of the castle as Christian Miller has described it. What sounds might you hear as you walked into the room? What different smells might you encounter?

---

[1]From "A Scottish Childhood" by Christian Miller. Copyright © 1979 by Christian Miller. Reprinted by permission of Wallace & Sheil Agency, Inc. and Anthony Sheil Associates Ltd. Originally published in *The New Yorker* Magazine.

Writing Practice 2: *Using Sense Details*

Write a notebook entry describing a common object you have at home or in your classroom, such as a pencil sharpener, record album cover, garbage can, or a water faucet. Use sense details to help readers see, hear, feel, taste, and smell what you describe.

When you describe an object from memory, you can easily recall how it looks, but you must imagine how it sounds, feels, tastes, and smells. For example, suppose you describe a pair of old tennis shoes. You can remember that the shoes are dirty and that one shoestring is very short.

To help you imagine how the shoes sound, feel, taste, and smell, think of wearing the shoes yourself. Ask questions like these:

1. How do the shoes sound when they are wet and you walk across the floor?

2. How do the shoes sound when you run on pavement?

3. How do the shoes feel if they are very wet when you put them on?

4. How do the shoes feel if they have been drying in the sun before you put them on?

5. A baby chews on a pair of tennis shoes. How do they taste?

6. How do the shoes smell when they are dirty?

7. How do the shoes smell when they have been drying in the sun?

Before you begin to describe an object at home or in your classroom, examine it. Ask yourself questions that will help you describe how it sounds, feels, tastes, and smells, as well as how it looks.

Writing About Feelings

Recording your feelings in your Writer's Notebook can help you find good subjects for future writing assignments. (You will probably write best about things you have feelings about.) Some of your feelings are private—you may not want to share them. So, when you keep a Writer's Notebook to share with others, write about less private feelings.

The following entry was written by Anne Frank, a young girl who lived in Amsterdam, Holland, before World War II. Because the Frank family was of Jewish descent, they were forced to hide from Nazi soldiers in secret rooms above Mr. Frank's former office. During their two years in hiding, Anne never went outside, and she lived in constant fear of being discovered.

For her thirteenth birthday, just before she and her family went into hiding, Anne's parents gave her a diary (a kind of notebook), which she named "Kitty." She wrote letters to it until the Franks and the friends who hid with them were discovered by the Nazis and sent to concentration camps. Anne died, but her father survived and later published her diary as *The Diary of Anne Frank*. It is now considered a classic.

Model: Writing About Feelings

In the entry that follows, Anne Frank writes about simple experiences, but ones of importance to her.

Dear Kitty,   23 February 1944

It's lovely weather outside and I've quite perked up since yesterday. Nearly every morning I go to the attic where Peter works to blow the stuffy air out of my lungs. From my favorite spot on the floor I look up at the blue sky and the bare chestnut tree, on whose branches little raindrops shine, appearing like silver, and at the seagulls and the other birds as they glide on the wind.

He stood with his head against a thick beam, and I sat down. We breathed the fresh air, looked outside, and both felt that the spell should not be broken by words. We remained like this for a long time, and when he had to go up to the loft to chop wood, I knew that he was a nice fellow. He climbed the ladder, and I followed; then he chopped wood for about a quarter of an hour, during which time we still remained silent. I watched him from where I stood; he was obviously doing his best to show off his strength. But I looked out of the open window too, over a large area of Amsterdam, over all the roofs and on to the horizon, which was such a pale blue that it was hard to see the dividing line. "As long as this exists," I thought, "and I may live to see it, this sunshine, the cloudless skies, while this lasts, I cannot be unhappy."[1]

[1]Excerpt from *Anne Frank: The Diary of a Young Girl* by Anne Frank. Copyright 1952 by Otto H. Frank. Reprinted by permission of Doubleday & Company, Inc.

Think and Discuss

1. In this entry Anne Frank describes experiences that were important to her. She writes about what she sees from the attic and about watching her friend Peter, who was also in hiding. Why were these experiences important?

2. What words tell about Anne's feelings?

Writing Assignment I: *A Writer's Notebook Entry*

Write a notebook entry about an experience that was important to you. Include details about your thoughts and feelings, as well as about the event. Select one of the experiences listed below or choose one of your own.

Your first day in school this year

Earning money for the first time

Losing a pet

Saying good-bye to a good friend

Celebrating a birthday

Being disappointed

Winning an honor in the classroom or in sports

Moving to a new apartment or house

Going to a party or dance

Cooking a meal by yourself

Follow the steps on the next page.

A. Prewriting

To help you recall your important experience, ask yourself questions like the ones below. Make notes to yourself on a sheet of paper as you answer the questions.

1. *What* exactly happened?

2. *Where* were you when the experience happened? Was the place important to the experience?

3. *When* did the experience happen? Was the time important for some reason?

4. *Who* were the other people involved in your experience? How were the other people important to you?

5. *Why* did the experience happen? Was the reason important to you?

6. *How* did the event make you feel? What were your thoughts about the event?

B. Writing

Using your prewriting notes, write the story of your important experience. Include sense details and other details that apply to your subject. Write in a natural tone, as if you were talking to a friend.

C. Postwriting

Revise your entry, using the following questions:

1. Is your entry about an experience that was important to you?

2. Did you use details that make the entry interesting for readers?

3. Did you omit details that do not relate to the experience?

4. Did you use sense details to help readers experience what you describe?

5. Did you write in sentences that your readers can easily understand?

Make changes in your notebook entry until you can answer *yes* to each of the above questions. Copy your entry over when you finish revising.

Finally, proofread your entry, using the Checklist for Proofreading at the back of the book.

More Notebook Writing

As you work through the writing chapters, you will find more suggestions for notebook entries. You will also read about using your notebook as a source of ideas for other kinds of writing.

The following writing practice will give you suggestions for more practice in keeping a Writer's Notebook. If your teacher does not require you to do the practice, you may wish to use the suggestions as ideas for notebook writing for your own pleasure.

Writing Practice 3: *More Notebook Writing*

1. What do seasons mean to you? Does fall, winter, spring, or summer have a special meaning for you? On a sheet of paper, write words that come to you when you think of one season. Then write an entry describing what that season means to you. Use sense details to capture the sights, sounds, textures, tastes, and smells of the season.

2. Think of a time you were frightened or worried. Perhaps you were at home alone one night, or perhaps you came to class without studying for a big test. Write an entry describing the situation and how you felt. Use sense details to capture the sights, sounds, textures, tastes, and smells of the experience.

3. Think of a time when you did something that made you physically feel very bad or very good. Perhaps you were outside at night when the mosquitoes were biting, or perhaps you went for a refreshing swim on a hot day. Write an entry describing the experience and how it made you feel. Use sense details to capture the sights, sounds, textures, tastes, and smells of the experience.

4. What would be your perfect day? If you could go anywhere or do anything you wanted to for one day, where would you go and what would you do? What would your day be like? Write an entry describing this perfect day. Use sense details to capture the sights, sounds, textures, tastes, and smells of your perfect day.

Sentence Variety: Joining Sentences

Using a Pair of Connectors

One kind of connector is a *pair of connecting words*. The pair of connecting words most often used is *either . . . or*. This pair of words connects sentences of equal importance.

Sentences: This shirt must be washed.
I can't wear it to the party.

Combined: *Either* this shirt must be washed, *or* I can't wear it to the party.

Sentences: That is my book.
I don't know it when I see it.

Combined: *Either* this is my book, *or* I don't know it when I see it.

Notice that when the two sentences are combined, *either* is placed in front of the first sentence, and *or* is placed between the two sentences. A comma always comes before the *or*.

The words *either . . . or* mean "one or the other." What is the difference in the meaning of the following two sentences?

This shirt must be washed, *and* I can't wear it to the party.

Either this shirt must be washed, *or* I can't wear it to the party.

The first sentence means that the person will not wear the shirt to the party. The second sentence means the person may or may not wear the shirt to the party. If the shirt is washed, it will be worn to the party. If the shirt is not washed, it will not be worn to the party.

Exercise 1: Using a Pair of Connectors

Combine each of the following sets of sentences by using the pair of connecting words *either . . . or*. Write each new sentence on a sheet of paper numbered 1–10.

Example

a. You leave the kitchen at once.
I'll chase you out.
Either you leave the kitchen at once, or I'll chase you out.

1. Victory was close at hand.
The scouts had given us poor information.

2. He's awfully smart.
He's just lucky.

3. The apples were exceptionally good.
The children were starved for fresh fruit.

4. Ms. Kenyon is a very shy, retiring lady.
She doesn't like her neighbors.

5. Juan will improve in mathematics.
Mother will hire a tutor to help him study.

6. The trail was particularly well marked.
Fernando was an excellent guide.

7. You will visit me while I baby-sit for my little brother.
   We won't have a chance to talk together today.

8. Michael and Carla rode their bicycles to school.
   They must have walked.

9. Swimming is Michelle's favorite activity.
   She is intent on winning the gold ribbon for our team.

10. Banks must continue to use computers.
    They will be swamped with paper work.

Adverbs That Connect Sentences

Another group of words that connect sentences are certain adverbs such as *however, therefore, instead, besides, furthermore, nevertheless, consequently, moreover, on the other hand, indeed,* and *in fact*.

These adverbs show that special kinds of relationships exist between two sentences.

However, instead, on the other hand, and *nevertheless* show that one idea is followed by an opposite idea.

Therefore and *consequently* suggest that a conclusion is being made.

Besides, furthermore, and *moreover* signal that some additional point, idea, or detail will follow.

Indeed and *in fact* help emphasize the writer's point.

These sentence connectors are more formal than *and*, *but*, and *or*. They need a semicolon just in front of them, and they are usually followed by a comma. The adverb connector in parentheses after each pair of sentences below is the signal that tells you which connector to use.

Sentences: The nurse rushed to the operating room.
He was too late to stop the operation. (*however*)

Combined: The nurse rushed to the operating room; *however*, he was too late to stop the operation.

Sentences: The lioness hunted all day and all night for fresh food.
No mother ever tried so hard to find food for her cubs. (*indeed*)

Combined: The lioness hunted all day and all night for fresh food; *indeed*, no mother ever tried so hard to find food for her cubs.

Sentences You could answer this advertisement for a job as a clerk.
You could put a "job wanted" ad of your own in the paper. (*on the other hand*)

Combined: You could answer this advertisement for a job as a clerk; *on the other hand*, you could put a "job wanted" ad of your own in the paper.

Exercise 2: *Joining Sentences with Adverbs*

Combine each of the sets of sentences on the following page into one sentence by using the adverb connector in parentheses at the end of the second sentence. Write each new sentence on a sheet of paper numbered 1–10. Use the semicolon (;) and comma (,) to punctuate the new sentences. Study the example before you begin.

Example

a. Elena decided it was too hot to walk to the library. She had already read the entire Monarch collection of books. (*besides*)
Elena decided it was too hot to walk to the library; besides, she had already read the entire Monarch collection of books.

1. Diane studied very hard for the test.
   She knew the lesson by heart. (*in fact*)

2. The supply of salmon in the river was dangerously short.
   Fishing was banned for the entire season. (*therefore*)

3. Tony had been very ill.
   He recovered faster than anyone had thought possible.
   (*however*)

4. Three times Gene had tried to win the Grand Prix.
   He had tried to win every major race on the circuit.
   (*indeed*)

5. We were told we could not see our friend Juan in the
   hospital today.
   We would have to wait at least a week to see him.
   (*moreover*)

6. Terry teased the dog by kicking at it.
   The dog bit him. (*consequently*)

7. The water was too deep and the current too strong to get
   through.
   The rafting party had to carry their equipment around the
   rapids. (*therefore*)

8. It seemed foolish for the explorers to go any farther that night.
   They might have better weather tomorrow. (*besides*)

9. An exotic animal such as an ocelot is difficult to care for. You should choose a more common pet such as a cat. (*instead*)

10. The herb garden we just planted may grow rapidly. It may wither and die shortly. (*on the other hand*)

Writing Practice: *Combining Sentences in a Writer's Notebook Entry*

Choose an entry from your Writer's Notebook and revise it for sentence variety. Use pairs of connectors and adverbs, as you learned in this lesson, to combine short sentences. When you have finished, your entry should have a variety of sentence lengths and patterns.

3 Writing from Experience

You write best about the things you know best—places you've seen, people you've known, experiences you've had. To write well about these things, you must observe them carefully or remember them clearly. In this chapter you will be guided in making careful observations of familiar places, people, and events. You will also practice writing descriptions and stories drawn from your own experiences.

Details in Description

All good descriptions have details that help readers see, feel, hear, taste, and smell what is being described. These kinds of details are called *sense details*.

Model: *Sense Details in Description*

In the following selection, Rose Wilder Lane describes a ravine that she explores on her parents' farmland in Missouri. As you read, notice the details that help you see, hear, and taste what the writer describes.

> The ravine was shadowy, darker in its narrow bottom. It ended in one huge rock, as big as a big house. Behind the rock was a hollow sound of running water, and water ran from beneath it into a little pool as round as a washtub and half as deep. Ferns hung over the darling pool, and from a bough above it dangled a hollowed-out gourd for dipping up the water.
> I drank a delicious cold gourdful, looking up and up the mountainside above the spring. It was all dark woods, only the very tips of the highest trees in sudden yellow light. All down the dark ravine the water chuckled eerily.[1]

[1]Text excerpts from *On the Way Home: The Diary of a Trip from South Dakota to Mansfield, Missouri, in 1894,* written by Laura Ingalls Wilder, with a commentary by Rose Wilder Lane. Copyright © 1962 by Roger Lee MacBride. By permission of Harper & Row, Publishers, Inc.

Rose Wilder Lane's use of sense details helps you share her experience. You can see the rock "as big as a big house" and hear the "hollow sound of running water." With the writer you can taste the "delicious cold" water she drinks from the gourd.

Some details in a place description may be *data*.

The word *data* is plural. The singular form is *datum*. Data are statements of fact or measurements of things:

There are 523 students in my school.

Harriet Tubman served as a nurse and as a spy for the Union Army.

In 1770 the population of the United States was 2,205,000.

Sometimes, data add to a description. In 1894 Laura Ingalls Wilder, the author of the *Little House on the Prairie* books and the mother of Rose Wilder Lane, traveled by wagon from South Dakota to Missouri. Laura Ingalls Wilder kept a record of her journey and often used data to describe her family's experiences.

Model: Data in Description

Below is Wilder's description of a scene near the James River in South Dakota.

> On this side of the James we have passed fields of corn 8 feet high. There are cottonwood hedges along the road, the trees 10 inches through and 35 or 40 feet tall. But it all seems burned and bare after our camping grounds by the river.
>
> 10 o'clock. It is 101° in the shade in the wagon, and hardly a breath of air.[1]

Think and Discuss

1. Which of the details in this description are data?

2. Which sentences contain sense details?

Writing Practice 1: *Describing a Place*

Study the picture on page 51. Imagine that you are a part of this place, perhaps sitting on the beach near the water. What do you see, hear, feel, taste, and smell? Write a description of the place as though you were there. Use sense details and data to help readers share your experience.

If you write about a real place, try to visit the place before you begin writing, even if you have recently been there or it is a place you see every day, such as your classroom. Take a pencil and paper with you and write notes about what you see, feel, hear, taste, and smell. Your notes might also include data. Later you can make these notes into sentences and organize your writing for your readers.

For Your Writer's Notebook

Imagine that you are traveling with your family in a covered wagon across your state and have stopped to camp at a site near your present home. Write a notebook entry describing your campsite as though you were seeing it for the first time. You can do this whether you live in a city or in the country.

[1] Ibid.

Writing About People

The purpose of writing about people is to make them seem real to readers. Readers want to be able to imagine how the people they read about look, so descriptions of people include details of physical appearance.

Model: Details of Physical Appearance

Loretta Lynn is one of the most famous entertainers in the United States today. In the following selection Robert Krishef describes how she looked when Loretta Webb met the man she would marry:

> She was a slender, pretty 13-year-old, with shiny black hair, bright blue eyes, and high cheekbones. Her spirited good nature and her clear, powerful singing voice impressed the stocky ex-soldier.

When you read the description of Loretta Lynn, you can imagine how she looked and how she sounded because the writer uses details to describe her. He writes about her "shiny black hair," her "bright blue eyes," and "her clear, powerful singing voice."

To help you think of details about physical appearance, ask yourself questions like these:

1. What physical features do you remember most? Everyone has features that stand out more than others: beautiful hair; a large nose; delicate, long fingers; a square chin.

2. How does the person usually dress? Does the person keep up with the latest styles? Does the person wear especially colorful clothes?

3. How does the person stand and move? Does the person stand very straight or tend to slump over?

4. What is the person's voice like? Is it loud or soft? Is the voice pleasant or in some way unpleasant?

5. Does the person have any distinctive habits, such as constantly twisting a lock of hair?

Another part of describing a person is telling what the person is like on the inside. Describing the inner part of a person means writing about personality. Personality is what makes one person think and act differently from another. One of your friends may be shy and another outgoing. Some people prefer quiet activities such as reading or painting, while others enjoy being outdoors. Some people may be known for their loyalty to friends, and others may be known for a good sense of humor.

One way to describe personality is to make direct statements about people: *Yim loves animals. Jane is very shy. More than anything, Maria enjoys being outdoors.* Another way is to reveal personality by showing how people behave and what they say.

Then you let readers decide for themselves what a person is like inside.

For example, instead of saying directly that Yim loves animals, you can describe the way he behaves:

> Yim is the only person I know who spends his allowance on dog food instead of on himself. So far he's picked up three strays, and his mother told him he would have to help feed them. He doesn't seem to mind though, even when he has to miss a movie or basketball game.

Model: *Details of Behavior*

In *A Scottish Childhood* Christian Miller describes her experience as a young girl living in a huge, ancient Scottish castle. In this selection the writer tells about the four ghosts who also lived there.

> There were four chief ghosts in the castle. The quietest was an old man in a velvet coat, who used to sit reading in the library. He was so peaceful that one could be in the room for several minutes without even noticing that he was there. As soon as one did notice, he would softly vanish, fading into the leather upholstery.
>
> The woman in a long gray dress was just as untroublesome. Her face was half covered with a sort of bandage similar to that worn by some orders of nurses. She would come through the wall of the nursery and bend over the babies in their cots, like a nurse checking to see if her charges were sleeping peacefully.
>
> Equally as quiet was the woman who regularly crossed one of the upper rooms of the tower and vanished into a loft. Her only fault was that she did not know that since her time the room had been converted into a bathroom, and her sudden appearance sometimes startled guests.
>
> Far from quiet, however, was the red-haired young man on the stairs. He was a ghost who loved parties, and he could be relied on to turn up whenever there was festivity. It was only when some elderly woman guest would ask my mother to tell "the young man with the red beard" not to push past people on the stairs that my mother would know he was out again. But anyone who slept in the tower could hear him on non-party nights as well, laughing and joking with his friends as he ran lightly up and down the steep spiral stairs.[1]

[1]Adapted excerpt from "A Scottish Childhood" by Christian Miller. Copyright © 1979 by Christian Miller. Reprinted by permission of Wallace & Sheil Agency, Inc. and Anthony Sheil Associates Ltd. Originally published in *The New Yorker* Magazine.

Think and Discuss

The first ghost is an old man in a velvet coat who likes to sit quietly and read. How does each of the other ghosts look and behave?

For Your Writer's Notebook

Imagine that your classroom has a ghost. How old would this ghost be? What would the ghost look like? How would it behave? When would it appear? How might different people in your school react to the ghost? Think about the answers to these questions, and then write a notebook entry describing your classroom ghost.

Writing Practice 2: *Describing a Person*

Write a description of an important person in your life. Describe both appearance and personality. Use specific details to help readers see and hear the person you describe.

To help you gather information for this assignment, ask yourself questions about the person's appearance and personality. Make notes to yourself on a sheet of paper. Then look over the notes to see if one detail reminds you of other details.

For example, suppose you make a note that your friend Paul always sticks the end of a pen in his mouth. This note might remind you of the time he bit into the pen and sat in class with blue ink staining his mouth and face.

When you finish, make your notes into sentences and organize your writing for your readers. One way to organize your description is to think of something that stands out about the character. Begin by telling about the outstanding part, and then use details to develop your description. Study the following example:

My father is a very large man, over six feet tall, but he is the most gentle person I know.

The other details in the description should illustrate your statement.

Writing About Action

When you write about your experiences, you often write about action. Action seems real to readers when they can see and hear it.

Your task as a writer is to help your readers see, hear, and feel the action.

Action words like *walk, sing, eat, pull,* and *throw* tell what people and animals do. By carefully selecting such words, you can help your readers share the experience that you describe.

Model: Writing About Action

The following poem by Edwin A. Hoey is about a boy making a foul shot in basketball. The poet writes how the boy "seeks out the line," "soothes his hands," and "gently drums the ball." These words help you experience the action—you see and hear what the boy does. What other action words help you see and hear the boy?

Foul Shot

With two 60's stuck on the scoreboard
And two seconds hanging on the clock,
The solemn boy in the center of eyes,
Squeezed by silence,
Seeks out the line with his feet,
Soothes his hands along his uniform,
Gently drums the ball against the floor,
Then measures the waiting net,
Raises the ball on his right hand,
Balances it with his left,
Calms it with fingertips,
Breathes,
Crouches,
Waits,
And then through a stretching of stillness,
Nudges it upward.

The ball
Slides up and out,
Lands,
Leans,
Wobbles,
Wavers,
Hesitates,
Exasperates,
Plays it coy
Until every face begs with unsounding screams—

And then,

    And then,

        And then,

Right before ROAR-UP,
Dives down and through.[1]

                        Edwin A. Hoey

[1]Reprinted by permission of *Read Magazine,* published by Xerox Education Publications © 1962, Xerox Corp.

The action words in this poem are *specific*. Specific words tell you more than what people and animals do; they also tell you *how* they do it. For example, suppose you want to describe how a person drinks something hot. The word *drink* tells you that the person swallows the liquid, but not how. The more specific word *sip* tells you that the person drinks the liquid *slowly, in small mouthfuls.*

Writing Practice 3: *Choosing Specific Words*

Many times when you use an action word such as *walk, sing, eat, pull,* or *throw,* another word can describe the same actions in a more specific way. The following words describe the actions *walk, sing, eat, pull,* and *throw* in specific ways.

walk	march	hike	trudge	pace
sing	chant	hum	warble	chirp
eat	nibble	devour	gulp	gnaw
pull	yank	tug	draw	drag
throw	cast	toss	hurl	fling

Which of these specific action words would you use to describe each of the following actions?

1. How you walk when you are on your way to school and have not studied for a big test

2. How you eat when you are on a day-long hike and stop to eat only once

3. How you sing when you are showing off

4. How you pull a heavy object behind you

5. How you throw your book to the floor when you are angry

6. How your parents tell you to walk when they see your torn blue jeans and send you back to change clothes

7. How you eat a food you cannot stand

8. How you throw your jacket on a chair when you come home in a good mood

9. How you pull the string on a package when you have tried three times and it will not come off

10. How you sing when you do not use words

57

Writing Practice 4: *Describing an Action*

Think of an action that is an important part of your life. Write several sentences describing yourself involved in the action. Use specific action words to help your readers see and hear the action you describe. Look through your notebook to see if you have described an action there. Use these details to help you with this assignment. Write about one of the following actions or one of your own choosing:

1. Catching a fish
2. Water-skiing
3. Playing soccer or some other sport
4. Dancing
5. Running or jogging
6. Playing a musical instrument
7. Swimming
8. Backpacking or going on a hike
9. Flying a kite
10. Having a snowball fight

Writing About Events

So far you have written about people, places, and isolated actions, but you have not yet told a story. To do this, you must also tell about the *events* in your life—the things that happen to you.

At first, it might seem very easy to write about events, since you write about them in order:

First On the way home from the library, I didn't watch what I was doing and got on the wrong bus.

Second I was too embarrassed to say anything, so I rode the bus to the end of the line and then got off.

Third By this time it was dark and beginning to rain. I saw only a few old houses, and they looked deserted.

To tell a story, however, you want to include more than just what happened. You also want to tell about the people and places involved in the event, and to tell about your thoughts and feelings.

One way to share your thoughts and feelings with readers is to state them directly: *I was sad when we had to move.*

Another way to share feelings and thoughts with readers is to describe how you behave and how you look. Below is a description of a student receiving an award. What details tell you what this student feels and thinks?

As the teacher handed me the trophy, I stood up straighter than usual and looked out over the audience where I could see my parents and many of my friends. After thanking the teacher, I bounced off the stage and took my seat, smiling the whole time.

Model: *Writing About Events*

Black Elk Speaks is the story of Black Elk, a holy man of the Lakota (Oglala Sioux) tribe, who told his life story through the poet John G. Neihardt. In this part of his autobiography, found on the next two pages, Black Elk tells about hunting for bison (buffalo) one winter when he was sixteen. As you read, think about how Black Elk feels and how he shows his feelings.

We stayed on Clay Creek in Grandmother's Land all that summer and the next winter when I was sixteen years old.

That was a very cold winter. There were many blizzards, game was hard to find, and after a while the papa (dried meat) that we had made in the summer was all eaten. It looked as though we might starve to death if we did not find some game soon, and everybody was downhearted. Little hunting parties went out in different directions, but it is bad hunting in blizzard weather. My father and I started out alone leading our horses in the deep snow. When we got to Little River Creek we made a shelter with our bison robes against a bank of the stream and started a fire.

The wind came up again with the daylight, and we could see only a little way ahead when we started west in the morning. Before we came to the ridge, we saw two horses, dim in the blowing snow beside some bushes. They were huddled up with their tails to the wind and their heads hanging low. When we came closer, there was a bison robe shelter in the brush, and in it were an old man and a boy, very cold and hungry and discouraged. They were Lakotas and were glad to see us, but they were feeling weak, because they had been out two days and had seen nothing but snow. We camped there with them in the brush, and then we went up on the ridge afoot. There was much timber up there. We got behind the hill in a sheltered place and waited, but we could see nothing. While we were waiting, we talked about the people starving at home, and we were all sad. Now and then the snow haze would open up for a little bit and you could see quite a distance, then it would close again. While we were talking about our hungry people, suddenly the snow haze opened a little, and we saw a shaggy bull's head coming out of the blowing snow up the draw that led past us below. Then seven more appeared, and the snow haze came back and shut us in there. They could not see us, and they were drifting with the wind so that they could not smell us.

The two old men were to shoot first and then we two boys would follow the others horseback. Soon we saw the bison coming. The old people crept up and shot, but they were so cold, and maybe excited, that they got only one bison. They cried "Hoka!" and we boys charged after the other bison. The snow was blowing hard in the wind that sucked down the draw, and when we came near them the bison were so excited that they backtracked and charged right past us bellowing. This broke the deep snow for our horses and it was easier to catch them. Suddenly I saw the bison I was chasing go out in a big flurry of snow, and I knew they had plunged into a snow-filled gulch, but it was too late to stop, and my horse plunged right in after them. There we were all together—four bison, my horse and I all floundering and kicking, but I managed to crawl out a little way. I had a repeating rifle that they gave me back at the camp, and I killed the four bison right there, but I had

thrown my mittens away and the gun froze to my hands while I was shooting, so that I had to tear the skin to get it loose.[1]

Think and Discuss

1. Black Elk describes many things that happened to him while he tried to find food. What were some of the problems Black Elk faced?

2. Black Elk often names his feeling directly: "We were sad." But he also shows feelings by describing behavior. How do you think Black Elk and his father felt toward the old man and boy they met? How do their actions show their feelings?

3. What details and actions in the last paragraph show how desperate the four hunters were for food?

4. What words in the story tell the order of events in time?

Writing Assignment I: *Writing About an Event*

Think of an event in your life that you could expand into a story. Write about this event. Tell about the people and places that were involved and about your thoughts and feelings.

A. Prewriting

Stories are interesting when they are about people solving problems. The event you select for this assignment should involve a problem. Taking a bus ride is an event, but it may not make interesting reading. Suppose, however, that you get lost on your ride and have to find your way home in the dark. Now your event is more likely to be interesting.

When you decide on an event, ask yourself questions like the following ones. Make notes to yourself as you answer.

1. What problem does your event involve?

2. What exactly happened?

3. What caused the event to happen?

4. What people were important to the event? What details about the people are important to share with readers?

5. Where did the event happen? What details about the place are important to share with readers?

6. What were the results of the event?

7. What were your thoughts and feelings about the event?

8. How did the event change you or someone else?

B. Writing

Make your notes into sentences, and organize a story by telling what happened first, what happened second, and so on. This is called *chronological organization*. As you write, think about making the event you describe seem real to readers.

C. Postwriting

Ask yourself these questions as you revise your writing.

1. Did you give important details about people involved in the event?

2. Did you describe the place where the event happens?

3. Did you write about thoughts and feelings as the event happens?

4. Did you *show* your readers how people feel by describing how they look and behave?

Also, consider how you have organized details in your story. Reread each sentence to be sure that details of action are arranged in the order that they happened. If any details of action are out of order, rearrange them during your revision.

Finally, proofread your story, using the Checklist for Proofreading at the back of the book. Share your story with a group of classmates, as your teacher directs. Read one another's stories for enjoyment.

Sentence Variety:
Joining Sentences

The Semicolon as Connector

The *semicolon* (;) can be a sentence connector. Use the semicolon as a sentence connector *only* when two sentences are equally important and make better sense joined than apart.

Sentences: Chicago was clean and cheerful.
Its people were friendly and smiling.

Combined: Chicago was clean and cheerful; its people were friendly and smiling.

Sentences: Manny plays and sings popular music.
His brother prefers jazz.

Combined: Manny plays and sings popular music; his brother prefers jazz.

Exercise 1: Joining Sentences with a Semicolon

Combine each of the following sets of sentences into one sentence with a semicolon (;). Copy each new sentence on a sheet of paper numbered 1–10.

1. To understand oneself is wonderful.
   To understand others is even more rewarding.

2. *The Big Sleep* is an excellent detective story.
   It has been read by millions since it was written in 1939.

3. The dictionary provides definitions, spellings, and pronunciations.
   It also has lists of abbreviations, special charts and graphs, and a guide for the use of the book itself.

4. Working busily all spring, a Baltimore oriole and its mate nested and raised a family in the tree branch outside Richard's kitchen window.
   Inside the house Richard's pet canary sang happily to its new neighbors.

5. Gnarled and weather-beaten, the cypress stood on the shoreline.
   Its age and form lent majesty to the wilderness scene.

6. The crystal chandelier tinkled as the door of the deserted mansion blew open.
   It played a song for the mansion ghost.

7. Apples, oranges, grapefruit, and bananas make a delicious, refreshing treat.
   They are also nutritious.

8. Watering the garden for Grandmother, Joe noticed that the roses were covered with bugs.
   They were bad this time of year.

9. Donald earned spending money by working a paper route.
   Ronald, his twin brother, earned his income caddying at the local golf course.

10. Ms. Welch encouraged her seventh-grade geography students to watch the news each evening.
    She wanted them to know about current events.

Adding Sentences in a Series

The sentence-combining exercises you have been doing asked you to join two sentences in a number of ways. Now you can begin to write sentences that join three or more sentences together. The first sentence in each set is called the *base sentence*. The other sentences are added to the base sentence.

Base Sentence: The monster reared back.

Add: The monster bellowed loudly.

Add: The monster beat its fists against its chest.

Combined: The monster reared back, bellowed loudly, *and* beat its fists against its chest.

The last sentence has been formed by combining the first three. The repeated words *The monster* have been taken out, and the word *and* has been added before the third sentence to join all three sentences together. Commas have been added to keep the parts from running together.

In this lesson you will learn new signals. The signal (,) tells you to put a comma *before* the added part in the new sentence.

The signal (,*and*) tells you to put both a comma and the word *and* before the last added part in the new sentence.

The (X) signal tells you to remove that word or words from the final combined sentences.

Base Sentence: Jackie picked up the baby.

Add: S̶h̶e placed it gently over her shoulder. (,)

Add: S̶h̶e patted it on the back. (, *and*)

Combined: Jackie picked up the baby, placed it gently over her shoulder, *and* patted it on the back.

When two verb forms ending in -*ing* are added to the base sentence, separate them from the base sentence with a comma, but use only an *and* between the two new -*ing* forms.

Sentences: The fountain was spurting high into the air.
T̶h̶e fountain w̶a̶s spilling over the sides of the basin. (,)
I̶t̶ w̶a̶s then splashing the feet of passersby. (*and*)

Combined: The fountain was spurting high into the air, spilling over the sides of the basin *and* then splashing the feet of passersby.

Sentences: The monkeys stared from the cage.
T̶h̶e̶y̶ w̶e̶r̶e̶ making wild noises. (,)
T̶h̶e̶y̶ w̶e̶r̶e̶ tossing peanut shells through the bars. (*and*)

Combined: The monkeys stared from the cage, making wild noises *and* tossing peanut shells through the bars.

The first sentence in a set is always the base. The other sentences are added to the base sentence in order. Notice that in the above examples the pronouns *it* and *they* are deleted in the combined sentences because they have the same meaning as the nouns *fountain* and *monkeys*.

Exercise 2: Adding Sentences in a Series

Combine each of the sets of sentences on the next page into one sentence by following the signals. Write each new sentence on a sheet of paper numbered 1–10. Study the example before you begin.

Example

a. The dog leaped madly about the beach.
The dog was playing with each new wave. (,)
The dog was sniffing at the seaweed. (and)
The dog leaped madly about the beach, playing with each new wave and sniffing at the seaweed.

1. The little boy jumped up and down on the trampoline.
He saw us watching him. (,)
He began to bounce even higher. (,and)

2. Ramon sat on the steps.
He was holding his head in his hands. (,)
He was crying softly to himself. (and)

3. Every chicken in the hen house squawked loudly.
It flapped its wings. (,)
It flew or ran through the door. (,and)

4. Casually, the man took out his wallet.
He unfolded a huge roll of bills. (,)
He selected a $50 bill for me. (,and)

5. Cathy approached the lion's cage.
She held out a huge bone. (,)
She quickly backed away. (,and)

Combine each of the following sets of sentences into one sentence. These sentences have no signals. Copy each set of sentences on a sheet of paper. Then cross out the words that are repeated in the second and third sentences. Add the words that are left to the first sentence. Use a comma (,) and the word *and* to separate parts of your new sentence. Write each new sentence.

Example

a. With great difficulty Silas hitched the old plow horse.
He got up on the wagon.
He started off toward the village.
With great difficulty Silas hitched the old plow horse, got up on the wagon, and started off toward the village.

6. Carlos tipped over the water jar.
He was spilling its contents all over the floor.
He was splashing liquid against the wall.

7. The road went on and on for miles across the desert.
   It was stretching out straight ahead of us.
   It was leading us toward the mountain in the distance.

8. Maria's father taught her all about race cars.
   He was giving her careful instruction.
   He was making sure she had plenty of driving practice.

9. The few people left in the room stood on chairs.
   They applauded wildly.
   They cheered for their candidate.

10. Over the weekend I cleaned up my room.
    I watched television.
    I played soccer when it wasn't raining.

Writing Practice: *Joining Sentences*

Imagine what your life would be like if you lived in an isolated cave deep in the forest. You would have no radio, television, telephone, or electricity. There would be no books, magazines, newspapers, or school. When you were hungry, you couldn't go to the grocery store; instead, you would have to find food in the forest and nearby river. Write a paragraph describing what an average day would be like for you in a place such as this. Use your imagination to make up other details about your life.

   As you write, use connectors to join your sentences. Underline each connector you use in your paragraph.

4 Writing Paragraphs

The Paragraph

Sometimes you write about an idea in one sentence.

I always knew roller-skating could be dangerous, and my accident last week proves it.

Star Wars is my favorite movie.

I think seventh-grade students should have school dances.

The directions for this test aren't clear.

Many times you add other sentences that develop or explain the idea in the first sentence. When you do this, you write a *paragraph.*

One definition of a paragraph is a group of sentences that develop or explain an idea or topic.

Each sentence in a paragraph is about the same idea or topic. If the sentences are not about the same idea, they are not a paragraph. The following group of sentences is not a paragraph. How many different ideas are there in this passage?

Baby-sitting isn't as easy as you might think. I have found sixth grade and seventh grade to be very different. Scientists are coming closer to finding a cure for cancer. I would like to get a job delivering newspapers, but I don't think I can get up at 4:00 A.M.

This group of sentences is not a paragraph because the sentences are not related to one another. There are four sentences in this passage, and each sentence is about a new idea.

Model: A Paragraph

This paragraph is from Maya Angelou's autobiography *I Know Why the Caged Bird Sings.* Until she was thirteen, Maya Angelou

lived in Stamps, Arkansas, and worked in her family's store. As you read the paragraph, notice how each sentence helps develop the idea that the store was her favorite place.

Topic sentence

Details

Until I was thirteen and left Arkansas for good, the Store was my favorite place to be. Alone and empty in the mornings, it looked like an unopened present from a stranger. Opening the front doors was pulling the ribbon off the unexpected gift. The light would come in softly (we faced north), easing itself over the shelves of mackerel, salmon, tobacco, thread. It fell flat on the big vat of lard and by noontime during the summer the grease had softened to a thick soup. Whenever I walked into the Store in the afternoon, I sensed that it was tired. I alone could hear the slow pulse of its job half done. But just before bedtime, after numerous people had walked in and out, had argued over their bills, or joked about their neighbors, or just dropped in "to give Sister Henderson a 'Hi y'all,'" the promise of magic mornings returned to the Store and spread itself over the family in washed life waves.[1]

---

[1]From *I Know Why the Caged Bird Sings* by Maya Angelou. Copyright © 1969 by Maya Angelou. Reprinted by permission of Random House, Inc.

Think and Discuss

In the first sentence Maya Angelou writes that the family store was her favorite place. The second sentence tells why she liked the store in the mornings. How does each of the other sentences in her paragraph help develop the idea that the store was the writer's favorite place?

For Your Writer's Notebook

> For Maya Angelou her family's store was a magic place. Think about a place in your life that at one time seemed magical to you. This may have been a place you liked to go, your home during a special holiday, or a tree house that you once had. Describe this place in your Writer's Notebook.

Writing Practice 1: *Writing a Paragraph*

Think of an idea or topic that interests you and write about this idea in one sentence. Then write four or five other sentences that develop or explain the idea in your first sentence. These sentences will make a paragraph.

To help you get started, you might use one of the following ideas and topics. If you prefer, make up one of your own.

1. Participating in sports is getting too expensive.

2. If I could, I would make a few changes in school.

3. Worms make good pets.

4. My grandparents (or parents) are very special people.

5. One day there may really be robots like R2-D2 in *Star Wars*.

To gather details for your paragraph, try brainstorming. For example, suppose you want to think about the idea *How I think a spaceship would look.* Try to empty your mind of any other thoughts except this one. Think of stories, movies, and television shows about spaceships.

As you concentrate, you will probably have many thoughts about spaceships. You may think of a very large object with a shape like a football. You may see rows of windows on your spaceship and a bluish glow coming from it. As you brainstorm, make notes to yourself on a sheet of paper.

When you finish, decide which notes you can use, and make them into sentences for your readers.

As you write your paragraph, think about each sentence. Can you tell how each sentence develops or explains the idea you wrote about in the first sentence? If some sentences do not develop or explain that idea, remove them. Add sentences that help develop or explain the idea in the first sentence.

Developing Paragraphs

The Main Idea and Details

Sentences in a paragraph develop or explain the main idea or topic of a paragraph by giving *details*.

Details in a paragraph answer the questions *who? what? where? when? why?* **and** *how?* **about the main idea.**

Model: Main Idea and Details

The following paragraph is from Ernesto Galarza's autobiography. Born in Mexico, he came to this country as a young boy and began school in Sacramento, California. What is the main idea of this paragraph? What details develop or explain it?

Topic sentence

Details

At Lincoln, making us into Americans did not mean scrubbing away what made us originally foreign. The teachers called us as our parents did, or as close as they could pronounce our names in Spanish or Japanese. No one was ever scolded or punished for speaking in his native tongue on the playground. Matti told the class about his mother's down quilt, which she had made in Italy with the fine feathers of a thousand geese. Encarnación acted out how boys learned to fish in the Philippines. I astounded the third grade with the story of my travels on a stagecoach, which nobody else in the class had seen except in the museum at Sutter's Fort. After a visit to the Crocker Art Gallery and its collection of heroic paintings of the golden age of California, someone showed a silk scroll with a Chinese painting. Miss Hopley herself had a way of expressing wonder over these matters before a class, her eyes wide open until they popped slightly. It was easy for me to feel that becoming a proud American, as she said we should, did not mean feeling ashamed of being a Mexican.[1]

---

[1] From *Barrio Boy* by Ernesto Galarza. Copyright 1971, University of Notre Dame Press, Notre Dame, Indiana 46556.

Think and Discuss

The main idea of this paragraph is the first sentence: *At Lincoln, making us into Americans did not mean scrubbing away what made us originally foreign.* The other sentences in the paragraph give details to show how the school did not try to take away the students' pride in their origins. These sentences answer the question *How did the school show respect for the students' national origins?* One way the teachers did this was to try to pronounce the students' Spanish or Japanese names as their parents did. In what other way did the school show respect for the students' backgrounds?

The Topic Sentence

A sentence that gives the main idea or topic of the paragraph is often called the *topic sentence.*

The topic sentence is not always the first one in a paragraph. What is the topic sentence in the following paragraph?

Model: Topic Sentence

A friend of mine was walking down a village street lined with maple trees, one summer morning, when a baby gray squirrel scrambled fearlessly down a nearby trunk. It came directly toward him in a series of little loping hops, its tiny tail flipping at every jump. When it was six feet away, it came to a sudden stop. An ear-piercing chatter had reached it from the branches overhead. Rattling over the bark, the mother squirrel came racing down the tree. She scurried to the baby, scolding at the top of her lungs. She gave him a nip that made him jump. Then she grabbed him by the back of the neck and lugged him, kittenwise, to the foot of the tree trunk. The youngster had learned a lesson in caution, a lesson that might save its life on a later day.[2]

The main idea of the above paragraph is that the young squirrel learned an important lesson in caution. This idea is expressed in the last sentence: *The youngster had learned a lesson in caution, a lesson that might save its life on a later day.* The last sentence is the topic sentence.

Writing Practice 2: *Writing a Topic Sentence and Details*

Think of something you have done that required courage, hard work, or discipline. Write one sentence telling what it was that required this effort. This sentence is the topic sentence of your paragraph. Here is an example:

Getting up to explore the empty, dark house after hearing strange noises was the hardest thing I have ever done.

Then write three or four other sentences that give details about your topic sentence. These sentences make a paragraph.

To help you get started, here are some things that might have required courage, hard work, or discipline from you:

1. Losing weight

2. Learning to swim (or ride a bicycle)

3. Keeping your room clean

4. Saving money

5. Making new friends

6. Keeping up with your homework assignments

7. Cooking a meal

8. Getting along with your brother or sister

9. Finding your way around in the city

10. Giving your cat a bath

---

[2]Excerpt from "A School for Foxes" from *The Lost Woods* by Edwin Way Teale. Copyright © 1954, 1973 by Edwin Way Teale. Reprinted by permission of Dodd, Mead & Company.

For Your Writer's Notebook

How much do you know about your origins? Are you a native American, or did your ancestors come from another country? Is your family a mixture of national origins? If you don't know your origins, talk with your parents or other relatives. Check the library for information about the country or countries that are a part of your heritage. Write in your notebook about the results of your study.

Developing Paragraphs with Incidents

An *incident* is a little story, usually about people. Writers often use incidents to develop or explain ideas because they know that people are interested in what happens to other people.

Model: Developing Paragraphs with Incidents

As a well-known poet, Langston Hughes traveled a great deal to read his poems. On his trips he often stayed in private homes. Excited by their famous guest, his hosts went to great lengths to prepare for his visit. This paragraph tells about an incident that happened on one of these visits. What is the incident?

Topic sentence

Details

Once, this household entertainment led to a most embarrassing situation. The hostess, in her zeal to have her house as shining and clean as possible for her guest, had painted the baseboards and all the more obviously soiled areas about the house. To top off her thoroughness, she had enameled the bathtub, both inside and out, but failed to tell Hughes what she had done. He went happily up to his room to rest before the evening's reading, drew a hot bath, and got into the tub. He had soaked for a comfortable length of time, when he found he could not get up! He was stuck to the enamel! Slowly, inch by square inch, he detached himself so as not to leave one patch of skin, but he said he did leave a very distinctive autograph on the bottom of the tub.[1]

---

[1]From *Black Troubadour: Langston Hughes,* by Charlemae H. Rollins. Copyright 1970 by Charlemae H. Rollins. Published by Rand McNally.

The topic of this paragraph is in the first sentence: *Once, this household entertainment led to a most embarrassing situation.* The rest of this paragraph develops this topic by giving details to help readers share Langston Hughes' experience: how the woman painted her house, and how Langston Hughes soaked in the hot tub and found that he could not get up.

Writing Assignment I: *Developing a Paragraph with an Incident*

Below are topic sentences that can be developed or explained with an incident. Select one of these topic sentences or make up one of your own. Then develop a paragraph by giving details about an incident that happened to you or to someone you know. Follow the steps on the next page.

1. I'm not very good at fixing things.

2. Sometimes, I have a strange imagination.

3. Summer has always been a special time for me.

4. Growing up means making some hard decisions.

5. Cooking is not one of my strong points.

A. Prewriting

To help you think of details about your incident, ask yourself questions like these:

1. *What* exactly happened?

2. *Who* are the people involved?

3. *Where* did the incident happen? Did the place have anything to do with the incident?

4. *When* did the incident happen? Did the time have anything to do with the incident?

5. *Why* did the incident happen? Did you or someone else do something to cause it to happen?

6. *What* were the results of the incident? Did it cause you or someone else to change in any way?

7. *How* did the incident make you feel?

Make a word cluster of specific details that will help your reader share the experience.

B. Writing

As you write your paragraph, use the details from your cluster. Tell about events in the order in which they happened. Build your paragraph around the topic sentence; do not use details that are unrelated to the main idea.

C. Postwriting

To revise this paragraph, think about the following questions:

1. Does each sentence in your paragraph tell about the incident you have chosen?

2. Did you use specific details to help readers share the story?

3. Did you use details to answer *who? what? where? when? why?* and *how?* questions about the incident?

Finally, proofread your paragraph, using the Checklist for Proofreading at the back of the book.

Coherence

When every sentence in it relates to the same idea, a paragraph has *unity.* Even though paragraphs must be unified, having unity is not enough. Paragraphs must be written so that readers can see *how* each sentence in the paragraph relates to every other sentence in the paragraph.

When the relationship of each sentence to the others is clear, the paragraph has *coherence.*

Readers can easily move from one sentence to the next.

Imagine trying to make hot cereal by using the directions in the following paragraph.

Bring to boil, reduce heat, and simmer 5 to 8 minutes, stirring occasionally, until cereal gets as thick as you like it. Mix together in a saucepan the wheat cereal, salt, raisins, and water. While cereal is cooking, chop the nuts. Remove cereal from stove and stir in nuts and honey. Serve with milk. Spoon into 2 cereal bowls.

Even though each of these sentences is about making hot cereal, these directions are confusing. The first sentence says to bring something to a boil, but what? The second sentence says to mix the ingredients but tells nothing about cooking them. Because you cannot understand how these sentences are related to each other, this set of instructions is not coherent.

One way to make paragraphs coherent is to arrange them in *logical order.* This means that the sentences are arranged for a reason.

Steps in a Process

One kind of logical order is *steps in a process.*

Paragraphs that explain how to do something often explain a process: cooking a dish or building a kite. The sentences are usually arranged by the steps you follow.

Model: *Steps in a Process*

The following paragraph, from the book *Song of Solomon* by Toni Morrison, tells how to cook a soft-boiled egg.

Details

Now, the water and the egg have to meet each other on a kind of equal standing. One can't get the upper hand over the other. So the temperature has to be the same for both. I knock the chill off the water first. Just the chill. I don't let it get warm because the egg is room temperature, you see. Now then, the real secret is right here in the boiling. When the tiny bubbles come to the surface, when they are as big as peas and just before they get big as marbles. Well, right then you take the pot off the fire. You don't just put the fire out; you take the pot off. Then you put a folded newspaper over the pot and do one small obligation, like answering the door or emptying the bucket and bringing it in off the front porch. . . . If you do all

Topic sentence

that, you got yourself a perfect soft-boiled egg.[1]

Think and Discuss

This paragraph, which gives a "common sense" way to cook a soft-boiled egg, is organized by steps in the process. The first step is to "knock the chill off the water." What are the other steps in the process?

Writing Practice 3: *Arranging Details by Steps in a Process*

Below are five topic sentences. Select one of these or make up one of your own. Develop the topic sentence into a paragraph by adding details. Arrange the sentences by steps in the process.

1. Changing a bicycle tire isn't hard if you know how.

2. Making a paper airplane is an art.

---

[1]From *Song of Solomon* by Toni Morrison. Copyright © 1977 by Toni Morrison. Reprinted by permission of Alfred A. Knopf, Inc.

3. Everyone should know how to call the fire department and report a fire.

4. Tying a shoelace is simple, but explaining how to do it isn't.

5. Putting together my ideal meal would take a lot of work.

Chronological Order

Another kind of logical order is *chronological*.

Chronological order is the way events happen in time. When you tell a story, you often arrange paragraphs by time order, telling what happened first, what happened next, and so on.

Model: Chronological Order

In the following paragraph from Toni Cade Bambara's story "Raymond's Run," a girl named Squeaky describes her thoughts and feelings during a race. Squeaky had been dreaming about being able to fly, and as the paragraph opens, the race is about to begin. (Amsterdam is a street in New York City.)

> Once I spread my fingers in the dirt and crouch over the Get on Your Mark, the dream goes and I am solid again and am telling myself, Squeaky you must win, you must win, you are the fastest thing in the world, you can even beat your father up Amsterdam if you really try. And then I feel my weight coming back just behind my knees then down to my feet then into the earth and the pistol shot explodes in my blood and I am off and weightless again, flying past the other runners, my arms

pumping up and down and the whole world is quiet except for the crunch as I zoom over the gravel in the track. I glance to my left and there is no one. To the right, a blurred Gretchen, who's got her chin jutting out as if it would win the race all by itself. And on the other side of the fence is Raymond with his arms down to his side and the palms tucked up behind him, running in his very own style, and it's the first time I ever saw that and I almost stop to watch my brother Raymond on his first run. But the white ribbon is bouncing toward me and I tear past it, racing into the distance till my feet with a mind of their own start digging up footfuls of dirt and brake me short. Then all the kids standing on the side pile on me, banging me on the back and slapping my head with their May Day programs, for I have won again and everybody on 151st Street can walk tall for another year.[1]

Think and Discuss

Toni Cade Bambara develops the above paragraph with chronological organization. As the paragraph opens, Squeaky is

---

[1]From *Tales and Short Stories for Black Folks* by Toni Cade Bambara. Copyright © 1971 by Doubleday & Company, Inc. Reprinted by permission of Joan Daves.

crouched down, ready for the signal to start. Name each event that happens after that.

Writing Practice 4: *Arranging Details Chronologically*

Below are five topic sentences. Select one of these or make up one of your own. Develop the topic sentence into a paragraph by adding details in chronological order. Before you begin, discover details for your paragraph by brainstorming or by using one of the other methods in Chapter 1.

1. I can easily describe what a perfect day would be like for me.

2. The early morning calm was suddenly shattered by the shrill ringing of an alarm bell.

3. I tiptoed quietly into the house, hoping I wouldn't wake anyone.

4. My dog got me into a great deal of trouble recently.

5. I've changed a great deal in the past five years.

For Your Writer's Notebook

In the paragraph from "Raymond's Run," Toni Cade Bambara describes a girl's thoughts and feelings during an exciting race. Think about something exciting that has happened to you recently. Write an entry describing the event and your thoughts and feelings about it.

Spatial Order

A third kind of order is *spatial order*.

Spatial order is the way objects appear in space. When you use spatial order in a paragraph, you describe people, places, or objects as you see them. Suppose you write a paragraph describing your English classroom. You might tell how the room looks as your eyes move from left to right or from top to bottom. With a large object such as a car, you might begin by describing the front of the car and then move to the rear or the outside, then the inside.

Model: Spatial Order

The following paragraph is from Maureen Daly's book *Seventeenth Summer.* (*Pete's* is a gathering place for the teenagers in the novel.)

> The lake behind Pete's lay flat and glassy in the sunlight. The lawn was green and lush near the water's edge, but farther from the shore it was littered with cigarette stubs, small bits of bottle glass, and faded scraps of red and green fire-cracker paper left from the Fourth of July. Sometimes people have wiener roasts here and on one side there was a patch of burnt litter where someone had made a fire, and around it lay bits of charred wood and a blackened beer can and the grass was burnt short like curly black hairs.[1]

Think and Discuss

Maureen Daly arranges the sentences of the preceding paragraph in spatial order. She begins by describing the lake that is located behind Pete's, and then she describes the two parts of the lawn. Why does she describe the green part of the lawn first?

Writing Practice 5: *Arranging Details by Spatial Order*

Below is a list of topic sentences. Select one of these or make up one of your own. Develop the topic sentence into a paragraph by adding details. Arrange the sentences in spatial order.

---

[1]Excerpt from *Seventeenth Summer* by Maureen Daly. Reprinted by permission of Dodd, Mead & Company.

1. When spaceships carry passengers on regular trips to the moon, the ships should be carefully designed.

2. If I could make any changes I wanted to in my own room, I would create the ideal room for teenagers.

3. A baseball field must be laid out according to a pattern.

4. Across the lake I could see people running around and waving their arms.

5. Everywhere I looked, I saw the terrible destruction that was caused by the earthquake.

Transitions

One way to help a paragraph have coherence is to use a logical order of organization. Another way is to use words that show the relationships between sentences.

Words that show relationships between sentences are called *transition words.*

When you arrange sentences in a paragraph by steps in a process, use transition words to show that you are moving from one step to another. These may be words such as *first, second, third, then, now, next, when, after.*

Model: Transitions

Notice the transition words in the following instructions:

Topic sentence
Details

Bathing a cat is never simple, but careful preparation can make the task a little easier. The first step is to dress correctly for the job. The best outfit is a raincoat and long rubber boots, somewhat similar to those worn by sailors during a storm at sea. Next, collect everything you could possibly need—pet shampoo, towels (lots of them), a brush, and first aid supplies such as bandages and ointment. The shampoo, towels, and brush are for the cat; the first aid supplies are for you (unless the cat has been declawed). Then, draw the water and have the bath ready before bringing the cat into the room. Only when everything is ready should you begin trying to capture your pet. If you are successful in getting it anywhere near the water, the last step is to lock the door. It's surprising how even the smallest kitten, when lowered into the water, can suddenly turn into a howling banshee and tear through a closed door.

Think and Discuss

The first transition words used in the paragraph are *first* and *Next*. Find three other transition words in the rest of the paragraph.

For paragraphs with chronological order, use transition words such as *when, then, in the first place, while, meanwhile, still, next, after, after that.*

> *When* I was little, I was afraid of leaves. *Whenever* I was taken near a plant or bush, I cried. *Later* I outgrew this fear, but I *still* don't like to be near large trees. Sometimes even *now* I dream about trees chasing me down the street.

For paragraphs with spatial organization, use transition words that show place such as *next to, on the left, on the right, above, below, around, between, behind, beside.*

> You can usually tell from the state of my room when cleaning day approaches. By that time dirty clothes are heaped *all around* the room. *Behind* the chair are assorted books and records I haven't gotten around to putting away. *Next to* that mess is the overflowing wastebasket. *Under* the bed are glasses and plates I forgot to take back to the kitchen. It's almost a relief when Saturday does come.

Other transitional words show how ideas relate. These are words like *because, however, moreover, furthermore, thus, yet, so, therefore.*

Writing Assignment II: *A Paragraph with Transitions*

Have you ever thought of an object, like Dick Tracy's two-way TV wristwatch, that you would like to invent? Perhaps you would like a robot that specializes in doing homework or a battery-operated device that zooms you along the sidewalk. Think of an object you would like to invent. Then write a paragraph describing the object and telling how it works. Underline each transition word in the paragraph.

A. Prewriting

Brainstorm answers to the following questions, writing notes to yourself as you do so. Concentrate on thinking of as many details as you can.

1. What is the exact size and shape of your object? Perhaps you would prefer a pocket-sized robot.

2. What parts does your object have? Does your imaginary robot have a "memory" to store your instructions to it?

3. Is your new object similar to any other object your readers know? Does your imaginary robot look like a windup toy?

4. How does your object work? Does your imaginary robot have batteries, or does it obey your spoken commands?

5. For what purpose do you use your object?

Next, look over your notes. Decide what kind of organization would work best to tie these notes together.

B. Writing

Write your paragraph. Use appropriate transition words between sentences so that the organization of your paragraph is clear to the reader.

C. Postwriting

To revise your paragraph, use the following checklist. Make as many changes as needed. You may need to rewrite, add, or take out sentences. Your goal is to answer *yes* to each of the questions in the checklist.

Revising Your Paragraph

1. Does every sentence in your paragraph develop or explain your main idea or topic?

2. Did you use specific details to answer questions that readers might have about your main idea?

3. Are the sentences in your paragraph arranged by some kind of logical order?

4. Did you use transition words to help readers see how one sentence relates to another?

Finally, use the Checklist for Proofreading at the back of the book to proofread your paragraph. Underline each transition word you have used.

Sentence Variety:
Joining Sentences

New Ways to Add Sentences in a Series

Adding sentences in a series does not always mean attaching sentences to the *end* of a base sentence. Sometimes you will want to attach a sentence to the *front* of the base sentence. For example, the following sets of sentences can be combined in two ways:

Base Sentence: A little boy sat on the schoolhouse steps.
Add: ~~He was~~ gathering up his courage to go inside.

Combined: A little boy sat on the schoolhouse steps, gathering up his courage to go inside.
or
Combined: Gathering up his courage to go inside, a little boy sat on the schoolhouse steps.

You can even add sentences both at the front of the base sentence and at the end.

Base Sentence: Cheryl moved about the hospital ward.

Add: ~~She was~~ fluffing pillows.

Add: ~~She was~~ cheering up the patients.

Combined: Fluffing pillows, Cheryl moved about the hospital ward cheering up the patients.

Adding sentence to sentence gives you several ways to arrange the combinations. For example, you might have made the last combination in the following way:

Cheryl moved about the hospital ward, *fluffing pillows* and *cheering up the patients*.
or
Fluffing pillows, and *cheering up the patients*, Cheryl moved about the hospital ward.

Exercise 1: Joining Sentences in a Series

Combine the following sets of sentences by adding to the front or back of the base sentence. Let the sense of the final combined sentence be your guide. The cross-out signal (X) tells you which words to take out. Remember that the first sentence in each set is the base. Write each new sentence on a piece of paper. Study the example before you begin.

Example

a. Two mockingbirds sat on the telephone line.
They were singing a duet.
They were making the air ring with a sweet melody.
Singing a duet, two mockingbirds sat on the telephone line, making the air ring with a sweet melody.

1. Tina didn't study for her test.
She was not worried about her grade.

2. The kittens tumbled around on the floor.
They were rolling over each other.
They were scratching at each other playfully.

3. Superman leaped from building to building.
~~He was~~ racing against the clock.
~~He was~~ making his finest effort to save Lois Lane.

4. The dog sat quietly.
~~It was~~ hoping for some attention.
~~It was~~ looking at its owner sadly.

5. The speckled trout lay quietly beneath the shade of the trees.
~~It was~~ watching a water bug on the surface.
~~It was~~ waiting for a chance to snatch the bug for dinner.

Combine the following sets of sentences by adding to the front or to the end of the base sentence. Let the sense of the final sentence be your guide. Since these sets do not have signals, you must decide which words to remove when you make the combinations. Write each new sentence on a sheet of paper. Study the example before you begin.

Example

a. The players trooped back to the locker room.
They were shouting with joy.
They were pounding each other gleefully.
Shouting with joy and pounding each other gleefully, the players trooped back to the locker room.

6. The woman finished the picture.
   She was throwing paint against the canvas.
   She was hoping for quick results.

7. The children enjoyed their holiday.
   They were playing happily in the mud puddle.
   They were not caring that summer would soon be over.

8. The turtle finally righted itself.
   It was straining mightily.
   It was rocking back and forth.

9. The explorers knew they were doomed.
   They were searching for shelter that wasn't there.
   They were praying for water that didn't exist.

10. The dogs were dangerous.
    They were running in a pack.
    They were becoming desperate for food.

Joining Sentences Unequal in Meaning

A group of connecting words called *subordinators* will allow you to join sentences that are not of equal importance. In sentence writing, *subordinate* means two things:

1. One idea in a sentence is emphasized and made more important than another.

2. The group of words that follows the subordinator does not form a complete sentence. It depends upon the rest of the sentence to make sense.

Words such as *because, although, since, after, before, if, until, as soon as, when,* and others subordinate the less important idea in a sentence to a more important one.

Sentences: You will never learn how to dance.
                You learn how to keep time to the music. (*until*)

Combined: You will never learn how to dance *until you learn how to keep time to the music.*

The word *until* is the subordinator in this example. It shows that there is a relationship between learning to keep time and learning to dance, but *until you learn how to keep time to the music* depends upon the rest of the sentence to make complete sense.

Sentences: Tobias likes fruit and milk for breakfast. (*because*)
He has both nearly every morning.

Combined: *Because Tobias likes fruit and milk for breakfast*, he has both nearly every morning.

Because Tobias likes fruit and milk for breakfast is not a complete sentence. It is subordinate to the more important idea *He has both nearly every morning*. It also shows that Tobias's liking fruit and milk is the *cause* of his having both nearly every morning.

Notice how the meaning would change if the subordinator were placed before the second statement in the combined sentence: *Tobias likes fruit and milk for breakfast because he has both nearly every morning.*

Exercise 2: *Joining Sentences Unequal in Meaning*

Combine each of the sets of the following sentences by using a connecting word that subordinates one sentence to another. If the signal follows the first sentence in the set, place that word in front of that sentence. If the signal follows the second sentence, place that word in front of the second sentence when you join the two. Write each new sentence on a sheet of paper numbered 1–5. Study the examples before you begin.

Examples

a. My great-grandfather was a boy. (*when*)
He learned how to shoe a horse.
When my great-grandfather was a boy, he learned how to shoe a horse.

b. Meals have not been the same at home.
Ginger learned to cook. (*since*)
Meals have not been the same at home since Ginger learned to cook.

1. The bus pulled over to the shoulder of the road.
Cars behind it could pass safely. (*so*)

2. Rafael will turn over the committee report.
It is needed. (*when*)

3. Jeff pays close attention to the instructor. (*unless*)
He will miss important instructions.

4. The desert flowers blossom into bright colors.
    It rains in early springtime. (*whenever*)

5. You want to give your dog good, healthy exercise. (*if*)
    Walk it around the lake twice.

The following sets of sentences have no signals, so you must decide which sentence to subordinate to the other. Choose a connecting word from the list below to join the sentences. Write each new sentence on a sheet of paper numbered 6–10.

since	when
if	until
because	although
whenever	after
unless	while
before	

6. People from the town helped to fill the sandbags.
    The river was about to overflow its banks.

7. You can find a needle in a haystack.
    You take time to look for it.

8. It's useless to change the tire on this car.
    I'm not even going to try.

9. This job can be finished quickly.
    We learn how to cooperate with one another.

10. Min-Sun can speak two languages already.
    She wants to study several others.

Writing Practice: *New Ways of Joining Sentences*

One of the most popular kinds of early radio shows was the soap opera. Often sponsored by companies that made soap, these shows told the continuing story of a set of characters, whose lives were usually unhappy. Invent a cast of characters and think of some events that might happen to them during a week or two of episodes. Use some of the sentence-combining skills you have learned so far to describe your imaginary soap opera.

5 Writing Compositions

The Composition

A *composition* is a group of related paragraphs.

Below is Phyllis Hollander's composition about the sprinter (short-distance runner) Chi Cheng. From it you learn how the young woman began racing, about important moments in her career, and why her career ended. Writing this composition involved a series of steps. You will learn about these steps in this chapter.

Model: A Composition

The paragraphs in Phyllis Hollander's composition are numbered. As you read, decide what each paragraph tells about Chi Cheng.

The Agony of the Short-Distance Runner

[1] The roar of the fans was deafening. A tall, slim, Oriental girl, pushing herself to the limits of endurance, was stretching her legs toward the victory tape. With one last supreme effort, her graceful, rhythmic body reached the finish line first and she collapsed in a heap.

[2] This was the way Chi Cheng ran in fifty-nine out of sixty races during the summer of 1970. Although running was the most important thing in her life, every stride she took in competition caused her untold agony. According to an old Oriental saying, a journey of a thousand miles begins with the first step, but for this victorious sprinter, every step seemed to be a thousand miles.

[3] Actually Chi Cheng's first step in competition began when she was a junior high school freshman in Taiwan. She had never run in an official race before, but the long-legged student had been chosen by her classmates to represent them in a provincial meet. She had often demonstrated her speed in games the youngsters played in the rice fields around their native town of Hsinchu. Although Chi Cheng came in last in

that provincial race, she discovered that she had a special skill in sprinting and began to train in earnest.

[4] In 1962, when she was eighteen, American track and field coach Vince Reel went to Taiwan for the Asian Games. He was so impressed with the speed and potential of this lovely young racer that he convinced her to come to the United States and train with him for the 1964 Olympics in Tokyo.

[5] Chi Cheng made it to the Olympics, representing her homeland, but she had trouble from the very start. In the 80-meter hurdles, she was running head-to-head with the leader, Russian star Galina Bystrova, when she hit the fifth hurdle and felt something snap in her thigh. The pain was severe and this Olympics was over for Chi Cheng.

[6] In spite of the injury, Chi was determined to keep training. In 1967 she underwent an operation on her knee, and in 1968 she pulled muscles in both legs. Still she managed to make it to the 1968 Olympics in Mexico City, where she placed third in the hurdles and seventh at 100 meters.

[7] By the beginning of 1970, Chi's legs finally healed and her incredible speed and talent burst forth. In the next seven months she set world records at 100 yards, 100 meters, 220 yards, and 200 meters. All told, she broke or equaled seven world marks and lost only one race until December, when she once again suffered from a bad knee plus the permanent complication of a snapping hip.

[8] She was named Woman Athlete of the Year for 1970, but her competitive days were nearing an end. The pain of her injuries was so great she could hardly walk. In the hope of finding some relief she went home to Taiwan for surgery. Doctors removed 14 inches of muscle from her left thigh and 11 inches from her right. After fifty-two days in the hospital, the champion sprinter returned to America, not to run, but simply to learn to walk again.

[9] Sadly, the "world's fastest woman" had to abandon her racing career. But spunky Chi Cheng found other hurdles to challenge her. With her husband and former coach, Vince Reel, she became co-track coach at Redlands University in Redlands, California, teaching other sprinters and hurdlers to follow in her footsteps.[1]

Think and Discuss

The topic of Phyllis Hollander's composition is Chi Cheng's racing career. Which paragraphs in this composition develop each of the following parts of the topic?

1. How Chi Cheng began her racing career

2. Important moments in Chi Cheng's racing career

3. Problems in Chi Cheng's racing career

4. The end of Chi Cheng's racing career

Note: A paragraph may have information about more than one part of the topic.

Preparing to Write a Composition

Like any other piece of writing, a composition is the product of many prewriting steps. It requires thought, organization, and careful development. This section will take you through the steps that lead to a successful final product.

Discovering Subjects for Writing

For many people, finding a subject is the most difficult part of writing. However, if you stop to think about your many experiences, you will discover that you have many subjects for

[1]From *100 Greatest Women in Sports* by Phyllis Hollonder. Copyright © 1976 by Associated Features, Inc.

writing. If you have written about some of these experiences in your Writer's Notebook, you can use your entries as a source of ideas for writing a composition.

A good subject for writing is one that you know about from your experience or from ideas that you have.

Some of the subjects you write about may be from your job, hobbies, or interests. You may have had some funny or interesting experiences taking care of other people's pets, or you may have become an expert baby-sitter. You may want to write about a person you admire or a favorite place. Other subjects for writing may be from ideas you have. You may want to explain how to build a prize-winning model railroad layout, or you may want to explain the reasons why you feel your junior high or middle school should have a student council. All of these could be excellent subjects for compositions.

Writing Practice 1: *Discovering Subjects for Writing*

On a sheet of paper, make a list of five subjects that you could write about for a composition. To help you make your list, read through your Writer's Notebook to find experiences and ideas you have written about there. Next to each subject write the reason why you think the subject would be a good one for a composition. Here are three examples:

1. Model railroading—I've been building model railroads for four years. I've also learned a lot about this hobby from reading. One of the layouts that I built won three prizes, so I'm something of an expert.

2. Television—If there's anything I know about, it's television. I like many of the shows, but there are some commercials I just can't stand. I wrote a notebook entry about some of these commercials.

3. Origami—My grandfather taught me about the Japanese art of paper folding. This is a hobby not many people know about. Some of the things you can do by folding paper are amazing.

From Subject to Topic

Two of the sample subjects in Writing Practice 1 are model railroading and television. In some libraries you will find hundreds of books on these two subjects. When a subject is so large that people write entire books on it, you know you cannot tell much about it in a short paper.

Subjects such as model railroading and television are too large because they have too many parts. The following list shows just a few of the parts of the subject *Television:*

1. The millions of television sets in the world

2. The millions of people in the world who watch television

3. The millions of programs and commercials that have been on television since its beginning.

To do a good job of writing about a subject in a short paper, you must discuss the subject thoroughly. You cannot do this with a subject that has too many parts.

The subject for a short paper must be limited. This limited subject is called a *topic.*

A topic has fewer parts than a subject. A good topic for writing from the subject *Television* is *My choice for the three worst commercials on television.* If you wrote on this topic, you would write about *one* television viewer—yourself—and only *three* examples of commercials that you consider unworthy of broadcast.

A topic also gives the writer's *point of view* about the subject.

A point of view is a way of looking at a subject.

For example, the topic *My choice for the three worst commercials on television* says that the writer has an *unfavorable* point of view toward these commercials. The most interesting writers are often those who have unusual points of view toward subjects.

Model: *Point of View*

Jean Kerr writes about everyday experiences such as cooking, taking care of pets, and living with children, but millions of people enjoy her books because she writes about these experiences from a humorous point of view. In the following paragraph she describes her dog Kelly.

> I never meant to say anything about this, but the fact is that I have never met a dog that didn't have it in for me. You take Kelly, for instance. He's a wire-haired fox terrier and he's had us for three years now. I wouldn't say that he was terribly handsome but he does have a very nice smile. What he *doesn't* have is any sense of fitness. All the other dogs in the neighborhood spend their afternoons yapping at each other's heels or chasing cats. Kelly spends his whole day, every day, chasing swans on the millpond. I don't actually worry because he will never catch one. For one thing, he can't swim. Instead of settling for a simple dogpaddle like everybody else, he has to show off and try some complicated overhand stroke, with the result that he always sinks and has to be fished out. Naturally, people talk, and I never take him for a walk that somebody doesn't point him out and say, "There's that crazy dog that chases swans."[1]

[1]From *Please Don't Eat the Daisies* by Jean Kerr. Copyright © 1957 by The Conde Nast Publications, Inc. Reprinted by permission of Doubleday & Company, Inc.

Think and Discuss

What is the writer's point of view about her pet?

Writing Practice 2: *From Subject to Topic*

On a sheet of paper, write the five subjects you chose for Writing Practice 1. Limit each of these subjects to a topic. Write the topic beneath the subject from which you developed it. To be certain that you have a limited topic, check to see that it does not have more parts than you can discuss in a short paper, and that it has a point of view. Your teacher may ask you to explain how you limited the subject and what your point of view will be. Here are two examples:

1. Subject: Model railroading
    Topic: The layout that won
             (I limited the subject of model railroading to one particular layout. My point of view is that this is a prize-winning layout.)

2. Subject: Origami
    Topic: How to fold a paper flower
             (I limited the subject of origami to how to fold one shape. My point of view is that origami is an interesting and unusual art.)

Gathering Information

In the first chapter of this book, you learned methods to help you gather information about your topic. Once you have thought of a topic for writing, use one or more of these methods to help you gather the information you will include in your short paper. As you think of ideas, make notes about your topic on a sheet of paper.

Suppose, for example, that one writer lives in a neighborhood where dogs are allowed to run freely. These dogs frequently wander onto nearby highways and are sometimes struck by passing cars. The writer feels that neighbors are not accepting responsibility for their pets and decides this opinion would make a good topic for a composition.

The first step is to use a prewriting method. The writer decides to brainstorm and discovers the following ideas:

Dogs running loose
Often hit by cars
Tear up shrubbery and plants

870027

870028

My first dog, Fluffy, dug holes in our backyard.
Small children frightened by dogs
Dogs in garbage cans looking for food
Neighbor's dog that was poisoned
Ticks and fleas
Litters of puppies
No shots
Large dogs kept in small apartments and left alone all day
I read an article in our community newspaper about a dog that died when its owner left it on a hot day inside a car with the windows rolled up.
One of my favorite books is *Old Yeller*.

Some of the ideas in these notes do not relate to the topic and must be eliminated before writing. Even after taking out unrelated ideas, however, the writer has enough material for a short paper. In fact, the problem with dogs in the neighborhood is even bigger than it first seemed. It involves people not only allowing dogs to run loose, but also not taking responsibility for their pets in other ways. The writer decides on the topic *A dog owner's responsibilities*.

Writing Practice 3: *Gathering Information*

Select one of the topics you developed for Writing Practice 2. Use one or more of the prewriting methods introduced in Chapter 1 to find ideas for your writing. As you brainstorm, free write, cluster ideas, or ask questions, make notes.

Planning a Composition

Once you have gathered information about a topic, the next step is to decide how to use the information. To do this, ask yourself three questions:

1. What is my purpose in writing this paper?

2. Who are my readers for this paper?

3. What is my point of view?

Of course, one reason for writing a paper is to complete an assignment and get a good grade, but that purpose does not help you decide how to use your information.

Every composition has a purpose that is related to the topic.

For the topic *A dog owner's responsibilities*, the writer's purpose will be to *explain* the responsibilities of a dog owner. With this purpose in mind, the writer can decide which information to include in the paper. On pages 100–101 are the notes the writer made while brainstorming this topic. Since the purpose of the paper is to tell about a dog owner's responsibilities, the writer will not use the notes *My first dog, Fluffy, dug holes in our backyard* or *One of my favorite books is* <u>*Old Yeller*</u> because this information is not related.

Your reader affects the way you write.

Unless your teacher tells you otherwise, the readers for your composition are your teacher and your classmates. Keep these readers in mind as you write your composition. If you write about a subject they may not know, such as origami, you may need to define words and give examples. Drawings or diagrams may also help your readers.

Your point of view also affects the way you write.

The last question to ask yourself is about your point of view—your relationship to your subject. Are you an authority on your subject? Do you know more about your subject than your readers? If you do know more than your readers, you will be giving them information that they do not know, and your composition is more likely to be interesting. If you do not know any more about your subject than your readers, you will probably have to do some research. You can still make your subject interesting if you have an unusual or humorous point of view.

Writing Practice 4: *Planning Your Composition*

On a sheet of paper, write the purpose for your composition. Then look back at the information that you gathered for Writing Practice 3. Make a list of the information that fits the purpose of your paper and will be included in your composition. Also, make a list of information that you will *not* include because it does not fit the purpose of your paper.

Next, write the words you will need to define for your readers. Make a note of places where a diagram or drawing might be helpful to your readers.

Finally, decide whether you know more about your topic than your readers. If you do, write down the information you will give your readers that they do not already have. If you do not know more about your topic than your readers, explain why your unusual point of view will make the composition interesting.

Organizing a Composition

Details in a composition must have a logical order. To decide how to arrange details, look back at your topic and at your purpose for writing. Consider the topic *A dog owner's responsibilities*. Ideas about this topic fall into the following three groups:

1. Responsibilities for a dog's health

2. Responsibilities for a dog's safety

3. Responsibilities for the harm that a dog could cause

In a composition on this topic, the writer may devote one or more paragraphs to each group of details. The first part of the composition will be about the owner's responsibility for the dog's health. The second part will be about the owner's responsibility for its safety, and the third part will be about the owner's responsibility for the harm a dog could cause.

Writing Practice 5: *Organizing a Composition*

Look at the information you gathered about your topic and decide on a logical order for the information. On a sheet of paper, copy the information in the order in which you will use it in your paper.

Making an Outline

In the last section, you made some general decisions about arranging information in your composition. For example, the writer of the paper on *A Dog Owner's Responsibilities* decided on three large groupings of details.

The next step is to arrange the details within each large grouping. One way to decide how to arrange details is to make an *informal outline.*

An informal outline is a plan for arranging information.

An informal outline shows how the main parts of a paper will be arranged, and it shows the details that develop each of these parts.

The following example is an informal outline for the topic *A dog owner's responsibilities.*

A Dog Owner's Responsibilities

Responsibilities for a dog's health
    Shots
    Medical care
    Balanced diet
    Exercise
Responsibilities for a dog's safety
    Dangerous streets
    Poisoned food
    Unattended dog
Responsibilities for the harm that a dog could cause
    Rabies
    Small children
    Property

The example is called a *topic outline* because its parts are not sentences. In a topic outline the headings should have the same form. In the outline above, for example, each heading is a noun or a noun plus modifiers. If your teacher prefers, you can write a *sentence outline,* but you should not mix topics and sentences in the same outline. The following example is a sentence outline for the topic *A dog owner's responsibilities:*

A Dog Owner's Responsibilities

Dog owners are responsible for a dog's health.
    They should give the dog the necessary shots to keep it healthy.
    They should provide medical care for the dog when it is ill.
    They should feed the dog a balanced diet.
    They should exercise the dog.
Dog owners are responsible for a dog's safety.
    They should keep the dog away from dangerous streets.
    They should keep the dog away from poisoned food.
    They should not leave dogs alone in cars.
Dog owners are responsible for the harm a dog could cause to other people and to property.
    They should get the dog a rabies shot.
    They should see that the dog does not harm small children.
    They should see that the dog does not harm neighbors' property.

Chapter 6 of this book tells how to write a *formal outline*. A formal outline uses letters and numbers to order its parts. As you can see, there are no numbers in an informal outline, but some parts are indented.

The three parts of the above outline that are not indented are the *major headings*. Details that develop these headings are indented below each of the headings. In the composition, each major heading can be a separate paragraph.

After you have decided which main ideas you will include in your composition and which details you will use to explain them, you are ready to write a *thesis sentence*. This sentence will present the central theme of your composition. For example, a good thesis sentence for the composition about dog owners' responsibilities (outlined on page 105) would be: *Although caring for a dog's health is important, it is only one responsibility of a dog's owner; other responsibilities are for the safety of the dog and for the harm the dog may cause to others.* This sentence not only names the topic of the composition, but also summarizes the three main points that will be made about the topic.

Writing Practice 6: *An Informal Outline and Thesis Sentence*

Using the ideas you gathered for Writing Practice 3, write an informal outline. To show which thoughts are major headings and which are details, indent the details under the major headings. Then write a thesis sentence that tells what your composition will cover.

Writing a Composition

Writing a composition means more than putting several paragraphs together. You must also decide how to introduce your topic, how to use paragraphs to develop your topic, and how to end your paper.

Writing the Introduction

An *introduction* names your topic and says something interesting about it.

Your introduction should make readers look forward to reading your paper. The first paragraph of Phyllis Hollander's composition at the beginning of this chapter introduces the topic of Chi

Cheng by showing her in a race. As you read the paragraph, you can hear the people cheering. In her introductory paragraph, Phyllis Hollander uses sense details to describe one part of her topic—Chi Cheng's racing career. This use of sense details is one kind of introduction. In this composition, it is especially appropriate since the sense details immediately give the reader access to Chi Cheng's experience.

To help you decide what part of your topic would make an interesting introduction, look back at your informal outline. For example, a composition about a dog owner's responsibilities could begin with sense details describing a healthy dog. This would relate to a major heading: *Responsibilities for a dog's health.*

Model: An Introduction Using Sense Details

A healthy dog is an attractive dog. It has a shiny coat and clear, alert eyes. An unhealthy dog, on the other hand, is a miserable sight. Its dim eyes and its dull coat betray its lack of care. Although caring for a dog's health is important, it is only one responsibility of a dog's owner; other responsibilities are for the safety of the dog and for the harm the dog may cause to others.

Note that this introduction ends with the thesis sentence. A good introduction often contains the thesis; this tells readers what to look for in the rest of the composition.

Writing Practice 7: *Writing the Introduction*

Use sense details to write an introductory paragraph for a composition on the topic you have selected. Your teacher may ask you to explain why you think your paragraph would interest readers. Include your thesis sentence in your paragraph.

Writing the Body

The *body* **of the composition is the part that actually develops your topic.**

In the body of the composition, each main heading of your informal outline may become a separate paragraph.

Good compositions are *unified* **and** *coherent.*

A composition is *unified* when each paragraph develops the topic of the composition. A composition is *coherent* when the reader can easily tell how the paragraphs relate to the topic and to each other.

Look back again at the informal outline on page 104. When making the outline, the writer took out the notes *My first dog was Fluffy* and *One of my favorite books is Old Yeller* because these items did not apply to the topic. If the writer had written a paragraph about either one of these items, the composition would not be unified. Unity is an important feature of any composition.

Model: Body of a Composition

The following body is for a composition on the topic *A Dog Owner's Responsibilities.* As you read pay attention to the structure of the body and take note of its unity.

This paragraph develops the major heading *Responsibilities for a dog's health.*

A dog's health should be its owner's first concern. Dogs need regular shots, a balanced diet, medical care when they are ill, and exercise. Because the first three items are expensive, many dog owners ignore them. They give their dogs only the shots required by law, feed their dogs table scraps, and ignore signs that their pets aren't feeling well. Also, because exercising animals is an effort, many dogs stay cooped up in small houses or yards practically all the time.

This paragraph develops the major heading *Responsibilities for a dog's safety.*

Another important responsibility of a dog owner is the dog's safety. Unless owners live on a farm or other open land, dogs should not be allowed to run loose. Unsupervised dogs often wander onto highways where they are struck by passing cars. Sadly, people have been known to leave poisoned meat out for dogs that make a nuisance of themselves by roaming around neighborhoods. Also, dogs should not be left alone in cars or trucks, especially during hot weather. An article in a local newspaper told about a woman who left her dog inside a car on a day when the temperature was almost 100°F. The windows were rolled up, and the dog could get no air. The animal died from suffocation.

This paragraph develops the heading *Responsibilities for the harm that a dog could cause.*

Dog owners also have a responsibility for the harm their pets might cause to people and to property. At the very least, owners should be certain that their dogs have the yearly rabies shot every state requires. This shot protects anyone the dog might bite from rabies, a serious illness, which only a few people in the United States have survived. Dog owners should also be especially careful with their pets around small children. The dog may mean no harm, but even a playful dog jumping up on a small child can cause an injury. Finally, dog owners should keep their pets from harming other people's property. A dog that digs up shrubbery or flowers in neighbors' yards is an unwelcome visitor, to say the least.

This composition has unity because each paragraph develops the topic that was selected: *A Dog Owner's Responsibilities*. The composition is coherent because the reader can easily tell how the paragraphs relate to the topic and to each other. The first paragraph of the body is about an owner's responsibilities for a dog's health. The second is about the owner's responsibilities for the dog's safety, and the third is about responsibilities for the harm that a dog could cause to people and to property.

The writer also uses transition words and phrases to make the composition coherent. Some of these words and phrases show that the writer is moving from one point to another:

> A dog's health should be its owner's <u>first</u> concern.
>
> <u>Another</u> important responsibility is for the dog's safety.
>
> Dog owners <u>also</u> have a responsibility for the harm a dog could cause <u>to</u> people and to property.

The writer also connects paragraphs by repeating key words and phrases from previous paragraphs. For instance, the key words *dog, owner,* and *responsibility* appear in each paragraph in the body.

Writing Practice 8: *Writing the Body*

Write the body of the composition that you began in Writing Practice 7. Use the informal outline you made for Writing Practice 6 to help you decide which headings to develop in separate paragraphs. Your teacher may ask you to explain how each paragraph develops your topic and to tell which words or phrases help the coherence of the composition.

Writing the Conclusion

A *conclusion* is a final paragraph that comes after the body of the composition—it brings the work to a close.

In a short paper the conclusion should do more than restate what the writer has already said. A good conclusion should tie together the various points you have made and help you achieve the purpose of the paper. The conclusion should also relate to the thesis and give the reader a sense of reaching the end of a discussion.

Model: A Conclusion

The following paragraph is a conclusion for the sample composition *A Dog Owner's Responsibilities*.

> The results of the carelessness of some dog owners are obvious. In some places dogs run in packs, scrounging for food, scratching furiously from ticks and fleas. Female dogs are allowed to have litter after litter of puppies, only adding to the problem. Neglecting animals in this manner is a crime. It's time that dog owners lived up to their responsibilities.

Think and Discuss

1. How does the conclusion refer to the thesis?
2. What sense details in this conclusion will leave readers with vivid mental images?

Writing Assignment I: *Writing a Composition*

For this assignment you will take all the pieces of the composition you have been developing in the Writing Practices throughout this chapter and write a complete composition. Your audience will be your teacher and classmates.

A. Prewriting

Gather your Writing Practices and reread them. Jot down ideas you could include; cross out ideas that don't apply. Free write to find ideas for a conclusion for your composition.

B. Writing

Using your notes and the introduction and body you wrote for the Writing Practices, write a complete composition. Use transition words between sentences and paragraphs, and strive for unity and coherence in your composition. Keep your audience in mind as you write. Use details that will interest them, and explain terms they may not know. Finally, using your free writing notes, write a conclusion. Use sense details to leave readers with mental images, and refer to your thesis.

C. Postwriting

Use the following checklist to revise your paper.

Checklist for Revising a Composition

1. The introductory paragraph introduces the topic and interests the reader in the composition.

2. The paper has a clear purpose, stated in a thesis sentence.

3. The topic is thoroughly discussed.

4. Either the information is new to readers, or the composition has an unusual point of view.

5. Each paragraph develops the topic; the composition is unified.

6. Readers can tell how the paragraphs relate to each other and to the topic; your work is coherent.

7. The concluding paragraph tells the reader that the discussion is completed.

After revising your composition, proofread it. After all errors are corrected, make a neat final draft. Finally, share your composition with your classmates; then tell one another which parts you like best, and why.

Sentence Variety:
Inserting Sentences

Building Sentences by Inserting

*I*nserting means "putting one thing into another." You insert a letter into an envelope in order to mail it, and you insert an ink cartridge into a pen in order to refill it. When you insert one sentence into another, you take a *part* of that sentence and fit it into another sentence called the *base sentence*. The part that you have inserted may be changed in some way.

Inserting Modifiers

Modifiers are words that limit or describe other words. In this lesson you will practice inserting modifiers into a base sentence. Consider the following sentences:

The news about our school was on television.

The television was local.

In the second sentence the word *local* modifies the word *television*. You combine sentences by moving modifiers to the front of the word they modify in the base sentence.

The news about our school was on *local* television.

It is possible to insert almost any number of modifiers into a base sentence, as the following example shows:

The day was long.

The day was hot.

The game was boring.

The basketball was one-on-one.

In these sentences the modifiers are the words *long, hot, boring,* and *one-on-one. Long* and *hot* modify *day; boring* modifies *game; one-on-one* modifies *basketball.* These modifiers can be inserted into a base sentence such as *Throughout the day we played a game of basketball,* with the following result:

Throughout the *long, hot* day we played a *boring* game of *one-on-one* basketball.

The signals you will use in this lesson are (,) and (*and*) and (*,and*). The signal (,) means to place a comma *before* a modifier when you insert it into the base sentence. The signal (*and*) means to write the word *and* before a modifier when you combine sentences. Use both a comma and the word *and* when you see the signal (*,and*).

Exercise 1: *Inserting Modifiers*

Study the examples and on a sheet of paper, combine the following sentences. The first sentence in each set is the base.

Examples

a. Her face gave away her age.
   Her face was wrinkled.
   Her face was weather-beaten. (,)
   Her age was advanced.
   Her wrinkled, weather-beaten face gave away her advanced age.

b. The clerk dropped the crystal on the floor.
   The clerk was hurried.
   The clerk was inefficient. (*and*)
   The crystal was beautiful.
   The crystal was fragile. (,)
   The floor was stone.
   The hurried and inefficient clerk dropped the beautiful, fragile crystal on the stone floor.

1. The notebook is on the desk.
   The notebook is loose-leaf.
   The desk is oak.

2. The scouts returned from their hike.
   The scouts were exhausted.
   The scouts were famished. (*and*)
   The hike was long.
   The hike was difficult. (,)

3. She was a child.
   She was strong.
   She was intelligent. (,)
   She was wiry. (*,and*)

113

4. The cats were fighting in the alley.
   The cats were battered.
   The cats were stray. (,)
   The cats were calico.
   The alley was nearby.

5. His eyes peered out from under his eyebrows.
   His eyes were beady.
   His eyes were green. (,)
   His eyes were alert. (,and)
   His eyebrows were bushy.

The next five sets of sentences do not have signals. Read each set carefully and decide how you think the modifiers should be inserted into the base sentence. Copy each new sentence on a sheet of paper numbered 6–10.

Example

a. Now he saw the fire—a thread between him and the location of the voice.
   The thread was tender.
   The thread was rosy.
   The thread was creeping.
   The voice was frightened.
   Now he saw the fire—a tender, rosy, creeping thread between him and the location of the frightened voice.

6. The air was filled with wings of birds.
   The air was stifling.
   The air was summery.
   The wings were beating.
   The birds were multicolored.
   The birds were crested.

7. She sat in the dark, a figure of despair.
   The dark was gloomy.
   The dark was depressing.
   The figure was spiritless.
   The despair was awful.

8. She held an armful of clothing and a washboard as she stood motionless at the steps, looking into the lot.
   The armful was huge.
   The clothing was dirty.
   The clothing was ragged.
   The washboard was metal-rimmed.
   The steps were rotten.

9. When the dragon bore down on him again, he hoped for one minute that his armor would protect him.
   The dragon was scaly.
   The dragon was fire-breathing.
   The minute was wild.
   The armor was rusty.
   The armor was second-hand.

10. Through the window half-stuffed with rags in the house across the alley, Bella saw a woman holding what appeared to be a child wrapped in a quilt.
    The rags were dirty.
    The house was decayed.
    The woman was proud.
    The woman was erect.
    The child was small.
    The quilt was tattered.

Writing Practice: *Inserting Modifiers*

Reread the introductory paragraph of the composition you wrote for Chapter 5. Revise the paragraph by inserting modifiers. Using the sentence variety techniques you have just learned, combine short sentences in your paragraph and add sense details. Strive for a variety of sentence lengths and patterns.

115

6 Writing About Ideas

When you write about ideas, you are usually writing for one of two reasons: to explain or to inform. Although you can also explain and inform by talking, writing has advantages. Unlike speech, written ideas, directions, and information of all kinds can be preserved. If a reader does not understand the information at once, he or she can read it again and absorb it more fully. In addition, writing ideas and information often makes a person think more clearly and carefully.

In this chapter, you will work to express ideas clearly and carefully by writing for the following purposes:

Writing messages
Giving directions
Giving instructions about a process
Explaining an opinion
Writing a report

Writing Explanations

One kind of writing you do often, perhaps even daily, is writing explanations. If you write a message telling your parents when you will be home, you write an explanation. You also do this when you write directions and when you write instructions such as you find in a recipe. In this section you will learn how to write messages, directions, and instructions. You will also learn how to explain an opinion clearly.

Writing Messages

Suppose your parents have gone out for the afternoon and have left you at home. Shortly after they leave, a friend calls to invite you to a basketball game. You are certain your parents will not mind your going, so you make your plans and leave them the following note:

Mom and Dad,

Have gone to Johnson game with Kiyo and her parents. They will bring me home after game. Should be back by 6:00.

Mary

Because you were in a hurry, you made your note as brief as possible, but you included all the important information. You told your parents where you went, who went with you, and when and how you were coming home, but you left out unimportant information. You did not tell your parents what time Kiyo called or what she had to say about a certain television program because these items had nothing to do with the information you wanted to give your parents.

Consider your reader when you write a message.

Decide what your reader needs to know, and provide only that information in your message. Mary did this when she wrote her note. If she had written it for someone other than her parents, she might have given more or different information.

Your reader also affects *how* you write a message. Because Mary wrote a message for her parents, she wrote *Have gone to Johnson game* instead of *I have gone to the Johnson Junior High School basketball game.* Suppose, however, you are answering the telephone for your principal. A message for your principal might look like the one following.

May 3, 1984

Dear Mrs. McPherson,

Mr. Folger called to say that he cannot be at the meeting this afternoon because of an emergency. He would like for you to return his call when you have time. He called at 3:00 P.M.

Mary Williams

Messages should be *clear* and *accurate*.

Clear writing is easy to understand because it does not contain unimportant information. It is also organized with the most important information first. For example, in the message to the principal above, the most important information is that Mr. Folger cannot be at the meeting.

Accuracy means that the information in the message is correct. Giving inaccurate information in an important message could have serious results. One way to be certain that your messages are accurate is to write down the information you need as you are given it. This is especially important when you are taking a message over the telephone.

Writing Practice 1: *Writing Messages*

The following two situations involve writing messages. For each of these situations, decide what information the reader needs. (Make up any information you think is missing.) Organize the information so that you give the most important details first; then write the messages.

1.   Your classmate and friend is ill and will be out of school for several weeks. Your science teacher asks you to write a

note to your friend giving the assignments for that time. The following information is what your teacher wants your friend to know:

a. The class will cover Chapters 10 and 11 of the science book.

b. Students are to answer all of the discussion questions at the end of Chapter 10, but only questions 1, 4, and 6 at the end of Chapter 11.

c. Each student is to select a book about a well-known scientist and begin reading it.

d. Each student is to select one of the experiments in the two chapters to do for the class. Students may work together on this assignment.

The teacher says your friend does not have to worry about the experiment, but might want to begin reading the book. If so, you can bring your friend a book from the library.

2. You are answering the telephone in the school library while the librarian, Mr. Jones, is out to lunch. While he is gone, he gets an important call from the head librarian at the State Department of Education, Mrs. Mary Kersey. Mrs. Kersey calls to tell Mr. Jones that she will visit your school library on Tuesday, April 16. She would like Mr. Jones to call the other librarians in the system and ask them to meet at 10:00 that morning in your library. The meeting should last no more than two hours. Mrs. Kersey will arrive in your school at 9:00 A.M. Write the message to Mr. Jones.

Writing Directions

Have you ever tried to follow directions that were not clear? Unclear directions have an immediate result: you become lost. One important part of writing clear directions is to give the information your reader needs.

Suppose you write directions for getting to your house for a friend who lives in your town. Because your friend knows the names of many streets, large buildings, and other landmarks, you could write directions such as the following:

Go north on the Strip and take a left at Cochran's.

Being familiar with the area, your friend knows that the *Strip* is the local name for your town's main highway and that *Cochran's* is a large roller-skating rink several miles down the highway.

Suppose, however, that you write directions for an out-of-town friend. In this case you must give more complete information about streets and buildings:

Go north on Highway 57. About three or four miles from where you entered the highway is a large roller-skating rink named Cochran's. Turn left there.

Another key to writing clear directions is to give step-by-step directions. Giving step-by-step directions means beginning at a place your reader knows and listing each new direction from that place:

Starting from the school, go three blocks north on 6th Street. Then turn right onto Celeste Avenue.

It is often helpful to mention buildings or other landmarks in the area:

About a mile down Celeste Avenue, you'll see a fire station on the right. Just after the fire station, you'll come to a fork in the road. Take the right fork.

Small maps, such as the one on the next page, showing names of streets, east/west and north/south directions, and buildings or other objects are also helpful.

A last point to remember is to be precise. Precise directions give exact information. They do not read *Drive down the street for a while;* instead, they read *Drive three blocks east on Summer Street.* They give exact information about distance, directions, and names.

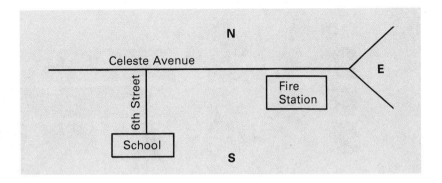

Writing Practice 2: *Writing Directions*

Write directions from your school to your house or apartment for a new classmate. Your classmate has lived in your area for only a few days. Use a map or diagram to illustrate your directions.

Writing About a Process

You write about a process when you write step-by-step instructions for doing something. Instructions on packages tell how to prepare the food inside, and instructions in the front of the telephone directory explain long-distance calling.

Instructions that are not clear can result in wasted time and money and much frustration. A badly written recipe can ruin a meal; confusing directions for operating a new calculator can ruin your grade in math.

The first step in writing clear instructions is to think about your reader.

When writing step-by-step instructions, never assume that your readers have the same level of familiarity or expertise as you do. As much as possible, use words that your readers already know. Define any terms that readers may not know and give clear examples.

Young readers, for instance, often need more and simpler information. Read the following instructions for making a local telephone call. If you were writing these instructions for a group of nine-year-old children, what changes would you make?

To make a local call, do not dial the area code. Dial only the telephone number. For example, dial 555-8679.

Nine-year-olds may not know what the terms *local* and *area code* mean. Such words would have to be defined. The following instructions might be more appropriate for nine-year-olds.

The three digits in front of a telephone number are the *area code*. For example, in the number (312) 555-8679, the digits *312* form the area code. The area code is the same for all telephone numbers within a certain area.

A *local* telephone call is one made to a number within your billing area. To make a local call, dial only the telephone number. Do not dial the area code. For example, for the number (312) 555-8679, dial 555-8679.

Give instructions step-by-step and arrange them in the order in which they are done.

Before writing instructions, be certain that you understand the steps. You could not explain to someone how to operate a hot-air popcorn popper unless you understood how the popper worked. Before you can give information on heating frozen pizza, you must understand how to do it. One way to be certain you understand the steps is to write each of them in order on a sheet of paper: step 1, step 2, step 3, and so on. Be certain that you have not left out any steps. Then you can organize your notes into sentences for your readers.

Instructions may be written as a list or they may be written in paragraph form. Instructions in paragraph form may need transition words—such as *first, second, third, then, next, after, when,*—to help readers follow the steps.

Model: Written Instructions

The following paragraph gives instructions for making a lean-to fire.

Making a Lean-To Fire-Lay

Hikers caught in a sudden mountain thunderstorm can get warm and dry quickly by making a simple lean-to fire. The first step is to collect several thin sticks, dry weed stalks, or other kindling. Under logs or rocks and around the bases of trees are good places to look for dry kindling. The next step is to start the fire-lay by pushing a green "lean-to stick" in the ground at a 30-degree angle. The top of the stick should point in the direction from which the wind comes. Next, a good amount of tinder is placed well in under the lean-to stick. Thin sticks and dry weed stalks, broken into short lengths, are leaned carefully against the lean-to stick. When the small, thin sticks or twigs are in place, thicker fuel sticks can be leaned against the thinner kindling. Now the fire-lay is ready to ignite. A good steady match flame thrust into the center of the fire-lay will fire the dry kindling, and there will soon be a warm, bright fire.

Think and Discuss

What transition words in the paragraph help readers move from one step to the next? For example, sentence two contains the words "The first step . . . "What other transition words appear in the paragraph?

Writing Practice 3: *Writing Instructions*

Think of something you know how to do well enough to write instructions for another person. First, on a sheet of paper, write down the materials a person would need to follow your instructions. Next, write down each step in the process. Finally, select one of the readers in the Readers list on page 124, and decide what information that person needs. Write the instructions for your reader, either as a list or as a paragraph.

To help you get started, the following list suggests subjects:

Subjects

How to go from your house or apartment to another location on public transportation

How to find the best fishing holes

How to find the Big Dipper constellation

How to bathe a cat

Readers

Your new robot that automatically programs simply word-ed instructions when you read them aloud

A foreign-exchange student who is living with your family and does not know much about American life

A new classmate who is blind and to whom you will read the set of instructions

A close friend

An older relative

Writing to Explain an Opinion

A statement such as *A junior high or middle school should have a student council* is an opinion that may not be shared by everyone. If you were to write on that topic, your readers would naturally expect you to know why you have that opinion.

An opinion is based on reasons.

Giving reasons is not difficult if you stop to consider why you hold an opinion and how you came to believe it to be true. The following reasons are some that might explain the opinion *A junior high or middle school should have a student council.* You might want to add others of your own.

Students at this age should have practice in making decisions.

Student councils help teach students the responsibilities of living in a democratic society.

Many school problems, such as keeping the halls and lunchrooms clean, can be discussed in a student council.

Special projects to help the school can be planned in a student council.

Writing a *letter to the editor* is one way to express an opinion. A letter to the editor is a letter expressing your opinion in a school or community newspaper. Letters to the editor follow standard business letter form. They usually begin with a statement of the opinion, followed by reasons for it. If they are printed, you may find that they have been edited or cut.

Model: *A Letter to the Editor*

This letter was written to a school newspaper.

12 Bramwell Road
Ogden, UT 84009
January 22, 1984

The Editor
The Valley Weekly
Mount Valley Middle School
Ogden, UT 84009

Dear Editor:

I think Mount Valley Middle School should have a student council. A student council would be helpful both to the students and to the school.

Students our age need practice making decisions. Since the purpose of a student council is to make decisions affecting the students and the school, the organization would help prepare us for our adult lives. Also, a student council is like a small democracy because student members discuss issues and then vote on them. We could learn a lot about living in a democratic society from such a group.

A student council would be a help to the school, as well as to the students. In the council we could discuss school problems such as noise in the cafeteria and the dirty hallways. With the help of faculty advisers, we might be able to think of practical solutions. We could also organize projects that would help the school. For example, we might sponsor a small store to sell supplies and paperback books at break and at lunch time. The profit from the store could be used for school activities.

When students feel that they are an important part of the school, they are more likely to take part in school activities. A student council at Mount Valley Middle School would make a big difference.

Sincerely yours,

Rosa Aguilar
Rosa Aguilar

Writing Practice 4: *Writing a Letter to the Editor*

Write a letter to the editor of your school newspaper. First, select one of the opinions listed below or make up one of your own. Next, make a list of your reasons for having the opinion. Then write a letter stating your opinion and explaining it with reasons. If you want your letter published, send it to the editor of your school newspaper.

1. Students should take more pride in our school.

2. Both boys and girls should take home economics and shop courses.

3. Homework should not be assigned over weekends.

4. Parents should restrict the amount of time that teenagers can watch television.

5. Junk foods should not be sold in schools.

Writing Reports

The purpose of a report is to give information about a subject.

Subjects for reports usually do not come from your own experiences. Instead, you report on such factual subjects as the first walk on the moon, the history of your school, or the story of peanut butter. Because you are not writing about your own experiences, you will use sources such as books, magazines, and interviews with people to gather information.

In the following sections you will study and practice how to organize and write clear and interesting reports.

Deciding on a Topic

In some of your classes, your teacher may assign a report topic. In other classes, however, you will be asked to choose your own topic. The guidelines for selecting composition topics apply to selecting report topics as well. If you do not remember these guidelines, review the material in Chapter 5. Remember that much of your information for a report will come from such sources as books, magazines, and interviews.

A good report covers its topic thoroughly.

It would take you many months of work to gather enough information to cover a subject such as *The history of Indiana* or *The United States space program*. Therefore, it is important to restrict your topic. For example, you could probably gather enough material in a short time to write a report on *The history of my school* or *The first space walk*.

Writing Practice 5: *Restricting Topics*

The following ten subjects are too broad for a short report. Decide how you would restrict each subject to a topic to develop in a short paper. On a sheet of paper, write the topic you have developed from each subject.

Example

Subject	Topic
The history of U.S. space exploration	Neil Armstrong's walk on the moon

Subjects

1. Food
2. Movies
3. Magicians
4. Heroes
5. Animals
6. Famous athletes
7. Education
8. Courageous people
9. Interesting inventions
10. Music

Writing a Preliminary Thesis Sentence

After deciding on a restricted topic, you need to compose a preliminary *thesis sentence*—a single sentence that tells exactly what point you are going to make about a topic. *Neil Armstrong's walk on the moon* is a restricted topic, but it doesn't reveal the point you are going to make. On the other hand, *Neil Armstrong's walk on the moon is one of the "firsts" that will always be included in American history books* reveals exactly what your paper is about. A reader who sees this thesis sentence at the beginning of your paper can expect the paper to center on the historical significance of the first walk on the moon.

A thesis sentence is important not only to readers, but also to writers. Once you have a thesis sentence, you can better decide which information to include in your paper. For example, a paper using the thesis sentence above would not include information about Neil Armstrong's personal life.

Writing Practice 6: *Writing a Thesis Sentence*

Using the list of restricted topics you composed for Writing Practice 5, think of a clear thesis sentence for each topic. Write these thesis sentences on a separate sheet of paper. Concentrate on making each interesting to readers.

Gathering Information

Once you have a restricted topic and a preliminary thesis sentence for your report, you can begin gathering information. Since you may not know much about your topic, it is a good idea first to find some general information in order to get familiar with your topic. The encyclopedia, which has articles on thousands of subjects, is a good place to begin. (For help in using an encyclopedia, see Chapter 26.)

Suppose you want to write a report on the famous American Harriet Tubman, but do not know much about her. You begin by looking for general information in the *T* volume of the encyclopedia, where you find that she lived from 1820 to 1913. She was once a slave, but she escaped in 1849. She risked her life many times to help other slaves to freedom on the "Underground Railroad." She was also a nurse and spy for the Union forces. At the end of the article, the encyclopedia gives the names of two books about Harriet Tubman. This is called bibliographical information.

Now that you have general information, you want to find sources that can give you more specific information. These sources should answer questions about the general information that you found in the encyclopedia.

Sometimes, as with Harriet Tubman, an encyclopedia gives names of books where you can find more specific information about a topic. Another way to find specific information is to look in the card catalogue for books on your subject and in the *Readers' Guide to Periodical Literature* for magazine and newspaper articles on your subject. The chapter on "Library Skills" tells how to use the card catalogue and the *Readers' Guide*. With some topics you will also find such reference books as almanacs and special encyclopedias helpful.

Writing Practice 7: *Finding Information*

From the list of topics and thesis sentences you developed for Writing Practices 5 and 6, select one that you are interested in learning more about. Locate an encyclopedia article on your topic and read the general information you find there. Using the general information you now have about your topic, make a list of specific information that you want to find about your topic. List three books and three magazine articles you could use to find information on your topic.

Taking Notes

For reports, you read what others have written about your topic and use their information. When you do this, you must give these people credit for their information and be able to show your readers, including your teacher, where you got the information. Using the words of other writers without giving the writers credit for their words is dishonest.

To keep a record of your sources of information, you follow certain steps when taking notes. These steps will help you avoid *plagiarism* (using someone else's work without giving credit), and will make the preparation of a *bibliography* easier. A bibliography is a list of sources used in writing a report. It goes at the end of a report.

As you gather information for your report, use a separate sheet of paper or a 3″ × 5″ note card to take notes from each source. At the top, list the title of the book, the author, the place of publication, the publisher, and the date of publication. This information is found at the front of a book. For magazines, list the title of the article, the author, the title of the magazine, and the date of publication.

As you take notes, use your own words. Limit the notes on each page or card to one idea. If you use a direct quotation, place quotation marks around the exact words. To make it easy for you to find the information again, note the exact page number at the bottom of each page or card.

> The Peanut Butter Cookbook.
> William I. Kaufman.
> New York: Simon & Schuster, 1977.
> peanut butter first made in
> St. Louis in 1890.
>
> p. 7

Writing Practice 8: *Taking Notes*

For this assignment use the sources of information you selected for Writing Practice 7. Follow these directions:

1. Locate each of your sources in the library.

2. If you cannot locate one of your sources, use the card catalogue or *Readers' Guide* to select another one.

3. Using sheets of paper or note cards, take notes from each of your sources. Add other information if it relates to your topic.

Organizing Your Information

The questions you ask yourself about your topic will help you organize your information. The following questions are ones a writer asked about the story of peanut butter. Below the questions is the information the writer found to answer them:

1. *Who* first made peanut butter?
    A doctor in St. Louis

2. *What* was the first peanut butter like?
    Ground-up peanuts with salt added—oil floated to top

3. *What* was later peanut butter like?
    Factory-made peanut butter had ingredient added to keep oil mixed in

4. *Where* does peanut butter come from?
   From peanuts

5. *Where* do peanuts come from?
   First eaten and grown in Peru
   Taken to West Africa from Peru
   Came to U.S. from West Africa

6. *Where* is peanut butter made?
   First made at home
   Later made in factories
   Often made at home today

7. *When* were peanuts first eaten and grown?
   Over 1,200 years ago in Peru

8. *When* did peanuts first come to U.S.?
   In 1600s from West Africa

9. *When* was peanut butter first made?
   1890

10. *Why* was peanut butter first made?
    For a healthy food

11. *Why* is peanut butter a healthy food?
    Has protein

12. *How* is peanut butter made?
    Peanuts shelled, sorted, and graded
    Outer skin removed
    Peanut split
    Heart of peanut removed
    Peanuts ground
    Other ingredients added

The *where?* and *when?* questions give an idea of the history of peanut butter. Answers to the *how?* questions describe the process of making peanut butter. Now the writer has at least two main headings for a report on peanut butter:

1. The history of peanut butter

2. How peanut butter is made in factories

In reading about peanut butter, the writer also found interesting information about the peanut. Since peanut butter is made from peanuts, the writer decides to add this heading first:

1. The history of peanuts

2. The history of peanut butter

3.   How peanut butter is made in factories

Another interesting fact the writer found is that many people today are going back to making peanut butter at home. They do this because they do not want the artificial ingredients that are added to peanut butter in factories and because peanut butter made at home is fresher. The information relates to the topic and would be interesting for readers. The writer adds it as the last heading:

1.   The history of peanuts

2.   The history of peanut butter

3.   How peanut butter is made in factories

4.   Back to homemade peanut butter

The first step in organizing information is to identify main headings. These headings are the main ideas about your topic. Arranging your information by *who? what? where? when? why? how?* questions will help you do this.

Writing Practice 9: *Answering Questions About a Topic*

Divide a sheet of paper into six columns. Give each column one of these headings: Who? What? Where? When? Why? How? Decide what kind of question about your topic each piece of information that you have found answers. List that piece of information under the proper heading. Read the example before you begin.

Example

Who?	*What?*	*Where?*
Doctor in St. Louis	Early peanut butter just ground-up peanuts	Early peanut butter made at home

When?	*Why?*	*How?*
Peanut butter first made in 1890	Doctor wanted healthy food for patients	Peanuts shelled and sorted

Writing a Formal Outline

A formal outline is a plan for writing a report.

A formal outline organizes material according to main and supporting ideas. A main idea is made up of many more parts than a supporting idea. *The history of peanuts,* for example, covers hundreds of years and many countries. However, one of its supporting ideas, *Peanuts in the Inca civilization,* covers only one region and one time period.

A supporting idea tells something specific about the main idea.

1,200 years ago names a specific time; *the Incas of Peru* names a specific group of people; *Peru, West Africa,* and the *United States* are regions that trace the spread of the peanut.

In a formal outline main ideas become headings with Roman numerals (I, II, III, IV, V). Supporting ideas become subheadings with capital letters (A, B, C, D, E).

Here is the way the main idea *The history of peanuts* and the supporting ideas are arranged in a formal outline:

I. The history of peanuts
    A. Peanuts in the Inca civilization
    B. Their spread to West Africa
    C. Their move to the United States

If supporting ideas are further broken down, these new subheadings are shown by Arabic numerals (1, 2, 3, 4, 5).

On this page and the next is a sample formal outline:

The Story of Peanut Butter

I. The history of peanuts
    A. Peanuts in the Inca civilization
    B. Their spread to West Africa
    C. Their move to the United States
II. The history of peanut butter
    A. Its invention in 1890
    B. The spread of its popularity
        1. The making of peanut butter at home
        2. Problems with homemade peanut butter
III. The making of peanut butter in factories
    A. Shelling, sorting, and roasting
    B. Removing the skin and splitting
    C. Removing the heart

    D.   Grinding
    E.   Adding other ingredients
 IV. The trend back to homemade peanut butter
    A.   Concern about artificial ingredients
    B.   Desire for freshness

Notice that each subheading is indented under the heading above it:

  I. A main idea goes here.
    A.   The first supporting idea goes here.
    B.   The second supporting idea goes here.
 II. The second main idea goes here.

Indenting helps you see which ideas are main and which are supporting.

A heading must be divided into at least two parts.

In the last part of the sample outline, the writer gives two reasons for the trend back to homemade peanut butter: concern about artificial ingredients and desire for freshness. If the only reason for the trend back to homemade peanut butter were freshness, the writer would not divide the heading. Instead the writer could have a heading such as this: *IV. The freshness of homemade peanut butter*.

A formal outline arranges ideas in the order they will have in the report.

The first two headings of this sample outline are arranged by time order. The peanut comes first and then peanut butter. The third heading of the sample outline is arranged by steps in the process of making peanut butter. The fourth heading of the outline comes at the end because it is the most recent event in making peanut butter.

The sample outline is called a *topic outline* because the headings are topics, not complete sentences.

Writing Practice 10: *Writing an Outline*

Prepare a formal topic outline for your short report. Read the list of information you wrote for Writing Practice 9. Choose four or five main headings from it for your outline. Add supporting ideas as subheadings.

Finally, reread your preliminary thesis sentence. Does it state the main idea shown by your outline? If not, revise the thesis sentence so that it tells exactly what your report now covers.

Reading a Short Report

Each main heading in your outline should be at least one paragraph in your report. Main headings with a number of supporting ideas may need more than one paragraph.

Model: A Short Report

The example that follows is a short report on the story of peanut butter. As you read the report, notice how the writer explains the main and supporting ideas.

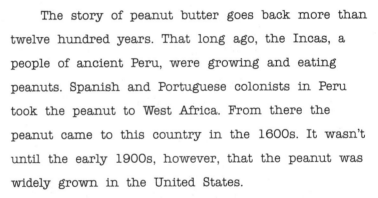

The Story of Peanut Butter

The story of peanut butter goes back more than twelve hundred years. That long ago, the Incas, a people of ancient Peru, were growing and eating peanuts. Spanish and Portuguese colonists in Peru took the peanut to West Africa. From there the peanut came to this country in the 1600s. It wasn't until the early 1900s, however, that the peanut was widely grown in the United States.

The first peanut butter was made in 1890 by a doctor in St. Louis who wanted a healthy food for his patients. The idea caught on, and before long, people all over the country were making peanut butter in their kitchens. This early peanut butter was little more than ground-up peanuts and salt. Peanuts have a lot of natural oil, and the oil would rise to the top of the homemade peanut butter, so the peanut butter had to be constantly stirred.

Peanut butter has come a long way since 1890. Much peanut butter today is made in factories with machinery doing most of the work. The peanuts are shelled, sorted for size and quality, and then roasted. After the cooking, the thin, red outer skin of the peanut is removed and the peanut is split. A small piece called the heart is then removed. This step is important because if the heart is left in, the peanut butter will be bitter.

The final step in making peanut butter is to grind the peanuts with large grinding disks. The peanuts are ground the same for all kinds of peanut butter. Chunky peanut butter is made by adding small pieces of peanuts to the mixture. At this time other ingredients are also added to the mixture. These include salt, honey or some other sweetener, and an artificial ingredient that keeps the oil from rising to the top.

Today, many people are conscious of healthy food. They are often concerned about artificial ingredients that are added to most processed foods, and they want food that is as fresh as possible. For these reasons many people buy small machines and grind their own peanut butter at home. In less than one hundred years peanut butter is back where it started!

Think and Discuss

1. The first paragraph in this report explains the history of peanuts. What does the second paragraph explain?

2. Where in the report do you find the thesis sentence?

3. What are the topics of the third and fourth paragraphs in the report?

4. Why have people today gone back to making their own peanut butter?

5. How does the last sentence summarize the report?

Unity and Coherence

Reports are easier for readers to follow if they are *unified* and *coherent*. *Unity* means that each paragraph explains or develops the topic. *Coherence* means that readers can see how the paragraphs are related to the topic and to each other. Look at the first sentences of the first four paragraphs from the sample paper on peanut butter:

1. The story of *peanut butter* goes back more than twelve hundred years.

2. The first *peanut butter* was made in 1890 by a doctor in St. Louis who wanted a healthy food for his patients.

3. *Peanut butter* has come a long way since 1890.

4. The final step in making *peanut butter* is to grind the peanuts with large grinding disks.

Because the word *peanut butter* appears in each of these sentences, readers can easily tell that the paragraph will explain or develop the topic *The story of peanut butter*. It is also helpful to see the thesis sentence at the beginning of the report: *The story of peanut butter goes back more than twelve hundred years.* This tells the reader what the focus of the report is. The report centers on the historical development of peanut butter. Every paragraph then relates to the history of peanut butter.

Time words also help readers follow the story. In the second paragraph the time word is *1890,* and in the third paragraph the time words are *since 1890.* Readers can tell that the report traces the history of peanut butter.

Writing a Bibliography

To give credit to your sources and to tell readers where they can learn more about the topic, you should include a bibliography at the end of your report. A bibliography is a list, in standard form, of the sources used.

A bibliography entry for a book consists of three kinds of information: the author, the title, and the publication data. This information appears in a special order. First comes the author's name, with last name first. Next is the underlined title of the book. The publication information comes last. It consists of the place of publication, the name of the publisher, and the latest copyright date. Study the following example of a standard book entry, noting especially the punctuation used. Also notice that the second line is indented.

Michener, James A. Sports in America. New York: Random House, 1976.

A bibliography entry for a magazine requires five items of information: the name of the author of the article (when given), the name of the article, the name of the magazine, the date of the magazine, and the page numbers of the article. Study the following example of a magazine entry.

Dickenson, J. Craig. "Tools for Home." The Color Computer Magazine, September 1984, pp. 60–65.

An encyclopedia entry in a bibliography usually includes just three items: the title of the article, the title of the encyclopedia, and the date of the particular edition used. Here is an example:

"Sponge." The New Columbia Encyclopedia. 1975 ed.

If the author's name is given, include his or her name at the beginning of the entry.

Bibliography entries are listed in alphabetical order.

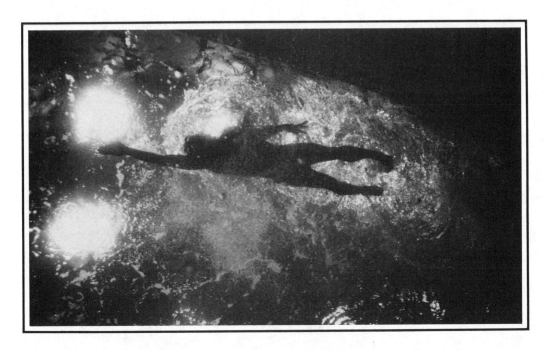

Model: Bibliography

Here is the bibliography for the report on peanut butter. Notice that the entries are in alphabetical order and in correct form.

Bibliography

Kaufman, William I. The Peanut Butter Cookbook. New York: Simon & Schuster, 1977.

"Peanut." The New Columbia Encyclopedia. 1975 ed.

Root, Waverly. "Now That Peanuts Are Important, Here's Their Story." Gourmet Magazine, April 1979, pp. 26–34.

Writing Assignment I: *Writing a Short Report*

Before beginning this assignment, gather the work you have done for Writing Practices 7–10. This information will be valuable to you as you start writing your report for this assignment.

A. Prewriting

You have already done many of the prewriting activities for your report. You brainstormed or used some other method to come up with your topic and thesis sentence. You took notes and organized them. You wrote a formal outline. Before you

begin writing, however, review your outline. Add or delete items to make the outline logical and complete.

B. Writing

Using your formal outline and notes as a guide, write the first draft of your short report. Don't try to make it perfect the first time; remember that you might need to write several drafts. Just concentrate on presenting all the information from your outline as completely as possible.

Include your thesis sentence at the beginning of the report, and aim for an interesting presentation. Use specific details and precise nouns and verbs to make your report both interesting and accurate. Remember to include a bibliography at the end.

C. Postwriting

Use the following checklist as a guide in revising your report.

Checklist for Revising a Short Report

1. The topic is limited enough to be thoroughly discussed.

2. Either the information in the report is new to readers, or it is presented with an unusual or humorous point of view.

3. The topic is developed with specific information that answers the *who? what? where? when? why? how?* questions.

4. Information is arranged in a logical order.

5. Each main idea is developed with supporting details, and each paragraph relates to the thesis.

Next, check your bibliography entries against the models in this chapter. Make sure you capitalize, punctuate, and alphabetize correctly.

Finally, proofread your report, using the Checklist for Proofreading at the back of the book. If you need to make more than one or two corrections, recopy your report.

Sentence Variety:
Inserting Sentences

Inserting (with)

The *with-phrase* is often used to give more information about subjects. A *with-phrase* is the word *with* and a series of words after it:

> The peacock *with the long, flowing tail*

> A river *with a rapidly moving current*

In the following example, the insert sentence becomes a *with-phrase*, which is inserted into the base sentence. The signal (*with*) tells you to make a *with-phrase* from the insert sentence.

Base Sentence: The parrot looked at us steadily.

Insert: The parrot had a long tail. (*with*)

Combined: The parrot *with a long tail* looked at us steadily.

Notice that the phrase *with a long tail* directly follows the word *parrot* in the new sentence because it is the parrot that is being described.

However, the *with-phrase* does not always directly follow the word it describes. Sometimes it sounds better at the beginning or end of a sentence.

Base Sentence: JoJo was short and stocky.

Insert: He had a smooth coat of short hair. (*with*)

Combined: JoJo was short and stocky *with a smooth coat of short hair.*

Exercise 1: Inserting (with)

Using the second sentence as a *with-phrase*, combine each of the following sets of sentences into one sentence. Insert the *with-phrase* into the first sentence, deciding for yourself where you think it belongs. Copy each new sentence on a sheet of paper numbered 1–10 and underline the *with-phrase*. Study the examples before you begin.

Examples

a. The American hockey team went to the Olympics.
   The American hockey team had high hopes. (*with*)
   The American hockey team went to the Olympics *with high hopes.*

b. I'm probably going to make an A in English.
   My marks are high. (*with*)
   With my high marks I'm probably going to make an A in English.

1. I decided to buy the puppy.
   The puppy has a small white mark on its nose. (*with*)

2. Gulf Shores is an attractive place for tourists.
   Gulf Shores has miles of sparkling white beaches. (*with*)

3. The boa constrictor swallowed its victim.
   The boa constrictor made a great gulp. (*with*)

4. Many countries have problems today.
   Many countries have low oil reserves. (*with*)

5. The cat is my favorite.
   The cat has gray-and-white fur. (*with*)

6. My favorite food is a hamburger.
   The hamburger has mustard, catsup, mayonnaise, onions, lettuce, cheese, and pickles. (*with*)

7. Joan, an accident victim, fought to regain the use of her legs.
   She fought with great courage. (*with*)

143

8. We'll make it through this bad time.
   We'll have a little luck. (*with*)

9. Maria is always dashing to her seat just as the bell rings.
   Maria has a huge stack of books in her arms. (*with*)

10. The monkeys kept visitors at the zoo entertained.
    The monkeys had clever tricks. (*with*)

Inserting (-ing)

A modifier is a word that describes somebody or something. The *-ing* forms of many verbs can be used as modifiers.

Verbs	Modifiers
The baby *sleeps*.	the *sleeping* baby
The flower *fades*.	the *fading* flower
The choir *carols*.	the *caroling* choir
My stomach *rumbles* when I'm hungry.	my *rumbling* stomach

You can combine sentences by first making the verb in the insert sentence a modifier with *-ing*. Then insert the new modifier into the base sentence before the word it modifies.

Base Sentence: Jim's gesture might start a fight.

Insert: The gesture threatens. (*-ing*)

Combined: Jim's *threatening* gesture might start a fight.

Base Sentence: Gradually, the top slowed its spin and toppled over.

Insert: The top whirls. (*-ing*)

Combined: Gradually, the *whirling* top slowed its spin and toppled over.

When two or more verbs appear in the insert sentence, each of them changes to the *-ing* form in the new sentence.

The victim was at Dracula's mercy.
The victim screams and cries. (*-ing*)
The *screaming and crying* victim was at Dracula's mercy.

144

Exercise 2: Inserting (-ing)

Combine each of the following sets of sentences into one sentence. Change the verb in the second sentence to a modifier with *-ing* and place the new modifier before the word it modifies in the insert sentence. In the first four sets, the word to be changed into the *-ing* form is *italicized*.

1. The swan's wings were spread out wide in a graceful movement.
   The wings *flap*. (*-ing*)

2. The committee selected three names as candidates for president.
   The committee *nominates*. (*-ing*)

3. Whenever I hear that sound, I know Mom has just come home from work in our new car.
   The sound *purrs*. (*-ing*)

4. Just past the next corner and a little way through the empty field is the best trail in the world.
   One *hikes* on the trail. (*-ing*)

5. Ms. Johnson, the lawyer in the case, tried to make her client feel comfortable.
   The lawyer examines. (*-ing*)

6. The parrot was the most popular attraction in the shop.
   The parrot talks. (*-ing*)

7. The tail showed the dog's happiness at its owner's arrival.
   The tail wags. (*-ing*)

8. No one seemed alarmed by the engine.
   The engine sputters and coughs. (*-ing*)

9. The next morning the neighbors complained that the dog had kept them awake all night.
   The dog whines and barks. (*-ing*)

10. The radiator kept us awake all night.
    The radiator hisses and clanks. (*-ing*)

Writing Practice: *Inserting Sentences by Using* (with) *and* (-ing)

Choose one or two paragraphs from the short report you wrote in Chapter 6, and revise them for sentence variety. Use (*with*) and (*-ing*) to combine short sentences. If necessary, add descriptive details to your sentences as you rework them.

7 Persuasive Writing

Have you ever heard or used statements like these?

Cruncho Bran Flakes are the world's favorite breakfast!

Rock stars set a terrible example for young people.

Peoples' Telephone Company is better because its rates are lower.

My weekly allowance should be raised!

Each of these statements aims to *persuade*—to influence the actions or beliefs of others. An advertiser tries to convince people to eat Cruncho Bran Flakes by making them sound popular. The second statement asks people to believe something negative about rock stars. Peoples' Telephone Company wants business. And you want your parents to raise your allowance.

You hear, see, and use persuasion every day. In this chapter you will learn several techniques for writing persuasively, and you will compose a persuasive letter.

Using Language to Persuade

People use persuasion in order to convince others of their point of view, to get a thing done, to make change, or to sell a product or service. You, too, use persuasive arguments in both speech and writing. The language you choose for your arguments partly determines how successful you will be.

Many words appeal to emotions because words can make people feel happy, sad, warm, insecure, or safe. Advertisers know which words will create the desired impression on buyers. For example, phrases such as "thick and rich," "a special treat," "velvety smooth" and "light and airy" create good feelings about a dairy product. But words such as "lumpy," "sour," or "stale" make that same product seem unpleasant.

Writing Practice 1: *Words That Appeal to Emotions*

The following is a list of words often found in advertisements. Choose three or more of these words and write an advertisement for a real or imaginary product. Give a name to your product. Your purpose is to make your readers feel good about the product by appealing to their emotions.

fancy	fast-acting	amazing
mysterious	snappy	inexpensive
sweet	rich	casual
colorful	hard-working	handsome
effective	young	super
exciting	splendid	easy to clean
wonderful	spellbinding	special
positive	tasty	smooth
long-lasting	natural	dependable
good-looking	clean	mature
refreshing	sparkling	

Misleading Uses of Language

L anguage can mislead by making claims that are too general. If you read that a product is "everyone's favorite," how can you be sure that the claim is true? It is impossible to poll everyone in the world. Below are several claims. Which claim in each pair is too general?

1. CycleRide bikes never need repair.
   CycleRide bikes seldom need repair.

2. Californians prefer our tasty avocados.
   Many Californians prefer our tasty avocados.

3. Cancel bug spray will forever rid your home of pests.
   Cancel bug spray will help rid your home of pests.

In the first statement of each pair, words such as "never" and "forever" make the claims too general. Example 2 does not use the word "all," but it *suggests* that "all Californians" prefer the product.

Words such as "only," "always," and "never" do have important uses, of course. For example, such words are appropriate in the following expressions.

Never dart across a street from between parked cars.

Always be careful when crossing a street.

It is important to think carefully before making a general statement.

Writing Practice 2: *Identifying Misleading Language*

In newspapers and magazines, find three advertisements that you think make overly general statements. Copy the wording of these advertisements. Write the source of each advertisement (name of the magazine or newspaper) and the kinds of readers you think it is directed to (for instance, teenagers, children, adults). Then write a brief statement saying why you think the language of each advertisement is too general. In class, compare your findings with those of your classmates.

Using Facts and Giving Opinions

Facts

A *fact* is an act or statement that is true. A fact can be proved by demonstrating, testing, or observing it. If it is a fact that 10 students in a class received A or B grades on the last test, you need only see those grades on their papers to prove the fact. Some facts, such as those about measurements, are commonly agreed upon. *One pound equals 16 ounces* is a fact because it is commonly accepted in our system of weights and measures.

In informative writing, facts are often used to explain, demonstrate, or describe a topic. Writers also use facts to support statements in persuasive writing.

Model: *Facts in Persuasive Writing*

The author of this fund-raising letter uses facts to show why people should be concerned about a serious situation.

Dear Animal Lover,

Last week as I was walking to my friend's house, I noticed a piece of old clothing on the curb, moving in an odd way. I lifted a corner of it and found a small puppy that was whimpering sadly. When I picked it up, I noticed it was very thin and perhaps sick. I couldn't leave an abandoned animal there in the street, so I dropped it off at the Animal Shelter where it would be cared for. The director there told me that this puppy was the third one they'd received that day, and the fifteenth one that week. In fact, over 200 abandoned dogs and 300 abandoned cats are brought into the Animal Shelter every year. But the shelter cannot afford to care for so many animals until they can be adopted, and so over 50 percent of them must be destroyed. I hope that the puppy I left there last week will not be destroyed and that others like it won't suffer from lack of care. I hope you will contribute to the Fund for a Better Animal Shelter.

Sincerely,
Tom Marin

Think and Discuss

1. What facts did the writer use to persuade readers to support the Animal Shelter?

2. Do you think those facts would impress readers? Why?

3. What other facts might the writer have used to be more persuasive?

4. What words did the writer use to appeal to readers' emotions?

5. How effective do you think this letter is? How would you have made it more persuasive?

Opinions

An *opinion* expresses a point of view, a belief, or an attitude. You need to read or listen carefully to distinguish between facts and opinions. In the following pairs of statements, *a* is a statement of fact; *b* is a statement of opinion. How could you prove the facts are true? What reasons would convince you to agree with the opinions?

---

a. The Old Erie Canal State Park is 35 miles long.
b. The Old Erie Canal State Park offers the best snowmobile trail in New York State.

---

a. The cigarette industry spends $1.5 billion a year to promote its products in magazines, newspapers, and billboards.
b. Cigarette smoking is America's #1 health problem.

---

a. Comedian Jack Benny not only starred in his own radio programs but made 22 films as well.
b. Jack Benny was America's favorite comedian from the early 1930s to the mid-1950s.

150

a. LOGO and BASIC are computer languages.
b. Students who work with personal computers should learn LOGO rather than BASIC as their first computer language.

Writers use opinions as well as facts in persuasive writing. Writers usually support those opinions by *giving reasons* for them.

Model: *Giving Reasons for Opinions*

This writer suggests a new service at the Community Center and gives reasons why it would help students like herself:

Babysitting can be a great way to earn money and to learn about raising children, having a job, and managing money. To learn what is expected of a babysitter and how to properly care for children, we need a class that will teach us how to become good babysitters. Sitters need to know how to be alert to possible dangers, how to prevent accidents, and where to get emergency help. They also need to understand how to handle small children and babies, how to choose safe toys or games for them, and how to help them eat and get to sleep easily. A class in babysitting or child care at the Community Center would help students like me, who want to earn money as sitters and learn how to do a responsible job.

Think and Discuss

1. What opinion does the writer express at the end of the letter?

2. What reasons support that opinion?

3. The writer begins by stating an opinion about the benefits of babysitting. Do you agree with that opinion? Why or why not?

4. What other reasons would you add to make this argument more persuasive?

Writing Practice 3: *Working with Facts and Opinions*

Read and think about each of the following statements. On a sheet of paper, write *fact* if the statement expresses a fact; write *opinion* if the statement expresses an opinion. If the statement is a fact, write a sentence telling how it can be proven. If it is an opinion, write two reasons that could support it.

1. Girls have longer hair than boys.

2. Women live longer than men.

3. If a black cat crosses your path, you will have bad luck.

4. Tall people make excellent basketball players.

5. There are 24 chairs in this room.

6. A cat is a furry, four-legged feline.

7. Criminals must be punished for their crimes.

8. I have no talent.

9. Broccoli is a healthful food for everyone.

10. Running is better for you than race walking.

Sound and Faulty Reasoning

Your readers or listeners will be more easily persuaded if you give *sound reasons* for believing you. Often, simple common sense helps you sort out sound reasoning from poor reasoning. Can you see why the second paragraph in each of the following pairs shows sounder reasoning than the first?

a. Model car kit A is a better buy than Model car kit B. You should buy kit A.

b. Model car kit A contains 30 separate pieces, a stand on which you can mount the completed model, two kinds of model paint, and a money-back guarantee. It costs $10.95 on sale. Kit B has no stand, no paint, and no guarantee. It costs the same amount. Kit A is the better buy.

a. Sign up for service clubs today. Twenty-five service club members are on the honor roll. Wouldn't you like to be on the honor roll, too?

b. Twenty-five service club members are on the honor roll this term. If you join a service club, you'll work with outstanding students and learn how they are motivated to do well.

Jumping to Conclusions

One common mistake in reasoning is to come to a hasty conclusion without giving enough evidence. This is often called *jumping to conclusions*. Study the following example.

Our club opposes election of officers by voice vote. How do I know? I talked to Carol and Jim about it, and that's what we think.

To avoid this kind of poor reasoning, remember that you cannot make a generalization based on information from only a few people or instances.

False Authority

Another mistake in reasoning is to use an authority who may not be an expert on the subject or who may be prejudiced in some way. Here is an example:

> Dr. Joan Callahan, an international expert in sports medicine, says children should not attend school until they are seven years old.

Dr. Callahan is an expert on sports medicine, not on children and school age.

You often see sports or entertainment stars sponsoring a product. Remember that, while they may sincerely believe in the product, most of these stars are paid large sums of money to make the ads. How might that affect their attitudes toward the products?

Cause-and-Effect Errors

A third error in reasoning is to claim that a certain action will surely produce a particular effect. Here is an example:

> When a community does not enforce a curfew on teenagers and younger children, crimes such as vandalism will increase.

To counter this kind of false reasoning, ask whether the action necessarily *causes* the effect. Faulty reasoning of this kind often results from lack of information or from prejudice.

Writing Practice 4: *Identifying Faulty Reasoning*

Read each of the following statements. What kind of false reasoning does each involve?

1. Station XYZB never plays good rock records. There's nothing good on radio any more.

2. I know Rousters jeans are the best. TV's new teen star, Tim Shue, wears them.

3. Cary used to be a top student. But since he started going to video arcades on weekends, his grades have gone down. If he'd give up playing video games, his grades would certainly go up.

4. My sister and I eat oatmeal every morning for breakfast. That's why we're both in good health.

5. Mr. Anderson, Mr. Graves, and Senator Strong each earn over $25,000 a year. Each man drives an American-built car. It's easy to see that men who earn over $25,000 a year drive American-made cars.

6. On January 10 Tina and Catherine had an after-school snack at their favorite pizza place. The next day, both girls had to miss softball practice because they were ill. Don't eat at that pizza place, or you'll become ill.

7. Magic Johnson wears that brand of basketball shoes. If they're right for him, they're right for me.

Knowing Your Audience

Before you begin to write persuasion, you need to think about your audience. You can ask yourself these questions to help prepare a good argument:

1. Whom do I want to persuade?

2. What do they already know about my topic? What facts do I need to tell them?

3. What are their interests? What will appeal to them?

Thinking about your audience will help you choose the best language and the most persuasive arguments.

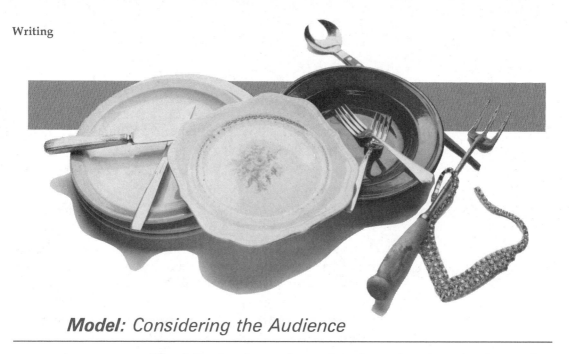

Model: Considering the Audience

The following letter shows that the writer thought about what facts her reader needed to know and what appeals to use.

Dear Aunt Margo,

I'm so glad you're coming to visit us during the week of our school's 25th anniversary celebration! A lot of things will be happening that week, and I know you'll have fun.

My class is running a booth at the celebration. We decided to try a "white elephant" sale to raise money for our library. We're asking people to donate old jewelry, household utensils, or personal belongings they don't want. I remember your saying last Christmas that you wanted to get rid of some old dishes and other items stored in your basement. Would you be willing to donate some of those things to our booth? I know you went to my school, too, when you lived in Minneapolis. Will you contribute to it now?

If you can contribute, you might bring the things with you. The whole family is looking forward to your visit.

Love,
Kris

This writer tells her audience (Aunt Margo) only the necessary facts. For example, she doesn't give the name of the school, because Aunt Margo already knows it. She uses friendly, informal language, appropriate for a family member. The letter writer also thinks about Aunt Margo's interests—since she went to the same school, she might be willing to help raise money for it.

Writing Practice 5: *Considering the Audience*

In each of the following situations, a person attempts to persuade others to act or believe in a certain way. Select one of these situations and write a sentence answering each of the three questions below.

Situations

a. A close friend has asked you to spend the weekend at his house while his parents are out of town. Your parents do not usually approve of your staying overnight at a friend's home unless there is an adult present. You want to persuade your parents to give their permission this time.

b. Your team or group plans a trip to a sports event but can't decide whether to attend a football game or a basketball game. Everyone must go as a group. Persuade them to attend the event of your choice.

c. A group of visitors from another nation has asked you and several other seventh-graders to talk to them about your school. They are interested in finding out whether schools in the United States offer worthwhile subjects that they might add to their own programs. Choose a subject you study in school and persuade the visitors that it is worthwhile.

Questions

1. How old are the people in your audience? How will their age affect your choice of language?

2. Do the people in your audience know you? How will their familiarity with you affect the way you write?

3. What reasons are most likely to persuade your audience? Why?

Writing to Persuade

Writers often express their opinions in editorials or letters to the editor in magazines and newspapers. The topics may reflect an individual's interests or those of a group or organization. The writers try to persuade other readers or listeners to adopt a point of view, change an attitude or belief, or take some action.

Model: A Persuasive Letter

This letter to the editor of a fashion magazine uses both facts and opinions supported by reasons to urge the editor to be more careful in setting a good example for consumer safety.

Dear Editor:

In your June issue, you featured an article about sportswear that showed a group of bicycle riders on a cross-country trip. The riders, posed on their bikes, showed that they knew about the latest fashions, but they must not have known about bicycle safety. Although the photos showed riders on multispeed touring bikes, the riders were not wearing helmets. In addition, two of the bikes did not have reflectors or front lights. One rider was wearing pants that fit loosely around the ankles. Although the pants are stylish, the fabric could get caught in the chain wheels or spokes and cause a bad accident.

Because many readers see your magazine, I think you should take care to show scenes that set good safety examples. In this case, three safety rules for bicycle riders were overlooked:

1. All bikes should have red rear reflectors so that they can be seen by motorists. If driven after dark, the bike must be equipped, or the driver must wear, a light that is visible from 500 feet. Many riders also equip their bikes with safety flags to make the bikes more visible.

2. When riding on a highway or at high speeds, a rider should wear a helmet to provide protection in case of an accidental fall or collision. A head injury could be fatal.

3. Loose-fitting pants should be secured around the ankle with a strap or piece of cloth to prevent the fabric from getting caught in the equipment.

Perhaps you could print an article on bicycle safety in one of your next issues to give readers bicycle safety tips.

Sincerely,
Virginia Pappas

Think and Discuss

1. The letter to a fashion magazine is addressed to a specific reader (the editor) and printed in a special section for other readers. Who do you think these other readers are?

2. Is the language in the letter suitable for these readers? Find some words or phrases you think will appeal to them.

3. Is the letter convincing? How does the writer make it convincing? How might the letter be made even more persuasive?

4. What actions does the letter ask for? Do you think the suggestion at the end of the letter will appeal to the editor of the magazine?

5. Virginia Pappas points out a problem: the magazine may be setting a poor example for readers by showing photos in which bicycle safety is overlooked. What facts or reasons does the writer use to persuade readers that following bicycle safety tips is important?

Finding a Topic

Writing to persuade involves several steps, just as does writing to explain, inform, or describe. First, you need to find a topic, gather information about it, and organize your material. Where do you find topics for persuasive writing? Look in newspapers and magazines for news about events or community problems that interest you and on which you have opinions. Listen to television or radio newscasts, special programs or documentaries, or talk shows on which people express their opinions about a problem. Think about a problem that worries you or concerns your school, community, or family. You and your friends have opinions about a number of things: sports, clothes, music, hobbies, or making and keeping friends. You probably have opinions about many subjects at school, too.

Stating an Opinion

Once you have chosen a topic, you need to make a statement about it that expresses your opinion. Opinion statements are written in complete sentences:

This class should publish a newspaper.

In hot weather, afternoon classes should be dismissed.

159

No one over 15 years old should have to attend school.

It is a student's responsibility to earn good grades.

Rock music expresses the feelings of young people better than reggae (or salsa, rockabilly, folk, etc.).

It is wrong to exclude another person from a group because he or she wears an odd hair style.

Writing Practice 6: *Finding Topics and Stating Opinions*

Over the next week, complete the following activities and make a list of at least five topics you would like to write about. Then write an opinion statement for each.

1. Begin reading the letters-to-the editor page in your community newspaper and in magazines. You can find these sources in your school or public library. In your Writer's Notebook, write down the topics these letters discuss.

2. Listen to the news, especially the short editorials most programs include. In your notebook, make a list of three or four topics that interest and concern you.

3. Pay attention to the arguments and discussions your friends have during the week. Perhaps some of you are working on a problem that is not yet solved. In your notebook, write down the topics that interest you most.

4. Ask your teachers, parents, and older brothers or sisters what they think about some of the topics you have found. Talking with them might bring up further topics or help you form your own opinions.

After a week, go over your list of topics and select five. Write an opinion statement for each topic. Write opinions that can be argued, not ones that nearly everyone already agrees with. For example, you would not argue that milk is a nutritious food because no one would be likely to disagree. But you might argue that milk should be distributed free by your school cafeteria. Save your work.

Making an Informal Outline

After you have chosen a topic and written an opinion statement, you can begin to develop the reasons you will use to support your opinion. You can organize your reasons by using an informal outline. You will need at least three sound reasons, and each reason must be backed up with facts. In addition, for the end of your outline, you will need a *call to action*—a definite statement of what you want your readers to do.

The following informal outline pattern is useful for organizing persuasive writing.

> Opinion statement
> > Reason
> > > Fact
> > > Fact
> > Reason
> > > Fact
> > > Fact
> > Reason
> > > Fact
> > > Fact
> Call to Action

Writing Assignment I: *A Persuasive Letter*

Write a letter to the editor of your school or city newspaper.

A. Prewriting

Preparing and stating your opinion: From the list of topics you made for Writing Practice 6, select one you feel strongly enough about to make it the topic for your letter to the editor. Your readers will be more willing to listen to your opinion if you are sincere and believe in what you say, if you give reasons why others should share your opinion, and if you show them how your proposal will benefit them.

Audience and Purpose: Before you begin your letter, write down your answers to each of these questions:

1. Who will your readers be? Be as specific as you can. Will they be adults? students? familiar or unfamiliar? older or younger?

2. What will your readers already know about your topic? What facts will you need to give them? Consult your Writer's Notebook for facts and details about your topic. If you need to find more facts and details, go to your school library.

3. What reasons do you have to support your opinion? List as many as you can. Then rank them in order from most important to least important.

4. Why is your topic important? Why should others care about it?

5. What result do you want from writing your letter? Do you want someone to take action, behave in a certain way, believe in something, or change in some way? Write a sentence that clearly states what result you want.

Next, organize your notes and ideas in a way that you think will be effective. You may find an informal outline useful.

B. Writing

Start your letter by explaining your topic and stating your opinion about it. Develop your letter by giving facts and reasons. Be sure your facts are accurate and your reasons are sound. Conclude by stating what you want your readers to do or believe. Here are other suggestions:

1. Don't worry about how your first draft looks. You can revise and correct errors during postwriting.

2. You may decide that your first outline could be improved or that one reason is not as good as you first thought. Don't hesitate to make changes while you write.

3. If you find it hard to get started, go back to the notes and ideas you jotted down in prewriting activities. Or try one of the prewriting techniques (such as clustering) described in Chapter 1. Once you get something down on paper, other words will come more easily.

C. Postwriting

Share your letter with your classmates or others whose opinions you value. Ask what impression your letter gives them. Do they understand your reasons? What reason is most convincing or least convincing to them? What improvements do they suggest? Use their responses and the following checklist to revise your letter.

Checklist for Revising a Persuasive Letter

1. Does your argument use facts and sound reasons to support your opinions?

2. Is the language of your letter suitable for your readers?

3. Is your topic clearly stated and your opinion clearly expressed?

4. Does your letter tell readers what result you want?

Proofread your revised draft and correct any errors. Remember, this letter is meant to be read by others. You want to make the best impression you can so that they will accept your opinion. Follow the form for writing a business letter in Chapter 10.

With your teacher's permission, submit your letter to the paper, magazine, group, or person to whom it is addressed.

Sentence Variety:
Inserting Sentences

Inserting ('s)

Y ou have learned to insert modifiers by using (*with*) and (*-ing*). Another way to form a modifier is to change a word to its possessive form. An apostrophe and an *s* show the possessive form of many words.

Word	Possessive Form
Henry	Henry's car
car	car's interior
pencil	pencil's eraser

If a plural word ends in *-s*, you form the possessive by adding an *apostrophe* only.

Word	Possessive Form
books	books' covers
stories	stories' plots
chairs	chairs' backs

Other words, such as *child, goose,* and *mouse,* change form to show their plurals but do not end in *s.* Add *'s* to form the possessive of these words: *children's, geese's, mice's.*

An *of . . . ,* or *by . . . ,* or *belongs to . . .* expression in the insert sentence tells you which word to make possessive. The (*'s*) signal tells you to make a noun possessive. The (*'s*) signal remains the same whether the noun is singular or plural.

Base Sentence: Here is a lost billfold.

Insert: The billfold belongs to Ginger. (*'s*)

Combined: Here is *Ginger's* lost billfold.

Belongs to Ginger in the insert sentence becomes *Ginger's*, which goes before the word it modifies in the new sentence.

The following example shows how the combination works with a plural noun:

Base Sentence: The plots were too complicated for Joan and me.

Insert: The plots were of the stories. (*'s*)

Combined: The *stories'* plots were too complicated for Joan and me.

Exercise 1: *Inserting* ('s)

Combine each of the following sets of sentences into one sentence. First, change part of the insert sentence to a possessive form. Second, put the new modifier before the word it modifies in the base sentence. Copy each new sentence on a sheet of paper numbered 1–10. In the first four sentences the noun you make possessive is italicized. In the other sentences you must find the noun yourself. Remember that the first sentence is always the base sentence.

1. The smokestacks were belching thick, black clouds of dusty smoke.
   The smokestacks belonged to the *factories*. (*'s*)

2. A city charter grants certain rights.
   The rights are of *citizens*. (*'s*)

3. On this wall is a photograph of my great-grandfather.
   The photograph is by *my cousin Ralph*. ('s)

4. Herb glanced down during the race and discovered that the tires needed air.
   The tires belonged to *his bicycle*. ('s)

5. The tail wagged furiously and happily as the pet waited for three-year-old Kenny to approach.
   The tail belonged to the brown-and-white collie. ('s)

6. The arrangement of springtime daffodils and irises was placed in the center of the banquet table.
   The arrangement was by a florist. ('s)

7. Audiences have been entertained for years by comedy.
   The comedy is by Red Skelton. ('s)

8. Several lyrics were composed by David Bowie.
   The lyrics belonged to songs. ('s)

9. Sunday Bob talked about winning the prize for his roses.
   The prize belonged to the Garden Club. ('s)

10. The plans had to be changed when it rained.
    The plans were of the afternoon. ('s)

Inserting (Where), (When), *and* (How)

In many sentences certain words or phrases (groups of words) tell *where, when,* or *how* something happened.

> Dusty Corners is a place.
> Dusty Corners is a place *in the middle of the desert.*
> (*In the middle of the desert* tells *where* the place is located.)

I eat two bananas and drink three cartons of milk.
I eat two bananas and drink three cartons of milk *at noon*.
(*At noon* tells *when* the person eats.)

Clare threaded the silver thread through the eye of the needle.
Clare threaded the silver thread through the eye of the needle *carefully*.
(*Carefully* tells *how* Clare threaded the needle.)

Groups of words that tell *where* and *when* often begin with words like the ones in the following list:

Where	*When*
in	before
at	after
by	in
near	during
beside	

Many single words that tell *how* often end in *-ly: happily, slowly, carefully, quickly, really, daily*.

In this lesson you will take details from the insert sentence that tell *where, when,* or *how* and insert them into the base sentences. The signals at the end of the insert sentence are (*where*), (*how*), and (*when*). These signals tell you the kind of details to take from the insert sentence, but you do not actually use the words *where, how,* and *when* in the new sentence.

Base Sentence: Susan stepped dramatically.

Insert: Susan stepped up to the microphone. (*where*)

Combined: Susan stepped dramatically *up to the microphone*.

In some sentences the insert words can be placed in more than one position.

Susan stepped dramatically *up to the microphone*.
  can also be
Susan stepped *up to the microphone* dramatically.

Exercise 2: *Inserting* (Where), (When), *and* (How)

Combine each of the sets of sentences on the following page into one sentence. The signal will tell you what kind of information to take from the insert sentence. Then insert the

167

information in the place that makes the best sense in the final sentence. Copy each new sentence on a sheet of paper numbered 1–5. Study the examples before you begin. Remember that the first sentence is always the base sentence.

Example

a. The entire family watched football games all afternoon. They watched football games on Thanksgiving Day. (*when*)

The entire family watched football games all afternoon on Thanksgiving Day.

or

On Thanksgiving Day the entire family watched football games all afternoon.

1. Jogging can be bad for your feet. The jogging is on pavement. (*where*)

2. All six loyal cheerleaders clapped as the bedraggled team left the gymnasium tired and defeated. They clapped proudly. (*how*)

3. Without complaining in the slightest, Teddie stretched out to check his brother's muffler. He stretched out under the old jalopy. (*where*)

4. Ronnie walked home with Marcia. They walked home after the Friday night dance at school. (*when*)

5. The coyote saw the jackrabbit.
   It saw the jackrabbit after a few minutes. (*when*)

The following sets of sentences ask you to insert more than one kind of information. Make the combination in any way you can, but use all of the information. Study the example before you begin.

Example

a. They checked the house to find the missing jewels.
   They checked carefully. (*how*)
   They checked in every nook and cranny. (*where*)
   They carefully checked the house in every nook and cranny to find the missing jewels.

6. Our town made a new soccer field.
   The soccer field is in Grant's Park. (*where*)
   The field was made this year. (*when*)

7. A museum of natural history stands.
   It stands near Temple Square. (*where*)
   It stands on the corner. (*where*)

8. The roller coaster climbed.
   It climbed slowly. (*how*)
   It climbed to the top of the ramp. (*where*)

9. Margaret turned and stormed.
   She turned quickly. (*how*)
   She stormed out of the room. (*where*)
   She stormed angrily. (*how*)

10. A small kitten stretched out and arched its back.
    It stretched out sleepily. (*how*)
    It arched its back across the pillow. (*where*)

Writing Practice: *Adventure!*

Think about something that would be the world's greatest adventure for you, even something quite impossible that you would like to imagine doing. Perhaps, like Superman, you would like to be able to fly or swim across the Atlantic or Pacific Ocean by yourself or travel to a planet in outer space. Describe your great adventure and tell about what you see, learn, and experience.

As you write, use some of the sentence-combining skills you have learned.

8 Writing Poems and Stories

Writing stories and poems helps you develop as a writer. Such writing involves playing with words, possibly to create an appealing sound, to invent a realistic dialogue, or to relay a sense of tension.

Writing Poems

What are the differences between the following pieces of writing about giraffes?

Model: A Definition and a Poem

1. Giraffe—Either of two species of large cud-chewing animals of Africa, with a very long neck and four legs.

2. **Giraffes**
   Stilted creatures,
   Features fashioned as a joke,
   Boned and buckled,
   Finger painted,
   They stand in the field
   On long-pronged legs
   As if thrust there.
   They airily feed,
   Slightly swaying,
   Like hammer-headed flowers.
   Bizarre they are
   Built silent and high,
   Ornaments against the sky.
   Ears like leaves
   To hear the silken
   Brushing of the clouds.[1]

   Sy Kahn

---

[1]"Giraffes" by Sy Kahn. Reprinted by permission of the author.

The first piece of writing is a dictionary definition of a giraffe, intended to give you a real-life description of the animal. The second piece is a poem that describes giraffes in an imaginative way. The poet Sy Kahn says that giraffes are "finger painted" and that they have "ears like leaves."

Poetry helps you to think about your world in an imaginative way.

In this section you will learn to use your imagination to express thoughts and feelings in poetry.

The Sounds of Words

In poetry, the sounds of words work with their meanings to create the effect of the poem. Read the poem on the next page. Notice how the sounds of words make the meaning clear. Look for the point where the sound suddenly changes.

Model: The Sounds of Words

The Stray Cat
It's just an old alley cat
that has followed us all the way home.

It hasn't a star on its forehead,
or a silky satiny coat.

No proud tiger stripes, no dainty tread,
no elegant velvet throat.

It's a splotchy, blotchy
city cat, not pretty cat,
a rough little tough little bag of old bones.

"Beauty," we shall call you,
"Beauty, come in."[1]

Eve Merriam

Eve Merriam knows that people react to the sounds of words as well as to their meanings. Words such as *silky, satiny,* and *dainty* do not sound like words for an old alley cat. Words like *splotchy, blotchy, rough,* and *tough,* however, seem to fit such an animal. The word *beauty* at the end of the poem surprises readers and makes them see the old alley cat in a different way.

Rhyme

Rhyme **is the repetition of end sounds.**

How many rhyming words can you find in the following poem by Robert P. Tristram Coffin?

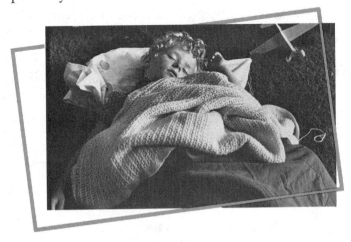

Model: Rhyme

The Secret Heart
Across the years he could recall
His father one way best of all.

In the stillest hour of night
The boy awakened to a light.

Sire means "father."

Half in dreams, he saw his sire
With his great hands full of fire.

The man had struck a match to see
If his son slept peacefully.

He held his palms each side the spark
His love had kindled in the dark.

A *semblance* means
"a likeness or
shape."

His two hands were curved apart
In the semblance of a heart.

He wore, it seemed to his small son,
A bare heart on his hidden one,

A heart that gave out such a glow
No son awake could bear to know.

It showed a look upon a face
Too tender for the day to trace.

One instant, it lit all about,
And then the secret heart went out.

But it shone long enough for one
To know that hands held up the sun.

Robert P. Tristram Coffin[1]

Think and Discuss

1. In this poem there are eleven pairs of rhyming words. *Recall* and *all* rhyme because the last sound in *recall* is the same as *all*. *Night* and *light* rhyme because the last sound (*-ight*) in each word is the same. Name the end sounds in each of the other nine pairs of words.

2. Knowing that sounds and meanings work together, poets do not use words merely to rhyme. They search for words with both the right sound and the correct meaning. You have found the rhyming words in "The Secret Heart." Now, explain what the poem means to you.

[1]"The Secret Heart" by Robert P. Tristram Coffin. Copyright 1935 by Macmillan Publishing Co., Inc., renewed 1963 by Margaret Coffin Halvosa. Reprinted with permission of Macmillan Publishing Co., Inc.

Writing Practice 1: *Sounds and Meanings*

In the poem on page 173, "The Secret Heart," a man describes a memory of his father. This memory was from a time when the father lighted a match in the dark to check on his sleeping son. Think about a special memory of your own that involves a parent, grandparent, or other relative. The memory might be about a time that the person said or did something that made you feel very happy. Then write in your notebook about your relative and about what happened to make the memory a special one for you. As you write, use details to help your reader share your experience.

Try to think of words that sound like your memory. For example, in the poem on page 173, Robert P. Tristram Coffin uses the word *stillest*. For many readers, this word has a quiet sound. The *s* sounds in *stillest* help readers share the quietness of the night. What words will help your readers feel what you felt at the time?

Figurative Language

One way that poets express their thoughts and feelings in poetry is by building "bridges" in readers' minds. These mental bridges connect what the poet wishes to describe with another person, animal, place, object, or event. For example, in the poem "Giraffes," on page 170, Sy Kahn builds a mental bridge from the giraffes to "hammer-headed flowers." He also builds a mental bridge to connect giraffes with "ornaments against the sky." These connections, called

figurative language, help the reader share the poet's feelings. When you read that giraffes are "Slightly swaying,/Like hammer-headed flowers," you may be able to see these "giraffe-flowers" in your own mind.

Model: *Figurative Language*

Here are two more examples of poems that contain figurative language.

November Day
Old haggard wind has
    plucked the trees
Like pheasants, held
    between her knees.
In rows she hangs them,
    bare and neat,
Their brilliant plumage at
    her feet.[1]

    Eleanor Averitt

A City Park
Timidly
Against a background of brick tenements
Some trees spread their branches
Skyward.
They are thin and sapless,
They are bent and weary—
Tamed with captivity;
And they huddle behind the fence
Swaying helplessly before the wind,
Forward and backward
Like a group of panicky deer
Caught in a cage.[2]

    Alter Brody

In the first poem Eleanor Averitt asks her readers to make a connection between trees when the winds pluck their leaves and pheasants when they are plucked. In the second poem Alter Brody connects trees in a city park with deer caught in a cage. These connections help many readers think of trees in new ways.

[1]"November Day" by Eleanor Averitt. Reprinted from *The Saturday Evening Post* © 1958 The Curtis Publishing Company. By permission of The Saturday Evening Post.
[2]"A City Park" from *A Family Album and Other Poems* by Alter Brody. Copyright 1918 by B. W. Huebsch, Inc., copyright renewed 1946 by Alter Brody. Reprinted by permission of Viking Penguin Inc.

In these two poems the poets use the word *like* to make the connections. Poets often use the word *as* in the same way. Connections made with *like* or *as* are called *similes*. Poets do not always use the words *like* or *as*, however. Connections made without *like* or *as* are called *metaphors*. The following poem uses a metaphor.

Model: *Metaphor*

What is the connection the poet wishes you to make in this poem?

Marbles
Marbles picked up
Heavy by the handful
And held, weighed,
Hard, glossy,
Glassy, cold,
Then poured clicking,
Water-smooth, back
To their bag, seem
Treasure: round jewels,
Slithering gold.[1]

Valerie Worth

Think and Discuss

1. The poet makes the connection between marbles and jewels when she writes that marbles "seem/treasure: round jewels,/slithering gold." How can marbles be compared with jewels?

2. How are marbles like gold?

Writing Practice 2: *Using Figurative Language*

Each of the phrases on page 177 describes a place, animal, or object. Write three phrases from this list in the left-hand part of a sheet of paper. Then, using the word *is*, *like*, or *as*, make a connection to another animal, place, object, or event.

To do a good job of making connections, carefully observe the person, animal, place, object, or event you select. When you write in your notebook, you often use your senses of sight,

---

[1]"Marbles" from *Small Poems* by Valerie Worth. Copyright © 1972 by Valerie Worth. Reprinted by permission of Farrar, Straus and Giroux, Inc. and Curtis Brown, Ltd.

hearing, touch, taste, and smell to create descriptions. These kinds of details are important in poetry, so before you write about something, ask yourself how it looks, sounds, feels, tastes, and smells.

You must also use your imagination. With imagination, you can turn everything around you into something else. A pet cat becomes a tiger; the blank sheet of paper before you is a limitless field of snow; and your hand changes into the powerful steel claw of a crane.

Example

a. My cat Sally   is a gray and white rag doll.

1. A supermarket on a busy Saturday morning

2. A roller-skating rink on Saturday evening

3. The first snowfall of the year

4. The city at 5:00 P.M. on a very hot weekday

5. The tiger in your local zoo

6. A flying disk when you have thrown it very far and very high

7. Your room when it hasn't been cleaned up in a long time

8. Your classroom when the final bell before summer vacation rings

9. A baseball when it's coming at you very fast

10. The sun when it breaks through on a cloudy day

The Rhythm of Words

thump
THUMP

thump
THUMP

The words above represent the sounds of an average heartbeat. There are two sounds in each beat, one louder than the other. The average heart beats more than seventy times a minute, and these two sounds are repeated over and over. When sounds are repeated in this kind of regular pattern, they form a *rhythm*.

Words can be arranged so that they, too, like heartbeats, can have rhythms. When you say a word of more than one syllable, you can hear that one syllable is spoken more loudly than the other:

describe	de SCRIBE
shadow	SHAD ow

Because words have soft and loud syllables, poets can put them together so that the sounds form a regular pattern.

The regular pattern of sounds in a poem is called *meter.*

Models: *Meter in Poetry*

Here is the first verse of Robert Frost's famous poem "Stopping by Woods on a Snowy Evening." The lines in this poem have a regular meter: softLOUD, softLOUD, softLOUD, softLOUD. The louder sounds in the first two lines are marked. Which words should be marked in the other lines?

Whose woods these are I think I know.
His house is in the village though.
He will not see me stopping here
To watch his woods fill up with snow.[1]

---

[1]From "Stopping by Woods on a Snowy Evening" from *The Poetry of Robert Frost* edited by Edward Connery Lathem. Copyright 1923, © 1969 by Holt, Rinehart and Winston. Copyright 1951 by Robert Frost. Reprinted by permission of the Estate of Robert Frost and Holt, Rinehart and Winston, Publishers.

Poets use many other kinds of sound patterns because meter is pleasing and often helps meaning. For example, in "The Highwayman," by Alfred Noyes, the meter is like the sound pattern of a galloping horse's hoofs. Here is one verse from that poem. Read it aloud, and notice the regular meter:

> *Tlot-tlot; tlot-tlot!* Had they heard it? The horse hoofs
> ringing clear;
> *Tlot-tlot, tlot-tlot,* in the distance? Were they deaf that
> they did not hear?
> Down the ribbon of moonlight, over the brow of the hill,
> The highwayman came riding,
> Riding, riding!
> The redcoats looked to their priming! She stood up,
> straight and still![1]

Writing Practice 3: *Using Meter*

Each of the following sets of words has a softLOUD sound pattern. The LOUD sound is marked with the symbol ('). Use each of the sets of words in a sentence that tells something about the person, place, object, or event. Select your words so that your finished sentence will have four sets of softLOUD sounds. Mark loud sounds in your sentences with the symbol ('). Remember that when a word has more than one syllable, each syllable is a sound: *PAS ture.*

Example

a. The horse
The horse approached the pasture fence.

1. The gift

2. A friend

3. The rain

4. A place

5. This boy

Next, add a second line to each of your sentences. The second line should continue the meaning of the first line and

[1]From "The Highwayman" in *Collected Poems in One Volume* by Alfred Noyes. Copyright 1934 by Alfred Noyes. Reprinted by permission of Harper & Row, Publishers, Inc. and Hugh Noyes, St. Laurence, Isle of Wight, England.

should have the same softLOUD softLOUD softLOUD softLOUD sound pattern.

Example

a. The horse
   The horse approached the pasture fence
   And nuzzled near for me to pet.

For Your Writer's Notebook

If you listen carefully, you can hear the rhythm of the world around you. When rain drums on a roof, for example, it may make a pattern such as softsoftLOUD softsoftLOUD. The sounds a woodpecker makes are often rhythmic. Listen in the world around you for examples of rhythms. When you do write about these rhythms in your notebook, use the words *soft* and *LOUD* to describe the sounds.

Describing with Poetry

Poets use *sense* details—sight, sound, touch, taste, and smell—to describe people, animals, events, and objects.

Model: Sense Details in Poetry

As you read the following poem about seals, look for details that help you see and hear:

Seal
See how he dives
 From the rocks with a zoom!
 See how he darts
 Through his watery room
 Past crabs and eels
 And green seaweed,
 Past fluffs of sandy
 Minnow feed!
 See how he swims
 With a swerve and a twist,
 A flip of the flipper,
 A flick of the wrist!
 Quicksilver-quick,
 Softer than spray,
 Down he plunges
 And sweeps away;
 Before you can think,
 Before you can utter
 Words like "Dill pickle"
 Or "Apple butter,"
 Back up he swims
 Past sting-ray and shark,
 Out with a zoom,
 A whoop, a bark;
 Before you can say
 Whatever you wish,
 He plops at your side
 With a mouthful of fish![1]

William Jay Smith

Think and Discuss

Words such as *dives, darts, swerve, twist, plunges, sweeps* help you see the seal as it moves. Other sight details help you see the seal when it is swimming underwater.

See how he darts
Through his *watery room*
Past *crabs* and *eels*
And *green seaweed,*

[1]From *Laughing Time: Nonsense Poems* by William Jay Smith, published by Delacorte Press, 1980, copyright © 1955, 1957, 1980 by William Jay Smith. Reprinted by permission of William Jay Smith.

Past *fluffs of sandy
Minnow feed!*

What details in the poem help you *hear* the seal?

Writing Assignment I: *Writing a Poem*

Write a poem that describes a person, animal, place, object, or event, using the following steps.

A. Prewriting

Writing a poem that *describes* is much like writing a description in your Writer's Notebook. You must begin by observing carefully what you describe. For this reason, choose a subject for your poem that you know well, that you can observe now, or that you have written about in your notebook.

When you have your subject, play a game of mental association. On a sheet of paper, write down your subject. Then let your mind wander and jot down details of sight, sound, taste, touch, and smell about the subject. Here are sense details about a cat named Sally:

My Cat Sally

Sight
Has gray-and-white fur
Looks like a porcupine when she needs a bath
Stretches and yawns in the sunlight
Sits and stares out the window
Has two shining yellow eyes

Sound
Makes a crunching noise when she eats her cat food
Wears a bell that tinkles when she moves
Lands in the middle of the table with a *plop*
Makes low purring sounds

Touch
Feels heavy when she sleeps and her limp body is next to me
Licks me with her rough tongue

Smell
Smells like the scented shampoo I bathe her with
Smells like tuna fish after she eats

B. Writing

Use the sense details to write your poem. If you like, use one of the poems in this chapter as a model for your own poem.

C. Postwriting

Revise your poem by looking again at the nouns and verbs you have used. Replace vague nouns like *thing, object,* or *stuff* with nouns that name items precisely. Replace vague verbs like *make* and *do* with words that give specific descriptions of actions. Finally, proofread your poem.

Humor in Poetry

Many of the nursery rhymes you enjoyed as a child, such as the following one, are humorous:

I asked my mother for fifty cents
To see the elephant jump the fence.
He jumped so high he reached the sky.
And didn't get back till the Fourth of July.

Model: Humor in Poetry

Readers especially enjoy humorous poems about animals. Here, for example, is Theodore Roethke's poem about a hippopotamus.

The Hippo
A Head or Tail—which does he lack?
I think his Forward's coming back!
He lives on Carrots, Leeks, and Hay;
He starts to yawn—it takes All Day
Some time I think I'll live that way.[1]

Theodore Roethke

Like many poems, this one gains its humor from *exaggeration.* You really can tell the front end from the back end of a hippo, and it does not take all day for one to yawn.

Another animal this poet thinks is humorous is the sloth, an animal that lives in the forests of Central and South America. It hangs upside down in trees and moves very slowly. As you read this poem by Theodore Roethke, think what qualities of the sloth the poet exaggerates. (*Peer* means "an equal.")

The Sloth
In moving-slow he has no Peer.
You ask him something in his ear;
He thinks about it for a Year;

And then, before he says a Word
There, upside down (unlike a Bird)
He will assume that you have Heard—

A most Ex-as-per-at-ing Lug.
But should you call his manner Smug,
He'll sigh and give his Branch a Hug;

Then off again to Sleep he goes,
Still swaying gently by his Toes,
And you just know he knows he knows.[2]

Theodore Roethke

---

[1]"The Hippo" copyright 1961 and 1950 by Theodore Roethke, from the book *The Collected Poems of Theodore Roethke* by Theodore Roethke. Reprinted by permission of Doubleday & Company, Inc.
[2]"The Sloth" copyright 1961 and 1950 by Theodore Roethke, from the book *The Collected Poems of Theodore Roethke* by Theodore Roethke. Reprinted by permission of Doubleday & Company, Inc.

Most humorous poems have very regular meter and rhyme. In "The Sloth," for example, the three lines of each verse rhyme, and every line has the same pattern of loud and soft sounds: *Then óff agáin to Sléep he góes.* Read "The Sloth" aloud, and you hear the singsong effect that this meter causes. Count the syllables (beats) softly with your fingers.

Writing Practice 4: *Writing a Humorous Poem*

Write a humorous poem about an animal. To help get started, think about an animal with characteristics that could be funny: the way an ostrich walks or the way a pig rolls in the mud. When you finish your poem, read it aloud to see if it has a regular rhythm and rhyme. To test for rhythm, tap your desk very lightly for soft sounds and a little heavier for loud sounds. If your poem does not have regular rhythm and rhyme, try changing some of your words.

or

Write a humorous poem about a characteristic that some animal has and that people do not, but should have. Should people hibernate during the winter as bears and other animals do? How about long necks like giraffes? Or armor like a turtle or armadillo?

Writing a Story

All stories have *character, setting,* and *plot.*

Characters are the people or animals in a story. *Setting* is the time and place of a story, and *plot* refers to the action and conflict in a story. Good story writers do more than tell about character, setting, and plot, however. They use vivid details to *show* the readers character, setting, and the action that makes up the plot.

A storywriter uses sense details of sight, sound, taste, touch, and smell to describe characters, setting, and action.

185

Model: Details Describing a Character

Here is the way Sally Carrighar describes an Eskimo woman.

> She was a really old person, her face webbed with lines, but she was dressed as prettily as a girl, in a pink, bell-shaped parka, with a pink and green scarf on her snow-white hair. She did not turn away but stood smiling, so radiantly that I was astounded by her sheer beauty. Travelers to the North always mention the smiles of the Eskimos, and during the day I had thought I knew why. For everywhere I had been greeted with smiles, which had been remarkable for the genuine welcome they seemed to express, and for the ease with which they had come. The old woman's smile was surpassing them all. What it conveyed was a transcendent kindliness. I believe that she realized I was a little lonely, and the thought moved her to tenderness of the purest sort. She smiled, and the loneliness melted.[1]

Think and Discuss

1. Which details in the description help you see the woman? What was her face like? How was she dressed?

2. Which details describe the woman's "transcendent (going beyond the usual limits) kindliness"?

---

[1]From *Moonlight at Midday* by Sally Carrighar. Copyright © 1958 by Sally Carrighar. Reprinted by permission of Alfred A. Knopf, Inc.

Writing Practice 5: *Describing Character and Setting*

Imagine that either the boy or the girl in the picture on page 186 is a character in a story you are writing. Using details that will help readers see and hear the boy or girl, write a description of him or her.

Next, imagine that the second picture on the facing page shows a scene in the setting of your story. Using vivid details, describe the setting.

Writing Dialogue

Dialogue **is the words people say.**

Good storywriters use dialogue that sounds like real speech. They write dialogue that sounds right for the ages, backgrounds, and personalities of the characters.

Model: Dialogue

Here is an example of dialogue from the book *Raising Demons* by Shirley Jackson. In this passage the mother and father are talking with their teenage son Laurie, who has lost his tennis shoes. (Laurie calls them *sneakers*.) As you read the conversation, look for differences in the way Laurie speaks and the way his mother and father speak. In the first line Laurie's mother asks him a question:

"Are you *sure* you looked under your bed?"

He looked at me in the manner his favorite television detective reserves for ladies who double-talk the cops. "Yeah," he said, "Yeah, lady. I'm sure."

"How about that little dark-haired girl?" my husband asked Laurie. "The one who keeps calling you so much?"

"Nah," Laurie said. "She's tipped, anyhow. Besides, how could she get my sneaker?" He slapped his forehead. "A madhouse," he said. "Lose a sneaker and they start criticizing your friends and trying to make out she stole it. Bah."

"Never find anything around here," he explained. "Nothing's ever where you put it. If *she*—"

"If by *she* you mean *me*—" I began.

"Always coming and picking things up and putting them away where a person can't find them. Always—"

"If you'd put things away neatly when you take them off

187

instead of just throwing everything under your bed—" I stopped to think. "Have you looked under your bed?"

Laurie threw his arms wide. "Why was I ever born?"

"When did you see them last?" I asked. "Seems to me if you could remember when you had them last—"

"Yeah. Well," Laurie said, scowling, "I *know* I had them last Saturday. But then I took them off and I remember they were on my bookcase because I had to remember to make that map for geography and that was for Wednesday when we had gym—say!" He opened his eyes wide. "Gym. I wore them Wednesday to school for gym. So I had them on Wednesday."[1]

Think and Discuss

The words these speakers use reveal their personalities and interests. Laurie talks about people putting things away so that other people can't find them. Laurie's mother talks about putting things away neatly. Laurie uses slang such as *yeah* and *madhouse* and expressions such as *she's tipped* and *why was I ever born?* Why would you not expect Laurie's mother and father to use words and expressions such as these?

When you write dialogue, read it aloud to see if it sounds the way people really talk. You can improve your ability to write dialogue by listening carefully to the way people of different ages and backgrounds talk.

Writing Practice 6: *Writing Dialogue*

Select one of the following situations and write a dialogue that might take place between the characters. The dialogue should fit the ages and personalities of the characters. For rules on punctuating dialogue, see Chapter 21.

1. A six-year-old boy comes into the house covered with mud. His thirteen-year-old brother, who is responsible for taking care of him, scolds him and the boy defends himself.

2. A seventh-grade student has failed to bring in her homework for the third time. The teacher, Ms. Ayo, is trying to find out why the student is not doing her homework.

3. An eight-year-old girl and an eight-year-old boy are playing marbles. The boy accuses the girl of cheating, and they have an argument.

[1]Selection from *Raising Demons* by Shirley Jackson. Copyright 1953, 1954, 1956, 1957 by Shirley Jackson. Reprinted by permission of Brandt & Brandt Literary Agents, Inc. and Farrar, Straus and Giroux, Inc.

4. At the door of the roller-skating rink, the manager stops a sixth-grade girl who is trying to leave without paying for a hamburger. The girl explains that her mother has already paid for the hamburger.

5. Use your imagination to create a situation that might take place in the photograph on this page. Think of the people who might be involved and then write their dialogue.

For Your Writer's Notebook

In your notebook, practice writing dialogue that you hear around you. Be careful not to violate other people's privacy by listening to their conversations, however. Write down dialogue that you hear on television or that you hear young children using as they play. Or write down conversations that you hear in grocery stores, on buses, at the beach, or in other public places.

Writing a Tall Tale

Jim Bridger, a hunter and trapper in the West during the 1800s, often told tall tales about his experiences. For example, he told about discovering an ice-cold spring at the top of a mountain.

According to this story, water flowed down the side of the mountain so fast that it was boiling hot when it reached the bottom.

Tall tales **are stories that are exaggerated and humorous.**

America is famous for its tall tales, which were often made up by cowhands, loggers, miners, and railroad workers. They are sometimes about real heroes, but as they were told over and over, the facts were stretched until finally there was little truth left in them.

Tall tales, like other stories, have characters, setting, and a plot. The storyteller uses details, often stretched, to describe the characters, setting, and plot.

Model: A Tall Tale

As you read the following tall tale from Arkansas, notice how the storyteller uses details to describe character, setting, and plot. Which of these details are exaggerated for humor? Tall tales were usually written in a *regional dialect.* (A regional dialect is a way of speaking shared by people in a certain part of the country.) In regional dialects the vocabulary and grammar differ from that of the Edited Standard English you write in school.

In Arkansas Stick to Bears: Don't Mess with Swampland Skeeters

A *squatter* is a person who settles on a piece of land without permission.

Back in the old days there lived a squatter in the Delta region not far from what is now the city of Helena. That squatter called himself Major Jones and he said he was slicker than a weasel, but his neighbors said he was a living bobcat that's dragged its tail through a briar patch. He wasn't a neighborly neighbor. He was forever complaining, but his biggest complaint was against Delta mosquitoes that were making life hard for man and beast.

They were as plentiful as ants at a picnic and big as wild turkeys. Some of them were nearly as big as deers in the woods.

One hot night the squatter set out to hunt bear. He was always bragging about his shooting strength. Truth to tell, he was lazy as pond water, so, instead of using his shooting piece on critters, he set bear traps deep in the swamps where he was sure bear were plentiful. After setting the contraptions he returned home. It was then nearly late candle-time, and it was mighty warm. Best time for mosquito-hunting. They were out thick as barn hay. They were zooming louder than frogs

croaking. The squatter was hopping faster than a fox with a
bumble bee in his tail, to steer clear of 'em. But those varmint
mosquitoes smelled blood and they were hot after it. And I tell
you when skeeters are on your trail, it's worse than snakes.

The man had come to his canoe, jumped in, and set down
to paddle. But the crick skeeters were after him like a mighty
army with banners, as it says in the Holy Book. Their zooming
seemed like thunder in the springtime. The squatter fought
them with paddle and gun to keep them off, but they were
coming at him like a herd of buffalo. Major Jones was getting
madder by the minute; he thought it was time to use powder
and lead. He raised his hunting piece and began to fire. He
brought down one or two of the zoomers and scared the rest,
but only for a short time. Pretty soon they were at him again.
By now he had come to where his cabin was. He leaped out of
the canoe, ran to the door quicker than a jack rabbit, and put on
the latch behind him, thanking the Lord for his safe escape.

The next morning early he went to the trap to see if it
had caught a fat brown bear, for he was in need of meat
and oil.

When he got there and saw what he saw, his face looked
like soot on a stick.

That bear trap had caught . . . a skeeter the size of a
young heifer.

Major Jones's face was fit to scare black cats at night. He
held his teeth tight, threw a rope round the neck of the
skeeter, tied a log to its borer, and hobbled its hind legs good.
Then he got the varmint out of the trap and dragged it home
slow-like. It wasn't easy, for that skeeter was bucking and
rearing to beat running fire.

"Jest you keep on rearin' and buckin'! I'm gonna train you
to be gentle as a lamb and I'm gonna train you to drill holes
with that borer of yourn. Maybe I'll find oil."

In the end he got the varmint in the barn, but he put the
boot on the wrong leg.

That critter began tearing and ripping around the barn like
a bull with hornets all over. It was making such a racket with
zooming, nobody could sleep. The third night the squatter
couldn't stand it any longer.

"I'll teach that toad blister somethin'," he said to his wife.
He took an old mule harness that was lying in the lot back of
the cabin and went cautiously into the barn. With dodging and
cross-running he got it on the skeeter, tied the skeeter to a
post, and went to his cabin.

The mosquito didn't like the queer contraption one bit. So
he began smashing it right and left and made enough noise to
wake the dead. In the end Major Jones went to the door of the
barn. Inside, the skeeter was banging and hitting away. Before
Jones's hand touched the wooden latch, the door came down

A *heifer* is a young
cow.

Hobble means "to
tie two legs
together."

with a bang. The critter had broken the door and had got the harness off its neck.

Major Jones's eyes popped open big as goose eggs, for the next thing that happened no man in Arkansas had ever seen.

Before you could say Jehoshaphat that skeeter was up in the air flying in the moonlight. It was aiming straight for the pasture where the squatter's cow was mooing for the calf. Down went that critter in the pasture and, come gunpowder!, if it didn't get hold of that cow with its hind legs and begin lifting it off the grass.

Now, it is common knowledge in Arkansas that it needs two Bear State mosquitoes to carry off a fair-sized cow, and here just one skeeter was doing it! Major Jones was so flabbergasted that he didn't even run for his shooting piece. It wouldn't have done him any good anyway.

That skeeter with the cow in its hind legs was so high up by then, no lead could catch it.

"Wal!" Major Jones growled like a bobcat with a thorn in its leg, "Wal, that'll teach me to stick to bears and not mess 'round skeeters in Arkansas swamplands."[1]

Think and Discuss

1. The storyteller uses details to tell the audience about Major Jones. In the first paragraph, for example, you learn that Major Jones "wasn't a neighborly neighbor." What are other details that describe Major Jones?

2. One detail you learn about setting in this tale is that the story takes place in the Delta region near what is now the city of Helena. What are details that describe this area?

3. The action in this tale begins when Major Jones goes out to hunt bears. What happens after that?

4. Writing a story in dialect means using words and phrases only people from that region use. This storyteller says that Major Jones was "slicker than a weasel" and that "he was a living bobcat that's dragged its tail through a briar patch." What are other phrases in this tale that only people from this region would be likely to know and use?

5. An important feature of a tall tale is exaggeration. In this tale the size of the mosquitoes is greatly exaggerated. What are other examples of exaggeration in this story?

---

[1]"In Arkansas Stick to Bears: Don't Mess with Swampland Skeeters" reprinted from *Folk Stories of the South* by M. A. Jagendorf by permission of the publisher, Vanguard Press, Inc. Copyright © 1972 by M. A. Jagendorf.

Writing Assignment II: *A Tall Tale*

Write a tall tale. Supply details of character, setting, and plot, and be sure to exaggerate enough of the details to make your tale humorous. If you like, write about one of the people or events listed below:

1. The adventures of a football (or other sport) star on the playing field

2. A fishing adventure

3. A bionic animal adventure

4. An adventure you might have at age twenty-five

5. An outer-space adventure

Use the following steps for prewriting, writing, and postwriting.

A. Prewriting

First, divide a page into four parts: *characters, setting, plot,* and *dialogue.* Brainstorm about each of these areas in relation to your topic. In the *characters* section, list the characters who will appear in your tall tale, and give descriptive details about their personalities and appearances. In the *setting* section, jot down phrases that describe the scene of the tale. Under *plot,* list possible events that may occur in the tale. Under *dialogue,* brainstorm words and phrases that your characters might use.

Next, order the information you have listed so far. Set up a time frame for your tale. Decide when to introduce the characters and how to order the events. Delete any notes that are not useful.

B. Writing

Using your time frame and model dialogue, write your tale. Vividly portray the characters, setting, and plot. Don't forget to let your sense of humor guide you as you write.

C. Postwriting

Use the following questions to help you revise your tall tale:

1. Are the descriptions appealing to various senses?

2. Does each character have a definite personality and appearance?

3. Are the events related in a logical order?

4. Is humor used appropriately?

5. Does the dialogue sound like real people talking?

Make changes in your tall tale until you can answer *yes* to each question.

Then use the Checklist for Proofreading at the back of this book to proofread your work.

Sentence Variety:
Inserting Sentences

Inserting (Who), (Which), *and* (That)

You can make a connection between two sentences by taking part of one sentence, adding the words *who*, *which*, or *that*, and inserting that part into a base sentence. In this way, you show how one sentence relates to the other.

Base Sentence: Maria heard a performance by Claudio Arrau.

Insert: Claudio Arrau is a concert pianist. (*who*)

Combined: Maria heard a performance by Claudio Arrau, *who is a concert pianist.*

Base Sentence: Irene finally found the book she wanted on the top shelf.

Insert: The top shelf was almost too high for her to reach. (*which*)

Combined: Irene finally found the book she wanted on the top shelf, *which was almost too high for her to reach.*

Notice that a comma separates the base sentence from the inserted sentence when the new part is added at the end. However, you add two commas, one before and one after the inserted part, when it is placed in the middle of the base sentence.

Base Sentence: Carl told a little lie and got me in trouble.

Insert: Telling a little lie made me angry. (*which*)

Combined: Carl told a little lie, *which made me angry*, and got me in trouble.

When you insert part of a sentence with *that*, you do not need to use a comma.

Base Sentence: We worked for twenty minutes on the problem.

Insert: The problem was in our math book. (*that*)

Combined: We worked for twenty minutes on the problem *that was in our math book.*

Exercise 1: *Inserting* (Who), (Which), *and* (That)

Using the signals as a guide, combine each of the following sets of sentences. Remember to use commas when they are needed. Place the inserted part in the base sentence where you think it belongs. Write each new sentence on a sheet of paper numbered 1–10. Study the example before you begin.

Example

a. The school band marched in the Founder's Day Parade. Founder's Day Parade is a local celebration. (*which*)
The school band marched in the Founder's Day Parade, which is a local celebration.

1. Peppermint Patty can twist Charlie Brown around her little finger.
Peppermint Patty is my favorite *Peanuts* character. (*who*)

2. Many products are now labeled according to the metric system.
The metric system may replace the system we use now. (*which*)

3. After the school play was over, Derek was surrounded by admiring friends.
   Derek had the leading role in Thornton Wilder's *Our Town.* (*who*)

4. A story by Rudyard Kipling is about a mongoose.
   A mongoose is a small, flesh-eating animal of India. (*which*)

5. The apples are beginning to ripen at last.
   The apples grow in our garden. (*that*)

6. Our relatives camped in Banff, Kootenay, and Jasper National Parks.
   These parks are north of Montana in the Canadian Rockies. (*which*)

7. My favorite cats are alley cats.
   Alley cats like to be free to roam wherever they choose. (*who*)

8. "We've won at last!" cried the team captain.
   The team captain had wanted to capture the trophy for the school. (*who*)

9. The guardrail may have prevented several accidents.
   The guardrail kept tourists from getting too close to the edge of the cliff. (*which*)

10. The title of the book is *The Call of the Wild.*
    The book provided me with long hours of entertainment last summer. (*that*)

Inserting (Whose), (Where), (When), and (Why)

Just as you combined sentences with *who, which,* or *that,* you can use *whose, where, when,* and *why* in place of the repeated word or words in the insert sentence.

Base Sentence:	Nancy was grateful to her friends.
Insert:	She had taken her friends' advice. (*whose*)
Combined:	Nancy was grateful to her friends *whose advice she had taken.*

Base Sentence:	James looked in every drawer and closet in the house.
Insert:	He might have left his woolen shirt. (*where*)
Combined:	James looked in every drawer and closet in the house *where he might have left his woolen shirt.*

Base Sentence:	Trouble seemed to come to Rosa at a time.
Insert:	She needed it the least. (*when*)
Combined:	Trouble seemed to come to Rosa at a time *when she needed it the least.*

Base Sentence:	Excuses will not explain the reason.
Insert:	Claudia arrived at school two hours late. (*why*)
Combined:	Excuses will not explain the reason *why Claudia arrived at school two hours late.*

Exercise 2: Inserting (Whose), (Where), (When), and (Why)

Combine the following sets of sentences by following the signals. You will not need to use commas in making the combinations. Write each new sentence on a sheet of paper numbered 1–5.

1. The conductor was not able to explain the reason.
   The train had stopped inside the tunnel. (*why*)

2. Our class had a party for those students.
   Those students' birthdays fell in December. (*whose*)

3. The twins could hardly wait for the day.
   On that day their father would be coming home again. (*when*)

4. It was so sunny and bright outdoors that we tried to find a place.
   We could shade our eyes and cool off a little. (*where*)

5. The Panama Canal was dug across the Isthmus of Panama.
   The distance between the Atlantic and Pacific Oceans is least. (*where*)

Writing Practice: *Sentence Variety in a Tall Tale*

Choose a paragraph from the tall tale you wrote in Chapter 8, and revise it for sentence variety. Use the words *who*, *which*, *that*, *whose*, *where*, *when*, and *why* to add details to your sentences.

9 Writing Friendly Letters

Writing to People You Know

A *friendly letter* is an informal letter to a friend, relative, or pen pal.

Years ago, people often wrote long friendly letters filled with news of family and community. Today, people can pick up a telephone and talk to a person hundreds of miles away in a matter of seconds. With this convenience, letter writing may seem to take too much time and energy.

Yet a personal letter is still an important way to communicate. A long-distance call is often expensive, but a letter costs only the price of a stamp, paper, and your time. Since a letter can be read over and over, it may be enjoyed many times.

In this chapter you will learn how to write a friendly letter.

Directing Letters to Readers

Think of coming home from school to find a letter from a close friend or relative waiting for you. As you open the letter, you feel a sense of excitement. Suppose, however, the letter has little more to say than *How are you? I'm fine and hope you are the same.*

If you have ever received such a letter, you were probably disappointed. You were anxious to hear all about your friend, but when you finished the letter, you did not know any more than before you read the letter. When you sat down to write a return letter, you could not think of anything to write about either.

Keep your reader in mind as you write your letter. Imagine a friend sitting across from you. Write about people, places, and events the two of you would talk about if you were together. You do not have to write about big events to make your letter interesting. Give news of your family, friends, and neighbors, your classes at school, your after-school activities, and anything special that happens to you.

Your Writer's Notebook is an important source of ideas for a personal letter.

In a notebook you write about your experiences, your thoughts, and your feelings. These are things a close friend or relative would want to know about. Remember that you also want to know about your reader. When you write a friendly letter, ask questions about your friend's or relative's interests and activities. These questions show your concern for your reader and help your reader begin the next letter to you.

Writing Practice 1: *Preparing to Write a Friendly Letter*

Think of a friend or relative to whom you would like to write a friendly letter. On a sheet of paper, make a list of your reader's interests. Now make a list of five subjects you could write about in a letter that would interest this reader: hobbies, activities, thoughts, feelings, or other subjects.

Writing an Interesting Letter

Interesting letters are like good notebook entries. They have details about people, places, and events and about the writer's thoughts and feelings.

Details help the reader share in the writer's experiences.

Model: Details in a Friendly Letter

Below is part of a letter written by a member of the Peace Corps. Since the early 1960s this organization has trained volunteers to work in nations around the world. In this letter the volunteer describes what a day for her is like in Addis Ababa, Ethiopia, in Africa where she lives and teaches. As you read this part of the letter, notice the writer's use of specific details.

In the morning now when we wake it is raining. Our roof, as most roofs in Addis, is tin and it is pleasant to wake at six to the heavy, amplified rain overhead. There are shutters on the two windows of my bedroom that keep it dark. It is cold, too, and in the mornings there is dew in the garden. The house is quiet. Today is Friday—my day to get up early and chop wood for the hot water heater.

My bedroom, like the other three, is big—twelve by twelve—with a high ceiling, a door out onto the front porch, wooden floor, dirty pale blue walls, and typical Peace Corps furniture. The mattress sags, as a hammock, in the bed; the wooden clothes closet has a warped door; the desk is small and shakes. I have constructed an artless but usable bookcase of stolen red bricks and unpainted planks; the walls are decorated with maps: Ethiopia, Africa, the world.[1]

In this part of the letter, the Peace Corps volunteer writing home describes her house. The details she includes allow you to hear the rain on the tin roof and to see the "dirty pale blue walls."

Use your notebook to help you recall details about your subject.

If you have written in your notebook about an experience while it was fresh in your mind, you will have a good source of specific, vivid details. Again, try to imagine your reader sitting across from you as you write. What specific questions might this person have about the experience you describe? In your letter use details to answer these questions.

The Form of a Friendly Letter

A friendly letter usually follows a standard form. The writer's address and date go in the upper right-hand part of the letter. The letter opens with a greeting such as *Dear Maria* and ends with a closing such as *Best wishes* and the writer's signature.

A friendly letter is called an *informal letter*. The form of an informal letter is not as important as it is with other kinds of letters because you usually write to a very close friend or relative. Such a reader probably cares more about what you say than how you say it.

A good skill to learn, however, is writing letters that follow standard form. If your teacher wishes you to use this form with the friendly letters you write now, turn to page 215, where you will find the proper form for friendly letters and for social letters. (Examples of social letters are thank-you notes and invitations.)

---

[1]From *Letters From the Peace Corps*, Iris Luce, ed., pp. 49–50. Washington 1964. Reprinted by permission of Robert B. Luce, Inc.

Writing Practice 2: *Writing a Friendly Letter*

Using the lists you composed for Writing Practice 1, write a letter to the friend or relative you chose. Include specific details about the subjects you think would interest your reader. Put your letter in standard form.

Writing to a Pen Pal

A *pen pal* is a friend you make through letters.

The purpose of writing to a pen pal is to share experiences with someone from another place. Pen pals may also be good company, and their letters are good ways to learn about a different part of the world.

In the early 1950s the United States was fighting the Korean War. During that time a group of ninth-graders wrote to President Harry Truman in behalf of the millions of boys and girls throughout the world who wanted peace. The result of their letter was World Pen Pals, an organization that helps boys and girls throughout the world become pen pals as a way to promote international understanding.

At the end of this section, you will find a list of organizations that you can contact for names of pen pals in other countries. Some of the organizations charge a small fee and ask you to send a self-addressed, stamped envelope. When you contact a pen pal organization, your letter should give information about yourself, such as your name, age, sex, and interests. If you want a pen pal from a particular state or country, you should also give that information in your letter. In return, the organization will tell you how to reach a pen pal.

Although most pen pals in other countries will write in English, their use of the language may seem strange to you at first. Your English may also be difficult for some pen pals to read. To help your pen pal, write in simple sentences and avoid using slang words. Remember that your pen pal's life may be different from yours. For example, pen pals in some countries may not listen to the same music you do or go to the same movies. In your first letter tell about yourself and your interests and ask for information about your pen pal. As you get to know each other, you will probably find that your lives are more alike than different and that you have many experiences to share.

If you write to a pen pal in another nation, it is best to use light-weight air mail stationery. The post office clerk can tell

you the postage rates for sending letters outside the United States.

Organizations for Pen Pals

League of Friendship
P.O. Box 509
Mount Vernon, OH 43050

International Friendship
League
22 Batterymarch
Boston, MA 02109

World Pen Pals
1690 Como Avenue
St. Paul, MN 55108

Writing Practice 3: *Writing to a Pen Pal*

The girl and the boy in the picture above are Japanese. The girl's name is Mitsuko Hayakawa, and the boy's name is Wada Mitsumoto. Mitsuko and Wada read and write English because they study it in school, but they do not know much about American teenagers or American schools. Write a letter to either Mitsuko or Wada. In your letter tell about yourself and about your interests and activities. Ask about your pen pal's interests and activities. Use the checklist at the back of the book to proofread your letter.

Writing Postcards

I magine that you are visiting an exciting place. You want to tell your friends hello, but you do not have time to write a long message. You also want your friends to share your experience with you. Writing a postcard is a good way to say hello when you do not have much time. Because many post-cards have pictures on one side, they can also be a way for friends to share your experience.

A *postcard* is a card the post office accepts without an envelope and for less postage than a regular letter.

The address of the person you are writing and your message go on the postcard itself. The U.S. Post Office sells a blank card with postage already on it. Write the address of the person to whom you are writing on one side of this card and your message on the other.

Another kind of postcard is a picture postcard. This postcard shows your reader some interesting or unusual part of the place you are visiting. The picture is one side, and the other side is divided into two parts: one for your message, and the other for the address of the person you are writing to.

Because you do not have much space on a postcard, your message has to be brief. You can make your postcard interesting by mentioning one or two specific things about your visit. You might also show an interest in what your friend or relative is doing at home.

Dec. 18, 1984

Greetings from Chicago!
I've never seen so many tall buildings. The most fun I had was in the Museum of Science and Industry. We walked through a real coal mine and saw a giant model railroad. It makes ours look like a toy.
It hasn't snowed yet, but maybe tomorrow. I'd bring you some snow if I could. Miss you!   *Love,*
Mary Ellen

Miss Chris Lee
603 Ellis Road
Little Rock, AR 72204

Writing Practice 4: *Writing a Postcard*

Siberia is a part of the Soviet Union 5,000 miles from Moscow. Imagine that you are spending two weeks this winter in Kyzyl-Syr, a town in Central Siberia.

On a sheet of paper, draw an outline of a postcard. Write a message to a friend or relative about your visit to Kyzyl-Syr. Use the following information for your message:

1. Kyzyl-Syr has a population of 6,000, and there are many young people.

2. Kyzyl-Syr has no roads to other towns. In the winter people drive on the river ice.

3. During the winter the temperature gets as low as −76°F (−60°C).

4. People in Kyzyl-Syr enjoy ice picnics. They dig holes in the ice, build tents over the holes, and catch fish through the holes. In a large tent on the ice, people gather to cook and eat the fish they catch.

5. Some animals you might see in Kyzyl-Syr are reindeer, bears, and wolves.

6. In the local market you can buy a pair of American jeans for $175.

Writing Assignment I: *Writing a Friendly Letter*

Imagine that you have been selected to make a guest appearance on your favorite TV show. You have been flown to the location and are now there, filming the episode. Write a letter to your best friend describing your fellow actors and actresses, the site of the filming, and your part in the show.

A. Prewriting

1. Brainstorm about the actors and actresses, the film site, and your part in the show. Write down every detail that comes to mind.

2. Underline the details that your best friend would be especially interested in. Add sense words so that your friend will be able to imagine sights, sounds, scents, textures, and tastes.

B. Writing

Using the standard form, write your friendly letter. Aim for a light, conversational tone, and use as many details as you can. You might mention the fun you and your friend could have if he or she were with you.

C. Postwriting

1. Read your letter. Does it sound interesting? Do you think your friend will feel like he or she is there with you? This is what you want your letter to accomplish. Revise it to make it more appealing.

2. Check your letter against the standard form on page 215. Is your letter neat and easy to read? Recopy it if it is too messy.

3. Proofread your letter, checking for correct spelling, punctuation, and capitalization.

Sentence Variety:
Inserting Sentences

New Ways to Combine (Who), (Where), (What), (Why), (When), and (How)

In this section (*who*), (*where*), (*what*), (*why*), (*when*), and (*how*) are again signals for combining sentences. But they will work with the new signal *something*. When you see the signal *something*, you insert some part of the second sentence in its place.

Base Sentence: Did Eloise ever figure out *something*?

Insert: Someone had knocked a hole in the wall. (*who*)

Combined: Did Eloise ever figure out <u>who had knocked a hole in the wall?</u>

After the insert sentence the signal (*who*) tells you to insert words from the second sentence that tell *who* is doing an action. Those words go in the place where the signal *something* appears in the base sentence.

Notice that in the combined sentence *who had knocked a hole in the wall* replaces the signal *something* in the base sentence. Notice also that the word *who* replaces the word *someone* because that word is no longer needed in the new sentence.

Study the following examples to see how other signals work with the signal *something*:

Base Sentence: I don't remember *something*.

Insert: The soccer coach told me. (*what*)

Combined: I don't remember <u>what the soccer coach told me.</u>

Base Sentence: I didn't know *something*.

Insert: Those people were standing in line for some reason. (*why*)

Combined: I didn't know <u>why those people were standing in line.</u>

Base Sentence:	Georgia couldn't say *something*.
Insert:	She would finish practicing her ballet sometime. (*when*)
Combined:	Georgia couldn't say <u>when she would finish practicing her ballet</u>.

Base Sentence:	Max, would you help me find *something*?
Insert:	I put my papers for science class somewhere. (*where*)
Combined:	Max, would you help me find <u>where I put my papers for science class</u>?

Base Sentence:	If nobody helps with this project, I don't know *something*.
Insert:	We will raise the money somehow. (*how*)
Combined:	If nobody helps with this project, I don't know <u>how we will raise the money</u>.

Exercise 1: *Inserting* (Who), (Where), (What), (Why), (When), *and* (How)

Combine the following sets of sentences by following the signal *something* in the base sentence and the signals (*who*), (*where*), (*what*), (*why*), (*when*), and (*how*) in the insert sentences. Write the new sentences on a sheet of paper numbered 1–5. Study the example before you begin.

Example

a. The officers didn't know *something*.
The thieves had not taken a valuable painting. (*why*)
The officers didn't know why the thieves had not taken a valuable painting.

1. Perhaps Mr. Chavez, an experienced art expert, could tell them *something*.
The painting had been overlooked. (*why*)
2. At least, he could tell the officers *something*.
The thieves entered the building. (*how*)
3. Mr. Chavez knew *something*.
Tools had been used by the thieves. (*what*)

4. Some people believed the building superintendent knew *something*.
   The thieves had got their break-in tools. (*where*)
5. Investigating detectives tried to determine *something*.
   The break-in happened. (*when*)

New Signals: (That), (The Fact That), (Join)

The new signals (*that*), (*the fact that*), and (*join*) work in the same way (*who*), (*what*), (*why*), (*when*), (*where*), and (*how*) work with the signal *something*. The signal word *something* in the base sentence is removed and the words *that* or *the fact that*, followed by some part of the insert sentence, are put in its place. When you see the signal (*join*), simply place the second sentence where *something* appears. No other word or words are added. Study the following examples to see how the combinations work:

Base Sentence: Carlotta believed *something*.

Insert: Tommy liked her very much. (*that*)

Combined: Carlotta believed <u>that Tommy liked her very much</u>.

Base Sentence: *Something* made Rosemary give up music lessons.

Insert: She hated to practice long hours. (*the fact that*)

Combined: <u>The fact that she hated to practice long hours</u> made Rosemary give up music lessons.

Base Sentence: The bus driver felt *something*.

Insert: The passengers were being too rowdy. (*join*)

Combined: The bus driver felt <u>the passengers were being too rowdy</u>.

Exercise 2: (That), (The Fact That), *and* (Join)

Combine the sets of sentences on the next page by following the signals (*that*), (*the fact that*), or (*join*) in the insert sentence and *something* in the base sentence. Write each new sentence on a sheet of paper numbered 1–5. Study the example before you begin.

Example

a. The hands on the clock told me *something*.
It was time to start dinner. (*that*)
The hands on the clock told me that it was time to start dinner.

1. The inspector found *something*.
Mice had eaten through the sacks of grain. (*that*)
2. *Something* made our holiday less happy.
George, Ralph, and Kerry were ill with the flu. (*the fact that*)
3. Annette felt *something*.
She deserved the same grades as her brother. (*that*)
4. *Something* was Mrs. Kellogg's main concern.
Her family would be able to save enough for the trip to Canada. (*that*)
5. Laurie and Tim truly believed *something*.
They could learn more about skiing on a full run down the face of the mountain than they could on beginner slopes. (*join*)

Exercise 3: *Choosing Your Own Signals*

The only signal in the following sets of sentences is *something*, so combine them in the way you think best. Write the new sentences on a sheet of paper numbered 1–10.

1. The Dolphins found *something*.
The best players were the most honest people.
2. Dr. Kenyon took time to give the reason.
Terry could not play hockey until her torn ligament had healed completely.
3. The student will be named class valedictorian.
The student's grades are the highest in the class.
4. Lupe said *something*.
It would not be fair to play when one was not eligible.
5. *Something* remained a mystery.
Chris had cleaned out her closet.
6. *Something* puzzled the street repair crew.
The dog got into the drain pipe.

7. The people of China gave a giant panda to the people of the United States as a symbol of friendship.
   President Nixon visited their country.
8. The beginners knew *something*.
   Someone would advance to the intermediate swimming class.
9. *Something* did not prevent Hiroshi's safe descent from the top of the mountain.
   His ankle had been sprained.
10. *Something* depended on how far the ancient bus could carry them.
    The passengers would end their journey.

Writing Practice: *Using New Techniques*

Look again at one of the friendly letters you wrote for Chapter 9. Choosing one paragraph from your letter, combine sentences and add details and descriptions. Use the new techniques you have learned in this section to vary the lengths and patterns of your sentences.

10 Writing Social and Business Letters

Social and business letters are written for specific reasons. Social letters officially thank someone for a gift or a visit; they are a courtesy to the addressee. Social letters also give or answer invitations. Business letters are used to apply for a job, to place an order, to make a request, and for other reasons. Unlike friendly letters, social and business letters are not casual. They always follow a standard form and always should be carefully checked for errors.

In this chapter you will learn how to write the different kinds of social and business letters and to follow the standard form for each.

Writing Social Letters

Carefully written social letters reflect good manners. They show that you care about and respect the feelings of others. There are many kinds of social letters, but they all follow one basic form. In the following sections you will learn first about the form, and second, about the specific types of social letters. Then you will be given the chance to practice what you have learned.

The parts of a social letter are the *heading,* the *salutation,* the *body,* the *closing,* and the *signature.*

Each part has a purpose in the letter and follows a standard form. You can tell where each part of the letter goes on the page by drawing imaginary lines called *margins* around the paper. The left-hand margin of the letter is about one and one-fourth inches from the left edge of the paper. The right-hand margin is about one inch from the right edge of the paper. Center a short letter so that you leave about the same amount of space at the top of the page as at the bottom of the page. If the letter fills up almost the entire page or if it runs over to another page, leave at least one inch at the top of the paper and one inch at the bottom.

Model: The Form of a Social Letter

The following thank-you letter shows the correct form for all social letters.

Heading

> 11 East Greenbay Avenue
> Pensacola, Florida 31705
> May 12, 1984

Salutation — Dear Aunt Helen,

Body

Thanks so much for the Washington Redskins poster. I've already got it hanging on my wall, and it looks great! You couldn't have made a better choice.

Mother tells me that you and Uncle John have a new litter of puppies. Any chance I could have one? I'm sure Mother won't mind. At least, I think I'm sure.

It was very kind of you to remember my interest in football. Thank you again.

Closing — Your nephew,

Signature — Sam

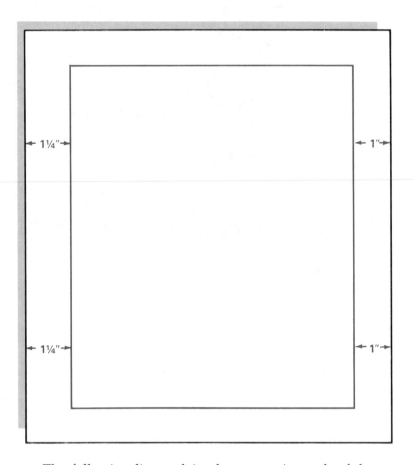

The following list explains how to write each of the parts for a social letter. Study the model thank-you letter that appears on page 215 as you read the explanation.

1. Heading

The *heading* of a social letter is the writer's street address, city, state, and ZIP code, and the date of the letter. The left-hand margins of these lines are even.

Place the heading in the upper-right corner of the letter. The longest line of the heading should not run too far past the right-hand margin of the letter.

2. Salutation

The *salutation* is the greeting to your friend or relative. It is customary to use the word *Dear* with the name of your friend or relative: *Dear Sara, Dear Uncle Bob.* Capitalize the first word and all nouns in the salutation, and put a comma after the salutation. Begin the salutation a space or two below the last line of the heading, even with the left-hand margin of the letter.

3. Body

The *body* of the letter is the main part. Leave a space between the salutation and the body. The left-hand margins of the body are even, but you may indent the beginning of each paragraph. To do this, begin each paragraph a few spaces to the right. The right-hand margins of the body are not exactly even, but they should not run too close to the edge of the page.

4. Closing

The *closing* begins a space after the last line of the body. The left-hand margin of the closing is even with the left-hand margin of the heading. *Sincerely* or *Sincerely yours* are always acceptable closings for a social letter. For a close relative or friend you might prefer a more casual closing such as *Your niece* or *Your friend*. The first word in the closing is always capitalized, but other words are not. A comma follows the closing.

5. Signature

The *signature* comes just below the closing and is always handwritten.

Your friend,

Janice Antini

The Envelope

The envelope for a social letter also has a standard form.

Model: *Form for an Envelope*

This form is the most widely used one for social letters.

Joan McPherson
848 San Bogue Lane
San Mateo, California 92647

Miss Ann Smith
17551 Robinson Road
Chicago, Illinois 60648

Write your name and address in the upper-left corner of the envelope, but leave some space at both the top and left-hand side. Do not use a title such as *Mr.* or *Miss* in front of your name. Center the name and address of the person to whom you are writing in the lower half of the envelope. Use a title such as *Mr., Ms., Mrs.,* or *Miss* before your friend's or relative's name. Capitalize and punctuate the addresses on the envelope just as you do those in the letter.

Folding the Letter

If you use a large size envelope (9½ × 4½), fold your letter in the following manner: Fold the bottom edge of the paper one-third of the way up the page and make a crease at the fold. Fold the top edge of the paper down to within one-fourth inch of the new bottom edge. Make a second crease in the paper. Place the letter into the envelope with the open edge up.

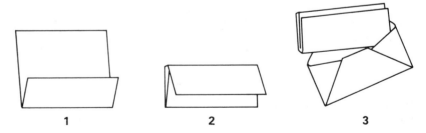

1   2   3

If you use the smaller size envelope (6½ × 3½), fold your letter in this manner: Bring the bottom edge of the paper within one-fourth inch from the top edge. Make a crease along the fold. Fold the right one-third of the page toward the left edge of the page. Crease the fold. Fold the left edge of the page to within one-fourth inch of the crease. Insert the letter into the envelope with the open side up, so that your reader can easily take the letter from the envelope.

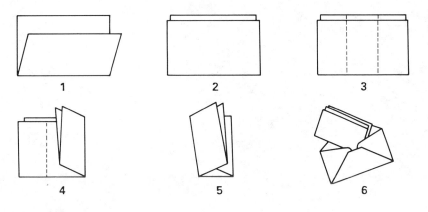

Writing a Thank-You Letter

The *thank-you letter* is written to thank a friend or relative for a gift or special favor.

Another important reason for writing a thank-you letter is to tell a relative or friend a gift has arrived safely through the mail. A thank-you letter should be written promptly. Delaying makes it seem as though writing the letter is a chore. The letter should be courteous and show genuine pleasure at receiving the gift.

When you write a thank-you letter, mention the gift you have received. A vague *Thank you for your gift* written across a note card might leave the sender wondering if you even knew whose gift you received. Your letter will seem much more sincere if you are able to tell your reader exactly why you like a gift.

A special courtesy in a thank-you letter is to show an interest in your reader as well as in the gift. Ask questions about your reader's well-being or mention some special activities or interests of the reader.

Writing Assignment I: *A Social Letter*

Select one of the following situations and write the thank-you letter that you might send to a friend or relative. If you prefer,

write a thank-you letter for a gift you actually received. Use the thank-you letter on page 215 as a model. Then address an envelope to go with your letter. If you do not have an envelope, draw an outline of one on a piece of paper and address it as you would an envelope. Use standard letter and envelope form.

1. A cousin you have not seen for years sent you some school pictures.

2. Your closest friend moved out of town and sent you a record for your birthday.

3. A brother in college sent you a funny poster for your birthday.

4. A friend who went to summer camp sent you a souvenir.

5. Your aunt gave you a gift certificate to your favorite hamburger place.

A. Prewriting

Make sure you have the correct address of the person to whom you are writing. Write the complete address of your real or imaginary reader so you will have it when addressing your envelope.

Next, jot down notes about what you want to say in your letter. Remember to include specific information about the gift and why you like it. Also, show in some other way that you are interested in your reader.

B. Writing

Using your prewriting notes, write a courteous thank-you letter. Keep your reader in mind as you write. After you finish the letter, address the envelope.

C. Postwriting

Read your letter. Did you explain in detail why you liked the gift? Does the letter sound courteous? Work on your letter until it is a message that you yourself would enjoy and appreciate receiving.

Next, check the form of your letter, using the following checklist.

Checklist for Proofreading Social Letters

1. The letter is neatly written on unlined paper in blue or black ink.

2. The parts of the letter are correctly spaced.

3. The left-hand margin of the heading is even with the left-hand margin of the closing, and the left-hand margin of the salutation is even with the left-hand margin of the body.

4. The first word and all nouns in the salutation are capitalized.

5. The first word of the closing is capitalized.

6. A comma comes between the city and the state in the heading.

7. A comma comes between the day of the month and the year in the heading.

8. A comma follows the salutation and the closing.

Finally, proofread your letter, using the Checklist for Proofreading at the back of the book. After you have made all necessary revisions and corrections, copy your letter neatly.

Writing a Bread-and-Butter Letter

A *bread-and-butter letter* is written after an overnight or longer stay at someone's home.

Although a friend of yours may have invited you, you usually write this letter to the adults most responsible for your comfort during your visit, the friend's parents, for example.

Model: A Bread-and-Butter Letter

Like other thank-you letters, the bread-and-butter letter should be written promptly. It should also mention specific parts of the visit you remember and appreciate, such as a special meal, a trip the family arranged for you and your friend, or some other special courtesy shown you.

> 1314 Weston Road
> Bridgeport, Connecticut 06606
> September 3, 1984
>
> Dear Mr. and Mrs. Osaka,
>
> Thank you for inviting me to your home. The weekend was a special time for me, and I appreciate your making it so enjoyable.
>
> Your dinner was delicious, Mr. Osaka. Maybe I could take cooking lessons from you. Even though John beat me badly, Mrs. Osaka, thank you for taking us to the tennis courts. I definitely need some lessons there.
>
> Thank you again for making me feel so welcome in your home.
>
> Sincerely,
> Paul Levine

Writing Practice 1: *Writing a Bread-and-Butter Letter*

Select one of the following situations or make up one of your own. Write a bread-and-butter letter to the hosts. Make up names, addresses, and any other details you need to write a good letter. Address an envelope to go with the letter. If you do not have an envelope, draw an outline of one on a piece of paper and address it as you would an envelope. Use the standard form for a social letter and envelope.

1. You spent a weekend night with a friend. Your friend's parents took you and your friend to the late horror movie.

2. You spent the night with your cousin. Your aunt and uncle took you to a model railroad show.

3. You spent the weekend at your scout leader's house. Your scout leader taught you to make candles and took you for a long walk.

4. You went with a friend's family to visit your friend's grandparents for a weekend. On the way you stopped at an amusement park.

5. You spent two weeks with your grandparents. They gave you some cooking lessons.

A Letter of Invitation

Although either using the telephone or filling out a printed invitation form is probably the easiest way to invite friends to a party, a handwritten *letter of invitation* is often better. It shows that you have made a special effort. Sending a handwritten letter also allows you to personalize each invitation. For example, you can give a person who has never been to your house detailed instructions, while leaving the instructions out for others. A form usually does not provide enough space for this kind of information, and a telephone call about such details may result in confusion.

Model: A Letter of Invitation

Letters of invitation should be precise about the time, date, and location of the event. The letter should also include information about any special activity or about the guest of honor. Your letter should make each guest feel really welcome.

You may want your guests to reply to an invitation so that you will know how many people to expect. If you do, place the letters *R.S.V.P.* in the lower left-hand corner of the invitation. Printed invitations may already have this abbreviation. If not, you may write it in. These letters are an abbreviation for French words meaning *Respond, if you please.* You may also write your telephone number after the *R.S.V.P.* so that guests can telephone their replies.

613 West Johns Road
Lexington, Kentucky 40502
May 2, 1984

Dear Maria,

Next weekend our friend Luis Paredes will be in town for a visit. I plan to have a few friends over to my house on Saturday, May 20, at 3:00 P.M., to give everyone a chance to say hello. I certainly would like for you to be there.

We will be cooking hamburgers outdoors, and we might even get another softball game going, so be sure to wear your comfortable clothes.

Sincerely,

Gail

R.S.V.P. 555-1929

Writing Practice 2: *Writing a Letter of Invitation*

Select one of the following five situations or make up one of your own, and write a letter of invitation for the occasion you select. Make up names, addresses, and any other details you need to write a good letter of invitation. Address an envelope to go with the letter. If you do not have an envelope, draw an outline of one on a piece of paper and address it as you would an envelope. Use the standard forms for a social letter and envelope.

1.   A bowling party to be held at a nearby bowling alley

2.   A birthday party for yourself

3. A party for a friend who is about to leave town

4. An end-of-school picnic to be held at a nearby park

5. A small, informal gathering of friends just for fun

Letters Accepting or Declining Invitations

Send letters accepting or declining an invitation as soon as possible after you receive the invitation. Responding promptly is especially important if the invitation contains an *R.S.V.P.*

Model: *A Letter of Acceptance*

23 Kirkland Drive
Lexington, Kentucky 40502
May 6, 1984

Dear Gail,

Thank you for the invitation to the cookout at your house on Saturday, May 20, at 3:00 P.M. There's nothing I would like more than to see Luis again, and the cookout sounds great.

See you on the 20th.

Sincerely,
Maria

Whether you accept or decline an invitation, you should express your pleasure at having been invited. When you accept, repeat the information in the original invitation about the occasion, date, time, and place in your letter. This lets your host know that you have the correct information. If you decline an invitation, you should, if possible, give your reasons for doing so.

Model: *A Letter Declining an Invitation*

23 Kirkland Drive
Lexington, Kentucky 40502
May 6, 1984

Dear Gail,

Thank you for the invitation to your cookout. There's nothing I would like more than to see Luis again, but May 20th is the date of our baseball game, and I will be out of town.

Please say hello to Luis for me and tell him I will see him the next time he is in town.

Sincerely,
Maria

Writing Practice 3: *Responding to an Invitation*

Exchange letters of invitation (from Writing Practice 2) with one of your classmates. Write a letter accepting or declining your classmate's invitation.

Writing Business Letters

Business letters are written to apply for a job, to place an order, to ask for information, and to communicate other matters of business. A good business letter makes a favorable impression on its reader and is often important in helping you achieve the results you want.

Model: A Business Letter

Thirteen-year-old Jenny Tanaka thought of a way to earn extra money. She typed and sent this letter to all of the people in her neighborhood:

Heading

1633 Wright Street
Stamford, CT 06902
May 3, 1984

Inside Address

Mr. and Mrs. Michael LaCavera
102 83rd Place, West
Stamford, CT 06902

Salutation

Dear Mr. and Mrs. LaCavera:

Body

If you are planning on taking a summer vacation, you may have wondered what to do with your house plants while you are away. I have a suggestion for you. For fifty cents a day, I will water and care for your plants during your vacation.

I have been raising plants since I was six years old. For the past three summers I have cared for the plants of several neighbors. One neighbor, Mr. John Price, will be happy to give you a recommendation if you call him at 555-4728 in the evening or on weekends. I am a seventh-grade honor student at Worth Junior High School and am very reliable.

If you would like me to take care of your plants this summer, please call me at 555-1929. I am usually home from school by 4:00 P.M.

Closing

Sincerely yours,

Signature

Jenny Tanaka

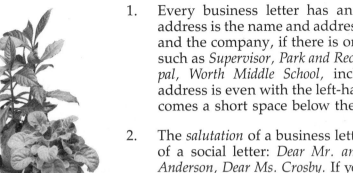

Jenny's letter, like all business letters, follows a customary form. In many ways the form of a business letter is the same as the form of a social letter. However, the form of a business letter differs from that of a social letter in the following ways:

1. Every business letter has an *inside address*. The inside address is the name and address of the person you write to and the company, if there is one. If the person has a title, such as *Supervisor, Park and Recreation Department* or *Principal, Worth Middle School*, include the title. The inside address is even with the left-hand margin of the letter and comes a short space below the heading.

2. The *salutation* of a business letter is more formal than that of a social letter: *Dear Mr. and Mrs. LaCavera, Dear Dr. Anderson, Dear Ms. Crosby*. If you do not know whether or not a woman is married, it is acceptable to address her as *Ms.* Sometimes you may write to a company or one department in a company without knowing anyone's name. In that case it is appropriate to address the department, the position, or the company:

   Dear Personnel Department:

   Dear Sunnyside Puppy Farm:

   Dear Record Department Manager:

   The salutation is always followed by a colon.

3. The *body* of a business letter should be businesslike. This means you should get quickly to the point and be as brief as possible without leaving out important information. Do not be so brief, however, that you are impolite. *Thank you* and *please* are not out of place in a business letter.

4. The *closing* of a business letter is more formal than that of a social letter. The following closings are acceptable:

   Yours truly,

   Very truly yours,

   Sincerely yours,

   Respectfully yours,

5. Sign your full name in a business letter, but do not use a title such as *Mr.* or *Miss.* If you wish your reader to know that you are a *Miss*, write this title in parentheses before your signature:

Write your business letter on plain, unlined stationery in your best handwriting. Center the letter on the page. If the letter is too long for one page, do not write on the back. Leave about an inch at the bottom of the first page and continue your letter about two inches from the top of the second page.

Abbreviations

The United States Post Office has approved two-letter abbreviations for states, possessions of the United States, and Canadian provinces to be used with ZIP codes. The list below shows the abbreviations. Notice that state abbreviations require no periods: *Wayne, NE 68787.*

Alabama **AL**	Montana **MT**	Wisconsin **WI**
Alaska **AK**	Nebraska **NE**	Wyoming **WY**
Arizona **AZ**	Nevada **NV**	Canal Zone **CZ**
Arkansas **AR**	New Hampshire **NH**	District of Columbia **DC**
California **CA**	New Jersey **NJ**	Guam **GU**
Colorado **CO**	New Mexico **NM**	Puerto Rico **PR**
Connecticut **CT**	New York **NY**	Virgin Islands **VI**
Delaware **DE**	North Carolina **NC**	Alberta **AB**
Florida **FL**	North Dakota **ND**	British Columbia **BC**
Georgia **GA**	Ohio **OH**	Manitoba **MB**
Hawaii **HI**	Oklahoma **OK**	New Brunswick **NB**
Idaho **ID**	Oregon **OR**	Newfoundland **NF**
Illinois **IL**	Pennsylvania **PA**	Northwest Territories **NT**
Indiana **IN**	Rhode Island **RI**	Nova Scotia **NS**
Iowa **IA**	South Carolina **SC**	Ontario **ON**
Kansas **KS**	South Dakota **SD**	Prince Edward Island **PE**
Kentucky **KY**	Tennessee **TN**	Quebec **PQ**
Louisiana **LA**	Texas **TX**	Saskatchewan **SK**
Maine **ME**	Utah **UT**	Yukon Territory **YT**
Maryland **MD**	Vermont **VT**	Labrador **LB**
Massachusetts **MA**	Virginia **VA**	
Michigan **MI**	Washington **WA**	
Minnesota **MN**	West Virginia **WV**	
Mississippi **MS**		
Missouri **MO**		

The Full Block Form for Business Letters

Many businesses use a letter form called the *full block form.*

With the *full block form* each part of the letter begins at the left-hand margin, and an extra space is left between paragraphs. Paragraphs are not indented, but the spacing of other parts remains the same.

Model: *Full Block Form*

The following sample is Jenny Tanaka's letter in block form.

Heading

1633 Wright Street
Stamford, CT 06902
May 3, 1984

Inside Address

Mr. and Michael LaCavera
102 83rd Place, West
Stamford, CT 06902

Salutation

Dear Mr. and Mrs. LaCavera:

Body

If you are planning on taking a summer vacation, you may have wondered what to do with your house plants while you are away. I have a suggestion for you. For fifty cents a day, I will water and care for your plants during your vacation.

I have been raising plants since I was six years old. For the past three summers, I have cared for plants of several neighbors. One neighbor, Mr. John Price, will be happy to give you a recommendation if you call him at 555-4728 in the evening or on weekends. I am a seventh-grade honor student at Worth Middle School and am very reliable.

If you would like me to take care of your plants this summer, please call me at 555-1929. I am usually home from school by 4:00 P.M.

Closing

Sincerely yours,

Signature

Jenny Tanaka
Jenny Tanaka

Businesses often use the full block form because their stationery already has a *letterhead,* which is the printed name and address of a company. You should use the full block form only for typewritten letters. If you hand write your letter, use the form on page 228.

Writing Assignment II: *A Business Letter*

Think of an interesting or unusual way to earn money. Then write a business letter to a parent, friend, neighbor, or some other person, selling your idea. Study the form of Jenny Tanaka's business letter before you begin. If you hand write your letter, use the form on page 228. The following suggestions may give you ideas:

1. Raise and sell "kitty plants." These are small plants that are harmless to cats. Many people who have cats cannot have houseplants because cats eat them and become sick. When cats have their own "kitty plants," they are more likely to leave regular houseplants alone.

2. Organize birthday parties for young children. This job would involve planning the party, organizing games, and cleaning up after the party.

3. Collect tin cans and other materials from your neighbors on a regular basis. You would then take the materials to a neighborhood recycling center.

4. Begin a dog-walking service for people who do not have time to walk their own dogs.

5. Begin a cleaning service for cleaning jobs such as washing windows or scrubbing walls.

A. Prewriting

Choose one of the suggested ideas, or use one of your own. Read the questions below, and think about them as you close your eyes and let thoughts freely come to you. When you're ready, write your thoughts in the form of a word cluster.

1. What will you do? Think of a variety of jobs you might offer to do. How can your idea be expanded to include more possibilities?

2. How does your experience especially qualify you for the job?

3. To whom can you send your letter? What specific people, or groups of people, might appreciate what you have to offer?

B. Writing

Organize your ideas, and then write a first draft of your letter. In the first paragraph, introduce what you are offering. Think of a clever opening line that will catch your readers' attention. In the second paragraph, describe your qualifications in a convincing way. Write a short concluding paragraph similar to Jenny's, giving information about how you may be contacted.

C. Postwriting

Read your letter, making changes that improve the power and economy of your language. Make a few words say a lot. Then proofread your letter carefully, using the checklist on page 234. After that, neatly copy your revised letter, using standard business letter form.

Finally, in small discussion groups, read each letter and discuss the following questions:

1. If you received this letter, what single feature about it would most interest you in what the writer has to sell?

2. Is there anything that needs more explanation?

3. Is there anything in the letter that seems unnecessary?

Checklist for Proofreading Business Letters

1. The letter is either neatly written on unlined paper in blue or black ink or neatly typed.

2. The letter is centered on the page.

3. The parts of the letter have the standard amount of spacing between them.

4. The left-hand margin of the heading is even with the left-hand margin of the closing.

5. The left-hand margin of the inside address is even with the left-hand margin of the body of the letter.

6. The left-hand margin of the salutation is even with the left-hand margin of the body of the letter.

7. The first word in the salutation is capitalized.

8. Titles and names in the salutation are capitalized.

9. The first word of the closing is capitalized.

10. A comma comes between the city and state in the heading and in the inside address.

11. A comma comes between the day of the month and the year in the heading.

12. A comma comes between the name of the person to whom you are writing and the person's title, if they are on the same line.

13. A colon follows the salutation, and a comma follows the closing.

The Business Letter Envelope

You prepare a business letter for mailing in much the same way you do a social letter. When you address a business envelope, copy the inside address in the center of the envelope just as it appears in the letter. Write your name and address in the upper left-hand corner of the envelope, just as you do for a social letter. Business letters today most often use the two-letter state abbreviation with ZIP codes.

Model: A Business Letter Envelope

```
Jenny Tanaka
1633 Wright Street
Stamford, CT 06902




                              Mr. and Mrs. Michael LaCavera
                              102 83rd Place, West
                              Stamford, CT 06902
```

Writing Practice 4: *A Business Letter Envelope*

Prepare an envelope for the letter you wrote for Writing Assignment II. If you do not have an envelope, draw the outline of one on a sheet of paper.

The Order Letter

An *order letter* is a business letter that is written to order something through the mail.

When you write an order letter, it is important to include all information necessary for filling your order. This information may include where you saw an item advertised, the catalogue number of an item, its size and color, and its price. Include any other information that might be needed to identify the item you want.

If you order more than one item, list each one with the necessary information on a separate line. Total the cost of the items, and add tax and postage to the total, if these are separate. Indicate the amount of money you are sending with the letter and whether you are sending a check or money order.

The order letter follows the same form as other business letters. Use the full block form only when you type your business letter.

Model: An Order Letter

16 San Vincenzo Place
Lakewood, CA 90713
April 16, 1984

Clearview Photo Shop
101 Crystal Rock Road
San Antonio, TX 78214

Dear Clearview Photo Shop:

In the April issue of Teen Talk magazine, you advertise posters made from photographs. I would like to order two posters from the photograph I am sending with this letter.

1 20 X 24 full-color poster		$4.95
1 14 X 17 black-and-white poster		$1.75
		6.70
Postage and tax		1.04
Total		7.74

I am sending a money order for $7.74 with this letter.

Yours truly,

Fred Esbelman

Writing Practice 5: *Writing an Order Letter*

Use the following information to write an order letter. Prepare an envelope for your letter. If you do not have an envelope, draw an outline of one on a piece of paper.

The February issue of *Pets Alive* advertises special feeding dishes for unusual pets at $3.95 each. The dishes come in green, yellow, blue, and brown. For an extra 25 cents you can have your pet's name on the dish in either red or white. The company is The Pet Place, 4533 17th Avenue, S.W., Ogden, Montana 84402. Order a dish for your unusual pet, with or without a name on the dish.

Sentence Variety: Inserting Sentences

('s) *and a New Use of* (-ing)

Adding an *-ing* can change a verb to a noun. In the following sentences the italicized words are verbs:

John *knits* while he watches television.

Everyone in my family *skates*.

Knits and *skates* are verbs because they show actions. In the following examples the words *knitting* and *skating* are nouns:

Knitting keeps John busy.

Skating is a family activity.

The words *knitting* and *skating* are nouns in the above sentences because they name activities.

When a verb becomes a noun, it can have a modifier like other nouns. The modifiers in the following sentences are italicized:

John's knitting keeps him busy.

The *family's* skating is a good activity.

Notice that each modifier has an *'s* form.

In this lesson you will learn the new signal (*'s + -ing*). You can use the signal (*'s + -ing*) to change an insert sentence like *the frog hopped* to *the frog's hopping*. When you do this, however, you no longer have a sentence; now you have a noun with a modifier in front of it. You then insert this phrase into the base sentence. The signal *something* tells you where to put the phrase in the base sentence.

Base Sentence:	*Something* frightened the little child.
Insert:	The dog barked. (*'s + -ing*)
Combined:	*The dog's barking* frightened the little child.

Base Sentence:	*Something* let him save the woman's life.
Insert:	John learned CPR. (*'s + -ing*)
Combined:	*John's learning CPR* let him save the woman's life.

Base Sentence:	Doctors had told the parents the child would never be able to sit up, so *something* surprised everyone.
Insert:	The baby walked. (*'s + -ing*)
Combined:	Doctors had told the parents the child would never be able to sit up, so *the baby's walking* surprised everyone.

Exercise 1: Using (*'s + -ing*)

Combine each of the following sets of sentences into one sentence. Follow the (*'s + -ing*) signal to change the insert sentence to a modifier plus a noun. Insert the new phrase into the base sentence where the *something* appears. Copy each new sentence on a sheet of paper numbered 1–5. Remember that the first sentence is the base sentence and the second sentence is the insert sentence. Study the example before you begin.

Example

a. The hunters listened to *something*.
The wolf howled. (*'s + -ing*)
The hunters listened to *the wolf's howling*.

1. *Something* created panic in the large crowd.
The earth trembled. (*'s + -ing*)

2. It's too bad that *something* has made her discouraged.
   Francine failed the test. (*'s + -ing*)

3. Unless we tie down the canvas shade, *something* will rip it off the patio.
   The wind blows. (*'s + -ing*)

4. Late at night *something* frightened Damien.
   The branches scraped against his bedroom window. (*'s + -ing*)

5. *Something* startled the girls and then made them laugh at their own nervousness.
   The door latched behind them. (*'s + -ing*)

A New Way to Use ('s)

The (*'s*) signal works differently on a certain group of words as shown on the following page. When you follow the (*'s*) signal, change the words in the first column to their possessive form in the second column:

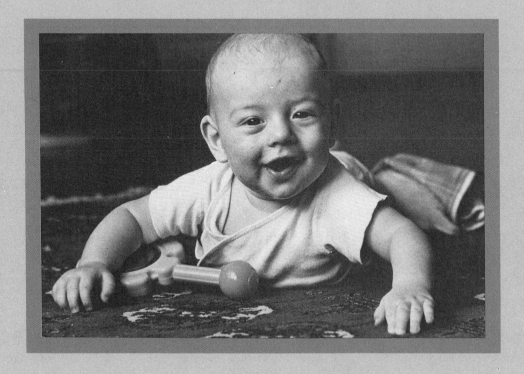

Column 1	Column 2
I	my
she	her
he	his
they	their
it	its
you	your
we	our

Consider the following sentences:

Base Sentence: The experienced sea captain insisted upon *something*.

Insert: They turn the ship around slowly. (*'s + -ing*)

From the list above, you can tell that the possessive form of *they* is *their*. The verb in the insert sentence is *turn*. The (*'s + -ing*) signal makes the insert sentence *their turning the ship around slowly*. Now add this phrase to the base sentence:

The experienced sea captain insisted upon *their turning the ship around slowly*.

Exercise 2: Using (*'s + -ing*) in a New Way

Combine each of the following sets of sentences into one sentence by following the (*'s + -ing*) signal. Insert the new phrase into the base sentence where the *something* appears. Copy each new sentence on a sheet of paper numbered 1–5. Study the example before you begin.

Example

a. *Something* disturbed the quiet evening.
   She cried. (*'s + -ing*)
   Her crying disturbed the quiet evening.

1.   *Something* has made Mom very pleased with you.
   You earned recognition on that important science report.
   (*'s + -ing*)

2. Everyone was impressed with *something*.
   She danced. (*'s* + *-ing*)

3. *Something* pleased the seventh-grade students.
   They won a school-wide contest. (*'s* + *-ing*)

4. *Something* is helpful to my mother.
   I get home early. (*'s* + *-ing*)

5. I am puzzled by *something*.
   He worries all the time. (*'s* + *-ing*)

Writing Practice: *Using* (*'s* + *-ing*) *to Improve a Letter*

Take the order letter you wrote for Writing Practice 5. Use the (*'s* + *-ing*) method to combine sentences in the letter. If necessary, add details as you combine the sentences. Strive for a variety of sentence lengths. Finally, rewrite the letter on a new piece of paper.

11 Filling Out Forms

Forms in Your Life

You have probably filled out many forms. You may have filled out a form to apply for a library card, or perhaps you have used the order blank on a cereal box or in a magazine to order something you wanted. Probably you have also filled out forms to register for classes at school and perhaps to register your bicycle with the local police department.

Most schools, businesses, and government agencies use forms because they are a convenient way to get information. In this chapter you will learn about different kinds of forms and about the proper way to fill them out.

Order Forms

The order forms you find in magazines and newspapers and on boxes and packages are usually very simple. Many ask only for your name and address and sometimes your age. To indicate the item you want, you usually make a check in a box or circle a number.

Even though an order form looks simple, a careful reading before you begin to fill it out can save you problems later. For example, many free gift offers require you to buy something later. Unless you read the form, you may not know this and will be asked to purchase something after you have received the gift.

Order forms usually have separate spaces for name, street address, city, state, and ZIP code. Many forms ask you to *print* this information because printing is easier to read than the handwriting of some people.

Sometimes a word or number in the order blank has a symbol called an *asterisk* (*) after it. This symbol tells you to look for another asterisk, usually at the bottom of the form. After this second asterisk is additional information or an explanation of the word or number. For example, in the sample

form, the $9.00 amount is followed by an asterisk. Following the asterisk at the bottom of the form is more information about the $9.00 subscription rate. Information with an asterisk often describes additional costs.

603 5th Ave., N.E.
P.O. Box 2254
Patterson, NJ 07502

Enclosed is $9.00. Please ☑ enter or ☐ extend my subscription to TEEN SCENE for 2 years at only $9.00* (a savings off the regular newsstand cost of $24.00 for 24 issues and $7.00 off the 2 year subscription rate of $16.00).

Name _MYRA LORENZINI_
(Please print)
Address _1602 LITTLE HARBOR ROAD_

City _GAINSVILLE_

State _GA_ Zip _30501_

* U.S. and Canada only. Other countries add $3.00 per year for postage.

Model: An Order Form

Some order forms are actually stamped postcards that you can detach and mail. If the order form is one that you must cut out and put into an envelope, address the envelope just as you would for a business letter. You will find the address of the company on the order form.

Writing Practice 1: *Filling Out an Order Form*

Find an order form in a newspaper or magazine or on a package or box. Cut the order form out or copy the form on a sheet of paper and bring it to class. Complete the form as though you were actually ordering the item. Finally, address an envelope (or draw a rectangle on a sheet of paper and address it as if it were an envelope) that could be used to mail the order form. Be sure to include the full address of the company you are ordering from, as well as your return address. Do not mail the form unless you actually wish to order the item.

Bicycle Registration Form

If you own a bicycle, you may fill out a registration form. Then, if your bike is lost or stolen, a description of your bicycle and its serial number will be on record with your local police department or school.

This form is organized in three sections. The labels in the first section are above the spaces where you write the information. The double line after the third space marks the end of this section. The second section, AFFIDAVIT, is for you to read. Then put the date and write your name in the blanks next to the labels. The third section, TRANSFER OF REGISTRATION, is for you to fill out only if you wish to give away or sell your bicycle.

The following list explains each of the labels on this form:

Rider means your first and last name. Even though the instructions do not say so, you should print the information. If your name is very long, begin immediately under the label *Rider*.

Address is your home address.

Model: A Bicycle Registration Form

BICYCLE REGISTRATION **—CITY OF EVANSTON—** **NO.** _____

RIDER Nicholas Hibbard	ADDRESS 1909 LINCOLN ST., Apt. A-1	PHONE 555-1929

BOY'S ✓	GIRL'S	SIZE 26"	FRAME COLOR Golden	MAKE Golden Races

SERIAL NUMBER SS42309	OTHER IDENTIFICATION Blue eagle on seat

AFFIDAVIT: I hereby certify that the above described bicycle is the property of the undersigned for use by the person named above.

DATE: 10/6/84 _____ Signature Nicholas Hibbard _____

KEEP THIS REGISTRATION RECEIPT IN A SAFE PLACE

TRANSFER OF REGISTRATION: The above described bicycle has been disposed by the above owner

New owner _____ Signature: _____

Address _____ Date: _____

Return Transfer to: RECORD SECTION
Police Department
1454 Elmwood Ave.
Evanston, Illinois 60201

STAMP THE REGISTRATION NUMBER INTO THE FRAME

FORM 315

Phone is your home telephone number.

Boy's/Girl's means whether your bike is a boy's or girl's, not whether you are a boy or girl. Place a check mark (√) in the correct box.

Size means the height of your bike or the wheel diameter.

Frame Color means the color of the part of your bike that is not the seat, handlebars, or wheels.

Make means the brand name of your bike. You will usually find the make of your bicycle in large letters on the frame.

Serial Number means the identification number of your bike. This number identifies the model of your bicycle and is usually found somewhere on the frame.

Other Identification means any special markings that will

help identify your bicycle.

Affidavit means a legal statement. This affidavit states that you are the owner and user of your bicycle.

Signature means your handwritten name. This is often the only part of a form that you write.

On many forms you will find spaces where you are not supposed to write. Sometimes, there is a *DO NOT WRITE IN THIS SPACE* note, and sometimes the label for that space is in darker ink. On the bicycle registration form the NO. label at the top of the form marks such a space. This is a space for the police department or school to enter your assigned number.

Writing Practice 2: *Filling Out a Bicycle Registration Form*

On a sheet of paper, copy the sample form on page 245. Do not enter the information about Nicholas Hibbard. Instead use information about your bike or information that you make up. Fill out the form completely, being sure to make your printing as neat as possible. After you have finished, read over the form carefully. Be certain that you have not omitted any information. Finally, proofread the information you have supplied; be sure your spelling and capitalization are correct.

Emergency Health Card Form

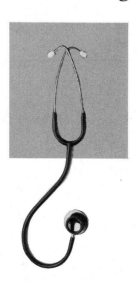

One very important form you may be called on to fill out at school is the *emergency health card*. The purpose of the emergency health card is to give the school the information needed to contact your family doctor or the adult responsible for you if you become ill.

Before you begin filling out the form, study it to see how it is organized. Like many other forms, the following sample form has different kinds of organization. The first line has a *Date* label followed by a space for you to write the date. The next two sections of the form have boxes with labels beneath them, and you are to write the information in the boxes.

Notice the double line separating these two sections from the rest of the form. A line like this often indicates that you must record your information in a different way. In the last part of the form, the labels are above or to the sides of the spaces where you write the information.

Model: Emergency Health Card Form

```
EMERGENCY HEALTH CARD
MOUNT PROSPECT SCHOOL DISTRICT
MOUNT PROSPECT, KANSAS
                                        DATE   9/10/84
```

Santos	Ricardo	11/28/70	555-1929
LAST NAME	FIRST NAME	BIRTH DATE	TELEPHONE

7	Pearson	1224 Chisolm Rd., Mount Prospect
GRADE	HR TEACHER	ADDRESS

NAME OF PERSON TO NOTIFY IN EMERGENCY   RELATIONSHIP
Mr. José Santos   Father
ADDRESS   WORK PHONE   555-8822
1224 Chisolm Road   HOME PHONE   555-1929
PERSON TO NOTIFY IF THIS PERSON CANNOT BE REACHED
Mrs. Rosa Johnson
ADDRESS   114 Winthrop St., Apt. 6   HOME PHONE   555-8597
          Mount Prospect   WORK PHONE   555-1632
NAME OF FAMILY PHYSICIAN
Dr. Anna Henderson
ADDRESS
23 Cole Mill Rd., Mount Prospect, KN

Before you begin filling in the form, be sure you know what the labels mean. The following list explains each of the labels on this form:

Date means today's date. You may abbreviate the date by using numbers and slash marks: 9/10/84.

Last Name means print only your last name in this box. When there are no directions telling you to print, do so anyway.

First Name means print only your first name in this box.

Birth Date means the date you were born. You may abbreviate this date also.

Telephone means your home telephone number. If you do not have a telephone at home, write *None* in this box.

Grade means your present grade level in school.

HR Teacher means the name of your homeroom teacher.

Address means your home address. If you live in the same city as the school, you do not have to write the name of the city. You may use abbreviations for such words as *Road, Street, Avenue, Boulevard, Rural Route.*

Name of Person to Notify in Emergency means the adult who is responsible for you.

Relationship means how the person is related to you. The person may be your mother, father, stepmother or stepfather, or other relative. If the person responsible is not related to you, write *Guardian* in this space.

Address means where the responsible adult lives. This address will usually be the same as your home address.

Work Phone means the telephone number of the business or company where the adult works.

Home Phone means the home telephone number of the adult.

Person to Notify if This Person Cannot Be Reached means the name of a second adult who is responsible for you. If you live with both parents, you can print here the name of the parent you did not use in the last section. If you live with one parent, you can print the name of a relative or other adult who lives nearby.

Address means the home address of this second adult.

Home Phone means the home telephone number of the second adult.

Work Phone means the telephone number of the business or company where the second adult works.

Name of Family Physician means the name of your family doctor.

Address means the address of your family doctor.

It is very important that all the information on this form be correct. If you do not know such information as the telephone number at work of the adult who is responsible for you or the name of your family doctor, ask at home before you fill out the form.

Writing Practice 3: *Filling Out an Emergency Health Card Form*

On a sheet of lined paper, copy the form on page 247, leaving out the information about Ricardo Santos. Fill in the form with information about yourself or with information about a person you make up.

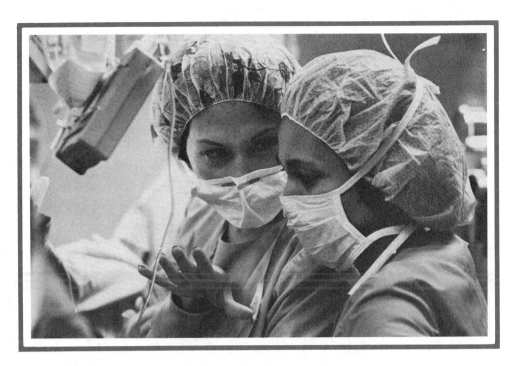

Writing Assignment I: *Filling Out a Membership Application Form*

The purpose of this assignment is to provide you with the opportunity to fill out a more complicated form than you may have dealt with before. On page 251 is a copy of a membership application form. Number a sheet of paper 1–14. On each line, write the information called for on that line of the application.

A. Prewriting

The major preparation for filling out a form involves reading it carefully all the way through. Do this for your form, and then answer the following questions:

1. Do you have all the information you need to fill out the form? Do you need information from another person? If you are lacking information, think of a way to obtain the information you need.

2. Are there any words on the form that you don't understand? If so, look the words up in a dictionary before completing the form.

B. Writing

Once you are satisfied that you have everything you need to complete the form, fill in the requested information on your numbered paper. Go slowly, writing neatly and providing information for each space.

C. Postwriting

1. Check over your paper, using the following guidelines:
    a. Is every question answered?
    b. Is my writing legible?
    c. Have I given correct facts?
    d. Have I followed instructions?

2. When you have completed the form as accurately as possible, sign your name as you normally sign it. Remember that your signature is your guarantee that the information given is correct.

Lemon Grove Racquet and Swim Club
Application for Membership

GENERAL INFORMATION

Name_____   Date_____

Address_____   Birthdate_____

_____

Telephone_____(Home)_____(Business)

CHOICE OF MEMBERSHIP PLAN

Place a √ next to the plan you want.   _____Single Membership

_____Family Membership

If family, names of all members of family   _____

_____

- -

_____Plan A—Swimmer Membership ($200 single; $350 family)

- • Unlimited use of swimming pool
- • Unlimited use of weight machines
- • Use of racquetball courts at per-hour fees of $8 nonprime time and $10 prime time

- -

_____Plan B—Racquet Membership ($200 single; $350 family)

- • Use of swimming pool at per-hour fee of $4
- • Unlimited use of weight machines
- • Use of racquetball courts at per-hour fees of $4 nonprime time and $6 prime time

STATEMENT OF FINANCIAL RESPONSIBILITY

Name of person responsible for payment:_____

Address:_____

Telephone:_____(Home)_____(Business)

I agree to make the payments for the person(s) named above according to the plan I have indicated. I understand that all statements are due and payable within 30 days of receipt. Late payments will be subject to a penalty fee of $10.00. Nonpayment after 60 days will result in loss of membership.

_____
Signature of responsible party

Sentence Variety:
Inserting Sentences

Inserting (To + Verb)

I n this lesson you will learn how to form a *to + verb* phrase from an insert sentence. The new phrase is inserted into the base sentence to replace the *something* signal.

Base Sentence: I want (to do) *something.*

Insert: I wash my hair. (*to + verb*)

Combined: I want *to wash my hair.*

Base Sentence: *Something* is what Carol likes to do.

Insert: Carol goes skating on Friday nights. (*to + verb*)

Combined: *To go skating on Friday nights* is what Carol likes to do.

In these sentences the form of the verb does not change. Sometimes, however, the verb changes to become the *to + verb* form. The following verbs are among those that change:

Verb	To + Verb Form
loves, loved	to love
sings, sang	to sing
minds, minded	to mind
wishes, wished	to wish
solves, solved	to solve
likes, liked	to like
cares, cared	to care
hunts, hunted	to hunt
shouts, shouted	to shout
visits, visited	to visit

Exercise 1: Using the (To + Verb) *Signal*

Combine the following sets of sentences by using the (*to + verb*) signal. Copy each new sentence on a sheet of paper numbered 1–10. Study the example before you begin.

Example

a. You prefer (to do) *something.*
   You go bike riding. (*to + verb*)
   You prefer to go bike riding.

1. I would like *something.*
   I spend my vacation in Miami, Florida. (*to + verb*)

2. *Something* would be fun, don't you agree?
   One rides a roller coaster. (*to + verb*)

3. We are pleased (to do) *something.*
   We announce the winners. (*to + verb*)

4. Our goal of winning the title means that we have the responsibility (to do) *something.*
   We train ourselves carefully. (*to + verb*)

5. A thesaurus is particularly helpful when you need (to do) *something.*
   You find synonyms for overworked words. (*to + verb*)

6. *Something* has been Nanette's dream since she was a small child.
   She travels through Europe alone. (*to + verb*)

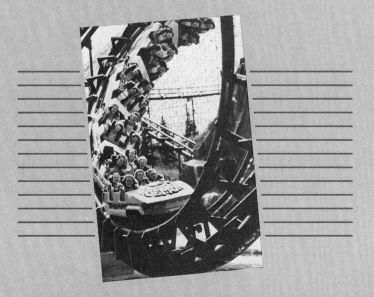

7. All of the Fourth of July picnickers were thrilled (to do) *something*.
    They watched the fantastic display of fireworks. (*to + verb*)

8. Our family saves the evening meal as a time (to do) *something*.
    We share the highlights of the day with one another. (*to + verb*)

9. *Something* is too strenuous for John.
    John runs six miles the first day of training. (*to + verb*)

10. My goal is *something*.
    I finish every homework assignment, turn it in on time, and never again forget to bring my books to class. (*to + verb*)

Exercise 2: Combining Sentences

Using any of the skills you have learned so far, combine each of the following sets of sentences to make a ten-sentence paragraph. The only signal in these sets is *something*. On a sheet of paper, write your new sentences as a paragraph.

1. The house stood.
    It stood for several days.
    It stood undisturbed.
    There was no sign of the ship's visit.
    The sign is visible.

2. The passersby saw only a house.
   The house was dark.
   The passersby were few.
   The passersby didn't suspect anything.
   The house was peaceful.

3. A smell seemed *something*.
   It comes from the house.
   The smell is faint.
   It was on the tenth day.
   It was after the visit.

4. A breeze carried the smell.
   The breeze is light.
   It carried across the fields.
   The fields are corn.
   The fields are wheat.

5. A dust appeared.
   The dust is sinister.
   The dust is orange.
   It appeared a few days later.
   It appeared on the crop.
   The crop is new.

6. The corn began *something*.
   The corn is straight.
   The corn is heavy.
   It drooped.
   It was soon.

7. The change happened.
   It was fast.
   It was in the fields.
   The fields are wheat.
   The fields are corn.

8. The wheat had stood the beating of winds.
   The winds are fierce.
   The wheat had stood the pounding of hail.
   The wheat had stood the lashing of rain.
   The rain is heavy.
   It now died.
   It died quickly.

9. The dust spread.
   The dust is evil.
   It spread now.
   It spread like wildfire.
   It spread from field to field.

10. People began *something*.
    They began soon.
    They are across the country.
    They feel the effects of the ship.
    The ship had come from so far away.

Writing Practice: *Improving Sentence Variety*

In the following list are some sentence-combining skills you have studied. Read the list and review those sections in the textbook if you are not certain how the combinations work. Then use some of the skills in the list to combine the sentences in the paragraph that follows.

1. Adding sentences in a series

2. Combining with subordinators

3. Inserting modifiers

4. Inserting *with-phrases*

5. Inserting (*-ing*)

6. Inserting (*'s*)

7. Inserting (*where*) (*when*) (*how*)

8. Inserting (*who*) (*which*) (*that*)

9. Inserting (*whose*) (*where*) (*when*) (*why*)

10. Inserting (*to + verb*)

Note: You may also want to use transition words such as *also, then, when*.

Paul Robeson was an actor. He was an outstanding actor. He became famous in the 1920s. He played football in college. He was named an all-American. Paul Robeson had a rich and powerful voice. He sang black spirituals. He sang them in his first concert. He appeared in *All God's Chillun Got Wings. All God's Chillun Got Wings* was a play. Paul Robeson became famous because of this role. Then he sang in *Porgy and Bess*. He sang in *Showboat*. He expressed deep feeling. The feeling was for a slave's life. Paul Robeson's father had been a slave. Paul Robeson performed in the play *Othello. Othello* was written by Shakespeare. The performer traveled around the world. His fame spread. It spread worldwide.

2
Grammar and Usage

12 Nouns

Understanding Nouns

Nouns are words that name. They name everything you can see and even things you cannot see, like thoughts. You can learn to recognize nouns in three different ways: through their definition, their division into classes, and their features that distinguish them from other parts of speech. In this section you will study and practice each of these ways to identify nouns.

Defining Nouns

A *noun* is usually defined as the name of a person, place, thing, or idea.

Alicia is the leader.	[name of person]
We live in *Chicago*.	[name of place]
A *hammer* is a useful tool.	[name of thing]
Peace in the world is our goal.	[name of idea]

Exercise 1: Identifying Nouns

Write the following sentences and underline all the nouns. Above each noun write whether it is the name of a person, place, thing, or idea.

Examples

    a. Jean lives in Austin.

        person   place
        Jean lives in Austin.

b. Happiness is a warm blanket.
   idea   thing
   Happiness is a warm blanket.

1. Maria reads books.

2. Barbara prefers good movies.

3. Jill saw a comedy at the Rialto.

4. The Rialto is the largest building in Centerville.

5. Eric enjoys westerns, especially if they're old.

6. The western usually portrays good against evil.

7. Many westerns were filmed in Arizona.

8. A famous director of westerns was John Ford.

9. Our teacher lets us review movies as well as books.

10. Ms. Ashida suggested that we watch a movie made without sound.

Grouping Nouns by Classes

Two large classes of nouns are *proper nouns* and *common nouns*.

Proper nouns **name specific persons, places, things, or ideas. All other nouns are called** *common nouns.*

Our *neighbors* visited Italy last summer.

The noun *neighbors* is a common noun because it does not name specific people.

The *Espositos* visited Italy last summer.

The noun *Espositos* is a proper noun because it names specific people.

Proper nouns are capitalized; common nouns are not.

We sang a *song*.	[common noun]
We sang "*The Star-Spangled Banner.*"	[proper noun]
My friend lives in the *capital*.	[common noun]
My friend lives in *Sacramento*.	[proper noun]

The *airport* was crowded and noisy.	[common noun]
Dallas-Fort Worth International Airport was crowded and noisy.	[proper noun]

Many proper nouns, and some common nouns, are *compound nouns*, because they are made up of more than one word.

Compound proper nouns have two or more words.

Golden Gate Bridge	[one thing]
Atlantic City, New Jersey	[one place]
Edgar Allan Poe	[one person]

A compound common noun may be closed (spelled as one word), open (spelled as two separate words), or hyphenated.

    Closed: airplane, barnyard, dishwasher

      Open: report card, station wagon, swimming pool

Hyphenated: sister-in-law, push-up, great-aunt

Exercise 2: Identifying Common, Proper, and Compound Nouns

Write the following sentences and underline each noun. Write *C* above each common noun and *P* above each proper noun. Be sure to underline the entire noun if it is a compound.

Example

a. We met Felicia Montez at the church.

             P   C

We met <u>Felicia Montez</u> at the <u>church</u>.

1. The Sullivans are great fans of the Pittsburgh Pirates.

2. Rock grew in England with the Beatles.

3. Old Faithful is a popular attraction for tourists.

4. A cave-in in the Appalachians alarmed the residents.

5. The sharpshooter in Buffalo Bill's Wild West Show was Annie Oakley.

6. The 1980 Winter Olympic Games were held in the town of Lake Placid, New York.

7. For many years the B-52 was one of the most important airplanes in the United States Air Force.

8. The editor-in-chief of the magazine is Marilyn DeZaurro.

9. Our class visited the Lincoln Memorial, a monument that shows honor and respect for President Abraham Lincoln.

10. Several months ago Uncle Maurice bought a cookbook from a restaurant in Kansas City, Missouri.

Finding Nouns by Their Features

Four features can help you identify nouns. A word that is a noun must have at least one of these features, and some nouns will have all four.

Nouns often have *determiners* before them.

Determiners are words like *a, an, the, this, that, these, those, some, many, one, two.* The most common determiners—*a, an,* and *the*—are also called *articles.*

many bananas	*the* moccasins
a friendship	*four* pizzas
this letter	*an* operation

Nouns may be either *singular* or *plural*.

Most nouns have different forms for singular and plural. The plural form is used for nouns that name more than one person, place, thing, or idea.

Singular	*Plural*
one *book*	five *books*
one *map*	several *maps*

Singular	Plural
one *tooth*	three *teeth*
one *loaf*	many *loaves*
one *lady*	two *ladies*
one *box*	six *boxes*

Nouns may show ownership or relationship.

Both singular and plural nouns have *possessive* forms that show ownership or relationship. A possessive noun ends with an apostrophe and -*s* (the boy's hat) or with only an apostrophe (the two girls' voices).

The bike that Frank owns is a ten-speed. *Frank's* bike is a ten-speed.	[ownership]
The pane of the window was frosted. The *window's* pane was frosted.	[relationship]

Nouns may be formed with a noun *suffix* such as -*ation*, -*ism*, -*ment*, -*ness*, -*ance*.

Consider becomes the noun *consideration* when the noun suffix -*ation* is added. The endings of many words give helpful clues that they are nouns.

imagine + *ation* ⟶ *imagination*

capital + *ism* ⟶ *capitalism*

assign + *ment* ⟶ *assignment*

lonely + *ness* ⟶ *loneliness*

accept + *ance* ⟶ *acceptance*

Exercise 3: *Identifying Nouns by Their Features*

There are twenty-five nouns in the following paragraphs. Use what you have learned about the features of nouns to identify at least ten of them. List each noun on a sheet of paper. Your teacher may ask you which feature or features you used to identify the nouns.

The airport was a madhouse. All the airlines' employees worked frantically. The storm was still raging, and all flights were canceled. Even worse, the highways were closed. People could not leave the area and would miss a holiday with their families.

Relaxation seemed the only answer. Many people sat in the aisles reading, while several executives played cards with some students. A few travelers just watched the snow falling outside the terminal's windows. Somehow the people managed to enjoy a feeling of togetherness.

Review: Understanding Nouns

There are twenty-five nouns in the following paragraph from the book *All Creatures Great and Small* by Daniel P. Mannix. Use what you have learned to find and list at least twenty. (Consider both *king cobra* and *garden hose* as compound nouns.)

I had first heard of Grace Wiley some years before when Dr. William Mann, then director of the National Zoological Park in Washington, D.C., handed me a picture of a tiny woman with a gigantic king cobra draped over her shoulders like a garden hose. The snake had partly spread his hood and was looking intently into the camera while his mistress stroked his head to quiet him. Dr. Mann told me: "Grace lives in a little house full of poisonous snakes, imported from all over the world. She lets them wander around like cats. There's been more nonsense written about 'snake charming' than nearly any other subject."[1]

Applying What You Know

From a magazine, newspaper, or book you have read, select a paragraph about five or six sentences long. Using what you have learned, identify all of the nouns and list them on a sheet of paper.

---

[1]From *All Creatures Great and Small* by Daniel P. Mannix. Copyright © 1963 by Daniel P. Mannix. Reprinted by permission of the Harold Matson Company.

Using Nouns

In this section you will practice forming the plurals of nouns, including compound nouns. You will also practice writing the possessive forms of nouns and capitalizing proper nouns.

Forming the Plurals of Nouns

Most nouns form their plurals by adding the suffix *-s* or *-es* to the singular form. These plurals are called *regular plurals*.

Form the regular plural of most nouns by adding the suffix *-s*.

Singular	Plural
one *song*	two *songs*
one *cake*	several *cakes*

Form the regular plural of nouns ending in *s, sh, ch, x,* or *z* by adding the suffix *-es*.

Singular	Plural
one *bus*	three *buses*
a *dish*	several *dishes*
a *church*	two *churches*
the *fox*	those *foxes*
one *buzz*	many *buzzes*

Form the plural of nouns ending in *o* preceded by a vowel by adding the suffix *-s*. Form the plural of nouns ending in *o* preceded by a consonant by adding the suffix *-es*.

Singular	Plural
a *stereo*	several *stereos*
the *patio*	some *patios*
one *tomato*	three *tomatoes*
an *echo*	some *echoes*

Exception: The plurals of nouns that end in *o* and have to do with music take only the suffix *-s* (*solos, pianos, trios*).

Exercise 4: *Forming Plural Nouns*

The nouns in the following sentences have been *italicized*. Write the sentences and change each singular noun to its plural form by adding *-s* or *-es*. Underline the nouns.

Example

a. The *mole* lived in the deep *tunnel*.
   The <u>moles</u> lived in the deep <u>tunnels</u>.

1. The *dieter* ate only the *sandwich*.
2. The *soprano* sat down at the *piano*.
3. Our *wish* may be the *dream* we share.
4. The *player* believed the *referee* to be mistaken.
5. The *crash* of the *glass* scared us all.
6. The *box* full of *paper* fell into the *furnace*.
7. The *hero* at the soccer *match* had been applauded.
8. The *gas* in the *balloon* came from the *tank*.
9. Our French *teacher* asked the *senior* to read the *novel*.
10. The best *player* on the *team* let the *substitute* play.

Forming the Irregular Plurals of Nouns

Many irregular plurals are formed by a spelling change plus the addition of the suffix *-s* or *-es*.

Form the plural of most nouns that end in *y* preceded by a consonant by changing the *y* to *i* and adding the suffix *-es*.

Singular	Plural
one *family*	several *families*
a *lady*	those *ladies*
the *hobby*	some *hobbies*

Form the plural of nouns that end in *y* preceded by a vowel by simply adding the suffix *-s*.

Singular	Plural
the *key*	many *keys*
a *valley*	two *valleys*
one *chimney*	several *chimneys*

If you are unsure about which plural ending to use with a noun ending in *y*, check your dictionary for the proper spelling.

Exercise 5: *Plurals of Nouns Ending in y*

The *italicized* nouns in the following sentences have singular forms ending in *y*. Write each sentence and change each noun to its proper plural form. Underline each plural noun.

Example

a. The spectacular *carry* of Franco Harris made the best *play* of the game.

The spectacular carries of Franco Harris made the best plays of the game.

1. At the zoo we feed the *monkey* on *Saturday*.

2. The *country* voted for *democracy*.

3. The *baby* threw the *penny* at the cat.

4. Our *journey* began in the *valley*.

5. The *key* to the *library* fell in the *entry*.

6. We read the *story* about the *jury* who found the *secretary* guilty.

7. The foreign *ally* broke the *treaty* by forming the *army*.

8. The *cry* of the *donkey* screeched across the *valley* and echoed in the hills.

9. The *family* walked through the *alley*.

10. The *duty* must be paid first.

Form some irregular plurals by changing a vowel sound.

Singular	*Plural*
woman	women
mouse	mice
tooth	teeth
goose	geese

Form the plural of some nouns ending in *fe* and *f* by changing the *f* to *v* and adding the suffix *-es*.

Singular	*Plural*	*Singular*	*Plural*
calf	calves	self	selves
elf	elves	sheaf	sheaves
half	halves	shelf	shelves
knife	knives	thief	thieves
life	lives	wife	wives
loaf	loaves	wolf	wolves

Form the plural of many nouns ending in *f* or *fe* by simply adding the suffix -*s*.

Singular	Plural
roof	roofs
safe	safes
belief	beliefs
reef	reefs

Some words have the same form for singular and plural.

We saw a *moose* in the forest.	[singular]
We saw two *moose* in the forest.	[plural]

The following words are included in this group.

bass	deer	grouse	pike	sheep
carp	fish	moose	salmon	trout

Use your dictionary to check plural forms that may be unfamiliar.

The plurals of some nouns fit no pattern. If you are unsure about the spelling of a plural, look up the singular form of the word in the dictionary. If the plural is irregular, the dictionary will give the plural spelling. Most dictionaries use the abbreviation *pl* for plural.

child *n. pl* **children**

phenomenon *n. pl* **phenomena**

larva *n. pl* **lar-vae** *also* **larvas**

Exercise 6: *Forming Irregular Plural*

Write each of the sentences on the following page and change each *italicized* noun to its proper plural form. Underline the nouns you change.

Example

> a. The *man* used the *knife* to cut the *loaf* of bread.
> The <u>men</u> used the <u>knives</u> to cut the <u>loaves</u> of bread.

1. The *woman* caught the *bass* by the icy *reef.*
2. The second *half* of the *story* bored us all.
3. The *thief* stole the *safe* on the top *shelf.*
4. The *wolf* hunted the frightened *moose* for days.
5. The sound of the *mouse* was like an *elf* on the *roof.*
6. He checked the *hoof* of the *calf.*
7. The *child* cried when the *tooth* came out.
8. The *chief* struggled to save the *life* of the *man.*
9. The *leaf* flew as high as the wild *goose.*
10. The *foot* of the *deer* touched the shore of the *gulf.*

Forming the Plurals of Compound Nouns

Form the plural of a closed compound noun as you would form the plural of the last word of the compound.

Singular	*Plural*
one *mailbox*	two *mailboxes*
one *cupful*	four *cupfuls*
the *basketball*	some *basketballs*
this *horsefly*	these *horseflies*

Exception: one *passerby*, but two *passersby*.

Form the plural of an open or hyphenated compound noun by making plural the most important word in the compound.

Singular	Plural
the *father-in-law*	these *fathers-in-law*
a *report card*	some *report cards*
one *push-up*	fifty *push-ups*
a *man-of-war*	several *men-of-war*

Sometimes it is difficult to know which is the main word in a compound noun (*merry-go-round, twelve-year-old, drive-in*). The plurals of these compound nouns are formed by the addition of the suffix *-s* to the last word (*merry-go-rounds, twelve-year-olds, drive-ins*). When in doubt, check your dictionary for the spelling of plural forms of compound nouns.

Exercise 7: *Forming Compound Noun Plurals*

The *italicized* compound nouns in the following sentences are singular. Write each sentence and change the compound noun to its plural form. Underline the compound nouns you make plural.

Examples

   a. A band from the *high school* led the parade.
      A band from the high schools led the parade.

   b. The *butterfly* flew close to the flowers.
      The butterflies flew close to the flowers.

1. Her favorite recipe takes the heaping *teaspoonful* of baking soda.
2. The *eight-year-old* hit the *tennis ball* well.
3. The *soccer ball* headed for the *goalpost*.
4. The *Dutchman* sailed the boat past the *man-of-war*.
5. My *brother-in-law* called the *attorney-at-law*.
6. The *earthquake* caused serious structural damage to the *skyscraper*.
7. The *runner-up* gave a speech to the *editor-in-chief*.
8. The *sergeant-at-arms* kept order at the meeting.

9. My *sister-in-law* made the *doghouse* with the *two-by-four*.

10. The *basketball* fell out of the *station wagon* and into the *swimming pool*.

Forming the Possessive of Nouns

The *possessive form* of a noun shows ownership or the relationship of one noun to another. One possessive noun can replace several words in a sentence.

The sweater that Joan owns is torn. *Joan's* sweater is torn.	[ownership]
The uncle of the girl won the prize. The *girl's* uncle won the prize.	[relationship]

Form the possessive of a singular noun by adding an apostrophe (') and an -s.

Noun	Possessive Form
the records of the *girl*	the *girl's* records
the bike of *Douglas*	*Douglas's* bike
the brakes of the *car*	the *car's* brakes

Form the possessive of a plural noun ending in s by adding an apostrophe (') only.

Noun	Possessive Form
the buttons of the *coats*	the *coats'* buttons
the stories of the *authors*	the *authors'* stories
the dunes of the *beaches*	the *beaches'* dunes
the books of the *teachers*	the *teachers'* books

Form the possessive of a plural noun not ending in *s* by adding an apostrophe (') and an *-s.*

Noun	Possessive Form
the toes of the *feet*	the *feet's* toes
the eyes of the *children*	the *children's* eyes
the wool of the *sheep*	the *sheep's* wool

Exercise 8: *Forming Possessive Nouns*

On a sheet of paper numbered 1–10, write the following sentences and supply the possessive form of each noun given in parentheses. Check whether the noun is singular or plural before you form its possessive. Underline the possessive nouns you form.

Example

    a. (Maya) house is larger than (Wes) house.
       Maya's house is larger than Wes's house.

1. I signed (Verla) autograph book and gave her my (sisters) book to sign.

2. (Florida) agriculture differs from (Ohio).

3. Grandmother knits socks for the (family) pets and makes tree houses for the (neighborhood) children.

4. Both (rodeos) champion was (Steve Lewis) younger brother.

5. The (skull) bones protect the (brain) delicate tissue.

6. The (men) team was called The (Lion) Paw.

7. The (children) toys filled Mr. (Jones) garage and he left his car parked in the driveway.

8. (Jess) advice saved (Marcia) life.

9. Each (stitch) length was over one millimeter; together they took many (hours) time.

10. The (bus) route followed the (officer) directions.

Capitalizing Proper Nouns

Proper nouns name specific persons, places, and things. They are always capitalized. The following guidelines tell how to capitalize proper nouns correctly.

Capitalize the names of specific persons, places, and things.

Common Noun	Proper Noun
my cousin	Donna Thomas
the mayor	Mayor Lester Gerry
my father's business	Riverside Press

Capitalize all the important words in the name of a specific building, landmark, or institution.

Note: Unimportant words are the articles *a*, *an*, and *the*. Prepositions and conjunctions with fewer than five letters are also unimportant words: *of, in, with, and, or.*

Common Noun	Proper Noun
this building	the Library of Congress
that monument	the Statue of Liberty
our college	the University of Colorado

Capitalize the first word and all important words in the title of a book, newspaper, magazine, poem, story, song, movie, or television series.

Note: Capitalize *a*, *an*, and *the* when these are the first words in a title. In the following examples, *The New York Times* is the official title. However, *the* is not part of the name *Atlanta Journal.*

Common Nouns	Proper Nouns
book	*The Pigman*
newspaper	*the Atlanta Journal* or *The New York Times*
magazine	*Time* magazine
poem	"The Return of the Rivers"
song	"America the Beautiful"
short story	"The Gift of the Magi"
movie	*The Empire Strikes Back*
television series	*Little House on the Prairie*

Note: The title of a longer work such as a novel, a magazine, newspaper, movie, or television series is *italicized* in print and underlined in handwriting. The title of a shorter work is placed in quotation marks.

Capitalize the name of a team, organization, business firm, or government body.

Common Noun	Proper Noun
your team	the Los Angeles Rams
our club	the Future Farmers of America
my uncle's store	Grayson's Drugstore
the agency	the Department of Commerce

Capitalize names of national origin and religions.

Common Noun	Proper Noun
a religion	Buddhism
our neighbors	the Canadians
a people	the Navajo

The chapter on capitalization in this book gives more rules for capitalizing proper nouns. The rules will help you with specific problems: Do I capitalize the name of a ship or train? A famous bridge? An important battle?

Exercise 9: *Capitalizing Proper Nouns*

Write the following sentences and capitalize the proper nouns. Underline the proper nouns that are printed in *italics* and each noun that you capitalize.

Examples

a. My brother mel joined the cub scouts when he was eight.
My brother Mel joined the Cub Scouts when he was eight.

b. jeremy clark works in his mother's office at the world trade center.
Jeremy Clark works in his mother's office at the World Trade Center.

1. While we were in austin, texas, we visited the lyndon b. johnson library.

2. If you are ever visiting new york city during the winter months, be sure to go ice-skating at rockefeller center.

3. The winter basketball play-offs were held at roosevelt high school in ann arbor, michigan.

4. My friends jose and reggie hoped to get summer jobs as attendents at lake geneva boat rental owned by lena wilson.

5. For our spring program jackie and kim decided to perform "the legend of sleepy hollow."

6. I read accounts of the snowstorm that paralyzed the city's transportation system in *newsweek* magazine and the *chicago tribune.*

7. On Saturdays marlo and leslie enjoy watching *hot hero sandwich* on television.

8. The swiss are quite famous for their luxurious ski resorts in the alps.

9. The hopi and navaho live in new mexico.

10. The ortega family visited their son at st. meinrad, a religious school in indiana.

Choosing Specific Proper Nouns

Some nouns may be common or proper, depending on their use in sentences. The noun is proper if its reference is *specific*. The noun is common if its reference is *general*. You must decide which way the noun is used to know whether it should be capitalized.

Common Noun	Proper Noun
My great-aunt	is Aunt Juanita.
We drove southwest	to see the deserts of the Southwest.
Our state representative	is Representative John Anderson.
My algebra course	is Algebra I.

Capitalize a title only when it is used as part of a name or in place of a name.

There is Justice Sandra O'Connor.

She is the first woman to serve as a justice of the Supreme Court.

I am looking for Judge Manchester.

I hope the judge is not late.

Capitalize words showing family relationship when they are used as part of a person's name or in place of a name.

My uncle is a good boss.

Paul works for Uncle Roberto.

My mother works in the city.

Can I go to the movies, Mother?

Capitalize geographical sections of the country, but not directions.

The people from the North visited Brownsville at the end of December.

The people from Miami went north for the summer.

Capitalize nouns that name one specific school course or have a numeral after the course name. The names of language courses are always capitalized.

Alexander liked chorus so much that he signed up for Chorus III.

I enjoy American government, so I am taking Civics I.

I'm taking a special course next semester called Modern Living.

Students are required to take English each year.

Exercise 10: *Capitalizing Proper Nouns*

Write the following sentences and capitalize the proper nouns. Underline the nouns that you capitalize.

Examples

a. Turn south at the next corner, dad.
Turn south at the next corner, <u>Dad</u>.

b. The specialist my brother saw was dr. lauren brummet.
The specialist my brother saw was <u>Dr. Lauren Brummet</u>.

1. Maureen's grandmother always went fishing in the northwest during the summer.

2. We did more work in french than we did in homemaking I.

3. The sing family settled first in the midwest, but later they went west to oregon.

4. It's the truth, judge; the other car was heading north.

5. Joe, uncle milton was once major milton of tyler, texas.

6. Wait a minute, father, and I'll call grandmother martin and aunt sue.

7. When we traveled west, we saw more vegetation in the deserts of the southwest than we expected.

8. Tomorrow congressman lyle chavez will speak at loyola university.

9. The math we studied in math II was harder than I thought it would be.

10. Our students wanted a city council official to speak, so we invited councilwoman tanaka.

Review: Using Nouns

In the following sentences the nouns in parentheses need to be made plural, or possessive, or both. On a sheet of paper write each sentence and underline the nouns you change.

Examples

a. We needed to buy two (loaf) of bread.
   We needed to buy two loaves of bread.

b. Let's read (Sheila) report.
   Let's read Sheila's report.

1. These (knife) cut bread well.

2. The (woman) locker room is down the main hall to your left.

3. (Carlos) corduroy jacket was much more colorful than my wool coat.

4. Two (tablespoon) of this should soothe your cough and sore throat.

5. Fourteen (child) feet scrambled up the stairs in order to get to class on time.

6. It was (Ross) paper that I graded.

7. The new books are on those four (shelf).

8. Several (diary) were found in the old trunk.

9. Frost on the window is (winter) handiwork.

10. Many (family) lives were in danger because of the fire.

Write the following sentences and capitalize each proper noun. Underline the proper nouns that you capitalize.

Examples

a. My favorite folk song is "this land is your land."
My favorite folk song is "This Land Is Your Land."

b. Coach waters has collected over a thousand dollars for the red cross.
Coach Waters has collected over a thousand dollars for the Red Cross.

11. People in mississippi hold to many traditions of the south.

12. Ms. elsa bergson suggests english mysteries to her visiting students from australia.

13. Mr. robert f. kennedy was one of the most active attorneys general of the united states.

14. We prepared for our trip to the austrian highlands by studying german.

15. One of the obligations of a mormon is doing missionary work.

16. Many residents of the southwest speak three languages: navaho, spanish, and english.

17. Many people are unaware that the islands of martinique and guadeloupe are actually part of france and that the language spoken on these caribbean islands is french.

18. We learned how to dissect a frog in biology I and a rat in biology II.

19. "The celebrated jumping frog of calaveras county" is one of mark twain's best stories.

20. Our trip highlight was a tour of the world trade center in new york city, where aunt sally works.

Writing Focus: *Using Specific Nouns in Writing*

Good writers use specific nouns to paint a clear and exact picture for readers. For example, the noun *shirt* is more specific than the noun *clothes*. As much as possible, use specific nouns to make your writing more precise, informative, and clear.

Assignment: *Clouds*

It's a warm summer day. You and your little brother or sister are lying in a meadow, arms crossed under your heads, gazing at the white, puffy clouds high in the blue sky. For a while you both pick out "animals" you see in the clouds. Then your sibling suddenly asks, "What are clouds?"

In one or more well-developed paragraphs, write an answer to your little brother or sister's question. Don't be scientific in your explanation, but include information about what clouds are, what they're made of, and why they change shape. Entertain your sibling with your answer. Your work will be evaluated for effective use of nouns.

Use the following steps to complete this assignment.

A. Prewriting

Imagine looking at some clouds. Notice their different shapes, textures, movements. Using the brainstorming technique described in Chapter 1, write down words or phrases that could explain what clouds are. Could they be a mad painter's white spray paint spattering on a blue wall? Could they be wisps of cotton candy clinging to the blue skirt of a *very* large girl? Perhaps a story will occur to you. Remember to account for the composition and changing shapes of clouds. Go back and underline details and associations you like that explain what clouds are.

B. Writing

Use your brainstorming list to write one or more paragraphs explaining to your little brother or sister what clouds are. Make

your account entertaining and fanciful. As you write, use specific nouns to make your explanation precise.

C. Postwriting

Use the following checklist to revise your work.

1. Have I actually explained what clouds are?
2. Have I used specific nouns effectively to make the writing precise?

Edit your work using the Checklist for Proofreading at the back of the book. If appropriate, share your writing with your classmates by sitting in a circle to read each other's work. Create and illustrate a booklet entitled *Clouds*.

13 Pronouns

Understanding Pronouns

Pronouns are words that take the place of nouns. There are several different ways to identify pronouns: by their definition, by the classes into which they can be grouped, or by the features that distinguish pronouns from other parts of speech. In this section you will study and practice each of these ways of identifying pronouns.

Defining Pronouns

A *pronoun* is usually defined as a word that takes the place of a noun or another pronoun. A pronoun refers to a specific noun or pronoun, which is called an *antecedent.* Antecedents usually come before the pronoun.

Daniel brought the *present* inside and gave *it* to his Uncle Harvey.
(*It* refers to *present; present* is the antecedent.)

Some of the students want *their* grades now before vacation starts.
(*Their* refers to *some; some* is the antecedent.)

Sometimes an antecedent follows its pronoun.

When *they* entered the clubhouse turn, the *horses* were neck and neck.

After *he* returned from the hike, *Carlos* was too exhausted to do his chores.

The antecedent of a pronoun may also appear in a preceding sentence.

Gene didn't answer the final question on the test.

He should have read more carefully.

A single pronoun can replace several nouns in a sentence.

Dictionaries, encyclopedias, and almanacs are available in the library, but *they* cannot be checked out.
(The word *they* refers to the nouns *dictionaries, encyclopedias,* and *almanacs.*)

Sometimes a pronoun can be used to replace a word group that functions as a noun.

The movement of the pendulum, *which* Janet thought was caused by a motor, was actually due to the rotation of the earth.
(The pronoun *which* replaces the word group *the movement of the pendulum.*)

A single pronoun can be used in place of an entire sentence.

The province of Quebec may secede from Canada. Many people do not want *this* to happen.
(*This* refers to the entire first sentence; the first sentence is the antecedent.)

Exercise 1: Identifying Pronouns and Antecedents

Write the sentences on the following page and circle each pronoun. Then underline the antecedent to which each pronoun refers.

Examples

a. Charlene finally got a dial tone, but by then she had forgotten the number.

Charlene finally got a dial tone, but by then (she) had forgotten the number.

b. Raul tried to reach the green with a five iron. That was simply an error in judgment.

Raul tried to reach the green with a five iron. (That) was simply an error in judgment.

1. Most cats are quite easy to take care of, but they must be trained a bit.

2. Even if a cat has been declawed, it will still make scratching motions.

3. Some cats claw furniture, and that is annoying and often costly to repair.

4. Lydia has a Siamese cat which has very short hair and a gentle temper.

5. When it was lost during vacation, one cat traveled many miles to get home.

6. People say cats have nine lives, but that certainly isn't true!

7. Alexander loves cats as pets, and he has recently adopted six kittens.

8. The crew of the *Mayflower* brought a cat along. It was supposed to bring good luck.

9. House cats rarely need bathing because they keep very clean.

10. In ancient Egypt laws protected cats, which were sacred animals.

Grouping Pronouns by Classes

In this section you will study five classes of pronouns: personal, possessive, interrogative, demonstrative, and indefinite.

Personal Pronouns

Speakers or writers use *personal pronouns* to refer to themselves, to the people they are speaking or writing to, and to the nouns they are speaking or writing about.

	Singular	*Plural*
First Person:	I, me	we, us
Second Person:	you	you
Third Person:	he/she/it him/her/it	they, them

The pronouns *I, we, me,* and *us* are the *first person pronouns.* These pronouns are used when speakers or writers refer to themselves.

Singular	*Plural*
I enjoy old movies.	*We* enjoy old movies.
The jury believed *me.*	The jury believed *us.*

You, the *second person pronoun,* refers to the person or people that are addressed.

Singular	*Plural*
You enjoy old movies.	*You* will all enjoy this old movie.
The jury believed *you.*	The jury believed both of *you.*

The *third person pronouns—he, she, it, him, her, they,* and *them*—are used in speaking or writing about other people, places, things, or ideas.

Singular	*Plural*
He enjoys old movies.	*They* all enjoy this old movie.
The jury believed *him*.	The jury believed *them*.

Some personal pronouns can combine with *-self* or *-selves*:

She hurt *herself* in the fall.

I like going to the movies by *myself*.

They enjoyed *themselves* at the party.

Exercise 2: *Identifying Personal Pronouns*

Write the following sentences and underline all the personal pronouns.

Example

a. Jaime can speak for himself.
Jaime can speak for <u>himself</u>.

1. Yolanda camped in Yosemite National Park for a week by herself.

2. The towering mountains amazed her; they seemed to touch the clouds.

3. Can you read the sign? It says "Do Not Feed the Bears."

4. They look cute but can be dangerous, especially if you have food.

5. If you see bears, leave them alone, and they may return the favor.

6. Garter snakes won't hurt you, but you should stay away from rattlers.

7. I wouldn't want to have a rattler bite me!

8. A family of raccoons visited us, and we gave them some food.

9. Would you hike through the meadow with me? I want you to see it.

10. He tried to carry the backpack himself, but it was too heavy for him.

Possessive Pronouns

Possessive pronouns are used to show ownership or relationship.

Singular	Plural
my, mine	our, ours
your, yours	your, yours
his her, hers its	their, theirs

Some possessive pronouns can be used in front of the nouns they possess.

Her report was the best by far.

I like *your* drawing better.

We'll go to the game in *our* car.

Would you like to borrow *my* dictionary?

Some possessive pronouns can be used alone.

Hers was the best by far.

I like *yours* better than *his*.

We'll go to the game in *ours*.

Would you like to borrow *mine?*

Exercise 3: Identifying Possessive Pronouns

Write the following sentences and underline each possessive pronoun.

Examples

    a. No one grows tomatoes that are larger than his.
       No one grows tomatoes that are larger than <u>his</u>.

    b. Their family tree begins in Czechoslovakia.
       <u>Their</u> family tree begins in Czechoslovakia.

---

1. The idea for the costume party was hers.
2. The guests knew their costumes should be white.
3. The white robe is his; he made it himself.
4. Kim, the sheet is yours.
5. Are the nurses' uniforms really costumes, or have the nurses come straight from their work?
6. The best disguise is my refrigerator costume.
7. We want to have the next party at our house.
8. Mark donated his soccer ball for our door prize.
9. Lauren, you're going to need your sunglasses to drive.
10. It's not surprising that the party lost some of its spirit after most of the guests left.

Interrogative Pronouns

Interrogative pronouns are used in asking questions.

Interrogative Pronouns

whom	whose	what
whom	which	

Who will be performing tonight?

Whom have you asked about the job?

Whose was the winning entry?

Which has the fewer calories?

What causes the earth to rotate?

Each interrogative pronoun in the sentences above is used in place of an unnamed person, place, thing, or idea.

> *Who* will be performing tonight?
>
> Jean Pierre Rampal will be performing tonight.

If an interrogative pronoun is used before a noun, it is used as a modifier, not as a pronoun.

Which is the most nutritious of the three?	[interrogative pronoun]
Which fruit is the most nutritious of the three?	[modifier]
What is the answer?	[interrogative pronoun]
What answer did you give?	[modifier]

Demonstrative Pronouns

Demonstrative pronouns are used to point out specific persons, places, things, or ideas.

> *This* is easily my favorite popular song.
>
> *That* used to be expensive.
>
> If you need some more, try *these*.
>
> On the other hand, *those* will do as well.

Demonstrative pronouns have both a singular and plural form.

Singular	*Plural*
this	these
that	those

When a demonstrative pronoun is used before a noun, it is used as a modifier, not as a demonstrative pronoun.

This would be my first choice.	[demonstrative pronoun]
This restaurant would be my first choice.	[modifier]
If you're hungry, try *these*.	[demonstrative pronoun]
If you're hungry, try *these* pizzas.	[modifier]

Exercise 4: Identifying Interrogative and Demonstrative Pronouns

Write the following sentences and underline each interrogative and demonstrative pronoun. Make sure the pronoun is not used as a modifier.

Examples

a. What would you like to do now?
   What would you like to do now?

b. I'll have four of those and two of these.
   I'll have four of those and two of these.

1. What is that dog's name?
2. By whom was the animal named?
3. Who would call a dark brown dog Snowflake?
4. These are Great Danes; those dogs are Dalmatians.
5. If you are looking for a doghouse, take this.
6. On what have you based your decision to own a dog?
7. You don't need much food to feed those.
8. These dogs are really skinny; those are fatter.
9. Take the ones you want from those. Which dogs do you like best, and which do you want to own?
10. Whose is the little dog with the big ears?

Indefinite Pronouns

Indefinite pronouns do not refer to specific persons or things. Indefinite pronouns may take the place of a noun in a sentence, but they often do not have antecedents.

Anyone can learn to cook eggs.

On the bus I saw *no one* who was familiar.

Each of the plants gets special attention.

Indefinite pronouns have singular or plural meanings.

Singular Indefinite Pronouns

anybody	everybody	nobody
anyone	much	one
each	neither	somebody
either	no one	someone·
everyone		

Plural Indefinite Pronouns

both	few	many	others	several

A few indefinite pronouns can be either singular or plural, depending on the nouns they refer to in the sentence.

all	any	most	none	some

All of the air in the city was polluted.	[singular]
All of the skaters were on the ice.	[plural]
Some of the canned food is past the expiration date.	[singular]
Some of our friends are coming over tonight.	[plural]

Exercise 5: *Identifying Indefinite Pronouns*

Write the sentences on the following page and underline the indefinite pronouns. Above the pronoun write *S* if it is singular and *P* if it is plural.

Examples

   a. From the roof we could see someone entering the building below.

                                S

   From the roof we could see <u>someone</u> entering the building below.

   b. Few of the trees still have their leaves.

     P

   <u>Few</u> of the trees still have their leaves.

1. Both of the princes moved their belongings to the royal palace.

2. Each of the princesses redecorated her room at the palace.

3. Several of the tourists left the main group and took their own tour.

4. One of the princes had built a theater for his amusement.

5. Each of the first floor rooms had its own entrance to the main hall.

6. One of the women said she was a fortune-teller.

7. Either of your palms will tell its story to the trained reader.

8. Someone on the women's team announced she wanted to challenge the men's team.

9. Neither of the boys would put himself on the line.

10. Few of the spectators thought they had ever seen a more exciting game.

Finding Pronouns by Their Features

Pronouns have three features that distinguish them from other parts of speech. Personal pronouns have all three features. Other kinds of pronouns usually have at least one.

A pronoun may be singular or plural.

Personal, possessive, demonstrative, and indefinite pronouns have singular or plural meanings.

	Singular	*Plural*
Personal:	I, you, he, she, it, me, him, her	we, you, they, us, them
Possessive:	my, mine, your, yours, his, her, hers, its	our, ours, your, yours, their, theirs
Demonstrative:	this, that	these, those
Indefinite:	anybody, everyone, nobody, each, one, someone	both, few, many, others, several

---

Pronouns may change form to show what they do in a sentence.

Only personal pronouns have both subject forms and object forms.

Subject Forms	Object Forms
I, we	me, us
you	you
he, she, it, they	him, her, it, them

Subject: *She* stopped by my house after school to pick up the schedule.
After the storm *we* cleaned up the yard.
Maria and *I* were the class representatives for the council.

Object: Sally will call *me* tonight about the assignment.
The winning poster for the annual fundraiser was drawn by *him*.
Dad helped *us* build our science project.

Pronouns may show gender.

Personal and possessive pronouns may be masculine, feminine, or neuter.

Masculine: he, him, his

Feminine: she, her, hers

Neuter: it, its

Some pronouns can be either masculine or feminine, depending on the speaker.

I, me, myself

Some pronouns refer to groups of men or women or to mixed groups, depending on the meaning of the sentence.

we, us, they, them, you, ourselves, themselves, yourselves

Exercise 6: Identifying Pronouns by Their Features

Write the following sentences and underline the pronouns. Be prepared to tell which features you used to identify the pronouns.

Examples

a. They put all of their equipment on the back porch.
   They put all of their equipment on the back porch.

b. Sandra wrote herself a note about the picnic and put it on the refrigerator.
   Sandra wrote herself a note about the picnic and put it on the refrigerator.

1. In 1965 a power failure blacked out almost all of New York City.

2. When it happened, no one knew why the power went out.

3. Many people were without lights; others were stranded in elevators and subways.

4. Radio and television stations went off the air; they were helpless without their source of power.

5. Radio stations improvised hookups; these let them begin broadcasting again.

6. Many of the people in darkened areas began calling the radio stations to pass along news about the blackout and its effects.

7. Everyone in the city had special stories to tell about that night; these were often better than those from a book.

8. A 91-year-old woman was trapped in a hotel elevator; three volunteers rescued her.

9. Other volunteers directed traffic when the city lost its electricity.

10. The people of New York City handled themselves well in this emergency; they should be proud of that.

Review: Understanding Pronouns

Write the sentences on this page and the next. Circle each pronoun and underline its antecedent.

Examples

a. Maria left school before she took the test.

  <u>Maria</u> left school before (she) took the test.

b. Bernice and Carlos thought their science project deserved an A.

  <u>Bernice and Carlos</u> thought (their) science project deserved an A.

1. Carol says she never eats potatoes.

2. Actually potatoes are not fattening, and they are rich in iron and in Vitamin C.

3. Many people don't like garlic, but it can add to the taste of food.

4. The boys worked hard in their garden.

5. Kim said that watermelon is her favorite summer fruit.

6. A gardener keeps very busy because plants can't take care of themselves.

7. Castroville, California, is famous for its artichokes.

8. Roger took his daughter to see the Golden Gate Bridge.

9. After working all summer, Georgette gave herself a vacation in New England.

10. Jack brought his mother a souvenir of his trip.

11. During Mardi Gras, New Orleans is flooded with tourists, and its hotels are full.

12. The tourists did all their shopping in New York.

13. The six children wanted to climb the lighthouse, but the guard wouldn't let them.

14. Kenny taught himself Spanish before he took a trip to Mexico.

15. After she had visited the Southwest, Melissa read every book she could find about the Navaho and Hopi.

16. Susan, can Richie borrow your notebook?

17. When they were in Italy, the Clarks spent most of their time in Venice.

18. Georgia O'Keeffe is best known for her paintings of the American Southwest.

19. The doctor asked her patient, "Have you had a rest lately?"

20. Since the choice was hers, Alice decided to spend the day at the beach.

Applying What You Know

In the following passage from the book *To Kill a Mockingbird* by Harper Lee, a young girl named Scout describes her father, Atticus. This passage contains several personal, possessive, interrogative, demonstrative, or indefinite pronouns. On a sheet of paper numbered 1–24, list each pronoun. Beside the pronoun write the class to which it belongs. Your teacher may ask you how you identified each pronoun.

Atticus was feeble: he was nearly fifty. When Jem and I asked him why he was so old, he said he got started late, which we felt reflected upon his abilities and manliness. He was much older than the parents of our school contemporaries, and there was nothing Jem or I could say about him when our classmates said, "*My* father—"

Jem was football crazy. Atticus was never too tired to play keepaway, but when Jem wanted to tackle him, Atticus would say, "I'm too old for that, son."

Our father didn't do anything. He worked in an office, not in a drugstore. Atticus did not drive a dump-truck for the county, he was not the sheriff, he did not farm, work in a garage, or do anything that could possibly arouse the admiration of anyone.

   Besides that, he wore glasses.[1]

Using Pronouns

Because some pronouns have many different forms, choosing the correct form is sometimes a problem. In this section you will learn how to use pronouns correctly and effectively in your writing and speaking.

Agreement of Pronouns and Antecedents

A pronoun must agree with its antecedent in number. When an antecedent is singular, the pronoun used to refer to it must be singular.

Each of my brothers has *his* own hair dryer.
(*Each* is the antecedent; *each* is singular.)

Someone on the girls' golf team lost *her* keys.
(*Someone* is the antecedent; *someone* is singular.)

When the antecedent is plural, a plural pronoun is used to refer to it.

Helen bought the apples and gave *them* to Karl.

The skiers unlocked *their* bindings.

We wanted to build the haunted house by *ourselves*.

Several of the students gave *their* opinions.

[1]From pp. 97–98 in *To Kill a Mockingbird* by Harper Lee (J. B. Lippincott). Copyright © 1960 by Harper Lee. Reprinted by permission of Harper & Row, Publishers, Inc. and William Heinmann Ltd., British publishers.

A pronoun must agree with its antecedent in *gender*. When a singular antecedent is clearly masculine, the pronouns *he, him,* or *his* are used.

Murray wrote a letter to *his* uncle in Germany.

Ricardo said that *he* would lend me *his* math book.

Jeff asked if *he* could go, but *his* mother told *him* no.

When a singular antecedent is feminine, the pronouns *she, her,* or *hers* are used.

Jennifer noticed that *she* forgot *her* notebook.

Juanita claimed that the jacket was *hers*.

When a singular antecedent is neuter, the pronouns *it* and *its* are used.

The snake shed *its* skin close to the rock.

During the rainstorm the rose lost *its* petals.

Exercise 7: *Making Pronouns Agree with Antecedents*

Write the sentences on the following page and supply the correct form of a pronoun that agrees with its antecedent in number and gender. Underline the pronoun you choose.

Example

a. When Uncle Arthur was in the army, _____ rose to the rank of captain.

When Uncle Arthur was in the army, <u>he</u> rose to the rank of captain.

1. The students enjoy watching *Buck Rogers*. _____ is an entertaining show.

2. Someone on the fathers' committee wanted to select the shows _____ son watched.

3. One of the television sets lost _____ picture twice last night.

4. Derrick wondered if the directors would pick _____ to star in the new show.

5. Elaine sold the script _____ had written to the network.

6. The plot was exciting because _____ had a lot of action.

7. The comedians gave _____ opinions about the script.

8. Although _____ knew the fire on the television show was not real, Alicia was frightened.

9. Maria hoped to direct the show by _____.

10. Both the actors were critical of _____ performance.

Agreement with Compound Antecedents

When two or more antecedents are joined by *and*, a plural pronoun is used to refer to them.

A martin and a wren have made *their* nests in the tree house.

Connie, Ed, and Marcella visited *their* friend Ramon.

Joan and the boys did *their* best on the test.

When two or more singular antecedents are joined by *or* or *nor*, a singular pronoun is used to refer to them.

An eagle or a hawk can spot *its* prey from a hundred meters in the air.

Either Sheila or Juanita will give *her* report.

Neither Yoshiro nor Kuni has received *his* magazine.

When two or more plural antecedents are joined by *or* or *nor*, a plural pronoun is used to refer to them.

Neither swans nor herons leave *their* nests unguarded.

Either the seals or the elephants will perform *their* tricks.

Exercise 8: Making Pronouns Agree with Compound Antecedents

Write the following sentences and choose the correct pronoun from those given in parentheses. Underline the pronouns you choose.

Example

---

a. Either Kate or Cheryl can finish that by (herself, themselves).
Either Kate or Cheryl can finish that by herself.

1. Neither Irene nor Lois could have done all the work by (herself, themselves).

2. Nancy and Judy said (they, she) would weed the garden.

3. Either sea otters or seals spend most of (its, their) time playing and doing tricks.

4. Angelo and his sisters decided to cook dinner for (himself, themselves, theirselves).

5. Jennifer, Kim, and Toby taught (herself, themselves) how to play the guitar.

6. Either Wyoming or Montana has (its, their) northern border next to Canada.

7. Neither Joanne nor her younger sister wants to clean the room by (herself, themselves).

8. Juanita and Jim both lost (her, his, their) tickets on the way to the game.

9. Neither the quart of milk nor the stick of butter will stay fresh unless you put (it, them) in the refrigerator.

10. Michael and David promised (he, they) would wash the car tomorrow.

Making Pronouns Agree

When the antecedent is an indefinite pronoun, you must decide whether it is singular or plural and make other pronouns agree with it.

Indefinite pronouns may be either singular or plural.

Singular			Plural	Singular or Plural
each	everyone	someone	several	all
one	everybody	somebody	few	none
either	anyone	no one	both	any
neither	anybody	nobody	many	most
much			others	some

When the antecedent is a singular indefinite pronoun, a singular pronoun is used to refer to it.

Each of the boys designed *his* own costume.

Everyone on the girls' tennis team played *her* match well.

A singular indefinite pronoun sometimes refers to a mixed group of men and women. In such sentences you may use the words *his or her*, or reword the sentence so that the antecedent is plural.

Anyone who is in the band should bring *his or her* music.

All of the band members should bring *their* music.

Band members should bring *their* music.

301

When the antecedent is a plural indefinite pronoun, a plural pronoun is used to refer to it.

Few of the players remembered *their* mistakes.

Many of the judges received *their* education at Harvard.

When the antecedent is an indefinite pronoun that can be either singular or plural, you must look closely at the meaning of the sentence to see how it is used.

None of this money is mine; *it* belongs   [singular]
to Bill.

None of these nickels, dimes, or   [plural]

quarters are mine; *they* belong to Bill.

Exercise 9: *Making Pronouns Agree*

Write each of the following sentences and then choose the correct pronoun from those that are given in parentheses. Underline the pronoun that you choose.

Example

a. Everyone in the men's glee club knew (his, their) part well.
Everyone in the men's glee club knew <u>his</u> part well.

1. Neither one of the boys wants (his, their) bicycle repaired.

2. Most of the high school band members have paid (their, his) dues.

3. None of the milk is good; (they, it) is sour.

4. None of these bottles have been sold; (they, it) will be left.

5. One of the American women skaters won (their, her) silver medal.

6. Most of the mistakes have been corrected, but (it, they) should all be changed.

7. Few people admit (his or her, their) own mistakes.

8. All of the boys who want to sign up for football should bring (his, their) uniforms.

9. Anyone who attends the play should buy (his or her, their) ticket early.

10. Either girl gives (their, her) best performance after much practice.

Using Subject Pronouns

The subject forms of the personal pronouns are as follows:

Subject Forms	
Singular	**Plural**
I, you, he, she, it	we, you, they

Use a subject form of the personal pronoun when the pronoun is the subject of a sentence.

> Margaret and *I* have a summer job at the bank.
>
> The Rosenbergs and *we* will be going on the trip together.
>
> Amanda and *she* have been best friends for years.

When using a personal pronoun to refer to yourself, always place the pronoun that refers to you last.

> Mary and *I* agree on very few things.
>
> Penny, Clipper, and *I* sat in the cockpit of the plane.

Use a subject pronoun when the pronoun follows a form of the verb *be* and renames or identifies the subject of the sentence.

The best swimmers on the team were *we*.

It's *they* who invited us.

The girl sitting on the stage was *she*.

When a sentence ends in an incomplete construction, use a subject form of the personal pronoun. An *incomplete construction* **is a sentence with part left for the reader to complete.**

You can persuade him more easily than *I*. (than I can.)

Now Patty is older than *he*. (than he is.)

Sometimes a pronoun is joined with a noun or other pronoun in a sentence. Use the form of the pronoun you would use if the pronoun were alone in the sentence.

My friends and I spend hours in the park.
(*I* spend hours in the park.)

Farmers can give important lessons to us city dwellers.
(Farmers can give important lessons to *us*.)

Exercise 10: Using Subject Forms of Personal Pronouns

Write each of the following sentences, and choose the subject form of the personal pronoun from those given in parentheses. Underline the pronouns you choose.

Example

---

a. Sue and (her, she) wore the same kind of skirt to school.
Sue and <u>she</u> wore the same kind of skirt to school.

1. The person who answered the phone was (I, me).

2. The girls' team and (us, we) will play an exhibition game.

3. A professional photographer will take better pictures than (them, they).

4. Sarah, Laurie, and (she, her) tried out for the leading role.

5. How did you know it was (he, him) at the next table?

6. Ms. Esposito can teach you geography quicker than (I, me).

7. The neighbors and (them, they) are organizing a garage sale.

8. Sonia spoke more often because she was more outgoing than (he, him).

9. The best spellers in the language arts class are (her, she) and (I, me).

10. Did the dogs and (them, they) arrive home safely?

Using Object Pronouns

Personal pronouns have both singular and plural object forms.

Object Forms	
Singular	*Plural*
me, you, him, her, it	us, you, them

Use the object form when the personal pronoun is the object of the verb. The object answers the question *whom?* **after the verb.**

Mother praised *me* for my grades.

Carrie called *us* from Alaska.

Chris and I saw *them* at the carnival last Saturday.

Use the object form when the pronoun answers the question *to whom?* **after the verb.**

My father gave *us* roses on Valentine's Day.

You should give *them* credit for their effort.

Mrs. Sing gave *him* a warning when he became too noisy.

Use the object form when the pronoun follows a preposition, such as *by, for, to, from,* and *with.*

Shelley drove with *us* to the beach.

Did you build that sand castle for *me?*

We arrived at the bus stop with *them.*

Exercise 11: *Using Object Forms of Personal Pronouns*

Write each of the following sentences and choose the correct personal pronoun from those given in parentheses. Underline the pronoun that you choose.

Example

a. The umpire glared up at (we, us) spectators.

The umpire glared up at <u>us</u> spectators.

1. Margo, Jared, and (I, me) were all born in August.
2. What do you know about (we, us) Leos?
3. The zodiac signs are interesting to Jeanette and (she, her).
4. Copernicus, Galileo, and (he, him) studied the stars.
5. The constellations in the night sky amaze (he, him).
6. Perhaps you and (they, them) will study astronomy.
7. Astrology is more interesting to you and (I, me).
8. (She, Her) and the other scientists think there is another planet in our solar system.
9. Do you believe (they, them)?
10. (We, Us) folks on earth seem very small compared with the whole universe.

Review: *Using Pronouns*

Write each of the sentences on the following page and choose the correct pronoun from those given in parentheses. Underline the pronouns you choose.

Example

a. I took our dog to have (it's, its) nails trimmed.
I took our dog to have <u>its</u> nails trimmed.

1. (She, Her) and (I, me) both entered the contest.
2. The entry forms were sent to (she, her) and (I, me).
3. (We, Us) contestants were excited about the prizes.
4. It was (he, him) who filled out the form so quickly.
5. Are you rooting for (they, them) or for (we, us)?
6. Zack, Deborah, and (I, me) decided to build three pyramids and a sphinx.
7. Deborah liked pyramids, and it was (she, her) who had the idea to build some.
8. Our sculpture will surprise Marta and (they, them).
9. The whole beach is available to (we, us) artists.
10. Will the water hit (we, us) or (they, them) first?
11. Either Atlantic City or Asbury Park has had (its, their) boardwalk rebuilt several times.
12. Every one of the Boy Scouts had (his, their) bags packed for the camping trip.
13. (Paula and I, Paula and me) wondered how long disco and roller-skating would keep (its, their) popularity.
14. A cow and two goats fed (itself, themselves) by munching on Abe's back lawn.
15. Peter gave tennis lessons to (Jenny and me, me and Jenny).
16. One of the champions on the men's tennis team drove (his, their) car in a parade.
17. Old horror movies can occupy (Jim and me, Jim and I) for hours.
18. Ken and Phil shouldn't fool (himself, themselves) into thinking the test will be easy.
19. Several of the cities had (its, their) power knocked out by the storm.
20. A few of the rough waves hit me with (its, their) full force.

Writing Focus: *Using Pronouns in Writing*

You can strengthen your writing by using pronouns to avoid unnecessary repetition and to vary the structure of your sentences. Be sure that the pronouns you use are in the correct form and agree with their antecedents in number and gender.

Assignment: *A Holiday Celebration*

Every family has a special way of celebrating a holiday. Perhaps your family opens Christmas presents on Christmas Eve after decorating the tree. Maybe your family invites less fortunate people to share Thanksgiving dinner. Or your family might even plan an all-day picnic for the Fourth of July. Whatever it is, you and your family celebrate holidays in your own special way.

Choose a holiday that you and your family especially enjoy celebrating. Write one or more paragraphs describing the special way you celebrate it. Which members of your family are included? Where do you spend your holiday? What does your family do that you consider special in celebrating this holiday? Include details so that your audience of classmates can imagine celebrating with you. Your writing will be evaluated for correct use of pronouns.

Use the following steps to complete this assignment.

A. Prewriting

Make a list of all the holidays you and your family celebrate and choose one to write about that seems special and important. Use the six basic questions method described in Chapter 1 to generate ideas for your description of the special way you celebrate. Jot down questions like the following: *Who* is involved in the celebration? *What* takes place? *Where* does it take place? *When* does it take place? *Why* does it take place? *How* does your family make the holiday special? Answer your questions specifically in words, phrases, or sentences. Review your answers and group them into an organization that will help your readers follow your description.

B. Writing

Using your answers, write one or more paragraphs describing the special way you and your family celebrate a particular holiday. Tell who is present, where and when you celebrate, and what you all do that you consider special. Be sure to include details in your account. As you write, pay particular attention to pronouns and to their antecedents.

C. Postwriting

Revise your first draft, using the following checklist.

1. Have I answered the questions *who? what? why? when? where?* and *how?* in describing the special way my family and I celebrate a holiday?

2. Have I used each pronoun in its correct form?

3. Does each pronoun agree with its antecedent in number and gender?

Edit your work, using the Checklist for Proofreading at the back of the book. If appropriate, share your writing with your teacher and the members of your class.

309

14 Verbs

Understanding Verbs

Verbs are the foundation words of sentences. Every sentence must have a verb. The verb gives the sentence meaning by saying something about the noun or pronoun that is the subject. You can identify verbs in three ways: by definition, by classification, and by the features that distinguish verbs from other parts of speech. In this section you will study and practice each of these ways to identify verbs.

Defining Verbs

A *verb* is defined as a word that shows action or a state of being about a noun or pronoun.

We *run* five miles each day.	[action]
That game *decided* the champion.	[action]
I *am* down in the dumps today.	[state of being]
The new students *became* our friends.	[state of being]

Exercise 1: Identifying Verbs

Write the following sentences and underline the verbs. Remember that a verb can show action or a state of being.

Examples

a. Carl climbed to the top of the tower.
   Carl <u>climbed</u> to the top of the tower.

b. All the letters were on the table.
   All the letters <u>were</u> on the table.

1. We planned the menu for our club's dinner.
2. Each of those boys was at school today.
3. We thought about the final exam.
4. The students concentrated on the test.
5. Nancy and Juanita swim after school.
6. My sister became the most popular member of the team.
7. Brian and Eric studied almost all night.
8. Mrs. Appleton seemed pleased by my answer.
9. Renaldo and Kay play tennis together well.
10. My brother was on the honor roll.

Grouping Verbs by Classes

Verbs are usually grouped into three main classes: *action verbs, being and linking verbs,* and *helping verbs.* These three classes help to identify verbs.

Verbs that show physical or mental action are called *action verbs.*

Physical Action	**Mental Action**
Ricardo *climbed* the rope.	I *concentrated* on the test.
Amy *started* the lawnmower.	We *hope* our team wins.
The fans *cheered*.	Hiromi *thought* hard.

Exercise 2: *Identifying Action Verbs*

Write the sentences on the following page and underline each action verb. Write *P* above verbs that show physical action. Write *M* above verbs that show mental action.

Example

a. The lightning flashed across the sky.

P

The lightning <u>flashed</u> across the sky.

1. Every Saturday we go to the movies.

2. The coach decided on the team's schedule.

3. Mother told us to be on time for dinner.

4. The crowd screamed for more home runs.

5. Slyly the cat crept along the fence.

6. We enjoyed the movie.

7. The children believed in magic.

8. Our family drove to California last summer.

9. My brothers share a room.

10. Jesse thought about his birthday party.

Linking verbs **do not show action. They link a noun or pronoun in the first part of a sentence with a word in the second part of a sentence.**

The oranges *were* delicious.   He *is* an artist.

The sky *became* cloudy.   The water *felt* cool.

Linking verbs include forms of *be* and a few other commonly used verbs. The following verbs are the most commonly used linking verbs.

Some forms of Be		**Common Linking Verbs**		
am	has been	taste	look	grow
is	have been	smell	feel	appear
are	had been	sound	become	remain
was	will be	seem	stay	
were	should be			
may be	would have been			
can be	shall be			

Some words can be either action or linking verbs. You must look at the way the verb is used in the sentence to decide which kind it is.

Action: We *grew* potatoes in our garden.

Linking: The children *grew* tired.

Action: The nurse *felt* the boy's forehead.

Linking: I *felt* good after some sleep.

Exercise 3: Identifying Linking Verbs

Write the following sentences and underline each linking verb. Draw arrows between the two words the verb links together.

Examples

a. The homemade pickles tasted sour.

The homemade pickles <u>tasted</u> sour.

b. The little puppy was afraid.

The little puppy <u>was</u> afraid.

1. The lawn smells fresh after an April shower.
2. My sister is captain of the team.
3. The sandpaper felt rough on my skin.
4. Charles Yang became president of the class by a margin of three votes.
5. The Reynoldses are my neighbors.
6. My mother looks very young.
7. The dough for the bread seems too stiff.
8. On Monday mornings I am usually sleepy.
9. Our dogs were the winners of the contest.
10. Jennifer stayed calm during the accident.

Helping verbs **help the main verb express an action or a state of being.**

The plane *will* arrive on schedule.

Our flight *had been* delayed two hours.

The bicycle chain *has* become rusty.

The paint *should* appear thick at first.

Helping verbs include the forms of *be* and many other commonly used words.

Forms of Be

am	were
is	be
are	been
was	

Commonly Used Helping Verbs

has	might
have	must
had	can
do	shall
does	should
did	will
may	would

Exercise 4: Identifying Main and Helping Verbs

Write the following sentences. Underline each main verb once and each helping verb twice.

Examples

a. Harold had played the trumpet solo.
   Harold <u>had</u> <u>played</u> the trumpet solo.

b. You should have come to the party.
   You <u>should have</u> <u>come</u> to the party.

1. Kara, Bill, Ricky, and Melissa must have gone to the circus.

2. Milo's plants had grown tall and green in the summer sunshine.

3. Our high school's soccer team should win the championship this year.

4. Our Constitution states that we must elect a President every four years.

5. Confidence can help your ability.

6. Ross has been selected for the solo part.

7. The painting was hung in the living room.

8. The ocean can become angry in a storm.

9. I could have been stung by that wasp if I hadn't moved.

10. Our Siamese cat has felt sick lately.

Finding Verbs by Their Features

Four features can help you identify verbs. A word that is a verb must have *at least one* of these features, but some verbs will have all four.

Verbs have *tense.*

Tense is the time expressed by a verb. There are two kinds of tenses: *simple* and *perfect.* The three simple tenses are *present, past,* and *future.* The three perfect tenses are *present perfect, past perfect,* and *future perfect.*

They *walk* to school in the morning.	[simple present]
The scout troup *walked* across the street.	[simple past]
Myron *will walk* to the movies with us.	[simple future]
Roger *has walked* the dog.	[present perfect]
The dog knew Myra *had walked* another dog.	[past perfect]
He *will have walked* five kilometers by dinner.	[future perfect]

The tense of the verb is formed with one of its three *principal parts: present, past,* and *past participle.* The *present* form is the form of the verb used with *to: (to) go, (to) swim, (to) play.* The *past* form is the one that shows past time: *went, swam, played.* The *past participle* form of the verb is the form of the verb used with the helping verb *has* or *have: (has) gone, (has) swum, (has) played.*

Present	Past	Past Participle
hope	hoped	hoped
close	closed	closed
look	looked	looked
run	ran	run
see	saw	seen

The following list shows how verb tenses are formed.

Tense	How Formed	Example
Simple present	present form of verb	I walk, he walks
Simple past	past form of verb	I walked, he walked
Simple future	present form + *will* or *shall*	I shall walk He will walk
Present perfect	past participle form of verb + *has* or *have*	I have walked He has walked
Past perfect	past participle form of verb + *had*	I had walked He had walked
Future perfect	past participle form + *shall have* or *will have*	I shall have walked He will have walked

Helping verbs are used to form the simple future and all the perfect tenses. The helping verb and the main verb together are called a *verb phrase*.

    verb phrase
I *shall walk* to school tomorrow.

    verb phrase
I *have walked* to school in the rain.

    verb phrase
I *had walked* to school until yesterday.

       verb phrase
On Friday I *shall have walked* to school for an entire week.

Exercise 5: *Identifying Verb Tenses*

Write each of the sentences on the following page and underline the verb or verb phrase. After the sentence write the tense of the verb or verb phrase. The tense will be one of the following:

simple present	present perfect
simple past	past perfect
simple future	future perfect

Examples

a. The ancient Incas lived in Peru.
   The ancient Incas <u>lived</u> in Peru. (simple past)

b. Inflation has caused problems for many people.
   Inflation <u>has caused</u> problems for many people. (present perfect)

1. For centuries no one knew how to find the key to Egyptian hieroglyphics.

2. Hieroglyphics had puzzled scholars for years.

3. In 1821 Jean François Champellion discovered the key to Egyptian hieroglyphics.

4. The key is in the Rosetta stone.

5. Ancient Egyptians had written on the stone in three languages.

6. The Greek language on the stone helped Jean François in his task.

7. Modern scholars have used the same approach to other languages.

8. Scholars will use a known language as a clue to an unknown language.

9. By the year 2000 scholars will have learned the meanings of many ancient languages.

10. Another interesting possibility for language study lies in outer space.

Verbs have an *-ing* form.

The *-ing* form is the verb's *progressive form*. The *progressive* form of the verb uses a form of *be* in the simple tenses. The future tense also uses *will* or *shall*.

I *am sewing* a costume.	[present tense]
I *was sewing* a costume.	[past tense]
I *will be sewing* a costume.	[future tense]

Verbs have singular and plural forms.

Whether a verb is singular or plural depends on the subject of the sentence. When the subject is singular, the ending -s or -es is added to the present tense form of the verb. When the subject is plural, the present tense form is used by itself. Helping verbs may also be singular or plural.

Shirley *plans* to study medicine.	[singular]
The three students *plan* to study music.	[plural]
My sister *flies* a plane on weekends.	[singular]
Many birds *fly* south for the winter.	[plural]
Joan *has seen* the movie three times.	[singular]
We *have seen* the movie three times.	[plural]

Verbs may be formed with suffixes such as *-fy*, *-ize*, and *-ate*, and many others.

The parent tried to *pacify* the crying baby.

Farmers *pasteurize* milk to kill bacteria.

Doctors *vaccinate* infants against whopping cough.

Exercise 6: *Identifying Verbs by Their Features*

Write each of the following sentences and underline the verb or verb phrase. Use the four verb features to identify the verbs. Your teacher may ask how you identified each verb.

Examples

    a. Pamela was attending the meeting.
       Pamela <u>was attending</u> the meeting.

       (This verb ends in *-ing* and uses a form of *be.*)

    b. Pedro knows the most about science.
       Pedro <u>knows</u> the most about science.

       (This verb has an *-s* for its singular form.)

1. The fox terrier hides its bone under the porch.
2. We will be waiting on the corner.
3. Cecelia received a record album for her birthday.
4. Jack was polishing his saxophone for the afternoon band performance.
5. Next weekend our family will go on a camping trip in the mountains.
6. The mail arrives at the same time every day.
7. The teacher has canceled tryouts for the play.
8. The flowering plants beautify the highways.
9. Wealthy patrons donate works of art to the museum.
10. I am planning a costume for the party.

Review: Understanding Verbs

The following paragraphs have twenty-five verbs or verb phrases. List twenty of them on a sheet of paper numbered 1–20. Use any of the ways you have learned about in this section to identify them. Your teacher may ask you how you identified each verb. Did you use the definition of a verb? The classes? The features?

My science teacher, Mr. Brice, assigned a report on a career in science. I chose the career of a pharmacist because my aunt is one. She and my uncle have owned a drugstore for twenty years. I was hoping for an interview with her for my report.

I had planned a visit to the library because I needed background information on this career. I found a lot of information. Pharmacists are pretty important people. They need a thorough knowledge of the chemistry of the human body and the chemistry of drugs. By the time they finish school, they will have studied the effects of drugs on the human body. Also, they will have learned about the effects of combinations of drugs. That is a lot of information! For that amount of knowledge, pharmacists will go to school for many years. But their salary will reflect all of this hard work.

Finally I interviewed my aunt. I had prepared well for my interview, and I impressed her with my research. Still, she offered more details for my report. She even explained the daily routine of a pharmacist to me. This first-hand information really added a new dimension to my report.

The next day I gave Mr. Brice my report. He was happy, especially with the interview. Now I am waiting, and not so patiently, for my grade.

Applying What You Know

Select several paragraphs from a newspaper, magazine, or book you have read. Read the paragraphs again paying special attention to the verbs in the passage. Use what you have learned in this section to identify the verbs in the paragraphs. Make a list of the verbs on a sheet of paper. Your teacher may ask how you identified each of your verbs. Did you decide that the verb expressed action or a state of being? Did you decide that it belongs to one of the classes of verbs? Does it have one or more of the four features that distinguish verbs from other parts of speech?

Using Verbs

This section will give you practice in forming and using the tenses and progressive forms of verbs. You will also practice making verbs agree with their subjects. Verbs have so many different forms that they are often difficult to use correctly. This section is designed to give you helpful practice in using all of the verb forms correctly. As you work the exercises, be sure to look back at the Understanding Verbs section when you need help. You may also check your work by comparing it to the appropiate section when you finish.

Using the Simple Verb Tenses

Form the *present tense* with the present form of the verb.

In the present tense the verb changes form in the third person singular by adding -s or -es.

Present Tense

I allow	we allow
you allow	you allow
he she it } allows	they allow

Form the *past tense* of *regular* verbs by adding *-d* or *-ed* to the present form.

Past Tense

I dreamed	we dreamed
you dreamed	you dreamed
he she it } dreamed	they dreamed

Form the *future tense* with the helping verbs *will* or *shall* and the present form of the verb.

Future Tense

I shall/will open	we shall/will open
you will open	you will open
he she it } will open	they will open

Exercise 7: Using Simple Verb Tenses

Rewrite each of the sentences on the following page, changing the verb tense to the one given in parentheses. Underline the verbs you form.

Examples

 a. The eagle always nested in the tallest tree. (present)
The eagle always <u>nests</u> in the tallest tree.

 b. I am the treasurer of our class. (future)
I <u>will be</u> the treasurer of our class.

1. We talked to Mayor Sanchez about more city parks. (future)

2. This small car used far less gas. (present)

3. Ms. Chang will frown at your paper. (past)

4. Gloria helps both her parents with their English lessons. (future)

5. Cindy surprised her mother at work. (present)

6. Jean and Nancy will display their 4-H projects. (past)

7. Peter whacked the ball straight down toward third base. (present)

8. The kite sails out of sight. (future)

9. Both stepsisters struggled with the glass slipper. (present)

10. The drought ends with the rains of spring. (future)

Using the Perfect Tenses

The *present perfect tense* is formed with the helping verb *has* or *have* and the past participle form of the verb. *Has* is used with the third person singular form of the verb.

Present Perfect Tense

I have watched	we have watched
you have watched	you have watched
he she it } has watched	they have watched

The *past perfect tense* is formed with the helping verb *had* and the past participle form of the verb.

Past Perfect Tense

I had walked	we had walked
you had walked	you had walked
he she it } had walked	they had walked

The *future perfect tense* is formed with the helping verbs *shall have* or *will have* and the past participle form of the verb. Either *shall* or *will* is used with the first person form of the verb.

Future Perfect Tense

I shall/will have walked	we shall/will have walked
you will have walked	you will have walked
he she it } will have walked	they will have walked

Exercise 8: Using the Perfect Verb Tenses

Rewrite each of the sentences on the following page and change the verb to the perfect tense given in parentheses. Underline the verbs you form.

Examples

a. The book remained on the shelf. (present perfect)
The book has remained on the shelf.

b. Three members of the swimming team competed in the finals. (past perfect)
Three members of the swimming team had competed in the finals.

1. Carol presented her report. (present perfect)

2. I asked my parents for permission. (past perfect)

3. She told me the answer three times. (future perfect)

4. Fresh peaches never tasted better. (present perfect)

5. The frogs jumped from lily pad to lily pad. (past perfect)

6. My friend played drums in a rock band. (past perfect)

7. Sam asked for a moment of total silence. (present perfect)

8. The weather suddenly turned very cold. (future perfect)

9. Gary and Luis watched Old Faithful in Yellowstone National Park. (present perfect)

10. Jack climbed to the top of the beanstalk. (future perfect)

Using Irregular Verbs

Irregular verbs are verbs that do not follow the regular pattern for forming their principal parts.

Some irregular verbs form their past and past participle forms by a change in spelling. Others are the same in both their past and past participle forms. The following list gives the three principal parts for commonly used irregular verbs.

Principal Parts		
Present	*Past*	*Past Participle* (*has, have,* or *had*)
begin	began	begun
blow	blew	blown
break	broke	broken
bring	brought	brought
build	built	built
burst	burst	burst

Present	Past	Past Participle
buy	bought	bought
choose	chose	chosen
come	came	come
dive	dove *or* dived	dived
do	did	done
draw	drew	drawn
drink	drank	drunk
drive	drove	driven
eat	ate	eaten
fall	fell	fallen
fly	flew	flown
forget	forgot	forgotten
freeze	froze	frozen
give	gave	given
go	went	gone
grow	grew	grown
keep	kept	kept
know	knew	known
lay	laid	laid
lie	lay	lain
ride	rode	ridden
ring	rang	rung
rise	rose	risen
run	ran	run
see	saw	seen
shake	shook	shaken
shrink	shrank	shrunk
sing	sang	sung
sink	sank	sunk

Present	Past	Past Participle
speak	spoke	spoken
spend	spent	spent
spring	sprang	sprung
steal	stole	stolen
swear	swore	sworn
swim	swam	swum
take	took	taken
teach	taught	taught
think	thought	thought
throw	threw	thrown
wear	wore	worn
write	wrote	written

Like regular verbs, the principal parts of irregular verbs form tenses.

Principal Parts

Present	Past	Past Participle
know	knew	known

Present Tense
(*add* -s *or* -es *in the third person singular*)

I know	we know
you know	you know
he she it } knows	they know

Past Tense
(*past form*)

I knew	we knew
you knew	you knew
he she it } knew	they knew

Future Tense
(will *or* shall + *present form*)

I shall/will know	we shall/will know
you will know	you will know
he she it } will know	they will know

Present Perfect Tense
(have *or* has + *past participle*)

I have known	we have known
you have known	you have known
he she it } has known	they have known

Past Perfect Tense
(had + *past participle*)

I had known	we had known
you had known	you had known
he she it } had known	they had known

Future Perfect Tense
(shall have *or* will have + *past participle*)

I shall/will have known	we shall/will have known
you will have known	you will have known
he she } will have known it	they will have known

Exercise 9: *Choosing the Proper Verb Form*

Write the following sentences and choose the proper verb form from those given in parentheses. If you are unsure about which of the given forms is correct, consult the list of irregular verbs. Underline the verb form you choose.

Examples

a. When I dropped the pane of glass, it (burst, busted) into a million pieces.

When I dropped the pane of glass, it burst into a million pieces.

b. Kay tried to open the door, but it had (froze, frozen) shut.

Kay tried to open the door, but it had frozen shut.

1. Ginger has (fell, fallen) off the ladder again.

2. The lake (froze, frozen) during last week's cold spell.

3. That jet always (breaks, broken) the sound barrier.

4. Janice has (ran, run) the track in record time!

5. The guests have (ate, eaten) all of the casserole.

6. We (saw, seen) the movie three times!

7. Raymond, Marsha, Gregory and I (gone, went) to the store together.

8. I have (drank, drunk) that kind of juice before.

9. Ricardo (steal, stole) second base.

10. After we (did, done) our work, we went skating at the rink in the park.

Using the Progressive Form of Verbs

The *progressive* is the *-ing* form of the verb plus a form of *be*. If you have spelling problems when adding *-ing* to the present form, use the rules given in Chapter 23 which is about vocabulary and spelling skills. You may also use a dictionary which provides the spelling of the various forms with the present form in the main entry.

The progressive form can be used in all six tenses. Form the progressive for each tense by using the correct tense of the verb *be* with the *-ing* verb.

Progressive Form of Present Tense
(*present tense of* be + -ing *verb*)

I am seeing	we are seeing
you are seeing	you are seeing
he she it } is seeing	they are seeing

Progressive Form of Past Tense
(*past tense of* be + -ing *verb*)

I was seeing	we were seeing
you were seeing	you were seeing
he she it } was seeing	they were seeing

Progressive Form of Future Tense
(shall/will + be + -ing *verb*)

I shall/will be seeing	we shall/will be seeing
you will be seeing	you will be seeing
he she it } will be seeing	they will be seeing

Progressive Form of Present Perfect Tense
(have *or* has + been + -ing *verb*)

I have been seeing	we have been seeing
you have been seeing	you have been seeing
he she } has been seeing it	they have been seeing

Progressive Form of Past Perfect Tense
(had + been + -ing *verb*)

I had been seeing	we had been seeing
you had been seeing	you had been seeing
he she } had been seeing it	they had been seeing

Progressive Form of Future Perfect Tense
(shall/will + have been + -ing *verb*)

I shall/will have been seeing	we shall/will have been seeing
you will have been seeing	you will have been seeing
he she } will have been seeing it	they will have been seeing

Exercise 10: *Using the Progressive Verb Forms*

Rewrite each of the following sentences and change the progressive form of the verb to the tense given in parentheses. Underline the verbs you form.

Examples

---

a. We students are dreaming about the high school. (future progressive)

We students <u>will be dreaming</u> about the high school.

b. Bobby and Carol were dancing both fast and slowly, depending upon the music. (past perfect progressive)
Bobby and Carol had been dancing both fast and slowly, depending upon the music.

1. The students in band are practicing every day. (past progressive)

2. Each year the women were sewing a quilt. (past perfect progressive)

3. The cars are turning that corner at dangerous speeds. (future perfect progressive)

4. In time with the music, we had been skating around the rink. (present perfect progressive)

5. The two new teachers will be grading compositions. (past progressive)

6. The shipwrecked sailors will be praying for land. (present progressive)

7. The pirates are burying the treasure. (future progressive)

8. On Memorial Day the veterans were parading in memory of their fallen comrades. (past perfect progressive)

9. Mom and Dad have been hurrying us off to school. (past progressive)

10. The fruit growers had been spraying their trees. (future progressive)

Making Verbs Agree

A verb must agree with its subject.

Verbs and their subjects can both be singular or plural. When a subject is singular, its verb must also be singular.

The boy walks his dog.	[singular subject, singular verb]
The elephant curls its trunk.	[singular subject, singular verb]

When a subject is plural, its verb must also be plural. Most verbs drop the *-s* ending to form the plural.

The <u>girls</u> <u>hang</u> the posters.	[plural subject, plural verb]
The <u>oranges</u> <u>are</u> fresh.	[plural subject, plural verb]

Exercise 11: *Making Verbs Agree with Subjects*

Rewrite each of the following sentences so that its subject is the noun given in parentheses. Without changing verb tense, change the form of the verb to agree with its subject. It may not be necessary to change the form of some verbs. Underline the verbs in the sentences you write.

Examples

    a. My three brothers play in the school band. (brother)
       My brother <u>plays</u> in the school band.

    b. The scientist has developed a new vaccine. (scientists)
       The scientists <u>have developed</u> a new vaccine.

1. The stones weigh several hundred kilos. (stone)

2. The whale appears off the coast of Long Beach in southern California. (whales)

3. My sister has figure skated in national competitions for several years. (sisters)

4. In springtime the farmer plows the fields. (farmers)

5. The crows circle the field of newly planted corn. (crow)

6. Have the students conquered verbs yet? (student)

7. Frightened and hungry, the boy wandered away from camp. (boys)

8. The police officers pry open the door. (police officer)

9. Now the campers will ford the stream to reach the supplies on the other side. (camper)

10. Had the guard already approached the gate before you called? (guards)

Problems in Agreement

Agreement of a verb with its subject is not changed by a phrase following the subject.

The <u>potholes</u> in the highway <u>cause</u> many accidents.

A <u>movie</u> about encounters with Martian space travelers <u>has opened</u> at our local theater.

Exercise 12: Making Subjects and Verbs Agree

Write the following sentences and choose the form of the verb given in parentheses that agrees with the subject in each sentence. Underline the subject once and the chosen verb form twice.

Example

a. The workers at a nearby plant (belongs, belong) to my union.

The <u>workers</u> at a nearby plant <u>belong</u> to my union.

1. An announcement about our services (bring, brings) in more business.

2. The mailboxes on the mall (has, have) an early pickup.

3. The snow on the fields (is, are) deep.

4. The shelf of glasses (were, was) falling down.

5. The boy in the front of the row (takes, take) attendance.

6. The light over the double doors (shine, shines) brightly.

7. Sometimes shadows in the dark of night (does, do) play tricks on you.

8. Theodore's pictures of the party (show, shows) how much fun we had.

9. The last carton of strawberries (have, has) not ripened.

10. The final exam in my hardest classes (falls, fall) on Monday.

When indefinite pronouns are used as subjects of sentences, their verbs must agree with them.

Singular Indefinite Pronouns		Plural Indefinite Pronouns	
each	either	both	few
one	neither	many	several
no one	everyone		
nobody	everybody		
anyone	someone		
anybody	somebody		

Everyone <u>likes</u> clean air.	[each single person likes]
No one in our town <u>likes</u> smog.	[not one single person likes]

Exercise 13: Making Indefinite Pronoun Subjects and Verbs Agree

Write the following sentences and choose the form of the verb given in parentheses that agrees with the subject in each sentence. Underline the subject once and the verb twice. Read the examples before you begin.

Examples

    a. Each of the cars (get, gets) good mileage.
       <u>Each</u> of the cars <u>gets</u> good mileage.

    b. All of us (was, were) late.
       <u>All</u> of us <u>were</u> late.

1. Somebody always (spoil, spoils) our fun.

2. Neither of the jockeys (have, has) finished first before.

3. Both of my sisters (likes, like) pizza with pepperoni.

4. Anybody with headphones (listen, listens) in privacy.

5. Several of the members (was, were) absent.

6. Nobody from our neighborhood (has, have) a fireplace.

7. Either of the dogs (receives, receive) the ribbon.

8. Many of the fans (was, were) in the stadium.

9. One of the winners (sits, sit) next to me on the bus.

10. Everybody in the long line (grow, grows) angrier by the minute.

The indefinite pronouns *all, any, most, none,* and *some* cause special agreement problems. These words can be either singular or plural, depending on the "sense" of the sentence.

If the pronoun refers to one person or thing, it is singular and takes a singular verb. If it refers to more than one person or thing, it is plural and takes a plural verb.

Some of the liquid remains in the filter.	[singular]
Some of the windows remain broken.	[plural]
Most of the lake measures over twenty meters in depth.	[singular]
Most of the lakes measure over twenty meters in depth.	[plural]

When *there* or *here* is used to begin a sentence, the subject will appear after the verb in the sentence. The subject and verb must still agree.

There are five cars in line.	[plural]
There is no milk left.	[singular]
Here is the book you wanted.	[singular]
Here are the winners of the game.	[plural]

Exercise 14: *Making Subjects and Verbs Agree*

Write the sentences on the next page and choose the form of the verb given in parentheses that agrees with the subject in each sentence. Underline the subject once and the verb form twice.

Examples

a. Part of this textbook (reads, read) like a novel.
   Part of this textbook reads like a novel.

b. Here (is, are) the keys that I lost.
   Here are the keys that I lost.

1. Some of the streets (has, have) streetlights.

2. None of the oranges we brought with us (have, has) been eaten yet.

3. (Is, Are) all of your interest in planes?

4. There (was, were) no clean towels left.

5. (Do, Does) any of those books have my name on them?

6. Most of my jewelry (come, comes) from my grandmother.

7. Part of the textbooks (has turned, have turned) brown with age.

8. Here (is, are) the title of the poem I need.

9. (Was, Were) there no fishing allowed on the bridges?

10. Some of the excitement of the circus acts (were produced, was produced) by the clowns.

Agreement with Compound Subjects and Collective Nouns

Subjects joined by _and_ take a plural verb.

Karen and Pedro were going on a hike.

The newspapers and the magazines appear to be recent.

Singular subjects joined by _or_ or _nor_ take a singular verb.

A tablet or a spiral notebook is good enough.

Neither Jack nor Carol stands a chance of winning.

When a singular subject and a plural subject are joined by *or* or *nor*, the verb agrees with the nearer subject.

Neither John nor the boys practice often.	[plural]
Either the boys or John practices every day.	[singular]

Collective nouns can take either singular or plural verbs.

If they refer to a group as a unit, they are singular. If they refer to the individual members of a group, they are plural.

The family is going on vacation.	[singular]
The family are packing their suitcases.	[plural]

Exercise 15: Making Verbs Agree with Compound Subjects or Collective Noun Subjects

Write the following sentences and choose the verb form given in parentheses that agrees with the subject of each sentence. Underline the subject once and the verb twice.

Examples

a. Sharon, Jamie, and Ken (plays, play) in the school band.
   Sharon, Jamie, and Ken play in the school band.

b. Neither the players nor the coach (has, have) the score.
   Neither the players nor the coach has the score.

1. Neither Mr. Rossi nor his children (drives, drive) the car.

2. The bowls, plates, cups and saucers (was, were) lined up on the counter.

3. (Has, Have) the jackets or sweaters come?

4. Neither the speakers nor the microphone (was, were) working.

5. Margo and her entire group of friends (yell, yells) cheers at the game.

6. After careful deliberation, the jury (give, gives) its verdict at the end of the trial.

7. The jury (was, were) from many different parts of the city.

8. A homemade card or flowers (is, are) a good Mother's Day gift.

9. The class (vote, votes) on its officers tomorrow.

10. A road atlas or a state map (is, are) what we need now.

Verbs Often Confused

Lie/Lay

The verb *lie* means "to recline" or "to remain lying down." This verb can be used to describe a person who is relaxing or an object that has been placed to rest.

Principal Parts		
Present	*Past*	*Past Participle*
lie	lay	(have) lain

Robert lies on a hammock in the yard.	[present tense]
The books lie on the table.	[present tense]
Yesterday Robert lay on the hammock.	[past tense]
Yesterday the books lay on the table.	[past tense]
Since noon Robert has lain on the hammock.	[present perfect]
Since noon the books have lain on the table.	[present perfect]

The verb *lay* means "to put or place something down." In using this verb, state the object that is being put or placed down.

Principal Parts		
Present	*Past*	*Past Participle*
lay	laid	(have) laid

The constitution lays the framework for democracy.	[present]
The guests lay their coats on the chair.	[present]
The constitution laid the framework for democracy.	[past]
The guests laid their coats on the chair.	[past]
The constitution has laid the framework for democracy.	[present perfect]
The guests have laid their coats on the chair.	[present perfect]

Exercise 16: Choosing The Proper Form of Lie or Lay

Write the sentences on the following page and choose the proper form of the verb *lie* or *lay* from those given in parentheses. Underline the subject once and the chosen verb form twice.

Examples

a. Each afternoon I (lie, lay) down for a nap.
   Each afternoon I lie down for a nap.

b. The workers already had (lain, laid) down their tools.
   The workers already had laid down their tools.

1. These books from the library have (lain, laid) here for one solid week.

2. The answer to our problem (lies, lays) in our willingness to work hard.

3. Joan could not remember where she (lay, laid) the missing keys.

4. Cats often (lie, lay) in strange places, such as the tops of refrigerators or on mantles.

5. After jogging all afternoon, the members of the team (lay, laid) down for a well-deserved rest.

6. Someone has (lain, laid) the basket in the middle of the floor for a special reason.

7. The manager of the hardware store had (lain, laid) in bed for several weeks recovering from an illness.

8. The workers (laid, lay) the stone for the Watson's new patio yesterday.

9. The defense attorney carefully (lay, laid) the foundation for the accused person's defense.

10. Before them, in the wilderness, (laid, lay) miles and miles of swamp.

Sit/Set

The verb *sit* means "to rest" or "to sit down," or "to remain undisturbed."

Principal Parts

Present	Past	Past Participle
sit	sat	(have) sat

Carmen *sits* at the very first desk.	[present]
The beagles *sit* obediently for a treat.	[present]
The town *sits* in the valley.	[present]
Carmen *sat* at the very first desk.	[past]
The beagles *sat* obediently for a treat.	[past]
The town *sat* in the valley.	[past]

Carmen *has sat* at the first desk all morning.   [present perfect]

The beagles *have sat* obediently for a treat.   [present perfect]

The town *has sat* in the valley.   [present perfect]

The verb *set* means "to put something" or "to place something." In using this verb, state the object that is being put or placed.

Principal Parts		
Present	***Past***	***Past Participle***
set	set	(have) set

We *set* the oven at 175° Celsius.	[present]
Marsha *sets* the music on the piano.	[present]
We *set* the oven at 175° Celsius.	[past]
Marsha *set* the music on the piano.	[past]
We *have set* the oven at 175° Celsius.	[present perfect]
Marsha *has set* the music on the piano.	[present perfect]

Exercise 17: *Choosing the Proper Form of* Sit *or* Set

Write the following sentences and choose the proper form of *sit* or *set* given in parentheses. Underline the verb form that you choose.

Examples

    a. I think I will (sit, set) down and rest.
       I think I will <u>sit</u> down and rest.

    b. George (sat, set) down his books and rested.
       George <u>set</u> down his books and rested.

1. The people in the darkened theater (set, sat) entranced as spaceships shot across the screen.

2. On a high, lonely mountain peak in western Colorado (sits, sets) a monument to early pioneers who worked so hard to settle in the West.

3. (Sit, Set) the delicate crystal down carefully; it can be easily broken.

4. Members of the House of Windsor have (sat, set) on the British throne for many years.

5. Will I be able to (set, sit) the table before you begin studying?

6. For many hours the panther had (set, sat) in the tree, waiting for its prey to pass.

7. Stars in a constellation look as though each has been (set, sat) carefully in place.

8. (Set, Sat) your watch carefully so we can meet at the correct time.

9. In the nursery rhyme, Humpty Dumpty (sat, set) on a great wall.

10. The new pilot (sat, set) the plane down exactly as he had been instructed.

Rise/Raise

The verb *rise* means "to get up," "to go up," or "to arise." *Rise* describes the motion of someone or something that is going up.

Principal Parts		
Present	*Past*	*Past Participle*
rise	rose	(have) risen

The sound level *rises* at the end of the performance.	[present]
The children *rise* late on Saturdays.	[present]
The sound level *rose* at the end of the performance.	[past]
The children *rose* late on Saturday.	[past]

| The sound level *has risen* at the end of the performance. | [present perfect] |
| The children *have risen* late on Saturdays. | [present perfect] |

The verb *raise* means "to lift up," "to force up," or "to bring up." In using this verb, state the object that is being lifted, forced up, or brought up.

Principal Parts

Present	*Past*	*Past Participle*
raise	raised	(have) raised

The champion *raises* the flag in victory.	[present]
High winds *raise* clouds of dust.	[present]
The champion *raised* the flag in victory.	[past]
High winds *raised* clouds of dust.	[past]
The champion *has raised* the flag in victory.	[present perfect]
High winds *have raised* clouds of dust.	[present perfect]

Exercise 18: Choosing the Proper Form of Rise or Raise

Write the following sentences and choose the proper form of *rise* or *raise* from those given in parentheses. Underline the verb form you choose.

Examples

    a. Yeast is what causes the dough to (rise, raise).
       Yeast is what causes the dough to <u>rise</u>.

    b. The early returns (rose, raised) our hopes for victory.
       The early returns <u>raised</u> our hopes for victory.

1. When the barometer (rises, raises), good weather is usually ahead.

2. Juan's good grade on the test (rose, raised) his hopes for a good grade in the course.

3. I doubt your temperature would have (raised, risen) so high if you had taken aspirin.

4. In the book *Where the Red Fern Grows,* a young boy (rises, raises) two hound pups.

5. I'll (raise, rise) the window if you'll turn down the heat in this room.

6. Before the trial is over, the prosecutor will have (raised, risen) a record number of objections.

7. Your favorable comments have caused my interest in the book to (raise, rise).

8. We awakened early, long before the sun had (risen, raised).

9. The expression "Surf's Up!" means the surf has (risen, raised) to a good level.

10. I don't mean to (rise, raise) doubts in your mind, but do you really think this will work?

Review: Using Verbs

Write the following sentences and change the verb to the tense given in parentheses. Underline the verb you form.

Examples

a. She is a police officer. (past)
   She was a police officer.

b. The students went to the museum. (present perfect)
   The students have gone to the museum.

1. The letter carriers deliver the mail in the morning. (future)

2. The tree will have grown three feet a year. (past perfect)

3. My grandfather believes in the value of hard work. (past)

4. Our company built the new bridge. (future)

5. We had talked half the night. (future perfect)

6. Our dog ate my slipper. (past perfect)

7. Soon Ms. Lewis will announce the winners of the contest. (future perfect)

8. Mother and Grandmother hurried to get ready. (present)

9. Bob and JoAnn will have given their reports. (present perfect)

10. Ramona has known about Michael's party for two weeks. (past)

Write the following sentences and choose the verb form given in parentheses that agrees with the subject. Underline the subject once and the verb form twice.

Examples

a. The firefighter (break, breaks) down the door.
   The firefighter breaks down the door.

b. Many of the babies (was, were) crying.
   Many of the babies were crying.

11. All of the clues (show, shows) that the speckled band is a highly poisonous snake.

12. Most of the endangered animals in this country (remain, remains) under special protection.

13. When a movie is really good, some of the people in the audience (stay, stays) until the lights come on.

14. All of the books on this shelf (need, needs) dusting even though they're new.

15. Most of the uses George Washington Carver found for the peanut (was, were) practical ones.

16. All of the cream (is, are) sour.

17. *Where the Red Fern Grows* and *The Yearling* (is, are) two of my favorite books.

18. The class (has, have) been approved for a field trip to the National Air and Space Museum in Washington, D.C.

19. A science fiction movie or a mystery movie (give, gives) me the greatest pleasure.

20. Recycling and conservation (is, are) two good habits to practice.

Writing Focus: *Using Vivid Verbs in Writing*

You can improve your writing by including vivid verbs to *show* action precisely and clearly. Let the subject of your sentence *giggle, chortle, hoot,* or *chuckle* rather than *laugh.* Avoid overusing such dull verbs as *is, are, was, do, does, have, has,* and *make.*

Assignment: *Oops!*

Notice the photograph on page 347. Imagine that you can enter the photo and be part of the continuing action. You're now the bucking bull rider, suspended in air between the bull's back and the ground. You're aware of everything around you—sounds, smells, sights—and within you—muscles, heartbeat, breath. Your ride has been incredible!

Write one or more well-developed paragraphs telling about your ride as though you are on it—now! What happens to make you fall? Use words to paint a picture of the action-packed ride for your audience of classmates. Your writing will be evaluated for correct and effective use of verbs.

Use the following steps to complete this assignment.

A. Prewriting

Study the photograph carefully. Use your imagination to enter the picture. Pretend you are the rider, falling off the bucking bull. Free write, described in Chapter 1, about what you're experiencing: what you see, what you hear, what you feel, what you think, what you do. Concentrate on the details of the action, and don't worry about putting them down correctly. Just let your imagination help you create the experience. Reread your free writing and underline the words, phrases, and sentences that best describe the action and convey your experience. Number them in the order that shows what happens.

B. Writing

Using your free writing to help you, write one or more paragraphs telling about your exciting, action-packed ride. Start

your account by setting the scene. Then create a moving picture of what happens before, during, and after the photo was taken. Consider using the present tense of verbs to help you relate the experience as if it were happening *now*. Be certain to use vivid, specific verbs to depict the action.

C. Postwriting

Revise your first draft using the following checklist.

1. Does my account include enough specific details so that readers can experience my ride with me?

2. Do I use vivid verbs to convey a clear picture of the action?

3. Is each verb in the proper tense, and does it agree in number with the subject?

Edit your work using the Checklist for Proofreading in the back of the book. If appropriate, share your writing with your classmates to enjoy each other's "rides."

15 Adjectives

Understanding Adjectives

Adjectives are words that describe and modify. They make what you say and write more interesting for others. You can use several ways to identify adjectives: their definition, their division into classes, and those features that distinguish them from other parts of speech. In this section you will study and practice each of these methods.

Defining an Adjective

Adjectives are usually defined as words that modify nouns and pronouns.

Carla collects *old* photographs of *famous* people.

The *scrawny, lost* dog searched for scraps of food.

We were *enthusiastic* about our team winning.

Adjectives answer the questions *what kind? which one?* or *how many?* about the words they modify.

rare coins	[What kind of coins?]
those coins	[Which coins?]
thirteen coins	[How many coins?]

Exercise 1: Identifying Adjectives

Write the following sentences and underline the adjectives used to modify nouns and pronouns. Draw an arrow from the adjective to the word modified. Your teacher may ask you which question the adjective answers. (Do not count *a, an,* and *the.*)

Examples

    a. The small, ambitious children tried to pull the heavy box up the stairs.

    The small, ambitious children tried to pull the heavy box up the stairs.

    b. We decorated the house with colorful balloons; they were green, yellow, orange, and blue.

    We decorated the house with colorful balloons; they were green, yellow, orange, and blue.

1. The autumn leaves fell to the ground; they were brown and crisp.

2. The crepe paper decorated the festive room for the birthday party.

3. The weary travelers waited in the crowded airport during the winter storm.

4. The clear sky tonight predicts good weather tomorrow for the game.

5. We were proud of the basketball team when they won.

6. The icy stream felt good on our tired feet after we hiked halfway up the trail.

7. The brisk wind blew the powdery snow into high drifts around our house.

8. The police car zoomed across the high bridge to the scene of the terrible accident.

9. When Carolyn cleaned out the junk drawer in her desk, she found seven pennies, one diary, eight pictures, two pencils, and three odd buttons.

10. In the early morning the ocean is calm and peaceful; it becomes playful only when the people arrive.

Grouping Adjectives by Classes

There are five classes of adjectives: articles, proper adjectives, nouns used as adjectives, pronouns used as adjectives, and predicate adjectives. However, many adjectives do not belong to any special class.

Articles—*a*, *an*, and *the*—are the most frequently used adjectives in the English language.

The letter that granted *a* pardon arrived *an* hour too late to do any good.

A and *an* are used to modify singular nouns and pronouns. *An* is used when the word following *an* begins with a vowel sound.

The fluorescent light is *an* energy-saving device.

It was *an* honor to be invited.

Proper adjectives are proper nouns used as adjectives.

Some proper nouns change form to become adjectives. All proper nouns that become proper adjectives must be capitalized.

We visited the country of *Iceland.*	[proper noun]
We read several *Icelandic* newspapers while we were there.	[proper adjective]
Many treasure ships sank while returning to *Spain.*	[proper noun]
Treasure hunters today still find *Spanish* coins on the ocean floor.	[proper adjective]

Exercise 2: Identifying Proper Adjectives

Write the following sentences. Capitalize and underline any proper adjectives. Circle any other adjectives in the sentence.

Examples

a. The italian dinner consisted of spaghetti and french bread.

(The) Italian dinner consisted of spaghetti and French bread.

b. The beautiful chalets in the colorado mountains reflect swiss architecture.

(The) (beautiful) chalets in (the) Colorado mountains reflect Swiss architecture.

1. The french newspaper reported the story of a courageous lifeguard who saved an injured swimmer from drowning last week.

2. We admired the ageless star who had had the title role in so many italian movies.

3. Both an american museum and an israeli museum wanted to keep a statue that had been dug up from an ancient ruin.

4. Maggie and Emma rented rooms in a spanish villa, but it was a noisy house.

5. The original painting by the dutch artist is in a european museum.

6. I ate so much delicious food at the chinese restaurant that I'm a lucky person not to have a stomachache.

7. Some mexican food has a spicy flavor, so be a careful eater.

8. The team of doctors treated the exhausted explorer who had caught a tropical disease while traveling in the brazilian jungle.

9. Our egyptian guides had a great deal of national pride about their ancient monuments.

10. Although fashions change, irish sweaters and english trench coats are timeless classics.

Common nouns used as adjectives modify other nouns or pronouns.

Summer is my favorite season.	[noun]
Our *summer* vacation was much too short.	[adjective]
Our girls' volleyball team made the *play-offs*.	[noun]
The *play-off* game was scheduled for Friday.	[adjective]
We could see an *animal* running through the woods.	[noun]
We could see an *animal* trainer through a hole in the tent.	[adjective]

Exercise 3: Identifying Nouns Used as Adjectives

Write the following sentences. Underline every common noun that acts as an adjective in these sentences and draw a circle around every other adjective.

Examples

a. We lugged an old kitchen table down the basement stairs.

We lugged (an) (old) kitchen table down (the) basement stairs.

b. Carol is the best woman skier on the Vermont team.

Carol is (the) (best) woman skier on (the) (Vermont) team.

1. Lois stored her wedding presents in the hall closet.

2. On the first cool September day, Carla packed summer clothes away in the attic closet.

3. On cold winter evenings we like to drink hot apple cider.

4. The new breakfast dishes are in the kitchen cabinet over the sink.

5. The painting of a dairy cow won first prize in the school show.

6. The afternoon matinee is the least crowded of the dance performances.

7. The museum guard stood near the entrance to the sculpture gallery.

8. You must get a permit from the town police if you want to have a fire at a beach party.

9. Madelaine ordered a roast beef sandwich, but Juanita wanted only a tomato salad and a Florida orange.

10. A morning swim in the icy Maine ocean will definitely wake you up and get you moving.

Pronouns used as adjectives modify nouns or pronouns.

Demonstrative pronouns (*this, that, these,* and *those*) act as adjectives when they modify a noun or pronoun.

This will be perfect for the party.	[pronoun]
This dress will be perfect for the party.	[adjective]
Grandmother gave me *these* for my report.	[pronoun]
Grandmother gave me *these* pictures for my report.	[adjective]

The interrogative pronouns *which* and *what* act as adjectives when they modify a noun or pronoun.

Which is the safest form of transportation?	[pronoun]
Which flight will you be taking?	[adjective]
What is your new address?	[pronoun]
What number did you call?	[adjective]

Indefinite pronouns can sometimes act as adjectives if they modify a noun or pronoun.

Both of the boys had thought about the idea.	[pronoun]
Both boys had given the idea *some* thought.	[adjective]

One of the cherished beliefs is that people
should be free.   [pronoun]

One cherished belief is that *each* person
should be free.   [adjective]

Possessive pronouns (*my, your, his, her, its, our,* and *their*)
are pronouns that act as adjectives to modify nouns.

Bob put *his* suitcase in the trunk.

The seat belt is there for *your* safety.

The plane had trouble with *its* engine before takeoff.

We made *our* reservations for the late night flight.

Exercise 4: Identifying Pronouns Used as Adjectives

Write the following sentences. Underline every pronoun that
acts as an adjective and draw an arrow from each pronoun
adjective to the noun or pronoun it modifies.

Examples

---

a. One of the many benefits of solar energy is its safety.

One of the <u>many</u> benefits of solar energy is <u>its</u> safety.

b. Few people have given this idea much thought.

<u>Few</u> people have given <u>this</u> idea <u>much</u> thought.

1. Both girls wanted that part in the play.

2. Neither dog gave a good performance at that kennel
   show, so neither had any chance of winning.

3. Driving at this speed will give us several extra miles from
   each tank of gas.

4. I know which car you want, but this car is a better buy
   than that one is.

5. Hector has run in several marathons, but this is the most difficult of any race he has entered.

6. What are you afraid of? If you keep the car windows shut, some animals might come near, but none will do you any harm.

7. Listen to what Anita says because she knows which trails are easy and which have several hairpin turns.

8. Each of those campers has a sleeping bag, but some campers don't have any cooking utensils.

9. Pat knows this teacher and took one of his classes one semester last year.

10. Each of these recipes is easy, but this one is easier to follow than that one.

Predicate adjectives follow a linking verb and describe or modify the subject of the sentence.

The entire meal tasted *delicious*.

An Australian kangaroo can be *playful* or *vicious*.

They have been *helpful* to us in the past.

She was *confident* about her chances of winning.

Exercise 5: *Identifying Predicate Adjectives*

All of the sentences on the following page have linking verbs. Write each sentence and underline each predicate adjective. Draw an arrow from each predicate adjective to the noun or pronoun it modifies.

Examples

---

a. Your voice sounds strange over the telephone.

Your voice sounds <u>strange</u> over the telephone.

b. This model is available but very expensive.

This model is <u>available</u> but very <u>expensive</u>.

1. The milk in this pitcher tastes sour.

2. Bring a warm coat because San Francisco is sometimes chilly.

3. It is an adorable kitten, and I know it is friendly.

4. Vanilla has a wonderful smell, but it doesn't taste good.

5. Japanese food looks beautiful on the table.

6. Dune grass is pretty and also useful because it helps keep the beach from eroding.

7. Just before the storm the warm summer air seemed still and muggy.

8. That professor has lived all over the world, and his stories are wonderful.

9. The lily of the valley smells sweet, but make sure no one eats it, for it is poisonous.

10. This assignment seems difficult, but it is really easier than the one you already did.

Finding Adjectives by Their Features

Two features can help you identify adjectives: degrees of comparison and suffixes. Most adjectives have at least one of these features.

Adjectives may change form to show degrees of comparison.

Adjectives have three degrees for comparison: *positive, comparative,* and *superlative.*

Positive (describes one noun)	Comparative (compares two nouns)	Superlative (compares three or more nouns)
old	older	oldest
pretty	prettier	prettiest
smart	smarter	smartest

Terry is a *fast* runner.	[positive]
Ralph is a *faster* runner than Terry.	[comparative]
Jesse is the *fastest* runner in the class.	[superlative]

The regular way to form the comparative and superlative forms is to add *-er* and *-est* to the end of the adjective. Sometimes there will be a slight spelling change: pretty, prett*ier*, prett*iest*.

Many two-syllable adjectives and all adjectives that have three or more syllables form their comparative degree with *more* and their superlative degree with *most*.

Positive	Comparative	Superlative
helpful	more helpful	most helpful
thorough	more thorough	most thorough
horrible	more horrible	most horrible
important	more important	most important

Some adjectives have irregular comparative and superlative forms.

Positive	Comparative	Superlative
good	better	best
bad	worse	worst
much, many	more	most

Kiyo has a *good* voice.	[positive]
Jessica has a *better* voice than Kiyo.	[comparative]
Molly has the *best* voice in the chorus.	[superlative]

Exercise 6: Identifying Comparative Forms of Adjectives

Write the sentences on the following page and underline the adjectives that show one of the three forms of comparison.

Label the adjectives *P* for positive, *C* for comparative, and *S* for superlative.

Examples

a. The young attorney presented a more convincing case than the older attorney.

The <u>young</u> attorney presented a <u>more convincing</u> case
    P   C

than the <u>older</u> attorney.
       C

b. The shortest boy on the team made the most foul shots.

The <u>shortest</u> boy on the team made the <u>most</u> foul shots.
   S   S

1. Three jugglers, who had the funniest act in the carnival, drew a larger crowd than the lion tamer did.

2. The most popular site for tourists in the United States is the beautiful Grand Canyon.

3. We wanted to travel the closest way to Los Angeles, so we planned a special route.

4. A healthful diet and regular exercise contribute to good health.

5. If you're going to eat cookies, it is a better idea to eat two cookies than to eat ten cookies.

6. Of the many beautiful sights we had seen on our vacation, the Golden Gate Bridge in San Francisco was the most beautiful of all.

7. A folk superstition predicts that if bears have thick coats of fur, a snowy winter lies ahead.

8. The tropical sun can give you a serious burn, so be sure to spend a shorter amount of time on the beach than you usually do.

9. The small family farm in the low valley next to us grows the best corn and soybeans in the entire state of New Jersey.

10. The largest volcano that ever erupted was on the Greek island of Thera.

Adjectives may be formed with suffixes.

The following list gives the most often used adjective suffixes:

Noun	+	*Suffix*	=	*Adjective*
coast	+	-al	=	*coastal* resort
fool	+	-ish	=	*foolish* idea
thought	+	-less	=	*thoughtless* comment
life	+	-like	=	*lifelike* statue
danger	+	-ous	=	*dangerous* mission
wind	+	-y	=	*windy* day

Exercise 7: Identifying Adjectives Formed with Suffixes

Write the following sentences and underline the adjectives that are formed with suffixes.

Examples

a. His thankless attitude was very rude.
His <u>thankless</u> attitude was very rude.

b. The poisonous substance is considered dangerous to everyone.
The <u>poisonous</u> substance is considered <u>dangerous</u> to everyone.

1. Six cats and four dogs are a ridiculous number of pets.
2. Leo has a boyish charm.
3. The President is often called upon to be a gracious host.
4. Raw vegetables are beneficial to one's health.
5. Jennifer quickly found a job with a large international firm because she spoke three foreign languages.
6. These vegetables are tasteless, but those are crunchy and good.
7. Candidates for positions as astronauts must survive long, rigorous training.
8. The Roths lived in a small city apartment during the winter, but they also had a luxurious summer house at a New England beach.

9. The characters in this story are so lifelike that they almost breathe.

10. Four trendy French designers spoke to the freshman class.

Review: Understanding Adjectives

Write the following sentences and underline each adjective. Your teacher may ask you if the adjective belongs to one of the five classes: articles, proper nouns as adjectives, common nouns as adjectives, pronouns as adjectives, and predicate adjectives.

Examples

a. Tiny, jagged cracks had appeared throughout the huge steel pipeline.
   <u>Tiny, jagged</u> cracks had appeared throughout <u>the</u> <u>huge</u> <u>steel</u> pipeline.

b. The five English students who attended the American university returned home on a German jumbo jet.
   <u>The</u> <u>five</u> <u>English</u> students who attended <u>the</u> <u>American</u> university returned home on <u>a</u> <u>German</u> <u>jumbo</u> jet.

1. A high-speed elevator carried the excited passengers to the top of the new, towering skyscraper.

2. Old, creaky floors and broken, rattling windows gave the run-down Victorian house a reputation for being scary.

3. During the exciting last quarter of the championship game, loyal, cheering fans almost ran onto the court.

4. Schools of tiny, sparkling fish filled the water.

5. The four American students lived in a small, quiet village not far from Paris.

6. A large, laughing crowd watched one playful seal perform tricks and then applaud itself.

7. An ornate ceramic pot was filled with an exotic red plant that gave off a heavy, sweet aroma.

8. The energetic, young coach promised to shape the nine inexperienced players into a powerful winning volleyball team.

9. Saint Augustine, Florida, is an old American city, and many historic buildings line the warm, tree-shaded streets.

10. Both small children watched while the awkward, young colt stood up and tried to support itself on four wobbly, thin legs.

Write the following sentences and underline each adjective. Your teacher may ask you how you identified each of the adjectives.

Example

a. Cinderella was happier than her stepsisters.
Cinderella was <u>happier</u> than <u>her</u> stepsisters.

11. Do you believe in the fairy tales they told us when we were young and childlike?

12. This curious story tells about a lady and seven dwarfs.

13. Goldilocks should have been careful about those bears.

14. She was foolish not to know that it is dangerous to bother bears.

15. The names of those dwarfs are humorous.

16. One bowl was smaller than the other bowl.

17. The big bad wolf pops up in a few stories and does ridiculous things.

18. Miss Red Riding Hood had her problems with the wolf, but Goldilocks was careless with the bears.

19. Who was clever—Miss Riding Hood or the wolf?

20. Grandma had bad luck; also, she had a weighty problem.

Applying What You Know

In the following selection about moon exploration from Arthur C. Clarke's story "The Sentinel," there are twenty-four adjectives. Please list each adjective on a sheet of paper numbered 1–24. Your teacher may ask you how you identified each adjective. (Hint: *Half a dozen* is one adjective.)

We had begun our journey early in the slow lunar dawn, and still had almost a week of earth time before nightfall. Half a dozen times a day we would leave our vehicle and go outside in the space suits to hunt for interesting minerals, or to place markers for the guidance of future travelers. It was an uneventful routine. There is nothing hazardous or even particularly exciting about lunar exploration. We could live comfortably for a month in our pressurized tractors, and if we ran into trouble we could always radio for help and sit tight until one of the spaceships came to our rescue.[1]

Using Adjectives

Using Comparative and Superlative Forms

There are three ways in which adjectives change to show the comparative and superlative degree:

1. with -er or -est added to the positive form.

2. with the words more and most before the positive form.

3. with irregular forms that are completely different from the positive form.

Using -er and -est to Form Degrees of Comparison

The suffixes -er and -est form the comparative and superlative degrees of most one-syllable adjectives.

Positive	Comparative	Superlative
high	higher	highest
strong	stronger	strongest
fresh	fresher	freshest

[1]From "The Sentinel" by Arthur C. Clarke. Reprinted by permission of the author and the author's agents, Scott Meredith Literary Agency, Inc., 845 Third Avenue, New York, New York 10022.

If the positive degree ends in the letter *y*, change the *y* to *i* before adding *-er* or *-est*.

Positive	Comparative	Superlative
pretty	prettier	prettiest
healthy	healthier	healthiest
salty	saltier	saltiest

If the positive degree ends in the letter *e*, drop the *e* before adding *-er* or *-est*.

Positive	Comparative	Superlative
noble	nobler	noblest
large	larger	largest
wide	wider	widest

If the positive degree ends in a single consonant preceded by a single vowel, double the final consonant before adding *-er* or *-est*.

Positive	Comparative	Superlative
fat	fatter	fattest
dim	dimmer	dimmest
wet	wetter	wettest

Exercise 8: *Using* -er *and* -est *with Adjectives to Show Comparison*

Write the sentences on the following page and supply the correct form of the adjective given in parentheses. Underline the adjective form you choose.

Example

a. Joan has _____ eyes than Jessica does. (blue)
   Joan has bluer eyes than Jessica does.

1. Gold is a _____ metal than silver. (heavy)

2. The Amazon is a _____ river than the Mississippi. (long)

3. The Nile is the _____ river in the world. (long)

4. The iron skillet is a _____ pot than the aluminum one. (big)

5. Grandmother's old soup pot is the _____ pot of all the ones in our kitchen. (big)

6. Of all the ways to walk between school and home, the straight path is the _____ route. (short)

7. Green olives have a _____ taste than black olives. (salty)

8. Angel Falls in Venezuela is the _____ waterfall in the world. (high)

9. A 20-watt bulb gives off a _____ light than a 75-watt bulb. (dim)

10. Lake Huron is a _____ (wide) lake than Lake Michigan, but Lake Superior is the _____ (large) lake of the five Great Lakes.

Using More and Most to Show Comparison

Many two-syllable adjectives and all adjectives that have three or more syllables form their comparative and superlative degree with *more* and *most*.

Positive	Comparative	Superlative
anxious	more anxious	most anxious
cheerful	more cheerful	most cheerful
terrible	more terrible	most terrible
difficult	more difficult	most difficult

To show lesser amounts instead of greater amounts, use the word *less* in the comparative degree and the word *least* in the superlative degree.

Positive	Comparative	Superlative
precise	less precise	least precise
honest	less honest	least honest
wealthy	less wealthy	least wealthy

Exercise 9: *Using* More, Most, Less *and* Least *to Show Comparison*

Write the following sentences and supply the comparative or superlative form of the adjective given in parentheses. Underline the adjective form you choose.

Examples

a. The pig is actually a _____ animal than the horse. (intelligent)

The pig is actually a <u>more intelligent</u> animal than the horse.

b. Sharon is constantly saying rude things to people. She is the _____ person I know. (polite)

Sharon is constantly saying rude things to people. She is the <u>least polite</u> person I know.

1. The exciting telecast of the astronauts landing on the moon was the _____ event I've ever watched on TV. (dramatic)

2. In general, a great white shark is a _____ fish than a sand shark, but all sharks are _____ fish as far as I am concerned. (dangerous)

3. Nothing unusual at all happened on our trip to Niagara Falls. The vacation was the _least_ trip we've ever taken. (eventful)

4. The unusual fish was the _____ one at the pet shop around the corner. (expensive)

5. The unusual Tasmanian devil was the _____ animal in the zoo. (peculiar)

6. Take the subway if you're in a hurry. It is a _____ means of transportation than the bus. (efficient)

7. Silver is less expensive than gold because gold is a _____ metal than silver. (precious)

8. Millions of people watch the Super Bowl, which is the _____ sports event of any on TV. (popular)

9. The pitcher was on guard, and the outfield moved back when Reggie came to bat. He is the _____ hitter on the team. (powerful)

10. Jake's business sense is so bad, he's the _____ shop-keeper in town. (successful)

Using Irregular Comparisons

A few adjectives change their form completely to show comparative and superlative degree.

Positive	Comparative	Superlative
good	better	best
bad	worse	worst
far	farther	farthest
many, much	more	most

Your artwork for the show is *good,* but Melissa's is even *better.*

I can eat *more* pizza than you can, but Janice eats the *most* pizza of anyone I know.

Tony lives *farther* away from school than his *best* friend Ricardo.

Last week's hurricane was the *worst* in five years.

Janet ran the *farthest* distance.

Exercise 10: *Forming Irregular Comparative and Superlative Adjectives*

Write the following sentences and supply the comparative or superlative form of the adjective given in parentheses. Underline the adjective form you choose.

Examples

a. This was a _____ game than the two teams played the last time they met. (good)

This was a <u>better</u> game than the two teams played the last time they met.

b. In the auditorium I want to sit in the seat _____ from the stage. (far)

In the auditorium I want to sit in the seat <u>farthest</u> from the stage.

1. This hurricane is the _____ storm of any in the last five years. (bad)

2. Hurricane Diane did a lot of damage, but Hurricane David destroyed even _____ homes. (many)

3. "Stay indoors" is the _____ advice of all to remember during a bad storm. (good)

4. Of the last seven hurricanes, this one did the _____ damage. (much)

5. My mother uses the more economical of our two cars because she drives _____ to work than my father. (far)

6. Orange juice is a good source of Vitamin C, but parsley is an even _____ source. (good)

7. Celery has _____ calories than water, but fewer than apples. (many)

8. The sun is the _____ source of energy we have. (good)

9. Because of all the cars and industry in the area, New York City has _____ air pollution than Philadelphia does. (bad)

10. Six tennis players entered the finals. They were all good players, but the finals would decide who was the _____ player in the group. (good)

Two adjectives that may cause trouble are *less* and *fewer*. Each word means "a smaller amount" of the noun it modifies.

The adjective *less* is used to modify singular nouns.

If panic occurs, there will be *less* gasoline for everyone.

I have *less* talent in music than he does.

The adjective *fewer* is used to modify plural nouns.

Less gasoline will mean that *fewer* people will be able to drive.

Marsha has *fewer* errors on her test than Audrey.

Exercise 11: Using Less and Fewer

Write the following sentences and supply either *less* or *fewer* in the space indicated. Underline the adjective you choose.

Examples

a. We had _____ time than we thought.
   We had <u>less</u> time than we thought.

b. We studied in the library because there would be _____ distractions there.
   We studied in the library because there would be <u>fewer</u> distractions there.

1. The city hall auditorium has _____ seats than the armory has.

2. Carmen's small book shop has _____ books than Blake's Book Supermarket.

3. The fan uses _____ electricity than the air conditioner.

4. My toy poodle eats _____ food than my boxer.

5. Cora's second typing test had _____ mistakes than her first one.

6. Her grandparents moved to a smaller apartment with _____ rooms than their house.

7. I wonder if the steam iron will stop leaking if I put _____ water in it.

8. Marc prefers living in the country to living in the city, but he has _____ friends in the country.

9. Mari bought a wood-burning stove to heat her house so she would use _____ heating oil.

10. Our new car uses _____ gasoline than our old one did, so we make _____ stops at gas stations.

Forming Adjectives with Suffixes

Adjectives may be formed by adding suffixes to other parts of speech such as nouns and verbs.

Noun	+	*Suffix*	=	*Adjective*
cloud	+	-y	=	*cloudy* morning
score	+	-less	=	*scoreless* inning
play	+	-ful	=	*playful* puppy
adventure	+	-ous	=	*adventurous* voyage
honor	+	-able	=	*honorable* judge
clown	+	-ish	=	*clownish* grin
coast	+	-al	=	*coastal* mountains
ghost	+	-like	=	*ghostlike* appearance
Verb	+	*Suffix*	=	*Adjective*
talk	+	-ing	=	*talking* doll
help	+	-ful	=	*helpful* guide
consider	+	-ate	=	*considerate* remark
train	+	-ed	=	*trained* musician
notice	+	-able	=	*noticeable* difference
view	+	-less	=	*viewless* window
rain	+	-y	=	*rainy* afternoon

Exercise 12: Using Adjectives Formed with Suffixes

By adding the suffixes in parentheses, form adjectives from the words on the next page. Write a sentence using each new word you form. Underline the adjective you form. (For some new words, there will be a slight spelling change. Check your dictionary for help in spelling the new word correctly.)

Examples

a. thought + (-ful)
   The road atlas was a <u>thoughtful</u> gift for our trip.
b. stretch + (-ing)
   <u>Stretching</u> exercises can help you wake up in the morning.

1. effort + (-less)
2. plan + (-ing)
3. measure + (-able)
4. fool + (-ish)
5. appoint + (-ed)

6. friend + (-ly)
7. sand + (-y)
8. envy + (-ous)
9. laugh + (-able)
10. comic + (-al)

Using Adjectives to Be Specific

Adjectives give specific qualities to nouns and pronouns, answering the questions *what kind? which one?* and *how many?*

The chair leaned against the wall.

The *tattered* chair leaned against the *velvet wallpapered* wall.

The *two Victorian* chairs leaned against the heavily *draped* wall.

Exercise 13: Using Adjectives to Be Specific

Write the following sentences. Fill in the blanks with an adjective of your own that answers the adjective question in parentheses. Underline the adjective you select.

Examples

a. Jeremy rode the bus to the _____ building. (Which one?)
   Jeremy rode the bus to the <u>YMCA</u> building.

b. On rainy days I like to read _____ books. (What kind?)
   On rainy days I like to read <u>mystery</u> books.

1. Gabriela's favorite cat had _____ kittens. (How many kittens?)

2. Julio's dog had _____ puppies. (What kind of puppies?)

3. The _____ player hurt his leg in the fourth quarter of the game. (Which player?)

4. Over the summer Paula had a _____ vacation. (What kind of vacation?)

5. The tower had _____ stairs leading to the top. (How many stairs?)

6. The _____ ending of the movie surprised everyone. (What kind of ending?)

7. The _____ building was in the center of town. (What building?)

8. Carmen drove the _____ car. (Which car?)

9. _____ sweaters are Allen's favorite type. (What kind of sweaters?)

10. Carla's team scored _____ runs in the first inning. (How many runs?)

Review: Using Adjectives

Write the sentences on the following two pages and supply the correct form of the adjective given in parentheses. Underline the adjective form you choose.

Examples

a. This is the _____ class of students that I have ever taught. (noisy)
   This is the <u>noisiest</u> class of students that I have ever taught.

b. Our school has fewer students than yours; consequently, we have _____ hallways than you do. (crowded)
   Our school has fewer students than yours; consequently, we have <u>less crowded</u> hallways than you do.

1. A chunk of gold discovered in 1869 is the _____ nugget ever found. (large)

2. Exercise is the _____ way I know to maintain a healthy body. (good)

3. Gold that is mixed with sand or gravel is an _____ ore for miners to reach than gold that is buried deep within the earth. (easy)

4. Earth is a _____ planet than Mercury, Venus, Mars, and Pluto. (big)

5. A Siamese cat is a _____ household pet than an ocelot. (common)

6. I'm going to wear my oldest pair of jeans to the birthday party tonight. They're the _____ pants I have. (comfortable)

7. Because the water is rough and there are no lifeguards, that section is the _____ part of the whole beach. (crowded)

8. Carlotta loves to paint, so membership in an art class is the _____ gift you could give her. (thoughtful)

9. The Regency Theater is a _____ walk than the Columbia Theater. (far)

10. The blue car was in the _____ condition of the three cars that were for sale. (bad)

11. The small shop that just opened had _____ dresses. (many) Unfortunately, I liked the _____ dress of all. (expensive)

12. Juan's cat is mean to everyone. It is the _____ cat of the three in the neighborhood. (friendly)

13. Hockey is a _____ sport than baseball. (rough)

14. Paul's restaurant always serves good food, but last night's dinner was a _____ meal than the one we had last week. (good)

15. The three bags of groceries are all heavy bundles, but that bag is the _____ package. (heavy)

16. Out of eight flavors of yogurt, we still think lemon is the _____ choice. (good)

17. For the last three weeks, Eleanor has had the _____ cold she has ever had. (bad)

18. I thought *Gone with the Wind* was the _____ (sad) book I had ever read, but I just read another book that tells an even _____ story. (sad)

19. Martha's father is always very serious about everything. I think he is the _____ person I know. (amusing)

20. A sheep dog is a _____ dog than a spaniel and consequently sheds more. (furry)

Writing Focus: *Using Fresh*

Adjectives in Writing

Fresh adjectives can give your writing life, color, and feeling by adding specific details of sight, smell, sound, taste, and touch. Too many adjectives, or overused ones such as *cute, super,* or *nice,* however, can deaden your writing. Use precise and effective adjectives consciously in your writing to make it interesting to the reader.

Assignment: *Designer Extraordinaire*

Imagine you can have all the money you want to create a perfect room for yourself. What will the new room be like? How will it be decorated? Will it have color television, stereo, electronic games, or other special features? How will it be similar to or different from your present room?

Think about the preceding questions, and write one or more paragraphs comparing your present room and your *perfect* room. Let the items you choose to write about describe both rooms and clearly show their similarities and differences. Write for the designer who will make the changes in the room. Your writing will be evaluated for correct and effective use of adjectives.

Use the following steps to complete this assignment.

A. Prewriting

Divide a piece of paper into two columns: Present Room and Perfect Room. In the Present Room column, list what you see in your room in as much detail as you can. You might start in one corner of the room and move around it in an orderly fashion. To the side of each point you have listed, put down in the Perfect Room column what you plan for the new room about that point. Go back over your list, and underline the key points or ideas that best describe and compare the two rooms. Decide on an effective order for your information. You might discuss points about your present room first, then discuss the same points about the *perfect* room. Or you might discuss both rooms together under main ideas like furniture, decoration, and features.

B. Writing

Write one or more paragraphs describing and comparing your present room with a *perfect* room you plan to create. Use your prewriting to help you. Remember that if you discuss a point about your present room, you must discuss the same point about the *perfect* room you're planning. Let your points illuminate both the similarities and differences of the two rooms. Use fresh adjectives to provide details.

C. Postwriting

Revise your first draft using the following checklist.

1. Does my work describe and compare the two rooms with details of their similarities and differences?

2. Have I used fresh, specific adjectives?

Edit your work using the Checklist for Proofreading at the back of the book. If appropriate, share your writing with your classmates and teacher. Draw a blueprint or map of your room.

16 Adverbs

Understanding Adverbs

Adverbs are modifiers that answer specific questions about words and add detail to your writing and speaking. You can identify adverbs by their definition, by the way they are divided into classes, and by the features that distinguish them from other parts of speech. In this section you will study and practice each of these ways to identify adverbs.

Defining Adverbs

Adverbs are usually defined as words that modify verbs, adjectives, or other adverbs.

Modifying a Verb:

The gorilla slept *soundly* in the corner of the cage.

All the ducks had flown *away*.

Modifying an Adjective:

Ken was *rather* short for a basketball star.

The comedian told some *very* funny stories.

Modifying Another Adverb:

The horse ran *somewhat* slowly at first.

We had arrived *too* early for the show.

Adverbs modify verbs, adjectives, or other adverbs by answering one of several questions. These questions are *how? how often? when? where?* and *to what extent?*

Kathy answered each question *correctly*.   [how?]

All of us take piano lessons *daily*.   [how often?]

We went on a field trip *yesterday*.   [when?]

The librarian told us to leave the books

here.   [where?]

The jury was *hopelessly* deadlocked.   [to what extent?]

Exercise 1: Identifying Adverbs

Write the following sentences and underline each adverb.
Draw an arrow from the adverb to the verb, verb phrase,
adjective, or adverb it modifies. Some sentences contain more
than one adverb.

Examples

    a. You can eat spaghetti easily with a fork.

    You can eat spaghetti <u>easily</u> with a fork.

    b. Tom very foolishly left the keys in his car.

    Tom <u>very foolishly</u> left the keys in his car.

1. This sweater is rather bulky.
2. I'm out of breath because I ran too quickly.
3. Yim moved the plants outside.
4. Jennifer walked so slowly that she missed the bus.
5. Last Tuesday was an extremely hot day.
6. Shirley bought nearly new furniture for her apartment.
7. The politicians argued their cause very convincingly.
8. Kelly's dog barks somewhat loudly for a small puppy.

9. The Perezes frequently cook a Mexican feast for their friends.

10. The little child smiled very innocently when asked about the broken dish.

Grouping Adverbs by Classes

Any word that is used to modify a verb, an adjective, or an adverb is classified as an adverb. Within this large classification of words, however, there are two groups of adverbs that are sometimes difficult to identify. These are *interrogative adverbs* and *negative adverbs*. Interrogative and negative adverbs are most easily recognized by the way they are used in a sentence.

An adverb that is used at the beginning of a sentence that asks a question is called an *interrogative adverb*. Each interrogative adverb is used to modify a verb, an adjective, or an adverb in the sentence.

How far did you run?	[modifies the adverb *far*]
When did the race begin?	[modifies the verb phrase *did begin*]
Where did I put that stopwatch?	[modifies the verb phrase *did put*]
Why am I so forgetful?	[modifies the verb *am*]

A helpful way to decide which word the interrogative adverb modifies is to rewrite the sentence with the subject at the beginning:

You did run *how* far?

The race did begin *when?*

I did put that stopwatch *where?*

I am so forgetful *why?*

Exercise 2: *Identifying Interrogative Adverbs*

Write the following sentences and underline each interrogative adverb. After each sentence write in parentheses the verb, verb phrase, adjective, or adverb that the interrogative adverb modifies.

Example

a. How many times must I ask you?
   <u>How</u> many times must I ask you? (many)

---

1. How often do you visit your grandmother?
2. Where can we catch a bus to Baltimore?
3. Why do leaves turn red in the fall?
4. When will the next Presidential election be held?
5. Where was Thomas Jefferson born?
6. How far is it from the earth to the moon?
7. When was the Declaration of Independence signed?
8. Where do snow leopards live?
9. Why did the chicken cross the road?
10. How do you speak pig Latin?

The word *not* is an adverb. It can be used to give verbs, adjectives, or other adverbs a negative meaning and so is called a *negative adverb*.

Modifying a Verb:

My biology notes were *not* in my locker.

Dr. Rogers will *not* be in her office all day.

Modifying an Adjective:

Not happy with her score, Nicole took the test again.

Not concerned with his own safety, Bill rushed into the fire to save his sister.

Modifying an Adverb:

Baseball records are broken, although *not* frequently.

Not far from home, there is a post office.

When *not* is used to modify a verb phrase, it is sometimes written as the contraction *n't* and added to the end of the first helping verb.

We have *not* found our missing cat.
We have*n't* found our missing cat.

It could *not* have gone very far.
It could*n't* have gone very far.

By adding *n't* to the end of a helping verb, you can make the following contractions:

isn't	don't	shouldn't	hadn't
aren't	doesn't	wouldn't	mightn't
wasn't	didn't	haven't	mustn't
weren't	couldn't	hasn't	

Note: will + n't = won't
can + n't = can't

The *n't* ending does not combine with *may* or *am:*

You *may not* be able to get a ticket.

However, I *am not* saying it is impossible.

To use *not* with most one-word verbs, you must add a form of the verb *do* as a helping verb.

We *grow* tomatoes in our backyard.
We *do not grow* tomatoes in our backyard.

This book *has* many stories about Ireland.
This book *does not have* many stories about Ireland.

My sisters *went* to the county fair.
My sisters *did not go* to the county fair.

Exercise 3: Using the Adverb Not

Write the following sentences and change each sentence by adding the adverb *not* to modify the verb or verb phrase. If *not* can be written as a contraction, use its proper form in the rewritten sentence. Underline the verb or verb phrase including the adverb *not* or *n't*.

Examples

  a. You should have turned at that intersection.
  You shouldn't have turned at that intersection.

  b. Julie mowed our lawn yesterday.
  Julie didn't mow our lawn yesterday.

  c. I may be home before dinner.
  I may not be home before dinner.

1. Derrick will drive to Houston.

2. Janice wants a ski parka.

3. You may visit Andrea on Sunday.

4. There is enough food for dinner.

5. Mariko should close all the windows.

6. John can take the exam next week.

7. I did buy a ticket for the five o'clock show.

8. Dolores finds a ghost in her aunt's living room.

9. Suzie and Don are moving in August.

10. I am going to Des Moines this summer.

Finding Adverbs by Their Features

Two features can help you to identify adverbs—degrees of comparison and suffixes. Most adverbs will have at least one of these features.

Some adverbs change form to show degrees of comparison.

Adverbs have three degrees of comparison: *positive*, *comparative*, and *superlative*.

Most adverbs form their comparative and superlative degrees with the words *more* and *most*.

Positive (modifies one word)	Comparative (compares two words)	Superlative (compares three or more words)
quickly	more quickly	most quickly
tightly	more tightly	most tightly
intelligently	more intelligently	most intelligently

Juan reads *quickly*.	[positive]
Juan reads *more quickly* than Pat.	[comparative]
Of all the students in his class, Juan reads *most quickly*.	[superlative]

Some adverbs add *-er* and *-est* to form their comparative and superlative degrees.

Positive	Comparative	Superlative
close	closer	closest
fast	faster	fastest
near	nearer	nearest

I am going to bed *early* tonight.	[positive]
I went to bed *earlier* last night than tonight.	[comparative]
I went to bed *earliest* of anyone in the house.	[superlative]

A few common adverbs form their comparative and superlative degrees in irregular ways. These adverbs and their different degrees must be memorized.

Positive	Comparative	Superlative
badly	worse	worst
far	farther	farthest

little	less	least
much	more	most
well	better	best

Allyson plays tennis *badly*.	[positive degree]
Vickie sings *worse* than she dances.	[comparative degree]
Of all the students, Terry lived *farthest* from school.	[superlative degree]

Exercise 4: Identifying Comparative Adverbs

Write the following sentences and underline the adverbs that show one of the three degrees of comparison. Label the adverbs *P* for positive, *C* for comparative, and *S* for superlative.

Examples

a. David speaks more softly than Richard.

                    C

David speaks <u>more softly</u> than Richard.

b. Of all the cats, that one howled loudest.

                    S

Of all the cats, that one howled <u>loudest</u>.

1. We are happy that our new car runs more efficiently.

2. Of the ten dancers in the troupe, Maria leaps most gracefully.

3. That typewriter is old, but it still types smoothly.

4. This persistent buzzer alarm rings more loudly than that musical alarm.

5. Let Lisa drive because she drives more carefully than her sister.

6. This ballpoint pen is easier to use, but it writes worse than the fountain pen.

7. Pete rehearsed his part more often and said his lines more confidently than Alex did.

8. Barbara has a sore throat, so she'll sing less loudly than you will; she's afraid she'll sing badly.

9. This digital watch keeps time less accurately than that old-fashioned pocket watch.

10. The thinner syrup pours less slowly than the thick syrup.

Adverbs may be formed with a suffix.

Many adverbs—especially those that answer the question *how?*—end with the suffix *-ly*. These adverbs are usually formed by adding the suffix to adjectives.

Adjective* + *-ly* = *Adverb

bright   + -ly = *brightly*
fierce   + -ly = *fiercely*

Not all words that end in *-ly* are adverbs. Only those that end in *-ly and* modify a verb, an adjective, or another adverb are adverbs.

      adj.   adv.

The daily chores are done daily.

Exercise 5: *Identifying Adverbs Ending in* -ly

Each of the following sentences contains one or more words that end in *-ly*. Write the sentences and underline each word ending in *-ly*. Draw an arrow from the word ending in *-ly* to the word it modifies. Above the word write *adj.*, if it is an adjective, and *adv.*, if it is an adverb.

Example

---

a. The sailors had been punished severely for their actions aboard the ship.

                                adv.

The sailors had been punished <u>severely</u> for their actions aboard the ship.

1. Our mail is delivered regularly at 9:30 A.M.

2. Mari quickly finished the dishes and then went to the movies.

3. The lovely petunias bloom annually.

4. Wayne usually works at the bakery after school.

5. We eat an early supper and frequently nibble a small snack later on.

6. The daily attendance sheet shows that Carol rarely is absent.

7. We laughed heartily at the jolly clowns.

8. The Presidential candidate calmly addressed the roomful of reporters.

9. The mayor's timely proposal pleasantly surprised everyone at the press conference.

10. We cautiously fed the billy goat some crackers.

Review: *Understanding Adverbs*

Write the following sentences and underline each adverb. If an adverb is written in its comparative or superlative form using the words *more, most, less,* or *least,* be sure to include this word as part of the adverb. Below each sentence list the adverbs it contains and tell what word or words each adverb modifies.

Example

a. We all marched slowly and somewhat timidly to the principal's office.
We all marched <u>slowly</u> and <u>somewhat</u> <u>timidly</u> to the principal's office.

slowly—marched
somewhat—timidly
timidly—marched

1. Though she campaigned energetically, the candidate wasn't very successful.

2. Mary searched frantically, but she couldn't find her light green notebook. computer.

3. A robin cannot fly faster than a falcon.

4. When was the first moon landing?

5. A very big dog will guard your house more efficiently than a small dog will.

6. The dark gray cat settled comfortably into the sofa.

7. I drive more cautiously at night than during the day.

8. The principal wouldn't accept my excuse, so I creatively invented another one.

9. The band tirelessly played its somewhat nostalgic music.

10. Why did you move the chair farther from the fireplace?

11. You may not go to Wyoming for the whole summer.

12. The rather old-fashioned vacuum cleaner whirred noisily.

13. Sharks must move constantly.

14. Rosa dived most gracefully of all the swimmers.

15. Allen didn't dial the phone correctly, so his call didn't connect.

16. Lobsters survive better in fairly cold water.

17. Lee arranged the flowers beautifully in a dark blue vase.

18. Why do cats and dogs fight fiercely?

19. I am not buying that very expensive sweater.

20. Manuel swung the bat hard, and the ball swiftly flew into the bleachers.

Applying What You Know

In the following bread-and-butter letter there are more than thirty adverbs. As you read the letter, use what you have learned in this section to identify the adverbs. Then, on a sheet of paper numbered 1–25, list at least twenty-five of the adverbs in the order they appear. (*Sukkoth* is a Jewish festival celebrating the fall harvest; a *sukkah* is a small, outdoor shelter.)

Dear Elaine,

I want to thank you and your mother for an absolutely wonderful week in North Miami Beach. You are certainly a good friend, Elaine, to share Sukkoth with me. I had never seen a sukkah before; it was so nice to sit under the willow and palm branches in yours. I hope the apples we hung on strings have not fallen. Did you finish the paper chain I started? I really enjoyed eating outside in the sukkah—a picnic under the stars! Tell your mom that I cooked acorn squash with cinnamon yesterday for my family.

I truly like the brightly colored butterfly you gave me Friday before I left. It traveled safely in my suitcase and is already mounted in a small gold frame. Looking at it, I can see your yard so clearly—the grapefruit hanging heavily on the tree, the hibiscus growing haphazardly along the fence, and the gnarled ficus tree. You are truly lucky to enjoy so much beauty daily and to swim in the ocean so often. Yesterday it was bitterly cold here, and soon our yard will be covered with snow. Your mother was right; my suitcase was so heavy that I could barely lift it, but I'm glad I packed the white coral from the beach. It reminds me of our day there, the funny pelicans, and all our good times together. Please write soon. I miss you.

Love,

Sara

Using Adverbs

In this section you will practice using the degrees of adverbs. You will also find practice exercises that will help you avoid problems caused by adverbs that look like adjectives and by negative adverbs.

Using Comparative and Superlative Forms

The majority of adverbs form their comparative and superlative degrees with the words *more* and *most*.

Positive (*modifies one word*)	Comparative (*compares two words*)	Superlative (*compares three or more words*)
quietly	more quietly	most quietly
distinctly	more distinctly	most distinctly
carefully	more carefully	most carefully

Adverbs can also show lesser amounts by using the word *less* in the comparative degree and *least* in the superlative degree.

Positive	Comparative	Superlative
quickly	less quickly	least quickly
swiftly	less swiftly	least swiftly
noisily	less noisily	least noisily

Richard cleared the hurdles at the track meet *more easily* than Harold.

Of the four groups of children, that group plays *most noisily*.

The juniors decorated their float *less attractively* than did the seniors last year.

The sophomores, however, decorated their float *least attractively* of all the classes.

Exercise 6: Using Comparative and Superlative Adverbs

Write the following sentences and supply the correct form of the adverb given in parentheses. Use either *more* or *less* for the comparative degree and *most* or *least* for the superlative. Underline the adverb form you use.

Examples

a. The reason the Bears should win is that they play defense _____ than do the Packers. (fiercely)

The reason the Bears should win is that they play defense <u>more fiercely</u> than do the Packers.

b. Train accidents are declining; in fact, they now happen _____ of all the accidents in transportation. (frequently)

Train accidents are declining; in fact, they now happen <u>least frequently</u> of all the accidents in transportation.

1. In order to be heard, you must speak _____ into the microphone. (distinctly)

2. The hare thought it could win because it could run _____ than the tortoise. (quickly)

3. The grasshopper was in trouble during the winter; of all the animals, it had prepared _____ for the coming cold weather. (carefully)

4. The kindergarten children were praised because they came into the room _____ than the group before them did. (noisily)

5. Her face flushed with excitement, the girl _____ blew out her birthday candles. (happily)

6. The gymnast who performs _____ of all the athletes wins the prize. (skillfully)

7. When you read for information, you should read _____ than when you read for pleasure. (slowly)

8. In the middle of my second period class, the fire alarm _____ rang. (suddenly)

9. The picture won a prize; it was the _____ drawn picture in the show. (creatively)

10. The last day before summer vacation passes _____ of all the days. (slowly)

Some adverbs add -er and -est to form their comparative and superlative degrees.

Positive	Comparative	Superlative
close	closer	closest
dark	darker	darkest
deep	deeper	deepest
early	earlier	earliest
fast	faster	fastest
hard	harder	hardest
high	higher	highest
late	later	latest (or last)

light	lighter	lightest
long	longer	longest
low	lower	lowest
near	nearer	nearest

We arrived at the party *late*.

We arrived at the party *later* than you did.

We arrived at the party *latest* of anyone.

A few common adverbs form their comparative and superlative degrees irregularly. The forms of these adverbs must be memorized.

Positive	*Comparative*	*Superlative*
badly	worse	worst
far	farther	farthest
little	less	least
much	more	most
well	better	best

Our house is *far* from the roller-skating rink.

Kevin swims *less* than I do in the summer.

Linda plays chess *best* of the three teammates.

Exercise 7: Using Comparative and Superlative Adverbs

Write the following sentences and supply the proper form of the adverb given in parentheses. Underline the form you choose.

Example

a. The first pitch of the inning was thrown much _____ than the second. (fast)

The first pitch of the inning was thrown much <u>faster</u> than the second.

1. In North America the sun sets _____ in the summer than in the winter. (late)

2. Margaret cries _____ of any newborn baby I've ever met. (little)

3. San Diego lies _____ to the Mexican border than Los Angeles does. (close)

4. Water-based paint dries _____ than oil-based paint. (fast)

5. Ivy grows _____ of all my house plants. (well)

6. A broken toe hurts _____ than a stubbed toe. (much)

7. Cheryl jumped onto the rope and climbed _____ of all the gymnasts. (high)

8. Tortoises live _____ than cats do. (long)

9. A nonstop flight will arrive _____ than one with stop-overs. (early)

10. Dry wood won't smoke so it is _____ to use than moist wood. (well)

Choosing Between Adjectives and Adverbs

Several pairs of adjectives and adverbs cause problems in writing and speaking. In selecting adjectives and adverbs remember the kinds of words each part of speech can modify.

Adjectives modify nouns and pronouns.
Adverbs modify verbs, adjectives, and other adverbs.

Bad/Badly

The adjective *bad* often follows a linking verb.

The fish tasted *bad* because it wasn't fresh.

I felt very *bad* about the accident.

The adverb *badly* modifies action verbs by answering the questions *how?* and *to what extent?*

The patient was injured *badly*. (*To what extent* was the patient injured?)

The horse ran *badly* but still won the race. (*How* did the horse run?)

The adverb *badly* also modifies adjectives.

The *badly* scarred face of the mountain showed the effects of erosion.

Easy/Easily

The adjective *easy* can modify nouns and pronouns, and may follow a linking verb.

To use this product, follow these three *easy* steps.

They are *easy*, but they are also very important.

The adverb *easily* almost always modifies a verb or verb phrase.

This will be *easily* the most important volleyball game of the year.

Do not use the adjective *easy* to modify a verb.

Exercise 8: Choosing Correct Adverbs and Adjectives

Write the following sentences. Choose the correct adjective or adverb from the words in the parentheses to complete each sentence. Underline the word you choose.

Example

a. This exercise is _____ if you think about what you have learned. (easy, easily)

This exercise is <u>easy</u> if you think about what you have learned.

1. Rosa felt _____ that she had missed the show. (bad, badly)

2. The drawer will open _____ after you oil it. (easy, easily)

3. If you have studied enough, the test should seem _____. (easy, easily)

4. Carrie played the set _____ and lost the tennis match. (bad, badly)

5. If you're just beginning to play the guitar, this is an _____ song to learn. (easy, easily)

6. The rusty lock didn't open _____. (easy, easily)

7. The new lock opened _____ than the old one. (easier, more easily)

8. The dog's poor performance was the result of _____ training. (bad, badly)

9. The old boat could not maneuver _____ through the rocky waters. (easy, easily)

10. Ken slipped and hurt his knee _____. (bad, badly)

Good/Well

The adjective *good* can follow linking verbs such as *be, taste, smell, become, look, seem,* and *sound.*

A hot bowl of chili tastes *good* on a cold winter day.

Your idea sounds *good* to me.

Our weather has been *good* all week.

However, when the meaning is "in good health" or "healthy," use the adjective *well*.

I feel *well* today. (meaning: feel "in good health")

You look *well* to me. (meaning: look "healthy")

Jack isn't *well* and can't come to school. (meaning: isn't "healthy")

The adverb *well* modifies verbs.

Arthur Mitchell dances *well*.

Billie Jean King plays tennis *well*.

Exercise 9: Using Good *and* Well

Write the following sentences and complete each by using either *good* or *well*. Underline the word you supply.

Examples

---

a. Burning leaves smell _____, but they also cause pollution unless the burning is carefully controlled.
   Burning leaves smell good, but they also cause pollution unless the burning is carefully controlled.

b. If you don't feel _____, don't come to work.
   If you don't feel well, don't come to work.

1. Ice water or cold lemonade tastes _____ on a hot summer day.

2. Jack's car handles _____ on bumpy roads.

3. Dana always feels _____ after exercising.

4. Don't go into the rough water unless you can swim _____, and even then, you should be very cautious.

5. A massage feels _____ when your muscles ache after a strenuous day.

6. Does Roberto have the flu? He doesn't seem _____.

7. I never sleep _____ the night before a big game.

8. That roast beef smells _____.

9. When you don't feel _____ because of a cold, you should get plenty of rest.

10. José's new stereo sounds _____.

Real/Really

The adjective *real* means "actual" or "true." It modifies nouns or pronouns.

The *real* cause of the accident was never discovered.

Would the *real* Mrs. Jones please stand up?

Is this one *real* or artificial?

The adverb *really* means "actually" or "truly." It modifies verbs, adjectives, and other adverbs.

We *really* had a good time.

The violinist gave a *really* fine performance.

We had to dive *really* deep to see the sunken wreck.

The adverb *really* often appears in front of an adjective or adverb it modifies. It has the same meaning the word *very* would have.

The violinist gave a *very* fine performance.

We had to dive *very* deep to see the sunken wreck.

Sure/Surely

The adjective *sure* modifies nouns and pronouns and has several different meanings.

We were about to suffer a *sure* defeat.

I was *sure* we would lose.

Surely **is an adverb that modifies verbs, adjectives, and other adverbs.**

The winners walked slowly but *surely* to the podium.

That *surely* was a delicious meal.

The adverb *surely* **often has the meaning "certainly." If the meaning of the word you want to use is "certainly," you may use the adverb** *surely.*

Will you help me move this bookcase?

Certainly, I'd be glad to help.

Surely, I'd be glad to help.

Exercise 10: *Using* Real/Really *and* Sure/Surely

Write the following sentences. From the pair of words given in parentheses choose the correct one. Underline the word you choose. Your teacher may ask you what the word modifies.

Examples

a. I am _____ happy to be home again. (real, really)
   I am <u>really</u> happy to be home again.

b. The attorney was _____ of her client's innocence.
   (sure, surely)
   The attorney was <u>sure</u> of her client's innocence.

1. Charley cooked a _____ delicious dinner. (real, really)

2. People _____ were hungry, because they finished everything. (sure, surely)

3. I'd rather have one _____ dependable friend than fifteen casual buddies. (real, really)

4. I _____ knew I had done well on the test. (sure, surely)

5. I was _____ I had not missed more than one question. (sure, surely)

6. When he heard the bus roaring toward him, Emilio knew _____ terror. (real, really)

7. After years of gymnastics, Carol's reflexes were _____ quick. (real, really)

8. If we work _____ hard all winter, we can take a long summer vacation. (real, really)

9. I _____ would like a bike for my birthday. (sure, surely)

10. Jackie handles the basketball with the _____ ability of an expert. (sure, surely)

Slow/Slowly

Slow is an adjective and can be used only to modify nouns and pronouns.

The snail was so *slow* that it seemed not to be moving.

The adverb *slowly* modifies verbs, adjectives, and other adverbs.

The snail was moving very *slowly*.

The *slowly* rising temperatures melted the snow.

Problems in using *slow* and *slowly* frequently occur when the comparative or superlative forms are used. (An asterisk [*] indicates a sentence with a feature that is not a part of Edited Standard English.)

	Positive	*Comparative*	*Superlative*
Adjective:	slow	slower	slowest
Adverb:	slowly	more slowly	most slowly

*I write *slower* when I am preparing my final draft.

I write *more slowly* when I am preparing my final draft.

Avoiding Double Negatives

The negative adverb *not* (or its contraction *n't*) gives a negative meaning to verbs.

Bernie should *not* have brought chicken to the picnic.

Bernie should*n't* have brought chicken to the picnic.

When two negative words are used where only one is necessary, the result is an error called a *double negative*. This error happens when writers forget that there are several other negative words besides *not* and *n't*. The words *no, never, none, no one,* and *nothing* all have a negative meaning. These words can be remembered because they all begin with the letter *n*. (An asterisk [*] indicates a sentence with a feature that is not a part of Edited Standard English.)

*No one told me *nothing* about it.	[double negative]
*You should*n't never* play with matches.	[double negative]

Double negatives can be avoided in two ways. You can take out one of the negative words, or you can change one of the negative words.

No one told me about it. (takes out the negative word *nothing*)

No one told me anything about it. (changes *nothing* to *anything*)

There are also a few negative words that do not begin with the letter *n*. The word *hardly* has a negative meaning, and the words *only* and *but* can sometimes have negative meanings.

I could *not* believe him after what he had done.

I could *hardly* believe him after what he had done.

**I could*n't hardly* believe him after what he had done.

When the words *only* and *but* mean "no more than," they also have a negative meaning.

He would be here *only* one day. (meaning: He would be here *no more than* one day.)

We had *but* two chances left. (meaning: We had *no more than* two chances left.)

A double negative results when another negative word is added to a sentence in which *only* or *but* mean "no more than."

*He would be here *no* more than *only* one day.

*We had*n't* *but* two chances left.

Exercise 11: Correcting Double Negatives

Each of the following sentences contains a double negative. Write the sentences and remove or change one of the negatives. Underline the negative word that is left in each rewritten sentence.

Example

a. Charlene never had no problem getting a summer job.
   Charlene <u>never</u> had any problem getting a summer job.

1. No one never said it would be easy to play the violin.
2. They didn't hardly have enough food for all of the guests.
3. Amelia wouldn't like none of the movies that are playing.
4. Kiyo hadn't missed but one day of school.
5. Elaine doesn't look nothing like her older sister.
6. There wasn't hardly room for all the people to sit.
7. I bet no one never saw *Jaws* without being scared.
8. I'm a vegetarian, and I don't want no lamb chops.
9. The kitten was so tiny that you couldn't hardly find it.
10. Yoshiro isn't interested in nothing that has to do with fishing.

Forming Adverbs

Many adverbs can be formed by the addition of the suffix *-ly* to adjectives. This formula for forming adverbs can help you add more detail and interest to your writing.

Adjective + -ly = Adverb

fond	+	-ly	=	*fondly*
severe	+	-ly	=	*severely*
regular	+	-ly	=	*regularly*
playful	+	-ly	=	*playfully*
quick	+	-ly	=	*quickly*

Not all words that end in *-ly* are adverbs. Only those words that end in *-ly* and modify a verb, an adjective, or another adverb are adverbs.

adj.   adv.
Our *family* picnic is held *annually* in June.

Exercise 12: *Using Adverbs Made from Adjectives*

Form adverbs from the following words and suffixes. Write a sentence using each new word you form and underline the adverb. Make sure that the new adverb modifies a verb, an adjective, or another adverb. Use your dictionary for help with spelling.

Example

a. sincere + -ly
   Marla's letter <u>sincerely</u> expressed her appreciation.

1. respectful + -ly
2. timid + -ly
3. imaginative + -ly
4. quiet + -ly
5. humorous + -ly
6. brilliant + -ly
7. honest + -ly
8. successful + -ly
9. final + -ly
10. tight + -ly

Placing Adverbs for Emphasis

When an adverb modifies a verb, its position in a sentence does not always have to be the same. It can usually appear wherever it is needed in the sentence to emphasize a particular meaning. Placing adverbs in different positions can also add interest, variety, and zest to your sentences.

Finally we were able to open the door.

We *finally* were able to open the door.

We were *finally* able to open the door.

We were able to open the door, *finally*.

Read the sentences above out loud and notice the emphasis in each. Since adverbs that modify verbs tell *how* and *when* something was done, where the adverb appears can change the emphasis of the sentence. Often there is more emphasis on *how* and *when* something was done when the adverb appears at the beginning of a sentence or at the end. However, sometimes you may not want the adverb emphasized as much. Emphasis depends on the meaning you want to convey.

Exercise 13: *Placing Adverbs for Emphasis*

Rewrite each of the following sentences in two different ways. Underline the adverb in each sentence.

Examples

a. We frantically rushed to catch the bus.
   We rushed <u>frantically</u> to catch the bus.

   <u>Frantically</u> we rushed to catch the bus.

b. We watch cartoons on Saturday mornings sometimes.
   <u>Sometimes</u> we watch cartoons on Saturday mornings.

   We <u>sometimes</u> watch cartoons on Saturday mornings.

1. Seldom the candidates request that all of the votes be recounted.

2. The principal spoke to the group frankly.

3. I timidly raised my hand to answer the question.

4. Eagerly ten people volunteered to taste the results.

5. Christina's eyes hopefully searched the stands for her friend.

6. The policewoman watched suspiciously as the two men entered the building.

7. The candidate for governor outlined the issues of the campaign forcefully.

8. Late again, Karl slid into his desk secretly.

9. The child cried loudly when its parents left the room.

10. Our family often visits our grandparents' dairy ranch.

Review: Using Adverbs

Write the following sentences and supply the correct comparative or superlative form of the adverb given in parentheses. Underline the form you choose.

Examples

a. Rhoda rides to school _____ than she walks. (often)
Rhoda rides to school more often than she walks.
or
Rhoda rides to school less often than she walks.

b. The track team practices _____ of all the athletic teams at our school. (hard)
The track team practices hardest of all the athletic teams at our school.

1. A cheetah can run _____ than a tiger, a lion, or a jaguar. (fast)

2. Ferns grow _____ in shaded light than they do in direct sunlight. (well)

3. Nancy Miller hasn't practiced on the electric typewriter for years, so she types _____ than Michelle Anderson. (quickly)

4. Amelia Chang jogged _____ on Tuesday than she had on Monday. (far)

5. You can dive _____ with scuba equipment than you can without it. (deep)

6. Juan Robinson is the star batter on our high school team and hits home runs _____ of all the players on the team. (often)

7. That ruler is very accurate and measures _____ than this one. (precisely)

8. Anita Lopez hopes to win a scholarship, so she is waiting _____ of all for the examination grades from last week. (anxiously)

9. A canary sings _____ than a pigeon. (sweetly)

10. If you're trying to lose weight, you should eat _____. (often)

Write the following sentences and choose the correct word or phrase from the words in the parentheses. Underline the word or phrase you choose.

Examples

a. To avoid hiccups, eat _____. (slow, slowly)
   To avoid hiccups, eat slowly.

b. Do you feel _____ enough to go back to work later this afternoon? (good, well)
   Do you feel well enough to go back to work later this afternoon?

c. He runs _____ as the race begins. (slower, more slowly)
   He runs more slowly as the race begins.

11. Hot tea tastes _____ with any type of Chinese food. (good, well)

12. Maria felt _____ that the Dodgers lost the World Series. (bad, badly)

13. Cross-country skiing doesn't look difficult, but it is a _____ rigorous sport. (real, really)

14. You can usually swim _____ in a lake than in the ocean. (easier, more easily)

15. The witness was poised and _____ of herself when she took the stand. (sure, surely)

16. If furniture is made _____, it should last a long time. (good, well)

17. Shouldn't you read those lines _____? (slower, more slowly)

18. I would think a horse _____ can run faster than a dog. (sure, surely)

19. The jumbo jet _____ soared above the clouds and avoided the storm. (easy, easily)

20. Ammonia doesn't smell _____. (good, well)

Writing Focus: *Using Exact Adverbs in Writing*

Appropriate and exact adverbs help writers in three main ways. First, they help make descriptions more exact and vivid. Second, they help organize material by showing time and space relationships. Finally, adverbs clarify the relationships between ideas. Let adverbs help you make your writing more effective and precise.

Assignment: *Out of This World*

It's eleven o'clock on a stormy night. You've just finished reading a book about visitors from outer space. You turn on your favorite TV show, but as you sit remembering the eerie things you've just read, you become convinced that the star of the show is really an alien.

Write one or more paragraphs explaining why you think your favorite TV star is really an alien. Write for a panel of scientists studying claims that aliens are living on earth. Your work will be evaluated for correct use of adverbs. Use the following steps.

A. Prewriting

Think of movies you've seen about aliens. Begin to imagine aliens that might pass for humans. Imagine the TV star being such an alien. Make a word cluster, described in Chapter 1, about the TV star. Add words or phrases that explain why you think he or she is an alien. Include details about mannerisms, behaviors, speech patterns or interests that "prove" your claim. Look over your word cluster and choose the details that best support your claim. Group and number your evidence points from the least to the most important.

B. Writing

Using your word cluster, write one or more well-developed paragraphs explaining why you think the TV star is an alien. Include details or examples to support your explanation. Use

adverbs like *consequently, also, besides, first, second, mainly, previously,* and *primarily* to help you connect and show relationships between your ideas and statements.

C. Postwriting

Use the following checklist to revise your first draft.

1. Have I included enough information so that my readers will understand why I think the star is an alien?

2. Have I used exact adverbs to describe, organize, and clarify?

17 Prepositions
Understanding Prepositions

Prepositions are words that show relationships between other words in a sentence. You can learn to identify prepositions by learning their definition and by looking at the way they work in a sentence. In this section you will study and practice each of these ways to identify prepositions.

Defining Prepositions

A *preposition* is usually defined as a word that shows the relationship between a noun or a pronoun and some other word in the sentence.

Notice how the meanings of the following sentences change with different prepositions.

Uncle Carl sat *at* the table.
Uncle Carl sat *on* the table.
(shows the relationship between *sat* and *table*)

The ball bounced *near* my head.
The ball bounced *off* my head.
(shows the relationship between *bounced* and *head*)

The space *above* it is empty.
The space *inside* it is empty.
(shows the relationship between *space* and *it*)

The following list gives the most commonly used prepositions:

aboard	among	beside	during
about	around	besides	except
above	at	between	for
across	before	beyond	from
after	behind	but	in
against	below	by	inside
along	beneath	down	into

like	out	till	up
near	outside	to	upon
of	over	toward	with
off	past	under	within
on	through	underneath	without
onto	throughout	until	

The noun or pronoun used with prepositions is called the *object of the preposition*. The object of the preposition (*OP*) usually follows the preposition (*P*).

           P   OP

The paths *through* the *park* are paved.

         P OP

People run *on them* all day long.

The preposition, the object of the preposition, and the object's modifiers are called a *prepositional phrase*.

The prepositional phrases in the following sentences have been *italicized*.

I like to read *about American history*.

The land *beyond my backyard* is vacant and has been ever since I can remember.

We jumped *into the cool, clear water*.

I can do that *by myself*.

Exercise 1: *Identifying Prepositional Phrases*

Each of the sentences on the next page has one or more *italicized* prepositions. Write the sentences and circle each prepositional phrase. Above the object of the preposition, write OP.

Example

a. This subway runs *underneath* the entire city.

                                          OP

This subway runs (underneath the entire city.)

1. There's a lake *behind* our house and a forest preserve *beyond* the lake.

2. A path winds *around* the lake and *to* the lodge.

3. The lake is deep *at* one end but shallow *at* the other.

4. Tall rocks *underneath* the water cannot be seen.

5. We dive boldly *into* the deep water.

6. Icy water splashes *over* us.

7. The lakes *in* northern Wisconsin freeze early.

8. We can skate *across* the glassy surface *of* the lake.

9. There's a cracked spot *near* the center *of* it.

10. It's nice to have a lake *at* our doorstep *during* any season.

Prepositions Used as Other Parts of Speech

Some prepositions can also be used as other parts of speech. The word *past,* for example, can be used as an adjective, a noun, or a preposition.

Tomorrow we will study the *past* tense.	[adjective]
Children were not allowed so much freedom in the *past.*	[noun]
We drove quickly *past* the scene of the accident.	[preposition]

The word *up* can be an adverb or a preposition.

Please stand *up* when your name is called.	[adverb]
The climb *up* this mountain takes three days.	[preposition]

The best way to decide whether a word is used as a preposition is to look for a noun or pronoun object. A preposition *always* has an object, while adjectives, adverbs, and nouns never have objects.

Exercise 2: Identifying Prepositional Phrases

Write the following sentences and underline each preposition.
Write *OP* over the noun or pronoun that is its object. Circle the
entire prepositional phrase.

Examples

a. The cars rolled slowly toward the starting line.

                                                 OP

    The cars rolled slowly (toward the starting line.)

b. The skater fell down but rose to her feet quickly.

                                             OP

    The skater fell down but rose (to her feet) quickly.

1. Did you put your tooth under your pillow?
2. Don't eat a snack before dinner.
3. Rock-and-roll really began during the 1950s.
4. We never sat down; we danced until midnight.
5. Really, it won't be Thanksgiving without a turkey.
6. Sue looked up and watched the sun disappear behind a cloud.
7. The police officers in our district are very friendly.
8. He's a nice person underneath his tough exterior.
9. They won the race against all odds.
10. After lunch, let's take a walk.

Prepositions with Compound Objects

A preposition can have more than one object. When
there is more than one object, the preposition has a
compound object.

                     OP   OP

I sent a letter *to Simon and Martha.*

                     OP   OP   OP

The bus left *without Tim, Suzanna, or me.*

Exercise 3: Identifying Compound Prepositional Objects

Each of the following sentences contains one or more prepositions with compound objects. Write the sentences, underline each preposition, and write *OP* above each object of a preposition that you find.

Example

a. An eclipse occurs when the moon passes between the earth and the sun.
   An eclipse occurs when the moon passes <u>between</u> the
                                             OP   OP
   earth and the sun.

---

1. The cat always hides under the sofa or the bed.

2. I can't choose between spaghetti and pizza for lunch and dinner.

3. Should I put the shirts in the closet or the dresser?

4. We jump over puddles and mud and run past fences and roads.

5. The movie will be shown on Friday and Saturday.

6. Pick a number between one and nine.

7. Would you rather have a room near the pool or the garden?

8. Jackie hung the picture above the table and chairs and put the plants against the fireplace and windows.

9. I'll support you through thick and thin.

10. I want a car with bucket seats and a stereo but without air conditioning and push-button windows.

Prepositional Phrases as Modifiers

Prepositional phrases are used as modifiers in the same way as adjectives and adverbs. They answer the same questions that adjectives and adverbs answer about the words they modify.

Prepositional phrases are adjectives when they modify nouns or pronouns.

In the following sentences the adjectives are *italicized:*

My brother gave me a *poetry* book.

My brother gave me a book *of poems.*

Prepositional phrases used as adjectives answer the questions *what kind? which one?* and *how many?*

Prepositional phrases are adverbs when they modify verbs, adjectives, or other adverbs.

In the following sentences the adverbs are *italicized:*

The missing boys played *there.*

The missing boys played *in the park.*
(*Where* did the missing boys play?)

Prepositional phrases used as adverbs answer the questions *where? how? how often? when?* and *to what extent?*

Sometimes one prepositional phrase follows another. The second prepositional phrase often acts as an adjective to modify the noun or pronoun object of the first phrase.

The bucket plunged *to the bottom of the well.*

The crystal vase *on the shelf by the fireplace* is fragile.

Exercise 4: *Identifying Prepositional Phrases as Modifiers*

Write the sentences on the next page and underline each prepositional phrase. Draw an arrow from the prepositional phrase to the word or words it modifies. Above each prepositional phrase write *adj.* if it acts as an adjective and *adv.* if it acts as an adverb.

Example

---

a. We launched our rocket from an empty lot.

adv.
We launched our rocket from an empty lot.

1. We watched them swing by their tails from the trees.
2. Let's take the path through the park.
3. The bloodhounds tracked the robber by scent.
4. If you follow the main road past the school, you'll soon see the football field on your right.
5. Miami is located at the southern tip of Florida.
6. Point your telescope toward the North Star.
7. Nikki's car skidded into the mailbox on the corner.
8. Joanna writes daily in her diary.
9. Oriental rugs covered the floors throughout the house.
10. Diana planted marigolds between the rows of tomatoes.

Review: Understanding Prepositions

Write the following sentences and underline each prepositional phrase. Draw an arrow to the word or words the phrase modifies. Write *adj.* above phrases that act as adjectives and *adv.* above phrases that act as adverbs.

Example

a. An argument started between John and him.

An argument started <u>between John and him</u>.
adv.

b. Water seeped underneath the floor of the bathroom.

Water seeped <u>underneath the floor</u> <u>of the bathroom</u>.
adv. *adj.*

1. Diana Nyad swam between Bermuda and Florida.
2. John had a party for his friends after graduation.
3. There is beautiful coral off the Bermuda coast.
4. The *Mariner* spacecraft traveled in its orbit around Mars.
5. The larger part of an iceberg lies below the water.
6. We sledded down the hill behind the barn.
7. Rachel's stories about her cruise made life aboard an ocean liner sound very relaxing.

8. Groundhogs dug under the porch and did a lot of damage.

9. The lion tamer stepped between the wild lions.

10. Stand up and put your hands above your head.

11. I can tell by your voice that you're angry with me.

12. Travel across the desert by jeep or by camel can be exciting.

13. There was so much argument among the members of the committee that they could never get anything done.

14. Sea lions dived off the rocks and swam around the pool.

15. John stored dishes in the cabinet over the refrigerator.

16. The witness turned toward the defense attorney and responded with honesty and directness.

17. I like all vegetables except lima beans and Brussels sprouts.

18. Many resorts in Maine open only during the summer.

19. The return trip up the river will take longer because we'll be paddling against the current.

20. Income tax returns must be filed before the fifteenth day of April.

Applying What You Know

The following selection is about a Scottish woman's experience as a child during World War II. On a sheet of paper numbered 1–20, list at least twenty of the prepositional phrases in the selection in the order they appear. (Hint: Consider *to* a preposition only when it has a noun or pronoun object. Also, each of the following is a prepositional phrase: *of being torpedoed* and *about being seasick*.)

> When I was about twelve years old, it looked very bad in the British Isles. We thought the Germans were on the verge of invading, and everyone was alerted that the church bells would ring and all kinds of signals would go off when the Germans actually landed. Since I was an only child and my mother was of a nervous temperament, she decided she'd like to send me out of the country. So she wrote to my father's brother and his wife, who lived in New York and had no children. She asked if they would take me temporarily until this crisis was over.

They wrote back and said, naturally, they'd be more than happy to take me. So I was shipped out on the Caledonian Line, along with a number of other young girls my age being sent to visit with relatives in the United States and Canada. We went in convoy and we could see the destroyers ahead and behind us as we went. We had to wear life belts the whole time we were on board, and we couldn't go up on deck after dark, and we had to be very careful with lights and so forth. Everything had to be kept very dark. I wasn't really alarmed about the possibility of being torpedoed; I was more concerned about being seasick, and I was curious about what it would be like in the United States.[1]

Using Prepositions

In this section you will learn how to use prepositions in Edited Standard English. You will also learn about the correct placement of prepositional phrases.

Using Pronouns as Objects of Prepositions

Only object forms of pronouns can be used as objects of a preposition.

Pronoun Object Forms

Singular	Plural
me	us
you	you
him her it	them
whom	whom

---

[1]Excerpt from *American Mosaic* compiled by Joan Morrison and Charlotte Fox Zabusky. Copyright © 1980 by Joan Morrison and Charlotte Fox Zabusky. Reprinted by permission of E. P. Dutton.

The judges finally decided upon *her* and *me*.

The person to *whom* I am speaking is my sister.

The Wildcats didn't stand a chance against *us* Buckeyes.

Our class received three postcards from *them*.

Exercise 5: Choosing Prepositional Pronoun Objects

Write each of the following sentences and choose the correct form of the pronouns given in parentheses. Underline the pronouns you select.

Example

a. The stories about (they, them) and (we, us) are simply untrue.
   The stories about them and us are simply untrue.

1. Emily Sue Lau gave Chinese-cooking lessons to Nadine and (I, me).

2. Using wooden chopsticks was very hard for (we, us) beginners.

3. The friendly calico cat rubbed up against Jaime and (he, him).

4. At the end of the dance contest, everyone formed a circle around Marc and (her, she).

5. The humorous television script was written by Mary, Ian, and (he, him).

6. The cottage near Kathleen and (they, them) was rented last week.

7. The mischievous children crept behind Bob and (I, me) and frightened us.

8. These sandwiches were ordered by someone in our office, but I'm not sure by (who, whom).

9. A huge wave washed over Angelo and (he, him), and for a minute they both disappeared.

10. The train passengers waved as they sped past (they, them) and (us, we).

Using Troublesome Prepositions Correctly

Among/Between

Use *between* when referring to exactly two people or things.

Carol was told to stand *between* Jack and me for the family portrait.

Use *among* when referring to more than two people or things.

Our company will divide its profits *among* all the employees in its plant.

Beside/Besides

Use *beside* when referring to a position "next to" something.

We found the missing red hammer *beside* the dilapidated, old tool shed.

***Besides* means "in addition to" or "other than."**

Besides the hammer we also found a rusty saw.

In/Into

***In* refers to a movement that happened "inside" or "within."**

The children jumped *in* the wagon. (while they were inside)

***Into* refers to a movement "from outside to inside."**

The children jumped *into* the wagon. (from outside to inside)

On/Onto

On has many meanings. Use *onto* only for the meaning "moving toward the top of something."

> Everyone scrambled *onto* the roof for a better look.
>
> I stepped *onto* the ladder and began to climb.

Exercise 6: Using Troublesome Prepositions Correctly

Write each of the following sentences and choose the correct one of the prepositions in parentheses. Underline the prepositions you choose.

Example

a. The votes were evenly divided (among, between) the four mayoral candidates.

The votes were evenly divided <u>among</u> the four mayoral candidates.

1. Be sure the children get (in, into) bed by six o'clock.

2. (Between, Among) you and me, I don't see why we should continue this project.

3. There was no one in the theater (besides, beside) a few small children.

4. (Onto, On) several occasions I thought about writing you.

5. The argument was (between, among) the four students with the highest grades.

6. (In, Into) the water we could see silver fish gliding just below the surface.

7. Please put the package (beside, besides) me; I'll open it when I can.

8. Children climbed (on, onto) boxes to have a better view.

9. (In, Into) every good meal go wholesome ingredients.

10. People working (in, into) the building suffered when the air conditioning broke down.

Using Prepositions in Edited Standard English

One feature of Edited Standard English is the use of prepositions. The following list shows how common prepositions are used in ESE. (An asterisk [*] indicates a sentence with a feature that is not part of ESE.)

about
Do not use *about* and *at* together in expressions of time. Use only the word that states the relationship you want to show.
> *We will be home *at about* 8:30.
> We will be home *at* 8:30.
> We will be home *about* 8:30.

at
Do not use *at* with *where*.
> *If you tell me where* it is *at*, I'll get it for you.
> If you tell me *where* it is, I'll get it for you.

by
Do not use *by* to mean *with*.
> *If that is your choice, it's all right *by* me.
> If that is your choice, it's all right *with* me.

except
Use *except* (not *outside of*) to mean "other than" or "excluding."
> *Nothing *outside of* winning would please him.
> Nothing *except* winning would please him.

of
Do not use *of* instead of the helping verb *have*.
> *I could *of* done that by myself.
> I could *have* done that by myself.

off
Use just the preposition *off* instead of *off of*.
> *It rolled *off of* the table and landed on the floor.
> It rolled *off* the table and landed on the floor.

on
Use the verb *blame* instead of *blame it on*.
> *I wasn't there, so you can't *blame it on* me.
> I wasn't there, so you can't *blame* me.

to
Do not use *to* as a replacement for *at*.
> *When I arrived *to* work, the office was closed.

When I arrived *at* work, the office was closed.

Do not use *to* when it is unnecessary.

*Where are you going *to* in such a hurry?
Where are you going in such a hurry?

Exercise 7: Using Prepositions in Edited Standard English

Write the following sentences and complete each one by choosing the necessary word or words in parentheses. Underline the words you choose.

Example

a. If we leave school _____ noon, we should be there on time. (about, at about)
If we leave school <u>about</u> noon, we should be there on time.

1. There's a tiny spare room _____ the kitchen. (in back of, behind)

2. Nothing _____ an earthquake will wake me up this morning. (except, outside of)

3. Tomorrow the sun will rise _____ 5:23 A.M. (at about, at)

4. If Carlotta wants to eat yogurt and honey instead of a hot fudge sundae, it's all right _____. (with me, by me)

5. We never remember where this restaurant _____. (is, is at)

6. When Alex arrived _____ the station, the train had already left. (to, at)

7. All my muscles ache. Could I _____ the weather? (blame it on, blame)

8. The golf ball rolled _____ the green and into a sand trap. (off, off of)

9. Where are you sending _____? (that package to, that package)

10. We _____ talked longer, but I had to go to work. (could of, could have)

Using Prepositional Phrases as Adjectives

Prepositional phrases can appear in many different positions in a sentence. In each position the prepositional phrase may have a different meaning.

> We voted on who should be our leader *during the trip.* (tells *who* would be the leader on the trip)

> We voted *during the trip* on who should be our leader. (tells *when* the vote was taken)

When a prepositional phrase is used as an adjective, it should be placed immediately after the noun or pronoun it modifies. Prepositional phrases that modify nouns or pronouns are called *adjective phrases*.

> The teacher gave a lecture *on a healthy diet* to all the students.

Any other position may make the meaning of the sentence unclear.

> Dr. Traveras gave a lecture to all the students *on a healthy diet.* (Are the students on a diet?)

> *On a healthy diet,* Dr. Traveras gave a lecture to all the students. (Is Dr. Traveras on a diet?)

Exercise 8: Using Prepositional Adjective Phrases

Each of the following sentences contains a prepositional phrase that acts as an adjective. The sentence is unclear because the phrase does not come after the word it modifies. Rewrite each sentence by moving the prepositional phrase to make the meaning clear. Underline the phrase.

Example

> a. Maria bought a hat for her cousin with a wide brim.
>   Maria bought a hat with a wide brim for her cousin.

1. The students quickly learned English from Denmark.

2. The apartment has a good view of the city on the top floor.

3. A small town is known for its cheese in Wisconsin.

4. The pond is a good place to fish near the fence.

5. A wedding should be held in a large church with many attendants.

6. Carmen gave a cat to her sister with yellow eyes.

7. The men were arrested with the printing press.

8. The long rest helped me to recover during my illness.

9. The girl sat as her mother made braids with long hair.

10. How accidents can be prevented is the topic of the officer's speech in the home.

Using Prepositional Phrases as Adverbs

Prepositional phrases that modify verbs—*adverb phrases*—usually can appear in a variety of places without confusing the reader.

The committee will announce its findings *in the morning.*

The committee will, *in the morning*, announce its findings.

In the morning the committee will announce its findings.

If the sentence contains two verbs, however, be careful to place the adverb phrase as near as possible to the verb you want it to modify.

Note: The location of an adverb phrase may change the meanings of some sentences.

We visited the student who was injured *after school.* (The student was injured after school.)

After school we visited the student who was injured. (The visit was after school.)

Exercise 9: Using Prepositional Adverb Phrases

Each of the sentences on the next page contains a prepositional phrase used as an adverb. The sentence is unclear because of the placement of the phrase. Rewrite the sentence and make the meaning clear by moving the phrase.

1. Nicole sat and watched the falcon soar majestically on the grass.

2. Oil was dripping, and Christopher was worried underneath the car.

3. Ms. Garcia promised by noon that the meeting would be over.

4. The students performed well and then had a party to celebrate on the test.

5. The reindeer clambered, and the man shouted in anger across the roof.

6. The candidate waved, and balloons fell to the crowd.

7. Around the track people cheered as the horses ran.

8. I dropped the clean laundry and had to wash it again in the mud.

9. Some people believe another Ice Age is possible, but I never think about it in several centuries.

10. The children stood and begged money from passersby on the corner.

Review: Using Prepositions

Rewrite each of the following sentences. Change pronoun forms that are misused as objects of prepositions, and change prepositions that would confuse your readers. Underline your changes.

Example

a. Let's keep this matter just between you and I.
   Let's keep this matter just between you and me.

1. The coat with the fur collar looked pretty onto the woman.

2. The children wanted to go where the giraffe was at.

3. Are there many jobs available to we graduates?

4. Just between you and I, I'd rather stay home than go out.

5. We strung the hammock among two big trees in the yard.

6. Will the tax refund be mailed to Manuel and we?

7. Wally is late, so the meeting will have to start without he and his assistant.

8. Ed moaned when the bowling ball rolled off of the alley and into the gutter.

9. We waved, but the bus zoomed past she and me.

10. Let's divide the work among Lauren, you, and I.

Each of the following sentences contains one or more prepositional phrases. Some of the sentences are clear, but some are unclear because of the position of a phrase. Number a sheet of paper 11–20. If the sentence is unclear, rewrite it and make it clear by moving a prepositional phrase. Underline the phrase. If it is clear, write *clear* beside that number on your paper.

Example

a. The coat looked pretty on the woman with the fur collar.
The coat <u>with the fur collar</u> looked pretty on the woman.

11. Those shoes are just the ones I want in the window.

12. The tree branches were hazardous during the storm above the porch.

13. The reporter ran past the police barricade with a press pass.

14. Everyone with the dancing bear applauded the trainer.

15. A spaniel barked at us visitors with brown spots.

16. By the dawn's early light Francis Scott Key wrote the song that became our national anthem.

17. Snoopy furnished his doghouse and demanded his dinner with stereo and wall-to-wall carpet.

18. Animals with very thick fur should not be kept in hot climates.

19. With his baggy pants and derby hat audiences grew to love Charlie Chaplin.

20. During the long years of the Civil War, families were divided and many people suffered.

Writing Focus: *Using*

Prepositional Phrases in Writing

As a writer, you can use prepositional phrases to make important distinctions in meaning, to add information to sentences, and to show relationships. Use prepositional phrases to make your writing clear and precise.

Assignment: *First Choice*

A new episode of a very popular adventure film has just been released, both as a movie and as a paperback novel. As a reward for earning good grades, your parents have offered to buy either your movie ticket or the book. Your choice is difficult because you like both movies and books. But you must decide which you will do first, see the movie or read the book.

After you have made a decision, write one or more paragraphs explaining it to your parents. Be clear about your reasons because your parents want to be certain that you will be happy with your choice. Your writing will be evaluated for correct and effective use of prepositional phrases.

Use the following steps to complete this assignment.

A. Prewriting

Imagine two voices in your mind, discussing your choices. One voice could speak for the book, the other for the movie. Write their conversation. For example, the book might say, "I can allow you to create scenes and action in your own mind," while the film could respond, "But I can make immediate and exciting pictures for you, and you don't have to do a thing!" Write it quickly, easily, and without judging the quality of the ideas. Let the two voices continue to argue their merits until you feel you have a decision.

Write your decision on a separate piece of paper. Go back over your dialogue and underline three points that offer the best reasons for your choice. Write them under your decision, leaving space between them. In the space, jot down details and more specific information to further explain your reasons. Number the reasons in this order: the second most important, the least important, and the most important.

B. Writing

Using your notes, write one or more paragraphs explaining your decision to accept either the ticket or book. Be specific. As you write, use prepositional phrases to add details and to explain your reasons.

C. Postwriting

Use the following checklist to revise your first draft.

1. Does my writing clearly state my decision?

2. Have I provided adequate reasons for my choice?

3. Have I used prepositional phrases to provide details and to show relationships?

Edit your work using the Checklist for Proofreading at the back of the book. If appropriate, share your writing with your classmates. Discuss with them the process you use in making a decision.

18 Conjunctions
Understanding Conjunctions

Conjunctions are words that join other words. You can learn to identify conjunctions by learning their definition and by looking at how they are grouped into classes. In this section you will study and practice identifying conjunctions in each of these ways.

Defining Conjunctions

A *conjunction* is usually defined as a word that joins words or groups of words.

The most commonly used conjunctions—*and, but, or, nor, for,* and *yet*—join individual words, word groups, or sentences.

When a conjunction is used to join individual words, the words must be of the same general type.

Joining Nouns

Linda (and) *Sid* have tickets for tonight's concert.

Joining Pronouns

None of the doctors (nor) *any* of the nurses could be found in time.

Joining Verbs

My head aches when I *write* (or) *read.*

Joining Adjectives

We were *tired* (and) *hungry* after the ordeal.

Joining Adverbs

The platoon moved *quickly* (but) *carefully.*

Sometimes the words that are joined will have other words modifying them.

I couldn't find the blue *jacket* (or) the gray *sweater*.

Exercise 1: *Identifying Conjunctions*

Each of the following sentences uses a conjunction to join two words. Write the sentences. Draw a circle around the conjunctions and underline the two words in each sentence that the conjunction joins.

Example

a. We paid our fine and quickly hurried off.

We <u>paid</u> our fine (and) quickly <u>hurried</u> off.

1. California and Texas border on Mexico.
2. The weather in Palm Springs, California, is very hot but very dry.
3. Is New Jersey or Pennsylvania known as the "The Garden State"?
4. In North America you cannot see tigers or leopards except in zoos.
5. Surfing is exciting but sometimes dangerous.
6. Yogurt is a healthy food and refreshing snack.
7. I'll wash but not dry the dishes.
8. Miss Marple studied all of the clues and solved the intriguing mystery.
9. Jaguars are beautiful yet impractical pets.
10. Shooting stars flash for a second in the sky and then disappear.

Grouping Conjunctions by Classes

The most commonly used group of conjunctions is the class called *coordinating conjunctions*.

Coordinating Conjunctions

and	or
but	nor
yet	for

Coordinating conjunctions are used to join similar words or groups of words.

We listened to the *thunder* (and) the *rain*.

Do you use *catsup* (or) *mustard* on your hot dog?

The breeze was *strong* (yet) *refreshing*.

None of my socks (nor) *any* of my shoes wear evenly.

Exercise 2: *Using Coordinating Conjunctions*

Write the following sentences and supply the coordinating conjunction that best joins each pair of words. Circle the coordinating conjunction you choose and underline the two words each joins.

Example

---

a. Oranges _____ kiwis are two of my favorite fruits.

Oranges (and) kiwis are two of my favorite fruits.

1. The storm raged all night _____ stopped early in the morning.

2. We should clean up our room _____ go outside.

3. None of the teachers _____ any of the students were injured in the bus accident.

4. We hope tomorrow will bring clear skies _____ warm weather for the picnic.

5. This will be a necessary _____ tiring trip.

6. Since I'm not going, maybe you can get a ride with Eileen _____ Hernando.

7. The manager's warning that we must behave in the theater was quiet _____ firm.

8. We dived off the pier _____ swam across the lake.

9. They tried to convince me to go skating _____ bowling.

10. None of these bananas _____ any of these pears is ripe enough to eat.

Coordinating conjunctions can be used to join two or more prepositional phrases.

We traveled *over the river* (and) *through the woods.*

The plane climbed *into the air* (and) *above the clouds.*

You can get to the museum *by bus* (or) *by train.*

Our campsite wasn't *on the mountain* (but) *near the lake* instead.

Coordinating conjunctions can be used to join complete sentences.

I didn't know the title, (but) I did remember the author's name.

I replaced all the spark plugs, (yet) the car still wouldn't start.

The summers are always too hot, (or) the winters are too cold.

We all studied hard, (for) no one wanted to fail.

Note: When a coordinating conjunction is used to join two complete sentences, a comma usually precedes the conjunction as the following examples indicate.

You will sit there today, and she will sit there tomorrow.

I remembered the address, but I forgot the phone number.

Exercise 3: Identifying Groups of Words Joined by Conjunctions

Each of the sentences on the following page uses a conjunction to join groups of words. Some of these word groups are prepositional phrases, and some would be complete sentences if they stood alone. Write the sentences and circle each conjunction. Underline each group of words that the conjunction joins.

Example

a. We jumped off the dock and into the water.

We jumped <u>off the dock</u> (and) <u>into the water.</u>

1. Kim slid down the slide and into the pool.
2. The dinner at the banquet was delicious, but we were still hungry afterward.
3. We went to the airport early, for we had to check our bags.
4. The rake is behind the garage or in the basement.
5. Store potatoes in the cellar, for they should be kept in a cool place.
6. Carlotta moved to Chicago, but her furniture is still in Santa Fe.
7. Do you jog before breakfast or after lunch?
8. Robin speaks Japanese, and she studies Chinese.
9. The post office is located around the corner and to your right.
10. The night was warm, yet we built a fire.

Review: Understanding Conjunctions

Each of the following sentences uses one or more conjunctions to join words or groups of words. Write the sentences and circle each conjunction. Underline the words or groups of words that each conjunction joins, and insert commas if they are needed.

Example

a. Ralph and Emma began the project and completed it on time.

<u>Ralph</u> (and) <u>Emma</u> began <u>the project</u> (and) <u>completed it on time.</u>

1. Is the museum open on the weekend or during the week?

2. Van Gogh was a great artist but he died without a cent.

3. Turnips taste good when served with other vegetables or by themselves.

4. We should see the exhibit soon for it is leaving next week.

5. Do you want your tea with your meal or after dinner?

6. Lynn only drinks fat-free milk for it has fewer calories.

7. Don't watch *The Haunting* alone for it's a very scary movie.

8. The air is warm but the water is freezing!

9. The cat jumped over the chair and onto the dresser.

10. Whenever Mari travels, she becomes excited but anxious.

11. You can drive to Boston or ride the bus.

12. The defense attorney argued her case convincingly and intelligently.

13. When Jenny missed work, her boss was understanding yet disappointed that she hadn't called.

14. Chinese food cooks quickly but it takes some advance preparation.

15. Mystery stories move quickly for they have strong plots.

16. The safecracker slowly and skillfully turned the lock and listened to the tumblers fall.

17. Please put the blanket over the sheet and under the quilt.

18. This broken pitcher cannot be mended by paste or glue.

19. Would you rather walk around the lake or across the field?

20. The storm damaged much property but injured no one.

Applying What You Know

The following selection contains over twenty coordinating conjunctions. List each conjunction on a sheet of paper. Your teacher may ask you which words are joined by the conjunctions.

> Tractors droned and gray dust rose on the horizon, yet my cousins and I had little interest in the plowing. For us, the Wheatland Plowing Match was an annual circus-in-a-field, and

we were much too preoccupied to care which sunburnt farmer carried off the huge silver trophy. First, we trotted stocky Shetlands around a ring marked by rope looped through red iron stakes—once around for a dime or three times for a quarter. From there, we headed toward the exhibits, bobbing under tent ropes but cutting a wide circle around the frightening black steam engine and its whirring belts. Filled with self-importance yet timid in front of the farm dealers, we moved along stashing tin pins shaped like ears of corn, wooden yardsticks, free pencils, and tiny notebooks filled with blank pages into the white shopping bags supplied by the Plainfield Grain Elevator. We stopped only to watch baby chicks hatching and to enter a drawing, for every year we hoped to win the scale model tractor. Stowing our treasures in the car, we trudged across the trampled weeds and ruts to inspect the new farm machinery glistening to the noonday sun. Up in the cab of a red combine, we twisted the steering wheel right and left or imagined ourselves grinding from first to second gear. We had exhausted our finances but not our energies, and we toured the Ladies' Fair, ducking under elbows and around ropes to peer at decorated cakes, embroidered pillows, or handmade sweaters. Proudly, I pointed to the plaid school dress my mother had sewn, for it now boasted a blue ribbon on its collar. Streaked with dirt and perspiration, we headed toward the dinner tent where my grandmother and her friends sat fanning their faces with upturned aprons. Bent over big plates of chicken and yeast rolls, we regaled these ladies with disconnected tales of our morning travels.

Using Conjunctions

Most common problems in using conjunctions involve punctuation. In this section you will practice using conjunctions and punctuating correctly.

Replacing Conjunctions with Punctuation

When more than two items are joined, some conjunctions should be replaced by commas.

Each new recruit was given a uniform *and* a hat *and* a pair of boots *and* a blanket.

Each new recruit was given a uniform, a hat, a pair of boots, *and* a blanket.

For tonight's main course you may have chicken *or* fish *or* turkey *or* lamb *or* spareribs, all of which will be grilled using mesquite chips.

For tonight's main course you may have chicken, fish, turkey, lamb, *or* spareribs, all of which will be grilled using mesquite chips.

Notice that commas never replace *all* the conjunctions in a sentence. When three or more items are joined by the same conjunction, commas can replace all but the last conjunction.

Use a comma and a conjunction between the last two items in a series.

Our hike took us around the pond, across the bridge, *and* through the forest.

You may enter one, two, three, *or* all four events at the church's fund-raising fair.

When the items in the series are word groups with conjunctions, use both commas and conjunctions.

The teams will be Juan and Carol, Ted and Alice, *and* Paul and Kiyo.

The choices for breakfast are bacon and eggs, ham and biscuits, *or* cereal and fruit.

The semicolon (;) can also be used to replace a conjunction.

Instead of a comma and a conjunction between two word groups that could be complete sentences, you may use a semicolon.

It was time to quit for the night, *for* I had begun to feel drowsy.

It was time to quit for the night; I had begun to feel drowsy.

Exercise 4: Replacing Conjunctions with Punctuation

Rewrite each of the following sentences. Replace the conjunctions *and* and *or* with commas to join items in a series. Replace a comma and the word *and* with semicolons to join two complete sentences. Circle the commas and semicolons and underline the conjunctions.

Example

a. You may write your report about a novel or a play or a short story.

You may write your report about a novel ⊙ a play ⊙ <u>or</u> a short story.

1. Lincoln's Birthday and Washington's Birthday and Valentine's Day are all in February.

2. The department store accepts cash or checks or personal charge accounts, and the store will also accept charge cards.

3. Would you rather have bacon and eggs or cream cheese and bagels or crackers and cheese for your breakfast this morning?

4. California has beaches and mountains and forests and deserts within its boundaries.

5. Gabe owned two dogs and six cats and two gerbils and a rabbit, and he decided to move his family to a farm in the country.

6. The tallest building in the United States is either in New York or Chicago or Boston or Dallas.

7. Ricardo traveled to Europe and visited Paris and Rome and London, but he didn't stop in Amsterdam or Brussels.

8. Linda sewed a blouse and a dress and a skirt and a pair of slacks.

9. Every week Lupe jogged two miles and swam fifteen laps and played tennis with her brother and coached a Little League team.

10. Elaine jumped onto the parallel bars, and she did a flip and a split and a handstand.

Using Too Many Conjunctions

Some speakers and writers join sentences with conjunctions without thinking whether they should actually be joined. The result may be too many conjunctions in a piece of writing.

> During this summer's County Fair an old biplane landed in a field next to the fairgrounds, and I ran over to talk to the pilot, and when he took off his goggles, I discovered that he was a she, and I talked with her for a while about her plane and about how it felt to fly, and she said that the best way to find out about flying was for me to hop in and take a ride, so for the next half hour, I had the time of my life, and we did spins and loops until we returned to the fairgrounds, and then I waved good-bye and watched her fly off, knowing that we would not meet again, but now I know the thrill of flying, and I know that it's a thrill I'll never forget.

In the following paragraph the overused conjunctions have been removed, making it easier for you to understand.

> During this summer's County Fair an old biplane landed in a field next to the fairgrounds. I ran over to talk to the pilot, and when he removed his goggles, I discovered that he was a she. I talked with her for a while about her plane and about how it felt to fly. She said that the best way to find out about flying was for me to hop in and take a ride. For the next half hour, I had the time of my life. We did spins and loops until we returned to the fairgrounds. Then I waved good-bye and watched her fly off, knowing that we would not meet again. But now I know the thrill of flying, and I know that it's a thrill I'll never forget.

Review: Using Conjunctions

Rewrite the following paragraph and remove the unnecessary conjunctions. Be sure to end each sentence with a period, question mark, or an exclamation point and to begin each new sentence with a capital letter.

> The ancient Egyptians buried their pharaohs with great treasures of jewelry and gold, and over the centuries, local robbers found and plundered many of the tombs, and then the robbers sold the valuables for vast fortunes, and once some brothers in a small village near the Valley

of the Kings found a pharaoh's tomb that was so rich in treasure that they could not take it all at once, so the brothers used the tomb like a bank, and whenever they needed some money, they would go to the tomb and take some jewelry or other valuables and sell them for cash, and when that money was used up, they would go back and take some more precious treasure. Eventually the local authorities became rather suspicious, and they tracked down the brothers, and they finally confessed, and their career of robbery came to an abrupt end.

Writing Focus: *Using* *Conjunctions in Writing*

Good writers use conjunctions to connect their thoughts and to make their writing flow more smoothly. Conjunctions tell readers how one idea or event relates to another, and they allow writers to express themselves in mature ways.

Assignment: *Morning Rush*

Uh, oh! While you were asleep last night, the electricity went off for thirty minutes. In the morning your whole family ran late for work and school. Write one or more well-developed paragraphs describing the panic of your family's rushing to get out of the house as quickly as possible.

A. Prewriting

Use brainstorming, described in Chapter 1, to jot down words and phrases that occur to you as you recall times everyone was running late. Include details about actions and sounds. Look back over the items on your brainstorming list, and underline the details that best describe your family's rush. Number them in chronological order.

B. Writing

Using your brainstorming list to help you, write one or more paragraphs describing the panic of your family's rushing to get to work and school after getting up late. Begin your description with your discovery that your alarm clock rang a half hour late. Then move to everyone's rushing around trying to get ready to leave the house. Include details that paint a moving picture. As you write, use conjunctions to combine ideas and to make relationships between ideas clear.

C. Postwriting

Use the following checklist to revise your first draft.

1. Have I included specific details?

2. Have I combined short sentences with conjunctions?

3. Have I used the appropriate conjunctions to show the relationship between my ideas?

Edit your paragraphs using the Checklist for Proofreading at the back of the book. If appropriate, share your description with your classmates by reading it aloud.

19 Interjections
Understanding Interjections

Interjections are usually defined as words that show a strong or sudden feeling.

You will notice that some interjections are followed by an exclamation mark.

> *Help!* I can't swim.

> *Ugh!* This tastes awful.

> *Hurray!* We made it.

Interjections show emotion or surprise. The feeling, however, may be very mild. Mild interjections are followed by a comma.

> *Oh,* I don't know about that.

> *Well,* you have your opinion, and I have mine.

> *Okay,* let's get this show on the road.

Some words (such as *ouch, whew, alas, oh, hey, yippee,* and the like) can be only interjections and never any other part of speech. Other words (such as *goodness, well, never, my, great,* and *nonsense)* can be either interjections or some other part of speech, depending upon how they are used.

My, that certainly is beautiful.	[interjection]
Are you referring to *my* painting?	[possessive pronoun]
Terrific! That is exactly what I wanted.	[interjection]
The coast was lashed by a *terrific* storm.	[adjective]

Many interjections (such as *Good grief!* and *Dear me!*) are made up of more than one word.

Exercise 1: *Identifying Interjections*

Write the following sentences and underline each interjection.

Example

a. After the explosion the professor cried, "Goodness gracious! What have you done?"

After the explosion the professor cried, "<u>Goodness gracious!</u> What have you done?"

1. Ouch! That cat just scratched me.

2. When it started to pour, Noreko declared, "Well, we'll just have to move our picnic indoors."

3. Yay! The office is closed on Friday, so we have a long weekend.

4. Oh, I don't mind waiting a little longer.

5. Help! The bookshelves in the north wing of the library just collapsed.

6. When he discovered the plans, Jack said, "Terrific!"

7. Whew! It was really a close race.

8. Nonsense! Toads do not give you warts. That is a fallacy.

9. Barbara argued, "Well, I'll never take that job after talking to him."

10. Hey! Don't pick those flowers. They can cause an allergic reaction in some people.

Review: *Understanding Interjections*

The selection on this page and the next is from the story "So Much Unfairness of Things," by C. D. B. Bryan. In this part of the story, two boys named P.S. and Charlie Merritt are talking about a Latin exam. During their conversation they use many interjections. On a sheet of paper numbered 1–5, list five interjections found in this selection.

"For Pete's sake, P.S.! I just made the bed!"

"O.K., O.K., I'll straighten it up when I leave." P.S. ran his fingers across the desk top. "Merritt, two demerits—dust. . . . Hey, the exam's at ten-thirty, isn't it?"

"Yep. If you flunk Latin again, will they make you go to summer school?"

Archaic means "old-fashioned."

"Probably. I really think it's archaic the way they make you pass Latin to get out of this place."

"Boy, I sure hope I pass it," Charlie said.

"You will. You will. You're the brain in the class."

"Come on, let's go to chow."

"That's what I've been waiting for, my good buddy, my good friend, old pal of mine." P.S. jumped off the bed, scooped up his notebook, and started out of the room.

"Hey!" Charlie said. "What about the bed?"[1]

Using Interjections

A speaker's voice shows the difference between mild and strong interjections. In writing, this difference is shown with punctuation. A mild interjection is usually followed by a comma. An exclamation point after the interjection shows a strong emotion or feeling.

Well, let me think about it until morning.	[mild]
Well! I have never been more insulted in my life!	[strong]

Do not use a comma or a period together with an exclamation point, even in a direct quotation. Capitalize the word following an exclamation mark only if the word begins a new sentence.

"Ouch!" he cried out.

"Charge! We have them on the run."

Exercise 2: Using Interjections

Write the following sentences and underline each interjection. Place an exclamation point after an interjection that shows a strong or sudden feeling. Place a comma after an interjection that expresses a milder emotion. Capitalize the first word after an exclamation point if that word begins a new sentence.

---

[1]From "So Much Unfairness of Things" by C. D. B. Bryan, *The New Yorker*. Copyright © 1962 by C. D. B. Bryan. Reprinted by permission of Brandt & Brandt Literary Agents, Inc.

Examples

a. Golly Mr. Wizard, how does that thing work?
   <u>Golly</u>, Mr. Wizard, how does that thing work?

b. Wow that was the longest home run I've ever seen.
   <u>Wow!</u> That was the longest home run I've ever seen.

1. Jonathan frantically yelled, "Watch out a car is coming."

2. Well I can give you a ride to school if you're ready to leave now.

3. Mark answered the door and said, "Oh I thought you were arriving tomorrow."

4. Grandfather moaned, "Gracious I've never seen such a mess."

5. Ouch I've just cut myself.

6. Fantastic you've just scored the touchdown that will win the game for us.

7. Oh I hung your coat in the hall closet.

8. Arlene yelled, "Hey someone just ran away with my purse."

9. Help I'm stuck in the elevator.

10. "Good grief" he cried. "The storm has turned cars upside down."

Writing Focus: *Using*

Interjections in Writing

Interjections are used to express strong emotions or sudden feelings, usually in dialogue. When you write dialogue, use interjections that are appropriate for the speaker. Your friends, for example, probably don't use the same interjections that your parents do.

Assignment: *A Pumpkin's Life*

Notice the photographs of the two pumpkins on these two pages. Imagine that the pumpkins have been put out on the steps after a Halloween party on October 31st. These pumpkins are special. They have been touched by the magic of Halloween night—they can speak!

Write the conversation/dialogue that the two pumpkins might be having on the steps. In it show their different personalities through topics of conversation and use of interjections. Let your audience of classmates and teacher have a glimpse of the pumpkins' lives from the pumpkins' point of view. Your work will be evaluated for effective and correct use of interjections.

Use the following steps to complete this assignment.

A. Prewriting

Study the pumpkins carefully. After especially noticing the different expressions on their faces, jot down your impression of the personalities of the two pumpkins. Then make a list of topics of conversation that they might discuss. (How they came to be at the Halloween party might be one fascinating topic!) Now make two word clusters, described in Chapter 1, about the conversation, one for each pumpkin. Add snippets of conversation about the topics that pumpkins might discuss that would be appropriate to their different personalities. Let your imagination help you create this unusual, magical dialogue. Choose two or three of the topics to write about at greater length.

B. Writing

Write a short dialogue between the two pumpkins. Begin with a few sentences describing the scene. Then write the dialogue, using the ideas from your word clusters. Let the dialogue develop naturally as the pumpkins discuss different topics. Include appropriate interjections.

C. Postwriting

Revise your first draft using the following checklist.

1. Have I captured two different speech personalities, one for each pumpkin?

2. Have I used interjections accurately to express emotion?

3. Have I punctuated and capitalized the interjections and other elements of the dialogue correctly?

Edit your draft using the Checklist for Proofreading at the back of the book. If appropriate, share your dialogue with your classmates, and discuss the human qualities students give to the pumpkins.

20 Sentence Structure

Understanding Sentences

Sentences are made by arranging words to form complete thoughts. You can learn to identify sentences in three different ways: by learning the definition, by looking at the kinds of sentences, and by studying the structure of a sentence to see how it is put together. In this section you will study and practice each of these ways.

Defining Sentences

A *sentence* is usually defined as a group of words that expresses a complete thought.

Played basketball until dark	[incomplete thought]
We played basketball until dark.	[sentence]
Neither Jeff nor Joanne	[incomplete thought]
Neither Jeff nor Joanne plays guitar.	[sentence]
For more than 10,000 meters	[incomplete thought]
Melissa swam for more than 10,000 meters.	[sentence]

A sentence that does not have a complete thought is called a *fragment*.

Exercise 1: Identifying Sentences

Some of the following groups of words are sentences, and some are not. Number a sheet of paper 1–10. If the group of words is not a sentence, write (*Fragment*) next to its number. If it is a sentence, write the sentence and place a period after it.

Examples

a. Coming home from the dance
   (Fragment)

b. The party was over at 11:00
   The party was over at 11:00.

1. Sometimes in the afternoon

2. On the sidelines by the players' bench

3. Christine will be elected president

4. The man who looked through the binoculars

5. My brothers never arrive late for dinner

6. The drama club will meet on Tuesday night

7. The player who hit the home run

8. The plants on the windowsill need watering

9. Makes that lay-up shot look easy

10. Neither the boys nor the girls in Mr. Chang's class

Kinds of Sentences

There are four kinds of sentences: declarative, imperative, interrogative, and exclamatory. Each conveys a different kind of thought and is written in a different way.

A *declarative sentence* makes a statement and ends with a period.

Human beings first walked on the moon in 1969.

The moon walk was a historic event.

An *imperative sentence* gives a command or makes a request, and ends with a period.

Tell me the name of our first astronaut.

Write his name on the blackboard.

An *interrogative sentence* asks a question and ends with a question mark.

What was the name of the first satellite to orbit the planet Earth?

Where did the rocket land on the moon?

An *exclamatory sentence* expresses a strong or sudden feeling, and ends with an exclamation point.

What a thrill it must be to walk in space!

Just imagine the view!

Exercise 2: Identifying and Punctuating Kinds of Sentences

Write each of the following sentences and use the correct end punctuation. After the sentence, write in parentheses whether it is declarative, imperative, interrogative, or exclamatory.

Examples

---

a. Raise your hand when you are finished
   Raise your hand when you are finished. (imperative)

b. When I finished, I raised my hand
   When I finished, I raised my hand. (declarative)

1. Who invented the parking meter

2. Carl Magee invented the parking meter

3. Please park your car by a meter

4. The traffic light was used first in Detroit

5. That light is red

6. Where can you find the most crooked street in the entire world

7. Lombard Street is in San Francisco

8. What a winding road

9. Drive slowly on Lombard Street

10. Do you have any more questions

The Parts of a Sentence

A sentence has two basic parts: a *subject* and a *predicate*.

Subject	Predicate
The pine cones on the lawn	cluttered the backyard.

The *subject* of a sentence identifies the person, place, thing, or idea that is being spoken about in the rest of the sentence. However, it does not always come at the beginning of the sentence. In the following sentences the subjects are underlined.

Herman plays chess.
A beautiful white stallion led the parade.
When was John F. Kennedy elected?

The *simple subject* is the main word in the subject of the sentence. In the following sentences the subjects are underlined, and the simple subjects are *italicized*.

The two oak *trees* had to be cut down.
Someone in the back of the room is whispering.

The *complete subject* is the main word plus its modifiers. In the following sentences the complete subjects are underlined:

Three students from our school spent the summer in France.
The beagle pups on the front porch are ours.

Sometimes the simple subject and the complete subject are the same.

Amelia Earhart was a famous flyer.
Did you forget your raincoat?

447

Exercise 3: *Identifying Complete and Simple Subjects*

Write the following sentences and underline the complete subject. Draw a circle around the simple subject.

Examples

---

a. Our favorite movie is playing at the theater.

Our favorite (movie) is playing at the theater.

b. Where are you going after school?

Where are (you) going after school?

1. Two noisy pigeons landed on the sill.

2. Florence Chadwick swam across the English Channel.

3. When did Arthur Ashe win at Wimbledon?

4. The famous Rosetta stone was discovered in Egypt in 1799.

5. Has anyone in your family ever run in a marathon?

6. Maria's favorite uncle starred in a Broadway play.

7. The silly dog ran around in circles after its tail.

8. Will you live in the dormitory this fall?

9. After studying for hours, Sui Ling fell asleep at her desk.

10. An action-packed western played at our neighborhood theater last week.

The Predicate

The *predicate* of a sentence is the part that says something about the subject.

In the following sentences the predicates are underlined twice.

The old library was torn down last year.

Janet received a track scholarship from the university.

The *simple predicate* is the verb or verb phrase in the complete predicate.

The predicates in the following sentences are underlined twice. The simple predicates are *italicized*.

My family *went* to Chicago for our vacation.

We *should have been* there by now.

Adverbs such as *not, never,* and *ever* sometimes separate parts of a simple predicate. These negative adverbs are never part of the simple predicate.

You must *not* quit until this afternoon.

You should*n't* go out in the rain.

The *complete predicate* includes the simple predicate and all the words and phrases that modify it.

The complete predicates in the following sentences are underlined twice.

The pouring rain filled the street with puddles.

Pearl Buck wrote the prize-winning novel *The Good Earth.*

Do you remember her new address?

Exercise 4: Identifying Complete and Simple Predicates

Write the following sentences and underline the complete predicate twice. Circle the simple predicate.

Examples

a. The two model planes collided in midair.

The two model planes (collided) in midair.

b. An electric car will not go far on a single charge.

An electric car (will) not (go) far on a single charge.

1. The ride to the city is longer during rush hour.

2. You shouldn't stand under a tree during an electrical storm.

3. Which television show has run the longest?

4. We must enroll for that popular course by the beginning of September.

5. Your sister did not call last night.

6. A baby is crying somewhere in the building.

7. Have you been driving all day?

8. We lived in Tucson for seven years.

9. Rosa already has typed the letters.

10. Haven't you ever overslept on a cold, rainy Monday morning?

Understood Subjects

The subject of a sentence can be *you* understood.

Understood subjects do not actually appear in the sentence. The reader understands that the subject is *you*. The subject of an imperative sentence is usually *you* understood.

Be sure to get there before five o'clock.
(*You*) be sure to get there before five o'clock.
understood subject: (*you*)

Please take your seats.
(*You*) please take your seats.
understood subject: (*you*)

The understood *you* is the simple and complete subject of the sentence.

Even when the name of the person or group that is being spoken to is given in an imperative sentence, the subject is still *you* understood.

Cheryl, tell us about your trip to Canada.
Cheryl, (*you*) tell us about your trip to Canada.
understood subject: (*you*)

Pass your papers to the front, class.
(*You*) pass your papers to the front, class.
understood subject: (*you*)

Exercise 5: *Identifying Simple Subjects and Simple Predicates*

Write the following sentences. Underline the simple subject once and the simple predicate twice. If the simple subject is *you* understood, write (*you*) after the sentence.

Examples

a. Listen to me very carefully.
   Listen to me very carefully. (you)

b. For tomorrow's class you will need a dictionary.
   For tomorrow's class you will need a dictionary.

1. Don't feed the animals!
2. Please put your name on your paper.
3. When were you born?
4. Please drive carefully.
5. Has anyone written to Denise?
6. Cross at the corner.
7. I stayed at the beach last weekend.
8. Don't fight with your sister.
9. Elaine, please answer the first question.
10. Please pass the ham, Maria.

Compound Subjects and Verbs

A *compound subject* consists of two or more connected subjects that have the same verb.

Compound subjects are usually connected by coordinating conjunctions such as *and* and *or*.

Jackie and I have worked at the same department store for two years.

The choir, the orchestra, or the band will perform at graduation.

Neither our basketball team nor our football squad is in the yearbook.

A *compound verb* consists of two or more connected verbs or verb phrases that have the same subject.

A compound verb or verb phrase is joined by a conjunction (usually *and, but, or,* or *nor*).

The teacher studied and worked all summer.

The class worked for days but could not finish the project.

A sentence with a compound verb may also have a compound subject.

Tim and Michael worked all day and slept all night.

Exercise 6: *Identifying Compound Subjects and Compound Verbs*

Some of the following sentences have a compound subject, some have a compound verb, and some have both. Write the sentences, underlining each subject once and each verb or verb phrase twice.

Examples

---

a. The wind and sun ruined our snow sculpture.
   The wind and sun ruined our snow sculpture.

b. Maria and Jim dance, sing, and play an instrument.
   Maria and Jim dance, sing, and play an instrument.

1. Schools and banks were closed for the election.
2. Both of the candidates and all of their friends waited anxiously.
3. Will Pamela and Glenn cook and serve dinner?
4. Many cabdrivers drive during the night and sleep during the day.
5. Someone called the fire department.
6. We washed and waxed the car yesterday.

7. Either Chicago or Los Angeles has the world's busiest airport.

8. Jack, Nancy, and some of their friends work at the store.

9. Neither gold nor silver weighs as much as lead.

10. One of the letters and both of the packages were late.

Simple and Compound Sentences

A *simple sentence* is a sentence that has only one subject and one verb.

The three exchange <u>students</u> <u>returned</u> home yesterday.

The <u>conductor</u> of the orchestra <u>walked</u> onto the stage.

A simple sentence may have a compound subject and a compound verb and still be a simple sentence.

Two <u>houses</u> and a <u>trailer</u> <u>were</u> damaged.	[simple sentence]
The store <u>opens</u> early and <u>closes</u> late.	[simple sentence]

A *compound sentence* is a sentence that consists of two or more simple sentences joined by a conjunction.

Compound sentences are formed by using a comma and the conjunctions *and, but, or, for, yet,* or *nor* between two or more simple sentences.

<u>Uncle Max</u> <u>arrived</u> at midnight, *and* we <u>met</u> him at the station.	[compound sentence]
We <u>worked</u> hard and <u>slept</u> outdoors, *but* <u>all</u> of us <u>enjoyed</u> our week at camp.	[compound sentence]

Exercise 7: Identifying Simple and Compound Sentences

Write the following sentences. Underline simple subjects once and simple predicates twice. Circle coordinating conjunctions. If the sentence is simple, write (*Simple*) next to it; if it is compound, write (*Compound*) next to it.

Example

a. Fresh fruit and vegetables should be washed and refrigerated.

Fresh fruit (and) vegetables should be washed (and) refrigerated. (Simple)

---

1. Lena brushed the cat and clipped its claws.

2. One of the tigers was stalking, but both of the lions were sleeping.

3. Will Pamela and Glenn cook and serve dinner?

4. Neither Nellie nor I could win a tennis match against Sandra, for she plays every day.

5. The storm broke on Friday, but by Saturday morning the skies cleared.

6. Someone called the fire department.

7. Will the concert be held tomorrow, or has it been post-poned indefinitely?

8. The grocery store was hiring salespeople, yet none of us got a job.

9. Is the movie still playing, or has it closed already?

10. Mari and Nell will drive to Jacksonville, and then they will fly to Miami.

Sentence Patterns

Sentences follow five different patterns. The following list shows these basic patterns.

1. **S-V**
   Subject-Verb

2. **S-V-DO**
   Subject-Verb-Direct Object

3. **S-V-IO-DO**
   Subject-Verb-Indirect Object-Direct Object

4. **S-LV-PN**
   Subject-Linking Verb-Predicate Noun (or Pronoun)

5. **S-LV-PA**
   Subject-Linking Verb-Predicate Adjective

The groups of words that follow the subject and verb in a sentence pattern are called *complements*.

A *complement* is a part of the predicate that completes the thought begun by the subject and verb.

S-V *Sentence Pattern*

Some groups of words can express a complete thought with just a subject and verb.

    S   V
Birds fly.

      S   V
The bell in the tower sounded.

         S   V
The ancient bell in the church tower sounded across the plains.

Even though several modifiers may be a part of a sentence, a sentence can still follow the S-V pattern.

S-V-DO *Sentence Pattern*

A *direct object* is usually defined as a noun or pronoun that follows an action verb and answers the question *what?* or *whom?* about the subject and verb.

DO
Janet recites *poetry*.   [Janet recites what?]

DO
We invited *him* to our party.   [We invited whom?]

A sentence may have more than one direct object.

  S   V   DO   DO   DO
We read several *poems, stories,* and *essays* by Stephen Crane.

Direct objects receive the action of the verb or show the result of that action. They cannot follow forms of the verb *be* or linking verbs.

Exercise 8: *Identifying* S-V-DO *Sentence Parts*

All of the following sentences contain direct objects. Write the sentences and label and underline the different parts of the sentence pattern.

Example

---

a. Grandfather carried Sally and pushed the baby.

        S   V   DO   V   DO
Grandfather carried Sally and pushed the baby.

1. Pedro and Maria performed magic tricks.

2. First Pedro clapped his hands.

3. Then he pulled a rabbit, a duck, and an egg from a hat.

4. Maria found a ring in her ear.

5. Maria chose a volunteer from the audience.

6. The assistant selected a card from the deck.

7. The magician discovered the card in his pocket.

8. Pedro changed a handkerchief into a long scarf.

9. Maria blindfolded Pedro and handcuffed him.

10. Pedro magically undid the handcuffs and amazed the audience.

S-V-IO-DO *Sentence Pattern*

An *indirect object* (IO) is a noun or a pronoun that answers the question *to what? for what? to whom?* or *for whom?* about the subject, verb, and direct object in a sentence.

The indirect object always appears between the verb and the direct object.

S	V	IO	DO

Suzanne sent *Mary* a thank-you note.   [sent to whom?]

S	V	IO	DO

I bought *her* a watch for her birthday.   [bought for whom?]

Note: Indirect objects are never part of a prepositional phrase.

Exercise 9: *Identifying S-V-IO-DO Sentence Parts*

Write the following sentences and label the parts of the sentence pattern. Underline the words you label. (If the subject is *you* understood, write *you* in parentheses in front of the sentence.)

Example

a. I gave the officer the license number of the truck.

S V   IO   DO
I gave the officer the license number of the truck.

1. Barney sent Diane flowers on her birthday.

2. Professor Manuelos showed his morning classes a documentary.

3. Our class wrote letters to the President.

4. The astronauts brought rocks from the moon.

5. Eleanor offered a prize to the winner.

6. Toby threw his dog a stick.

7. Maria brought some food for us.

8. The comedian told the audience some jokes.

9. Please don't give me any dessert.

10. Will your landlord give you a new lease?

S-LV-PN *Sentence Pattern*

A *predicate noun* (PN) or *predicate pronoun* is the noun or pronoun that follows a *linking verb* in a sentence and explains or identifies the subject of the sentence.

Predicate nouns and predicate pronouns are complements because they complete the meaning of the subject in the sentence.

```
   S   LV              PN
You are a very fine swimmer.
```

```
                 S        LV       PN
Our next President may be a woman.
```

```
S  LV                PN
I am the perfect person for that job.
```

```
  S   LV   PN
Emily is the one near the back.        [predicate pronoun]
```

```
     S          LV        PN
The winner should have been she.       [predicate pronoun]
```

Whenever a personal pronoun is used as a predicate noun, it should always be in its subject form.

```
          S                 LV   PN
The leading scorer on the team was she. [predicate pronoun]
```

Exercise 10: Identifying S-LV-PN *Sentence Parts*

Write the following sentences and label the parts of the sentence pattern. Underline the words you label.

Example

> a. Most ballet dancers are talented athletes.
>
>   S   LV   PN
> Most ballet <u>dancers</u> <u>are</u> talented <u>athletes</u>.

1. The first prize is a new car.
2. Our psychology professor once was an actor.
3. Jake is one of the finalists.
4. Your guide is either Shelly or he.
5. That horse is not a palomino.
6. Those houses are some of the oldest in town.
7. Elaine Coville must have been the youngest woman on the team.
8. The oldest member is either she or I.
9. The tabby cat is the one with stripes.
10. Juan will be an astronaut someday.

S-LV-PA *Sentence Pattern*

A *predicate adjective* (PA) is an adjective that appears in the predicate and follows a linking verb. The predicate adjective modifies the subject of the sentence.

        S   LV   PA
The <u>coins</u> <u>were</u> *rusty*.

     S   LV   PA
<u>Albert</u> <u>seemed</u> very *happy* about the test.

   S   LV   PA
<u>He</u> <u>became</u> *sad* upon hearing the results.

                               S   LV   PA
Throughout the winter the <u>army</u> <u>remained</u> *strong* and
   PA
confident.

                S   LV   PA   PA   PA
After the game the <u>team</u> <u>felt</u> *weak*, *tired*, and *beaten*.

459

Exercise 11: Identifying S-LV-PA *Sentence Parts*

Write the following sentences and label the words that form the sentence pattern. Underline the words you label.

a. Juanita has been cranky all day.

<pre>
   S   LV   PA
Juanita has been cranky all day.
</pre>

b. Do you feel hungry or thirsty?

<pre>
LV S   LV   PA   PA
Do you feel hungry or thirsty?
</pre>

1. The vacationers seemed relaxed and rested.

2. These hamburgers taste greasy.

3. The interviewer's questions were direct and challenging.

4. We felt frightened in the empty house.

5. Her clothes always look stylish.

6. Does this perfume smell too sweet?

7. Everyone on the jury was happy about the verdict.

8. That sunflower is enormous!

9. The city is exciting, but very noisy.

10. Some of the fruit tastes rotten.

Review: Understanding Sentences

Write the following sentences. If the sentence is a simple sentence, underline the complete subject once and the complete predicate twice. Circle the simple subject and the simple predicate. If the sentence is a compound sentence, write it as separate sentences, underlining each complete subject once and complete predicate twice, and circling each simple subject and simple predicate.

Example

a. Why didn't I think of that?

Why (did)n't (I) (think) of that?

1. Neither you nor I should carry those heavy cartons.

2. Ellen listens to rock-and-roll, but Marge prefers jazz.

3. One of those musicians played in a jazz band.

4. Did he play the saxophone or sing?

5. Kuni will cut the vegetables and make a salad.

6. Arnie wants Russian dressing on his salâd, but Louise wants French.

7. Mitchell roasted a turkey, made cranberry sauce, and baked potatoes.

8. Carolyn set the table, and she made some appetizers.

9. Have you written to your aunt or called your grandmother today?

10. Crowfoot, a great hunter and brave warrior, was born in 1821.

Each of the following sentences contains one or more complements. Write the sentences and label the words that form the sentence patterns. Be careful to check for compound subjects and verbs. Underline the words you label. (If the subject is *you* understood, write *you* in parentheses before the sentence.)

Example

a. I will mail you a check and bring you the form.

<pre>
S   V   IO   DO   V   IO   DO
I will mail you a check and bring you the form.
</pre>

11. I was once afraid of dogs.

12. Please bring both of the books to class.

13. The employment agency sent Luis and him the forms.

14. White roses are expensive.

15. The captains will be Irene and she.

16. We remained active in the tenants' association.

17. One of the best drivers is she.

18. Raul is always eager for adventure.

19. Peter will be president of the company within two years.

20. Our boss gave us a vacation.

Using Sentences

Two common errors in using sentences are the *sentence fragment* and the *run-on sentence*. This section will give you practice in correcting both of these errors.

Avoiding Sentence Fragments

> **A *sentence fragment* is a separated part of a sentence that does not express a complete thought.**

A sentence must have a subject, a verb, and sometimes a complement to be complete. (An asterisk [*] indicates a feature that is not a part of Edited Standard English.)

*With great courage and obvious ambition	[fragment]
José ran the race with great courage and obvious ambition.	[sentence]
*Losing her wallet on the beach	[fragment]
Losing her wallet on the beach, Lisa became depressed.	[sentence]
*After her wallet was found	[fragment]
Lisa celebrated after her wallet was found.	[sentence]

Sometimes a fragment has a subject and a verb, but it still does not express a complete thought.

S LV *The strawberry pie tastes (what? or how?)	[fragment]
The strawberry pie tastes sweet.	[sentence]

S V *When we arrived(what happened?)	[fragment]
When we arrived our parents were waiting.	[sentence]

Exercise 12: Correcting Sentence Fragments

If one of the following groups of words is a sentence, write (*Sentence*) next to its number on your paper. If the group of words is a fragment, add the words and punctuation necessary to make it a complete thought and write the new sentence on your paper.

Examples

a. Finding a needle in a haystack
   Finding a needle in a haystack is a difficult task.

b. After swimming all afternoon, we cooked hamburgers
   (Sentence)

1. When the coach blew the whistle
2. Flying in the helicopter above New York City
3. The charity tennis match was won by the former world champion
4. Seldom in the mysterious late hours of the night
5. The brisk mountain air and the crystal clear stream felt
6. The crumbling brick wall collapsed unnoticed in the neighborhood
7. Bored by seeing the same movie again, Hiromi fell asleep
8. Puzzled by the last problem on the math test
9. On the narrow ledge bordering the twenty-fifth story of the new bank building
10. Since the high-wire artist was blindfolded this time

Avoiding Run-On Sentences

A *run-on sentence* consists of two or more sentences separated by a comma or by no mark of punctuation.

An asterisk [*] indicates a feature that is not a part of Edited Standard English.

463

*My favorite snack is sunflower seeds I eat them all the time when I watch television.	[run-on]
My favorite snack is sunflower seeds. I eat them all the time when I watch television.	[correction]
*The audience applauded after the concert, then the orchestra stood up and bowed.	[run-on]
The audience applauded after the concert. Then the orchestra stood up and bowed.	[correction]

A run-on sentence can be corrected with an end mark to separate the two complete thoughts, with a comma and a conjunction, or with a semicolon to join two related sentences.

Adding End Punctuation

*I met my friends at the movie theater we bought our tickets and some popcorn, the front row was empty and waiting for us.	[run-on]
I met my friends at the movie theater. We bought our tickets and some popcorn. The front row was empty and waiting for us.	[correction]

Using Conjunctions and Proper Punctuation

*My brother and I worked at odd jobs all summer, we wanted money to spend on our vacation at the beach.	[run-on]
My brother and I worked at odd jobs all summer, *for* we wanted money to spend on our vacation at the beach.	[correction]

Using Semicolons

*Juan's sister wants to study art his brother wants to study music.	[run-on]
Juan's sister wants to study art; his brother wants to study music.	[correction]

Exercise 13: Correcting Run-on Sentences

Correct the run-on sentences in the following groups of words by adding end punctuation after complete thoughts or by joining related ideas with conjunctions or a semicolon. Rewrite the corrected sentences on your paper. Circle the punctuation and conjunctions you add.

Example

---

a. No one noticed our arrival, we were very quiet.

No one noticed our arrival, (for) we were very quiet.

1. Many people enjoy visiting Mexico, the Aztec ruins are particularly interesting.

2. Five resort hotels on the coast had to be rebuilt, the hurricane damaged them badly.

3. Where was all the noise coming from, she thought no one was home next door.

4. I could really use some help, my project is due tomorrow.

5. Most of us are excited about the space shuttle, others think it is a waste of money.

6. Sometimes I'm just too tired to jog in the morning, I guess I should get more sleep.

7. I cleaned my bedroom, then I raked the yard, then I joined my friends on the baseball field.

8. My brother is teaching me how to ski, he says it will strengthen my leg muscles.

9. This state park is a popular picnic area, we can't find a single empty table to use.

10. Few people believe the old superstition about the groundhog, we celebrate Groundhog Day every year.

Review: Using Sentences

Some of the following groups of words are fragments, some are run-ons, and some are complete sentences. Number a sheet of paper 1–20. If a sentence is correct, write (*Correct*) next to its number. If the group of words is a fragment or a run-on, rewrite the words as a correct sentence or sentences. Circle the punctuation and conjunctions you add.

Example

a. While driving along the road.

While driving along the road ⊙ we saw an armadillo.

1. Which told us there was a detour ahead.

2. After walking for hours, we found our way back to camp.

3. Ramero wanted to grow five inches in the summer, he wanted to try out for the basketball team next fall.

4. March is a great month for flying kites, I think I'll build one myself this year.

5. Dressed in a clown outfit and carrying a huge umbrella.

6. Tyrone inherited that saxophone from his uncle, he takes lessons every week.

7. Nervous about being late for the performance.

8. After the assembly Luis and Raoul found a jacket under the bleachers.

9. When the volume on the radio went up to full blast.

10. Last Saturday we went to the state fair, it will be at the fairgrounds for another week.

11. Last night's blizzard brought traffic to a standstill.

12. I mistakenly used the wrong ingredient, now I always read the label first.

13. Thinking that we might be late, Julio called our parents before we left.

14. After campaigning hard and giving speeches, Ty became.

15. The only difference between your report and mine.

16. As a surprise for his mother, Steve dug a garden, it was very small, it was just what she needed.

17. Nervously waiting in front of the train station.

18. The dogs begged and performed tricks for the bones, then they found their favorite place to chew on them.

19. The cat howling on the fence outside my window.

20. Highways were closed because motorists would freeze if cars stalled.

Writing Focus: *Improving*

Sentence Structure in Writing

You can strengthen your writing style by using a variety of simple and compound sentences. Make sure your sentences are not fragments or run-ons.

Assignment: *A Good Job*

To earn money for that special something you've always wanted, you've agreed to babysit all day Saturday for the three small children down the block. You like the two boys and the girl, but they are active and curious—a real handful. You need a master plan in order to amuse the children and to make the day a good one.

Write one or more well-developed paragraphs mapping out how to spend the day caring for the children. Write for yourself and for the children's parents. Explain what you'll do in the order you'll need to do it. Be as precise as you can. Your paragraphs will be evaluated for correct and varied sentences.

Use the following steps to complete this assignment.

A. Prewriting

Imagine yourself being an all-day babysitter. Picture the three young children, their house, and the physical surroundings of the neighborhood. List items you could use to amuse and care for the children. Then list the steps you'll need to follow in

order to get through the day. Don't worry about the order of the steps. For now, just jot down everything you can think of that will help you babysit. Use specific details. Group and number the steps in the order you'll need to perform them.

B. Writing

Using your list, write one or more paragraphs explaining how you'll spend the day with the three children. Begin by discussing any items you'll need to assemble, such as games, snacks, and soap, for example. Then go through the steps of what you'll do in the proper order. Use words like *first*, *next*, *then*, *while*, and *last of all* to help organize the time. As you write, pay particular attention to using a variety of complete sentences.

C. Postwriting

Revise your first draft, using the following checklist.

1. Have I included enough information so that I (and the children's parents) will know what will happen all day long?

2. Do my plans have a logical organization?

3. Have I varied the structure of my sentences?

Edit your draft using the Checklist for Proofreading at the back of the book. If appropriate, share your writing with your classmates to compare babysitting methods.

3
Mechanics

21 Punctuation

Punctuation Marks

Using voice alone, a speaker can give three different meanings to the words *Janet is here.* Spoken evenly and directly, *Janet is here* is a simple statement. If the speaker's voice rises at the end, *Janet is here* becomes a question. And if the speaker's voice is higher or louder than usual, *Janet is here* shows excitement.

Writers cannot use sounds to help communicate their meanings; instead they depend on symbols called *punctuation marks*. The spoken words *Janet is here* can be followed by three different punctuation marks, each with a different meaning:

Janet is here.	[simple statement]
Janet is here?	[question]
Janet is here!	[exclamation]

Writers must agree on how punctuation marks are used in order to communicate clearly. Imagine how difficult it would be to drive a car if a green light meant *Go* in one city and *Stop* in another. In this section you will learn the rules for using punctuation marks.

Using Punctuation

Punctuation marks have four main uses.

Punctuation marks separate.

Some punctuation marks show where to separate one word, group of words, or sentences from another. For example, the period (.) separates one sentence from another following it. The comma (,) separates items in a series.

Kevin squirted oil on his pet monkey. He wanted to see a monkeyshine.

Tina brought lettuce, a cucumber, a tomato, a green pepper, and a bunch of carrots to make a salad.

Punctuation marks link.

Some punctuation marks join words or numerals. For example, the hyphen (-) is often used to link the parts of a compound word or to link numbers.

Her father-in-law is a famous violinist.

The sixteen-inch softball broke her finger.

Punctuation marks show omission.

Some punctuation marks show that letters or words have been left out. For example, the apostrophe (') in the word *can't* shows that two letters have been omitted.

I *cannot* find my keys anywhere.

I *can't* find my keys anywhere.

Punctuation marks enclose.

Some marks of punctuation are used in pairs to show that the words they enclose belong together. For example, quotation marks (" . . .") enclose many titles.

We sang "The Star-Spangled Banner."

End Marks

Punctuation marks that come at the end of a sentence are called *end marks.* The three end marks are the *period,* the *question mark,* and the *exclamation point.*

Use a period after a sentence that makes a simple statement or mild command.

A sentence that makes a simple statement about something is called a *declarative sentence*.

I jog five kilometers every day.	[declarative]
Please turn to the next chapter.	[mild command]

Use a question mark after a sentence that asks a question.

What's a good name for my pet tarantula?

Use an exclamation point after a sentence that shows excitement or that is a strong command.

A sentence that shows excitement is called an *exclamatory sentence*.

You're standing on my hand!	[exclamatory]
Get those reindeer off my roof!	[strong command]

Exercise 1: Using End Marks

Each of the following groups of words contains two sentences that do not have end marks. Write the sentences and insert the correct punctuation. Circle the end marks you use.

Examples

a. Why don't you mend those ragged overalls They're a sight

Why don't you mend those ragged overalls (?) They're a sight (!)

b. You can help to conserve our resources Smash all your tin cans and save all your newspapers

You can help to conserve our resources (.) Smash all your tin cans and save all your newspapers (.)

1. This is really a blizzard The snow must be two meters deep

2. Can you drive to work in this snow Six more centimeters fell last night

3. Let's offer to help Mrs. Wong She's out shoveling her walks

4. Where are my snowshoes They were in the closet last week

5. School has been canceled for today The buses can't drive over the icy roads

6. Didn't you see that patch of ice Are you hurt

7. Let's build an igloo I'll draw the plans and you shovel the snow

8. Please don't go outside without your boots and mittens It's too cold

9. Look at that snowdrift Is there anyone inside

10. Did the weather forecaster really predict more than ten centimeters of snow That's terrific

Other Uses of the Period

Use a period after an abbreviation.

An *abbreviation* is a word or group of words that has been shortened by omitting some letters.

Unabbreviated Form	Abbreviation
First Avenue	First Ave.
Jefferson Street	Jefferson St.
ante meridiem	A.M.
post meridiem	P.M.
Doctor Ramirez	Dr. Ramirez
Sergeant Jones	Sgt. Jones

Note: The two-letter postal abbreviations for states do not have periods: *AL, CA, IL,* etc.

Use a period after the titles Mr., Mrs., and Ms.

Mr. Delasandro

Ms. Watkins

Exercise 2: *Using Periods with Abbreviations*

Write the following sentences, and place periods where they are needed. Circle the periods you insert.

Examples

a. We stayed awake until 11 P M to watch the horror film.

We stayed awake until 11 P⊙ M⊙ to watch the horror film.

b. Poor Dr Saito had the hiccups during her talk.

Poor Dr⊙ Saito had the hiccups during her talk.

1. Joyous Junk, Inc is the name of Aunt Tillie's new shop.

2. Her mom is up every morning at 6 A M to jog.

3. According to Dr Chu, I have perfect vision.

4. Now that my sister is an officer, most people call her Lt Loomis.

5. Sweeping floors at Acme Book Co is a nice summer job.

6. The new committee on snow removal is headed by Rev Rodriguez and Mrs Washington.

7. Dr Celia McIntyre makes rounds each day at 10 A M at Mercy Hospital.

8. The parade will start at the corner of Sixth St and Madison Ave exactly at noon.

9. Was 900 B C before or after A D 900?

10. Did you know that Sgt Wilson and Mr Wong are both in the city orchestra?

The Comma

A *comma* is often used to separate words or groups of words within a sentence.

Use a comma to separate words or word groups that are a series of three or more items.

We put lettuce, alfalfa sprouts, and tomatoes in the salad.

We have been studying American marches, work songs, hymns, and spirituals in music class this week.

Use a comma to separate two or more adjectives that come before a noun.

Pancho is a sensitive, talented musician.

A comma is not used unless the conjunction *and* makes sense when it is substituted for the comma. (Pancho is a sensitive *and* talented musician.)

Kiyo wore brown cowboy boots on Saturday.

(You would not say "brown and cowboy boots.")

Exercise 3: Using Commas

Write the following sentences. Place commas where they are needed to separate adjectives or to separate items in a series. Circle the commas you insert.

Examples

---

a. My mother traveled to New York Philadelphia and Washington on business.

My mother traveled to New York , Philadelphia , and Washington on business.

b. The large vegetable salad made a wholesome appetizing lunch.

The large vegetable salad made a wholesome , appetizing lunch.

1. In the summer boys and girls can play tennis baseball or soccer.

2. Our sightless neighbor plays cards cooks all his meals and walks to his job every day.

3. The silvery shining clouds stretched across the dark sky.

4. The quiet dazzling sunset over the ocean awed all of us.

5. I planted seeds watered them carefully and thinned the young plants to give them room to grow.

6. The prickly thin raspberry bushes grew quickly as the months passed.

7. I helped my grandmother pick the beans freeze the berries and cook the rhubarb.

8. How can you resist an intelligent attractive funny person like me?

9. The happy giggling children built a huge sand castle on the beach.

10. Jumping on the bed spilling food and teasing the dog didn't make the twins very popular with their baby-sitter.

Use a comma to separate complete statements that are joined by *and, but, or, for, nor, so,* or *yet* to form one compound sentence.

Everyone must work to conserve energy, or we may have a serious energy crisis.

My dad rides to work with two neighbors, for the car pool conserves gasoline.

We wanted to help conserve energy during the winter, so we agreed to keep the building temperature at sixty-five degrees.

Use a comma to separate brief interrupting elements at the beginning or end of a sentence.

The four interrupting elements are *nouns of address, appositives, mild interjections,* and *parenthetical expressions.*

The *noun of address* is the person or people addressed directly.

Boys, what do you know about the muddy footprints in the front hall?

What an attractive suit you're wearing, *Mildred!*

An *appositive* is a word or words with the same meaning as a nearby word.

A lonely area, the Arctic Circle is the home of many interesting forms of wildlife.

My aunt is taking photographs in Tasmania, *a large island.*

A *mild interjection* is a word that expresses mild emotion or feeling and has no other purpose in the sentence. Words such as *yes, no, well, why, still,* and *now* are sometimes used as interjections.

Now, we're all ready to start assembling this nifty Star Scan atomic space disintegrator.

Why, that isn't a catfish on your line; that's a dirty old rubber boot.

A *parenthetical expression* interrupts the flow of a sentence and can be removed without changing its meaning. The following list gives some of the most common parenthetical expressions:

as I was saying	I think
believe me	in my opinion
for instance	of course
I believe	mind you
I hope	to be honest
I know	to tell the truth
I suppose	truthfully

To tell the truth, I don't think I like this boiled eel with cheese sauce either.

Believe me, assembling this toy disintegrator is not an easy task.

We will all do well on this test, *I suppose.*

Use paired commas to separate an interrupting word or words in the middle of a sentence.

If you wait, *Maria,* we can play tennis together.

Hambone Jones, *the leader of our jazz combo,* is really talented.

The bad news is that, *well,* we can't get the space disintegrator put together.

477

Exercise 4: Using Commas

Write the following sentences. Insert commas before conjunctions or to separate interrupting words from the rest of the sentence. Circle the commas you insert.

Examples

a. Am I seeing things or is that hippo really purple?

Am I seeing things ⊘ or is that hippo really purple?

b. Well I've never seen a funnier film.

Well ⊘ I've never seen a funnier film.

1. Never tell a secret in a cornfield for the ears may be listening.
2. José offered to buy the book but I wouldn't let him.
3. We're going to the football game so we won't be home before dinner.
4. To save energy of course we ride our bikes to school.
5. Tom has distant relatives but he says they aren't distant enough.
6. Harriet Tubman I believe returned to the South many times to lead slaves to freedom.
7. May I sit by you Mrs. Sanchez?
8. Our car as a general rule gets twenty-two miles for each gallon of gas.
9. The garden flowers white daisies and roses are pretty.
10. Sure I'll clean my room after dinner Dad.

Use a comma to separate parts of geographical names and to separate the name of the street and city in an address. Use a comma to separate the address from the rest of the sentence.

Baton Rouge, Louisiana

4465 West Adams Avenue, Forest City, Pennsylvania

We have lived at 524 West Grant, Chicago, Illinois, for years.

Use a comma to separate the day of the week, the day of the month, and the year in dates. Use a comma to separate the date from the rest of the sentence.

We moved into this house on Tuesday, May 8, 1970.

These photos are from Easter, 1976.

On July 4, 1976, the United States of America celebrated its Bicentennial.

Exercise 5: *Commas with Dates and Addresses*

Write the following sentences, and insert commas where they are needed. Circle the commas you insert.

Examples

---

a. I boarded the train in Stumptown West Virginia and rode through the darkness toward Black Betsy.

I boarded the train in Stumptown ⊙ West Virginia ⊙ and rode through the darkness toward Black Betsy.

b. According to this certificate, your grandparents were married on August 31 1924.

According to this certificate, your grandparents were married on August 31 ⊙ 1924.

1. The next Presidential election will be held Tuesday November 8.

2. In the attic we found a yellowed letter written on January 1 1889.

3. My great aunt's book will finally be published May 3 1986.

4. Will this bus get me to Thistle Utah before sunset?

5. Our new address is Route 2 Commerce Texas.

6. Would you rather win a trip to Los Angeles California or to Hollywood California?

7. She left for Tokyo Japan on Friday July 30th.

8. Mrs. Shen's term of office begins March 4 1984.

9. Our address was changed on May 1 1982 to 306 Bloomingdale Road Kansas City Kansas.

10. On October 4 1957 the Russians startled the world by launching the first artificial earth satellite; it was called *Sputnik I.*

The Semicolon

The *semicolon* is a stronger mark of punctuation than a comma, but a weaker mark than a period.

Use a semicolon to link complete statements that are closely related.

Some of the students wrote nature poems; others wrote poems about people.

Elmer is on an onion diet; he's lost six pounds and most of his friends.

Use a semicolon to separate items in a series when one or more of the items contain commas.

I have friends in Hillsboro, North Carolina; Tip Top, Kentucky; and Spur, Texas.

My room contains an oak dresser; an antique, upholstered rocker; and a double bed.

Exercise 6: Using Semicolons

Write the following sentences, and insert semicolons where they are needed. Circle the semicolons you insert.

Examples

a. He painted the musty, old closet she built extra shelves for storage.

He painted the musty, old closet(;) she built extra shelves for storage.

b. Mr. Sanchez, the mayor of Oldenburg Marsha White, a biologist and Dr. Thomas spoke to our class about their careers.

Mr. Sanchez, the mayor of Oldenburg (;) Marsha White, a biologist (;) and Dr. Thomas spoke to our class about their careers.

1. My mother is an electrician she does all the wiring in our house.

2. This recipe requires three eggs, beaten one cup of fresh, chopped peppers and six tomatoes.

3. I've read this book twice it's about a family's courage.

4. Mr. Gomez wants us to come later he has company now.

5. Everyone in town looks up to Mr. Jones he is responsible for designing our city's efficient transportation system.

6. My uncle has invented a special kitchen knife it comes with a lifetime guarantee.

7. Daylight Savings Time begins today I must set my clock back one hour.

8. The hurricane caused high waves and severe damage in Biloxi, Mississippi Gulf Shores, Alabama and Pensacola, Florida.

9. I play chess with my grandfather every Friday afternoon he usually beats me, but I've learned a lot from him.

10. My sister was born June 3, 1973 my brother October 2, 1974 and I was born on November 25, 1970.

The Colon

The *colon* is used to separate elements within a sentence or to call attention to a word, phrase, or list which follows it.

Use a colon between an introductory statement and a list of items when the introductory statement contains the words *as follows, the following, these,* or a specific number.

There were seven dwarfs: Dopey, Doc, Grumpy, Happy, Sneezy, Bashful, and Sleepy.

Use a colon to separate hours from minutes when numbers are used.

Pick me up at exactly 8:03.

Exercise 7: *Using Colons*

Write the following sentences, and insert colons where they are needed. Circle each colon you insert.

Examples

a. The coach said the girls' track team will practice at 3 30 every day.
The coach said the girls' track team will practice at 3(:) 30 every day.

b. For the party we will need the following items a large table, some paper plates, some plastic knives and forks, and plenty of ice.
For the party we will need the following items(:) a large table, some paper plates, some plastic knives and forks, and plenty of ice.

1. This class will begin at 12 05 rather than 12 30.

2. These rooms in the house we bought need remodeling the upstairs bathroom, the kitchen, and the sun porch.

3. My doctor prescribed all of the following measures for my cold lots of fluids, bed rest, and a good mystery novel.

4. I'm taking the 8 20 bus downtown to the museum.

5. Dad fixed three great meals last week Swiss steak, Mexican chili, and spaghetti.

6. Do you watch the local news at 4 30 or the 6 00 national news?

7. I have to buy four things in town a birthday card, a notebook, white thread, and gym socks.

8. Hurry! The movie starts at 9 00, but it will take us twenty minutes to walk to the theater.

9. There are three things I want to do this summer visit Aunt Juanita, help my grandfather bale hay at the farm, and attend the summer music camp.

10. The train leaves at 8 05 in the morning and reaches Milwaukee at 1 25 in the afternoon.

The Hyphen

The *hyphen* is used to link two or more complete words in compound words or to link the syllables in a divided word.

Use a hyphen to link the syllables of a word when a word begins on one line of writing and continues on the next line.

Tina has already spent several weeks looking for yard work she can do this summer.

Although she seemed nervous, Rosa was not appre-
hensive about the tennis match.

There are three things you should remember about dividing words at the end of a line of writing:

a. Do not divide words of one syllable.

b. Do not leave just one letter on either line.

The twins do look the same, but they aren't alike in their interests.

(*Alike* cannot be divided *a-like.*)

c. A word that already contains a hyphen should be divided only at the hyphen.

My brother helped me carve a funny jack-o'-
lantern to take to the nursing home.

Use a hyphen to link the parts of some compound words.

son-in-law   ex-President

Not all compound words are hyphenated. Some are written as two words (*tennis shoe, peanut butter*); others are written as one word (*newspaper, homemaker*). Use your dictionary to find out how compound nouns are written.

Exercise 8: Using Hyphens

The following sentences contain compound words that have been written with slashes between the parts of the compound. Use a dictionary to find whether the compound word should be hyphenated or written as one or two words. Write each sentence, and use the proper form for the compound word. Underline the compound word.

Examples

a. I thought her comment was unkind and ill/mannered.
   I thought her comment was unkind and <u>ill-mannered</u>.

b. Flash Gordon peered into the eerie darkness of outer/space.
   Flash Gordon peered into the eerie darkness of <u>outer space</u>.

1. His declaration of love hit her like a thunder/bolt.

2. Miss Rodriguez is seeking a grant/in/aid for our teen center.

3. An ice/bag sometimes helps a bruise.

4. We need another two/by/four to finish this shelf.

5. I lost my luggage in the mix/up at the crowded airport, but it arrived at my hotel later.

6. My great/uncle, who is retired, works part of the day for an appliance store.

7. Joyce can do more push/ups than her older brother.

8. This walk/way must be cleared so people can get through.

9. We all thought the spy film at the Bijou was a real hair/raiser.

10. We need more thumb/tacks for this bulletin board.

The Apostrophe

The *apostrophe* is used to show the omission of letters and to show the possessive form of nouns.

Use an apostrophe to show that letters have been omitted in contractions.

Tom *isn't* playing baseball; *he's* at the drama club meeting.

Dad *won't* eat rich, gooey desserts; he says *they're* very unhealthy.

Note: Do not confuse certain contractions with the possessive forms of pronouns. Possessive pronouns are never written with apostrophes.

Contraction	Possessive Form
it's (it + is)	its book
who's (who + is)	whose book
they're (they + are)	their book
you're (you + are)	your book
there's (there + is)	The book is theirs.

Exercise 9: Using Apostrophes

Write each of the following sentences. Form a contraction from the words in parentheses and insert the correctly punctuated contraction in the blank. Underline the contraction you form.

Examples

a. _____ so absent-minded that yesterday she wore her slippers to school. (She + is)
She's so absent-minded that yesterday she wore her slippers to school.

1. The cannibal smiled and asked politely if I _____ join him for lunch. (would + not)

2. _____ love to go to the concert with you, but _____ busy Friday evening. (I + would) (I + am)

3. _____ you save money and energy if you added insulation to this house? (Could + not)

4. _____ sure they _____ mind if dinner is late? (You + are) (will + not)

5. If _____ in good shape, _____ enjoy the backpacking trip. (they + are) (they + will)

6. If _____ walking into town, perhaps _____ mail this letter for me? (you + are) (you + will)

7. _____ a beaver dam on this stream that _____ like to observe. (There + is) (we + would)

8. My legs _____ ache like this if _____ exercised before the hiking trip. (would + not) (I + had)

9. I _____ understand why we _____ cleaned this attic before. (can + not) (have + not)

10. Marge and her brother really enjoy soccer; _____ always enjoyed the game and _____ learning to play it. (she + has) (he + is)

Use an apostrophe in writing the possessive forms of nouns.

In writing the possessive forms of nouns, observe the following rules:

If the noun is singular, add an apostrophe and an *s*.

Singular Noun	Possessive Form
Jerry	*Jerry's* books
the *horse*	the *horse's* back
the *family*	the *family's* budget

If the noun is plural but does not end in *s*, add an apostrophe and *s*.

Plural Noun	Possessive Form
geese	geese's flight
people	people's habits

If the noun is plural and ends in *s*, add only an apostrophe.

Plural Noun	Possessive Form
boys	the boys' jackets
houses	the houses' roofs

Exercise 10: Using Apostrophes

Write each of the following sentences. Use apostrophes correctly in writing the possessive forms of the nouns in parentheses. Underline each possessive noun form.

Examples

a. I believe our new _____ name is Dr. Molar. (dentist)
   I believe our new <u>dentist's</u> name is Dr. Molar.

b. Their _____ luggage was stacked in the front hall. (parents)
   Their <u>parents'</u> luggage was stacked in the front hall.

1. Our _____ talents are sometimes shocking. (electrician)

2. My _____ friend Jody is a _____ apprentice. (daughter) (cabinetmaker)

3. We are all going to attend _____ graduation. (Pablo)

4. Our _____ favorite food is tapioca pudding. (cat)

5. The _____ efforts to clean up the brush in the vacant lot were admirable. (children)

6. The _____ mates must be here somewhere. (socks)

7. The local _____ club is having a seminar on home safety. (women)

8. Before the carpenters left the construction site, the _____ orders were carried out to the letter. (boss)

9. That plastic hydrant is our _____ favorite plaything. (dog)

10. My _____ fiftieth wedding anniversary was a happy occasion for the whole family. (grandparents)

Underlining (Italics)

Underlining is used most often to show titles.

In printed matter *italic* type is used to indicate underlining: *These words are in italics.*

Underline the titles of books, plays of any length, and long poems.

Both my brother and I enjoyed reading <u>Julie of the Wolves.</u>	[book title]
Pablo has a part in the junior high's next play, <u>Charley's Aunt.</u>	[play title]
Look! <u>The Song of Hiawatha</u> must be over fifty pages long.	[title of long poem]

Note: The words *a, an,* and *the* are underlined only if they are actually part of the title.

I have read <u>Little House on the Prairie</u>, but not <u>The Adventures of Tom Sawyer.</u>

Why don't you look up that information in the <u>Encyclopedia Britannica?</u>

Underline the titles of newspapers, magazines, and pamphlets.

Did you see your picture in the <u>Daily News?</u>	[newspaper]

Mother subscribes to Career Woman, but Dad often reads it more than she.	[magazine]
The pamphlet Jobs in Forestry answered Sheila's questions about becoming a ranger.	[pamphlet]

Note: Do not underline the words *magazine* or *newspaper* unless they are part of the title.

Underline the titles of films, radio programs, and television series.

Did you know there was a film called Santa Claus Conquers the Martians?	[film]
Sometimes I listen to the Radio Mystery Theater while I do my homework.	[radio program]
The only television shows Fran watches are Sixty Minutes and the nightly news.	[television series]

Underline the titles of paintings, sculptures, record albums, ballets, operas, musicals, and long works of instrumental music.

The painting in my bedroom is called Girl with Flowers.	[painting]
Who will dance the lead in Giselle?	[ballet]
The spring musical at the high school will be Hello, Dolly.	[musical]

Underline the names of ships, aircraft, and spacecraft.

Poor Great-aunt Maud went down with the <u>Titanic</u>.	[name of ship]
Janet enjoyed seeing the <u>Spirit of St. Louis</u> and <u>Pioneer 10</u> at the new museum in Washington.	[name of aircraft, name of spacecraft]

Exercise 11: Using Underlining (Italics)

Write each of the following sentences. Underline all words or groups of words that require underlining.

Examples

a. My sister reads the Wall Street Journal every evening.
   My sister reads the <u>Wall Street Journal</u> every evening.

b. We subscribe to U.S. News & World Report and other weekly magazines.
   We subscribe to <u>U.S. News & World Report</u> and other weekly magazines.

1. After he saw the play The Miracle Worker, Bob decided he might like doing volunteer work with disadvantaged children.

2. Manuel's poem will appear in Teen News magazine next month.

3. My dad reads several chapters of Winnie-the-Pooh to my little sister every night before she goes to bed.

4. For my birthday I hope to get tickets to the musical Annie.

5. Is that book about lemons really called The Big Squeeze?

6. Charlie Chaplin's The Tramp is a silent film classic.

7. I read part of Time magazine and the Cleveland Tribune while I waited in the airport for the next transatlantic flight.

8. During the flight to Seattle, I watched the film Star Wars.

9. After I saw Roots on television, I asked my grandfather to help me write a family history.

10. My neighbor, who reads books in Braille, especially enjoyed Witness for the Prosecution.

Quotation Marks

Quotation marks enclose or set off words that belong together.

Quotation marks are written in pairs at the beginning and end of the word or word group they enclose. Quotation marks are used most often to enclose exact words and some titles.

Use quotation marks to enclose the exact words spoken or written by another person.

It was Abraham Lincoln who spoke about a government "of the people, by the people, for the people."

"Do you know," Ted asked, "what happens at midnight?"
"No, I don't," Fred answered.
Ted said, "The next day begins."

Note: Do not use quotation marks unless a person's *exact* words are being enclosed.

Use quotation marks to enclose the titles of short stories, essays, and lectures.

Everyone thinks Mark Twain's "Story of the Old Ram" is hilarious.	[short story]
The assignment was to read "Great Mexican-American Leaders" for tomorrow's class.	[essay]
I used a quote from George Washington's "Farewell Address" in my essay.	[speech]

Note: Do not use quotation marks on your own paper for the title of a composition you write.

Use quotation marks to enclose the titles of songs and shorter poems.

Marian Anderson sings "My Lord, What a Morning" on this record.	[song]
We discussed Emily Dickinson's poem "I Never Saw a Moor" in my writing class today.	[poem]

Use quotation marks to enclose the titles of articles in newspapers or magazines, chapters in books, or episodes of radio and television series.

The newspaper article "Sources of Energy for the Next Century" raised some interesting questions.	[newspaper article]
Carlos found Chapter 10, "Making Career Decisions," an aid for planning his future.	[chapter in a book]
The funniest episode of *Little House on the Prairie* was the one called "County Fair."	[episode of television series]
This *Essence* article on the great trumpet player is entitled simply "Miles."	[magazine article]

Exercise 12: Using Quotation Marks

Write the following sentences. Use quotation marks where they are needed. Circle the quotation marks. Underline titles of longer works.

Examples

a. You're sure there are no alligators in this water? the tourist asked.

⟨"⟩ You're sure there are no alligators in this water?⟨"⟩ the tourist asked.

b. Because it describes the city where he lives, Manuel enjoyed Carl Sandburg's poem Chicago.
Because it describes the city where he lives, Manuel enjoyed Carl Sandburg's poem⟨"⟩ Chicago.⟨"⟩

c. You can find Lincoln's Gettysburg Address in the book Great Speeches of the World.

You can find Lincoln's⟨"⟩ Gettysburg Address⟨"⟩ in the book <u>Great Speeches of the World.</u>

1. My little sister can recite the poem I'm Nobody! Who Are You? by heart.

2. The funniest story we read this year in Miss Lehman's English Literature class was The Night the Bed Fell by James Thurber.

3. Mrs. Alvarez is teaching her music class to sing Silent Night in Spanish.

4. I recently read a fable called The Fairly Intelligent Fly by the humorist James Thurber.

5. We must wage an all-out war against the wasteful misuse of our nation's resources, the President said emphatically at today's press conference.

6. Carlos is reciting Lincoln's Second Inaugural Address in history class.

7. Dad has been humming Stardust under his breath for about three weeks.

8. The poem Fiddler Jones can be found in the book Spoon River Anthology.

9. I think Judy Garland sings Over the Rainbow in the movie Wizard of Oz.

10. I'm sorry, Tom answered, but I didn't know you were going out the front door.

Review: Using Punctuation

Write each of the following sentences. Add the marks of punctuation that are necessary. Circle the punctuation you add.

Examples

a. What a coincidence My brother was also born on June 3 1964

What a coincidence (!) My brother was also born on June 3 (,) 1964 (.)

b. Come to my house said Lee, and Ill help you with the math assignment

(")Come to my house (,") said Lee (,") and I(')ll help you with the math assignment(.")

c. The National League Eastern Division title won by the Chicago Cubs was highly publicized in the Chicago Tribune.

The National League Eastern Division title won by the Chicago Cubs was highly publicized in the <u>Chicago Tribune</u>.

1. Ms Saito our drama coach asked us to do the following things speak loudly and clearly use lively expression in our voices and react to what each character was saying

2. The package that arrived this morning shouldve been delivered to 1806 N Hampton Ave Dallas Texas not 1860 S. Hamilton our address

3. My sister actually made the batter but my brother was the cook

4. The editor in chief of the Washington Post was interviewed on the news program Meet the Press last Sunday morning

5. Ill be happy to let you borrow my copy of The Ghost Belonged to Me replied Carlotta after Ive finished the last chapter

6. At 11 15 AM Mrs Gomez our principal announced the following tornado drill procedures open the windows get under your desk and cover your head and keep very quiet

7. I cant go with you to see The Empire Strikes Back said Maria My mother isn't home yet and I have to watch my little brother

8. Id never really thought about anyone freezing to death until we read Jack Londons short story To Build a Fire

9. My great grandparents Mr. and Mrs. Gregory Anderson were listed as survivors of the Titanic in the book A Night to Remember

10. A tornado on the other hand usually has a narrower path than a hurricane explained the weather reporter in a speech to our class

11. I began my speech to the class with these words Students of Grover Cleveland Junior High wake up Do you know what time it is

12. Jana do you know where my blue jacket is asked Juan I cant find it in my locker Do you think its lost or has Tom borrowed it

13. Well we didn't invite the flies the mosquitoes or the ants to the picnic but they still came

14. The article Portlands Answer to the Energy Crisis in the Nov 24 issue of Time magazine really helped me with my report

15. Unfortunately Kuni thats not the right answer try again please

16. The hungry lost dog searched under the porch in the bushes and around the garbage can for food

17. Arthur Conan Doyle better known as the creator of Sherlock Holmes was born on May 22 1859 in Edinburgh Scotland

18. We sent a copy of the article Energy Hungry in our school newspaper The Crimson to the President of the United States the White House 1600 Pennsylvania Avenue Washington DC

19. These are the poems for tomorrows assignment Stopping by Woods on a Snowy Evening Rudolph Reed The Listeners and Chicago

20. Alicia is a good swimmer skier and tennis player her brother Marks talents lie in basketball baseball and racquetball

Writing Focus: *Improving Punctuation in Writing*

Punctuation marks are like road signs that writers use to guide readers through their writing. The marks can slow readers down, make them stop, and even point out items of interest. Like drivers who must learn to read and follow road signs to avoid accidents and to make traffic flow smoothly, writers must learn to use punctuation to avoid confusion and to make their writing easy to follow and understand.

Assignment: *Educational Entertainment*

Ever since the early days of television, animal films have been popular with the viewing public. Films about such specific animals as lions, beavers, pandas, and wolves, as well as documentaries about animals of the desert, the jungle, the ocean, and the rain forest have educated and delighted audiences of all ages.

Imagine that you have been chosen to produce a new animal film for television. Write a letter to the network president explaining and describing what you want to do. Include information about your choice of animal, where you want to film, how you want to film, and what you want to show and tell about in your film. Discuss your ideas in detail. Your writing will be evaluated for correct punctuation.

Use the following steps to complete this assignment.

A. Prewriting

Think about all the films or shows about animals you've seen over the years. Free write (described in Chapter 1) about films you've liked or shows you've thought worked well on television. Now let your mind wander. Think about doing a film on an animal of your choice. Continue free writing for at least five or ten minutes about how you want your animal film to be. Add details about the opening scene, action, facts, music, or closing scene that help explain or describe your film. Reread your free writing, and underline the details you wish to use in your letter.

B. Writing

Write a letter to the network president describing or explaining your animal film. Use your free writing to help you. Follow the guidelines for letter writing by including a heading, inside address, salutation, body, and closing. Make the body of your letter as detailed as possible so that the network president can actually visualize the film. As you write, pay particular attention to correct punctuation.

C. Postwriting

Use the following checklist to revise your first draft.

1. Is my letter in the correct form?

2. Have I provided sufficient details to explain or describe my film?

3. Is my punctuation correct?

Use the checklist at the back of the book to proofread your work. If appropriate, share your letter with your classmates. Create a classroom *TV Guide of Animal Films* using student work and illustrations.

22 Capitalization

Capitalization is a convention in the English language. For clarity, writers follow regular ways of capitalizing letters. In this chapter you will learn and practice the conventions of Edited Standard English for capitalization.

Capitalize the first word of a sentence.

Capitalize the first word of a sentence to separate it from the sentence before it.

The elderly lady carried both her bags to the taxi. Then she went back to the front porch for her golf clubs.

Capitalize the pronoun *I*.

After cleaning my room, I helped with the laundry.

Before math class could you and I discuss the assignment?

Capitalize the names of specific people (proper nouns).

Tom Rodriguez headed the city committee on recycling.

Tony, Leslie, and Kim help at the recycling center on Saturdays.

Capitalize words showing family relationship when they are used in place of a person's name and when they come directly before a person's name. Words like *Aunt*, *Grandpa*, and *Mother* are often used in place of a name.

Because she works every day, I often help Mother with the family laundry.

I wonder why Dad is late?

Will we see Grandpa Berg on Saturday?

The name of my grandmother is Martha Lance, but to me she is simply Grandmother.

Note: A word showing family relationship preceded by a possessive noun or pronoun (Jim's, my, your) is not capitalized.

See if Jenny's aunt has anything for the rummage sale.

I bet my grandfather can fix the swing.

To save money, her mother painted the back porch.

Exercise 1: Using Capital Letters

Rewrite the following sentences and add capital letters where they are needed. Circle each word you capitalize.

Example

a. oh, dad, i think you forgot to turn off the stove.

(Oh,) (Dad,) (I) think you forgot to turn off the stove.

1. your mother and i were on the winning volleyball team at the family reunion.

2. rob, who is aunt patty's oldest son, was married recently.

3. before the picnic lunch my cousin don broke his foot.

4. her uncle, robert johnson, is a chef in a tucson restaurant.

5. that's my mother's briefcase.

6. my mother and i plan to serve turkey.

7. my grandfather, george fry, has been a farmer for over fifty years.

8. the hit of the picnic was uncle dan's potato salad.

9. do you call all of your aunts by their first names?

10. the smiths' nephew mark sang in church today.

Capitalize a title when it directly precedes a person's name and when it replaces the name of a person being addressed directly.

At the university my aunt is called Professor Johnson.

I will talk to Senator Wong about this new legislation.

After dinner, Lieutenant, we will return to the city.

What is your opinion on this issue, Senator?

Note: When a title is used in a general sense and does not replace a person's name, do not use a capital letter.

The lieutenant peered into the darkness.

The senators debated the new bill for several hours.

Capitalize a title used alone only when it refers to a high official or to a person of national importance.

The words *President* and *Vice President* are capitalized when they refer to the leaders of the United States.

During the crisis no one was eager to be in the President's shoes.

The highest religious figure in England is the Archbishop of Canterbury.

Capitalize titles or abbreviations that appear with a person's name.

How are you today, Mrs. Alvarez?

The new school board members are Rev. Smith, Ms. Toomis, and John Bond, Jr.

We took our new puppy to Dr. Stevenson at the animal hospital.

Capitalize the names of specific animals and pets.

I named my new hamster Chirpy.

I think your collie looks like Lassie.

Exercise 2: Using Capital Letters

Write the following sentences. Add capital letters where they are needed. Circle the words you capitalize.

Example

a. Who was president during the Korean War?

Who was (President) during the Korean War?

1. have you asked governor hernandez about the new tax rates?

2. kelly has named her two pet hamsters tweedledum and tweedledee.

3. joshua is treasurer of our ecology club.

4. the president is elected every four years in a national election.

5. will dr. tanaka please report to the information desk.

6. my brother is a lieutenant in the police department.

7. won't you sign my leg cast, doctor?

8. in surgery, nurse ramirez is capable and efficient.

9. paul bunyan had a blue ox named babe.

10. after the lecture judge okimi answered several pertinent questions.

Capitalize the names of geographical places, specific buildings, and monuments.

Continents, Countries:	Asia, Africa, Nigeria
States, Counties:	Montana, Georgia, Kane County
Cities, Towns:	Broadview, Tucson, Oswego
Bodies of Water:	Pacific Ocean, Great Salt Lake
Islands, Points of Land:	St. John's Island, Cape Cod, Mt. McKinley
Special Regions:	the Arctic, the Ozarks, New England, the Everglades
Streets, Roadways:	Route 34, Elm Street, Northwest Highway
Parks:	Yellowstone National Park, Pioneer Park, White Pines State Park
Buildings, Monuments:	Rialto Theater, the Wilson Clinic

Note: Words such as *park, building, street,* and *county* are capitalized only when they are part of a specific name.

> The school I attend is Washington Junior High School.

> I wonder if that street is Jefferson Street?

Capitalize the words *north, south, east,* and *west* when they are part of an address or are the name for a specific region of the country.

> Do you live on Northwestern Avenue?

> When we lived in South America, I never wore a coat.

> Last summer we traveled in the West for three weeks.

> Do not capitalize the words *north, south, east,* and *west* when they are used as directions.

> The rain moved southeast in the afternoon.

> We have always lived in the northern part of the state.

> The church is just west of the shopping center.

Capitalize the names of specific institutions, businesses, organizations, and their abbreviations.

Institutions:	Franklin Grade School, USC, (University of Southern California), NYSE (New York Stock Exchange)
Businesses:	Meyer's Furniture Store, Car City, CBS
Organizations:	NFL (National Football League), YWCA (Young Women's Christian Association)

Note: Do not use a capital letter when an institution, business, or organization is referred to in a general sense.

> There are three grade schools in the city

> My aunt is an accountant for the furniture company.

Capitalize the names of political parties (but not the word *party*) and the names of government agencies, departments, and bureaus. Capitalize their abbreviations also.

You can call the IRS (Internal Revenue Service) for help with your income tax.

Although her family has always been Republican, Marsha voted with the Democratic party in the county election.

Kiyo has read so many mysteries that she wants to work for the CIA (Central Intelligence Agency).

Capitalize the names of specific products—that is, trade names, brand names, or trademarks. Do not capitalize the general name that often follows the brand name.

All I want for my birthday is a Peppy pogo stick.

Is that television program on the ABC network?

Exercise 3: Using Capital Letters

Write each of the following sentences. Add capital letters where they are required. Circle the words you capitalize.

Example

---

a. We camped several nights at electric peak in the northern portion of yellowstone national park.

We camped several nights at (Electric) (Peak) in the northern portion of (Yellowstone) (National) (Park).

1. I believe lake erie is on the border between the united states and canada.

2. We have a cabin on deer lake in jefferson county.

3. The middle east includes israel and many arab nations.

4. My little sister is a member of the oak hill safety patrol.

5. Write to the hillside chamber of commerce for more information.

6. Our electrician belongs to a union named electricians' local 16.

7. She attended both bennington college and the university of wisconsin.

8. Senator Long is a member of the democratic party.

9. Tina helped build the space shuttle, the enterprise, for nasa.

10. If you don't tell me where you hid my shoe, I'll call in the cia.

Review: Using Capital Letters

Write the following sentences. Add capital letters where they are necessary. Circle the words you capitalize.

1. we bought these used books at barney's bargain barn.

2. the reunion will be at whitewater park on eighth avenue.

3. john blackfeather has accepted a commission in the united states air force.

4. our new bronco automobile has power steering.

5. members of the oakhill kiwanis club tossed peanuts to us from their parade float.

6. do you prefer living in new england or the south?

7. is springfresh as good a shampoo as the ads suggest?

8. last Halloween we helped collect money for unicef.

9. when we were in the west, we attended a rodeo in laramie.

10. this magazine has an interesting article on the history of the united states treasury department.

11. which is farther from here—philadelphia or boston?

12. most of the students in our class see the pacific ocean every day, but few have seen the atlantic ocean.

13. to reach grand island, just take route 34.

14. Kiyoko does all the assignments for her college courses on the Braille typewriter the yorktown lions club rents to her.

15. isn't the university of north carolina in chapel hill?

16. the mississippi river flows south to the gulf of mexico.

17. in new york, we visited the national baseball museum.

18. the wind seems to be from the southwest.

19. if you travel in the south, try to visit the tuskegee institute, which booker t. washington founded.

20. the california historical society is located in san francisco.

Writing Focus: *Improving Capitalization in Writing*

In English, many single words and word groups are capitalized. Capitalizing words helps both writers and readers recognize the beginning of sentences and the names of specific people, places, and things. Capitalize correctly to help keep your writing clear.

Assignment: *Have Plans, Will Travel*

This summer you get to travel anywhere you want! Where will you go? Which cities, countries, and attractions will you see? Will you travel by car, boat, plane, or bus? Will you go alone or with friends? Will you visit anyone? What will you do?

For your classmates write several paragraphs telling about your proposed summer trip. Present your ideas in chronological order. Your work will be evaluated for correct capitalization.

Use the following steps to complete this assignment.

A. Prewriting

Imagine a whole summer of traveling anywhere you choose. Make a list of all the places you have ever thought about visiting. Choose the ones you most want to visit. Now make a word cluster (described in Chapter 1) about your trip. Include words and phrases about your itinerary, mode of transportation, activities, attractions, and the people involved. When your cluster is complete, go back over it, and number the items in the order they will occur on your trip. You might want to use an atlas of the world to help you decide the best way to proceed.

B. Writing

Use your word cluster to help you write one or more paragraphs telling about your summer trip. Don't just list the sights, people, and activities that will occupy your time. Present your plans in a conversational, detailed way. Help your readers visualize your trip so that they can be as excited about it

as you are. As you write, pay particular attention to correct capitalization.

C. Postwriting

Revise your first draft using the following checklist.

1. Is my work an interesting account of my proposed trip rather than just a list of sights, people, and activities?

2. Have I used capital letters correctly?

Proofread your work, using the checklist at the back of the book. If appropriate, share your paragraphs with your classmates. Make a map and indicate the places you'll visit or draw a picture of a special attraction you'll see.

4
Language Resources

23 Vocabulary and Spelling
Vocabulary

The Power of Words

I magine that you are walking through a gallery of famous paintings. When you look closely, you see that parts of the pictures are missing—perhaps the smile from the Mona Lisa or the lace cap of Whistler's Mother. Without these parts the paintings are spoiled. In the same way not knowing certain words can spoil a story for you. You will still understand what is happening, just as you can still look at the paintings with missing parts. However, what is missing may be very important.

The following paragraph is from a magazine article about the man who made the special effects for the science fiction movie *Star Wars*. Read it through carefully. On a sheet of paper, write down any words in the article that you do not know.

> Bearded, six-foot four-inch John Dykstra is on his knees on a darkened sound stage. His broad shoulders hunch against a 35-mm movie camera as he peers through the lens, softly whistling to himself. "Hm," he says softly, "I think we'd better cut back on the lighting. We're getting too much contrast." His camera points at the model of a spaceship, which scintillates under the studio lights. The spaceship model is no larger than one of Dykstra's massive hands. "Dennis," he says to a fellow worker, "let's angle the spaceship a little more. I'd like to show more underside as it begins to make its strafing dive." The model is tipped at a slightly more dramatic angle. "Lovely," says John Dykstra with a grin. "Let the dogfight begin."[1]

Some of the more difficult words in the paragraph are *hunch, scintillates, massive,* and *strafing.* If you do not know the meaning of those words, you are missing part of what is important in the article.

In this chapter you will read about words and their meanings. You will find ways to build a better vocabulary and to learn more about the words you already know.

---

[1]Adapted from "Special science creates illusions in sci-fi spectacles" by Leo Janos. Reprinted by permission of the author.

Words in Context

Many words have more than one meaning. The word *bat*, for example, may mean an animal or an object with which a baseball is hit. Until you put the word in context, you cannot tell the meaning of the word.

The *context* of a word is the other words that surround it. It is the *setting* of the word.

In the following sentences, the word bat has two different contexts. What does *bat* mean in each of these sentences?

A *bat* flew out of the broken window in the old house.

When she was at *bat*, Maria knocked the ball out of the park.

Now you know what the word means in each sentence. However, without the context of the sentence, you cannot tell whether the *bat* is an animal or a baseball *bat*.

Exercise 1: Identifying Words in Context

The following list has five words that can mean different things. Each word is used in two sentences. In each of these sentences, the meaning of the word differs because of its context. Number a sheet of paper 1–10. Beside each number write the correct meaning of the *italicized* word. Use your dictionary if you need help.

Examples

a. My baby-sitting money goes into the *bank*.
   A *bank* means "a place to deposit money."

b. I sat on the *bank* and fished for several hours.
   Bank means "the slope of land beside a river or lake."

1. At the *base* of the statue was a bronze plaque.

2. Maria wanted to *base* her decision on the facts.

3. We had to stay home Saturday morning until our rooms were *clean*.

4. When the saucer fell, it made a *clean* break, so I glued it back together.

5. The group sat around the campfire waiting for the flames to *die* down.

6. When a new coin is designed, a new *die* must be made for it.

7. Lisa and James brought enough food to *last* for the whole trip.

8. The boot-maker put the shoe onto the wooden *last*.

9. Will you write your name on this *scrap* of paper?

10. Kuni decided to *scrap* the project.

Using Context to Find the Meaning

When a word means more than one thing, context tells you which meaning is correct. When you do not know a word, the context may give you a clue to the word's meaning.

You can often tell the meaning of a word from your experience.

Based on your experience, what is the meaning of the word *commended* in the following sentence?

The local newspaper *commended* our school's honor roll students.

Perhaps you do not know the word *commended*. From the other words in the sentence, however, you can guess its meaning. Since you know from experience that students on an honor roll are usually praised, you can guess that *commended* has something to do with praise or approval.

Read the following sentence and try to guess the meaning of the word *dejected* by thinking about your own experience:

When the field trip to Sea World was canceled, the class was *dejected* all afternoon.

You would probably feel unhappy if a field trip to Sea World were canceled, so you can guess that *dejected* means "unhappy" or "in low spirits."

A sentence may state directly what a word means.

The following sentence tells you directly what the word *contusion* means. What is its meaning?

"This *contusion*, commonly called a bruise, will disappear within a week," said the doctor.

In this sentence the words *commonly called a bruise* tell you that *contusion* is another word for *bruise*.

What tells you the meaning of *ginseng* in the following sentence?

Ginseng, a plant whose root is used for medicine, grows in North America and in China.

The meaning of the word *ginseng* is in the phrase: Ginseng is *a plant whose root is used for medicine.*

Examples often help you to find the meaning of a word.

Examples are often introduced by the words *for example*, *such as*, and *like*. What is the meaning of *crinoline* in the next sentence?

Some materials that were once very popular, such as *crinoline*, are no longer used in making clothes.

The words *such as* are the clue here, telling you that *crinoline* is an example of the kind of material once used in making clothes.

See if you can figure out the meaning of the word *colloquial* in the following sentence. Which words give you the clue to its meaning?

Colloquial sayings such as "it's okay with me" are not used in formal writing.

The key here is *such as. It's okay with me* is an example of a *colloquial* saying, so you can guess that the term *colloquial* means "informal."

Comparisons may also give clues to word meanings.

Comparison means "showing how one thing is like or different from another." Comparisons showing likenesses are often introduced by the words *like*, *as*, and *as though*.

511

The *luminous* colors of the painting made it seem as though moonlight were coming through the canvas.

The clue here is the words *as though,* which tell you a comparison is being made. The writer of this sentence compares *luminous colors* with moonlight coming through the canvas. You can safely guess that *luminous* means "full of light" or "glowing."

Comparison showing a difference is often introduced by the word *but*.

At first, Celia was *indifferent* about the playoff, but soon her classmates' excitement rubbed off on her and she started cheering her team.

The clue here is the word *but* because it shows a comparison of opposites. First Celia was *indifferent,* but she changed. *But* means that getting excited and cheering are the opposite of being *indifferent.* You can guess that *indifferent* has to do with not caring and not showing interest.

Exercise 2: *Using Context Clues*

From the context clues, decide the meaning of each *italicized* word in the following paragraph. Write each word and its definition.

The forests of the Pacific Northwest can become *kindling.* In long periods of *drought,* the trails lie thick in dust, ankle deep and as fine as flour. Pine and fir needles become as *combustible* as paper. A campfire, unless circled with a trench, can spread along and under the surface. The chain that drags a log in lumber operations may scrape a rock and make a spark, igniting almost at once a whole forest. A cigarette or match carelessly tossed by the side of the trail can do the same. Lightning may make a flaming torch of any of the resinous evergreens. Even one spark can cause irreparable damage—a *smouldering* fire whipped to a blaze by a slight wind, racing up trees and through forests faster than a man can run, killing all life with its hot tongue, leaving behind *desolation* and a sterile earth that will not produce crops of timber for a generation or more.[1]

---

[1]Excerpt from p. 39 in *Of Men and Mountains* by William O. Douglas. Copyright 1950 by William O. Douglas. Reprinted by permission of Harper & Row, Publishers, Inc. and The Lantz Office Incorporated.

Using Structure to Find Meaning

You can learn about words that you do not know by looking at their setting or context. You can also learn meanings by taking words apart to see how they are made.

The *structure* of a word means "how the word is put together."

Each of the following words has a word inside it. What are the "hidden" words?

List A

undone	tenth
review	thinker
dismount	safely
injustice	comfortable
precaution	distortion

The "hidden" words are *done, view, mount, justice, caution, ten, think, safe, comfort,* and *distort.* These words are called *roots* because other words grow from them. The groups of letters added to these roots are *un-, re-, dis-, in-, pre-, -th, -er, -ly, -able,* and *-ion.* The first five sets of letters were added to the front of the root word. The last five sets of letters were added to the end of the root word.

Letters added to the front of roots are called *prefixes.* Letters that come after the roots are called *suffixes.*

The roots in list A are whole words. Prefixes and suffixes also combine with another kind of root. What are the roots in the following list of words?

List B

unkempt	ninth
rejoice	maker
distinct	truly
inject	likable
precise	attention

The words in this list have the same prefixes and suffixes as the words in list A. But when you take the prefixes and suffixes away from the words in list B, you do not have whole words left. You have groups of letters that look like this: *-kempt, -joice, -tinct, -ject, -cise, nin-, mak-, tru-, lik-,* and *attent-*. These groups of letters are also called roots.

Prefixes and suffixes go together with both kinds of roots to make new words.

The meanings of the prefixes and suffixes always stay the same. When you know the meanings of common prefixes and suffixes, you can guess the meanings of many new words. The prefixes *il-, im-,* and *in-* all have the same meaning: *not.* Use this information to guess the meaning of each *italicized* word in the following sentences:

The candidate's arguments were *illogical.*

Preparations for the long trip were *inadequate.*

The advice she gave was *impractical.*

To read these words, say *not* to yourself instead of the prefix.

illogical	*not* logical
inadequate	*not* adequate
impractical	*not* practical

You can look up the meaning of any prefix or suffix in the dictionary. They are listed in alphabetical order with other words. The following is a list of some of the most often used prefixes and suffixes and their meanings:

Prefix	Meaning	Suffix	Meaning
anti-	against	-al	having to do with
co-	with or together	-ish	like, similar to
dis-	not	-ful	full of
il-	not	-able	able to
im-	not	-er	one who

Prefix	Meaning	Suffix	Meaning
in-	not	-or	one who
mis-	wrong	-ess	one who
pre-	before, in advance	-fy	to make or to become
re-	again	-less	without
un-	not	-ly	in a certain way

When you use a prefix to make a new word, you add letters to a root word. The spelling of the root word does not change. When you use a suffix to make a new word, however, the spelling of the root word often changes.

Exercise 3: Using Structure to Find Meaning

By using the correct prefix, you can make each of the following groups of words into one word. Select a prefix from the preceding list of prefixes that can combine with one word in the group. Number your paper 1–5 and for each group of words, write the new word by the appropriate number. Study the examples before you begin.

Example

a. consider again
   reconsider

1. against slavery
2. exist together
3. pay in advance
4. not legal
5. not selfish

In the sentences on the following page, each phrase in parentheses can be made into a single word with a suffix. From the preceding list of suffixes, select a suffix to make the word. Write a sentence with the new word on a sheet of paper

6–10. Underline the new word. Check your dictionary to see if the spelling of the root word changes when you add the suffix. Study the example before you begin.

Example

a. The bear cubs at the zoo were very (full of play) when we saw them.
The bear cubs at the zoo were very <u>playful</u> when we saw them.

6. That morning the water was a pale (like green) gray.

7. Elena read her brothers a (full of fancy) story about a boy and his pet elephant.

8. The weather in the mountains is very (able to change).

9. The delicate crystal requires (with care) handling.

10. Lady Bird Johnson worked to (make beautiful) the highways of the United States.

Choosing the Best Word

A writer chooses words in much the same way a painter chooses color. A painter tries to find the colors that are just right to make the painting seem alive. In the same way the right words can bring a piece of writing to life.

As you read the following sentence, try to form a picture in your mind about the man:

The man *walked* down the street to the *store*.

The words in this sentence do not give you much help in forming a mental picture. When you read it, you know that a man walks to a store, but you do not know much about the man or the store. Here is the same sentence with two words changed. What mental picture do you get from this sentence?

The man *ambled* down the street to the *newsstand*.

The word *amble* means to walk in a slow, leisurely way. A *newsstand* is a kind of store that sells mostly newspapers and magazines. Now you have a better picture of what the man in this sentence is doing and how he is doing it.

Synonyms **are similar words that have almost, but not exactly, the same meaning.**

Walk and *amble* are synonyms, and *store* and *newsstand* are synonyms. Most words have several synonyms. When you write, try to choose the synonym that helps your reader form the best mental picture.

The words *ask, beg,* and *demand* are synonyms. Each word has the meaning "to request." If you wanted to show readers a picture of a spoiled girl being rude to her parents, which of the following sentences would you select?

Anita *asked* for her allowance.

Anita *begged* for her allowance.

Anita *demanded* her allowance.

Even though the words *beg* and *demand* are synonyms, they have different shades of meaning. *Beg* means "to ask humbly." *Demand* means "to ask firmly," so if you want to show how a spoiled girl would ask for her allowance, you would use the word *demand*. *Demand* is the word which best conveys your meaning.

Choose the synonym that conveys the correct meaning.

Many times a synonym will not fit into a sentence you are writing because it does not have the correct meaning. The words *smile* and *smirk* are synonyms, meaning "to move the mouth upward." However, which of the following sentences does not have the correct meaning?

She *smiled* happily when she won the award.

She *smirked* happily when she won the award.

Even though *smile* and *smirk* are synonyms, it is not correct to say *She* smirked *happily when she won the award,* because *smirk* has the exact meaning "to smile unpleasantly." It does not fit into the context of this sentence.

The words *loose* and *free* are also synonyms, meaning "not confined." In which of the following sentences is one of them used incorrectly?

She wore a *free,* comfortable sweater on the hike.

She wore a *loose,* comfortable sweater on the hike.

The word *free* in the first sentence would be correct only if you meant the sweater did not cost anything. If you are not certain about the meanings of synonyms, look the words up in your dictionary.

Exercise 4: *Using Synonyms*

Each of the following sentences has two synonyms in parentheses. Read each sentence and decide which synonym best fits the meaning of the sentence. Write each sentence with the synonym you select on a sheet of paper numbered 1–10. Underline the synonym in your sentence. Use your dictionary to find the meanings of synonyms.

Example

a. The punishment for a witness who (lies/fibs) under oath may be a prison sentence.
The punishment for a witness who lies under oath may be a prison sentence.

1. Jason's mother told him it was bad manners to (swallow/gulp) his breakfast.

2. When I dropped the crystal glass, it (shattered/cracked) into tiny pieces.

3. The lawyer wanted to (ask/interrogate) the prisoner about the crime.

4. When Susan's mother got her promotion, the entire family had to (drive/move) to Arizona.

5. From the lookout tower, the watchman (spied/saw) the enemy forces.

6. The driver slammed on the brakes, and the car started to (glide/skid).

7. On the horizon we saw the first (gleam/shine) of sunlight.

8. The eagle (flitted/soared) majestically through the clear, blue sky.

9. After the series the team celebrated their (victory/conquest).

10. The dog gave a short (cry/yelp) of pain when we took the thorn from its foot.

Special Vocabulary Words

When you were younger, perhaps you belonged to a secret club that had a password. Most passwords are ordinary words that everyone uses, but to members of the club, they have a special secret meaning.

Many words you read are like passwords, with an everyday meaning and also a special meaning for certain groups. These words are called *jargon*. Baseball players, for example, use many words that have different meanings to baseball players than in everyday speech. In daily speech *to hit* has the same meaning as *to strike*; the words are synonyms. But in baseball a *hit* is the opposite of a *strike*. A *strike* in baseball means "a miss." In baseball all the players *run* to get on base, but a *run* also means "a score."

Sometimes, to understand the meaning of a word, you must know the group using it. For example, the word *score* to a butcher means making cuts on a piece of meat. A *slide* is a kind of play in baseball, but to a photographer a *slide* is a kind of photograph. A *hit* in the record business is very different from a *hit* in baseball. A baker's *bun* in no way resembles a hairdresser's *bun*.

Exercise 5: Defining Jargon

In the following paragraphs about marbles champion Dean Feinauer, you will find many words that are marble players' jargon. On a separate sheet of paper, make a list of these words and their definitions.

Example

a. mibster
   A mibster is a slang word for marble player.

Dean Feinauer was down on all fours, head near the ground like a hound on the track of his quarry. Solemnly, Dean pushed back his visor, rolled the aggie around in his hand, planted a scratched and calloused knuckle, and unleashed his thumb. The aggie clickety-clacked across the concrete, and a commie ricocheted out of the ring.

The quiet mibster from Reading, Pennsylvania, exploded with pent-up emotion. After eleven grueling hours of shooting under a fiery sun, thirteen-year-old Dean was the new boys' marbles champion and winner of a $500 scholarship.

Each of the fifty-six competitors had played more than eighty games to determine the finalists of the 55th National Marbles Tournament, sponsored by International Telephone and Telegraph's "Big Blue Marble" TV series. The eight- to fourteen-year-old contestants represented nearly a dozen states along the Northeastern seaboard.

The official tournament marbles game is called ringer, and Dean explained how it's played:

"You shoot from outside a ten-foot circle at thirteen marbles in the shape of a cross in the middle. On your first shot, you try to hit one of the marbles out and stick in the ring. Then you have to shoot six more marbles out.

"As long as your shooter knocks a marble out, but stays in the ring, you keep shooting," Dean said. "But if you miss, your opponent gets to shoot from the outside of the ring. The first player to take seven out of thirteen marbles is the winner."

Dean and the other players naturally use the special slang of marbles. A taw is a shooting marble, and the best taws are aggies—made of polished agate. Some players have glass shooters. Commie is one name for the ordinary glass marbles that make up the cross in the ring. Mib is another name for a marble, and a mibster is a marbles player. When a player's shooter stays inside the ring after knocking a commie out, it is called a stick, and the player takes another shot.[1]

Spelling

Improving Your Spelling

Writing expresses ideas, but if you misspell words, your thoughts may not impress your readers. Spelling correctly shows that you are responsible and take pride in your work. In this chapter you will learn several ways to improve your spelling skills.

Develop good spelling habits.

Keep a list of your spelling problems on a separate page of your notebook. Write down each word you misspell and

---

[1]From "A Champ with Thumb-Thing Special" by Ken Fulton from *Boys' Life* Magazine, June 1979. Reprinted by permission.

underline the letters that cause you trouble. Keep your list of correctly spelled problem words up-to-date and review the list when you proofread your next written assignment.

Avoid mispronunciations.

You may be misspelling words because you pronounce them incorrectly. Many spelling problems can be remedied quickly if you learn to say the word correctly. Most good dictionaries include information on how a word is pronounced (usually enclosed within slant bars or parentheses) immediately after entry words.

Include on your spelling list the words you are misspelling because of mispronunciation, and work on saying these words clearly and correctly.

Write neatly and slowly and proofread to avoid careless errors.

Many people spell poorly because they write too quickly and do not form each letter in a word carefully. Proofread your work slowly, looking at the spelling of each word. Note words you think may be misspelled and check them.

Use a dictionary frequently.

Look up the word as you have spelled it. If you do not find the word in the dictionary, you may be misspelling it. Consider other ways the word might be spelled and look these up, too. If you are unsure about the beginning letter or letters, ask your teacher for help.

Several terms relating to spelling are used frequently in this chapter. If you are uncertain about what a term means, refer to the following list:

vowel The letters *a, e, i, o, u,* and sometimes *y* are the vowel sounds in the English alphabet.

consonant Letters of the English alphabet other than the vowels are called *consonants* (*b, c, d, f,* and so on).

syllable A *syllable* is one unit of language spoken in one breath that contains a vowel sound (*par-a-keet, el-e-phant*).

accent   *Accent* is the stress or emphasis placed on one syllable of a word to make that syllable sound louder than other syllables. (*par'a-keet, em-bar'ráss*)

Words Often Confused

Some spelling errors happen because writers confuse closely related words that are pronounced alike but spelled differently. There are many such words, including *their* and *there*, *principle* and *principal*, and *capital* and *capitol*. Devote one section of your spelling list to these words. Learn which words or pairs of words confuse you and practice using these words correctly. Always proofread your writing and pay attention to the words from this group that have given you problems in the past.

Helpful Spelling Rules

The following rules can help you improve your spelling. Although there are exceptions to some of these rules, they hold true in many cases. Learn each rule and then concentrate on the few exceptions.

Words with ie *and* ei

If a word is spelled with an *ie* or *ei* combination and sounds like the long ē in *feet*, write *ie* except after the letter *c*.

ie sounded as long ē: chief, brief, believe, yield

ei after *c:* receive, deceive, ceiling

Exceptions: neither, either, seize, sheik, leisure

If a word is spelled with an *ie* or *ei* combination and is pronounced with a vowel sound other than long ē, write *ei*, especially if the word has a long ā sound as in *weigh*.

ei sounded as long ā: eight, freight, rein

ei not sounded as long ē: their, foreign

Exceptions: friend, mischief, handkerchief

Exercise 6: Spelling Words with ie *and* ei

Write the following sentences and supply the correct *ei* or *ie* combination that is missing in each underlined word. Underline the complete word. Your teacher may ask you the rule you used for the correct spelling.

Examples

a. The tardy student hoped the talk with the principal would be br__f.

The tardy student hoped the talk with the principal would be brief.

b. Since Roberto began coaching the basketball team for the partially sighted children at the YMCA, he's had less l__sure time.

Since Roberto began coaching the basketball team for the partially sighted children at the YMCA, he's had less leisure time.

1. The accountant reached into her br__fcase for the figures on the company's taxes.

2. The tiny tiger cub w__ghed only three pounds at birth.

3. N__ther my father nor my mother enjoys rock music.

4. Santa stubbed his toe getting into the sl__gh.

5. I wonder where the last p__ce of this puzzle is?

6. Carlotta and Mark have been close fr__nds for many years.

7. Good gr__f! Did you see that jump shot?

8. It was just a tiny mouse, but they all shr__ked when they saw it.

9. If I organize th__r games, I can usually keep the twins busy.

10. Ch__f Brownfeather rode proudly across the plains.

Words with the seed *Sound*

Words with a syllable that is pronounced like the word *seed* are spelled in one of the following three ways:

1	**2**	**3**
supersede	exceed	accede
	proceed	concede
	succeed	intercede
		precede
		recede
		secede

Exercise 7: Spelling Words with the seed *Sound*

Write the following sentences, and supply the correct *-sede, -ceed,* or *-cede* form that is missing in each underlined word. Underline the completed word.

Examples

a. I think the senator will con___ the election only when all the votes are counted.
   I think the senator will concede the election only when all the votes are counted.

b. If you're through with the minutes, we will pro___ with the meeting.
   If you're through with the minutes, we will proceed with the meeting.

1. Do you think I'll ever suc___ at chess?

2. Grandpa's hair has not even started to re___.

3. Does a state have the right to se___ from the union?

4. If you don't ex___ the speed limit, you can conserve fuel.

5. I think the city will suc___ in its plan to build a small museum.

6. The lecture will pre___ the film on African wildlife.

7. After the jump shot, the ball game pro___ed.

8. Because of the seriousness of the problem, the break in the pipes super___d all other school business.

9. According to the radio, the flood waters are beginning to re __.

10. Profits from the rummage sale ex __ ed all the scouts' expectations.

Adding Prefixes

A prefix added to a root word does not change the spelling of the root word.

Prefix	+ *Root*	
mis-	+ spell	Good writers don't *misspell* common words.
im-	+ moral	Do you think telling a lie is always *immoral?*
un-	+ like	That is *unlike* you.

Adding Suffixes

If the root word ends with an *e,* drop the *e* before adding a suffix that begins with a vowel.

Root Word	+ *Suffix*	
use	+ -ing	I am *using* your notes.
live	+ -ing	Dad will vacuum the *living* room.

If the suffix begins with a consonant, do not drop the final *e* from the root word.

Root Word	+ *Suffix*	
use	+ -ful	This pamphlet on energy conservation is *useful.*
live	+ -ly	My grandfather is a *lively* card player.

Exercise 8: Spelling Words with Suffixes

Write the following sentences. In each blank, supply the correctly spelled form of the root word and suffix given in parentheses. Underline the new word. Read the example before you begin.

Example

a. Mrs. Brian, who is _____ years old, works in her garden every morning for several hours. (nine + -ty)
  Mrs. Brian, who is <u>ninety</u> years old, works in her garden every morning for several hours.

---

1. The angry fans _____ at the referee, but she didn't seem to care. (glare + -ed)

2. Since she got the female lead in the school play, *Romeo and Juliet*, little Rosaria always seems to be _____. (smile + -ing)

3. What is that stealthy _____ in the dark underbrush? (move + -ment)

4. Cindy is always _____ when she uses power tools. (care + -ful)

5. Most of the students were _____ before the test. (nerve + -ous)

6. Alfredo and my sister are _____ a slide series on child abuse. (prepare + -ing)

7. I thought her decision to take up sky _____ was rather serious. (dive + -ing)

8. _____ prices when we grocery shop takes time, but we do save on many items. (compare + -ing)

9. Please stop singing; you're _____ the baby. (scare + -ing)

10. He has so many problems with the old jalopy that belonged to his father that I've stopped _____ about them. (care + -ing)

If a root word ends with a *y* preceded by a consonant, change the *y* to *i* before adding a suffix that begins with any letter other than *i*.

Root Word	+ Suffix	
worry	+ -ed	Juan *worried* about his performance with the city orchestra.

Exceptions: gaily (gay + -ly), daily (day + -ly), wryly (wry + -ly), shyly (shy + -ly), dryly (dry + -ly), slyly (sly + -ly)

If the suffix begins with an -i, do not drop the final y.

Root Word	+ Suffix	
marry	+ -ing	Only after she finishes college will Julie think of *marrying* Dave.
worry	+ -ing	Juan is still *worrying* about the concert and his solo.

Exercise 9: *Spelling Words with Suffixes*

Write the following sentences. In the blank, insert the correctly spelled form of the root word and suffix given in parentheses. Underline the word you form.

Example

a. Although Marlo's sight is impaired, she _____ a full load of classes at the university. (carry + -es)

Although Marlo's sight is impaired, she carries a full load of classes at the university.

1. I have never been _____ than I was yesterday when I forgot your anniversary. (sorry + -er)

2. Sara says jogging with her dad makes her _____. (hungry + -er)

3. My great-grandmother is a _____ storyteller and an excellent bridge player. (live + -ly)

4. Jack is a considerate and _____ baby-sitter. (rely + -able)

5. We are _____ for the broken window little by little. (pay + -ing)

6. Winter is always dreary, but the holidays are _____. (joy + -ous)

7. The two couples were _____ in a double ceremony. (marry + -ed)

8. Last Saturday was the _____ day of my life. (happy + -est)

9. Ramon is the _____ player in the jazz band. (peppy + -est)

10. Our family helps several _____ organizations. (charity + -able)

If the root word is one syllable and ends with a single consonant preceded by a single vowel, double the final consonant before adding a suffix that begins with a vowel.

Root Word	+ Suffix	
plan	+ -ed	We *planned* an economical but relaxing family vacation.
stop	+ -ing	We are *stopping* at several state parks and museums along the way.

Exercise 10: Spelling Words with Suffixes

Write each of the following sentences. In each blank, supply the correctly spelled form of the word and suffix given in parentheses. Be careful to determine whether or not it is really necessary to double the final consonant. Underline the word you form.

Example

a. The profits from the garage sale really _____ the library fund. (help + -ed)

The profits from the garage sale really <u>helped</u> the library fund.

1. Raul _____ the avocados into the soup very carefully. (stir + -ed)

2. I think bacon would be a fine _____ for the casserole. (top + -ing)

3. Julio is _____ Algebra I; he says it's just an additional problem. (drop + -ing)

4. In the dark Willie couldn't avoid _____ into the lamp. (bump + -ing)

5. Raul and Maria _____ the children's football team to a victory. (coach + -ed)

6. The waves _____ steadily against the shore. (slap + -ed)

7. Saturday at the game I _____ my wool blazer. (rip + -ed)

8. At yesterday's game Scotty _____ in three runs. (bat + -ed)

9. Yoshiro has a job as a house _____. (paint + -er)

10. Juan is an excellent _____ and hopes to win the district diving championship. (swim + -er)

24 Changes in Language

The History of English

If you could go back to the England of 1,500 years ago, the speech of the people would perhaps surprise you. It would sound like a foreign language. However, it would be an early form of the English language. This early form is called *Anglo-Saxon* or *Old English.* It is the language from which modern English developed.

The history of the English language begins in about A.D. 449, when tribes from northern Europe, called the *Angles, Saxons,* and *Jutes,* began to invade the island of Britain. Eventually, they conquered the Celts and replaced the Celtic language with their own *Anglo-Saxon* or *Old English.*

As the following example shows, the written form of Old English seems as strange today as the spoken form. The Modern English word is written beneath each Old English word. Find the Old English words that are the same or almost the same as the Modern English form. See if you can figure out how the Old English words were pronounced.

Wē	wyllað	ēow	gereccan	θǣra	fēowertigra
We	want	[to] you	to tell	of the	forty

cempena	ðrowunge	θæt	ēower	gelēafa	θē	trumre
soldiers	[the] suffering,	that	your	belief	the	firmer

sȳ.	θonne	gĕ	gehȳrað	hū	θegenlice	hī	θrōwodon
may be,	when	ye	hear	how	thanelike	they	suffered

for	crīste[1]
for	Christ.

Thanelike means "like a great person."

A translation of the passage into modern English reads: "We want to tell you about the suffering of the forty soldiers, so that your belief may be firmer when you hear how nobly they suffered for Christ."

---

[1]From *The Origins and Development of the English Language* by Thomas Pyles, copyright © 1964 by Harcourt Brace Jovanovich, Inc. Reprinted by permission.

Exercise 1: Reporting on the Angles, Saxons, and Jutes

Use an encyclopedia and other sources to prepare a short report on the Angles, Saxons, and Jutes. In your report tell where these people lived before they invaded England and why they did so. Describe what life in England was like for these tribes.

Old English

Old English was spoken and written from about A.D. 449 to A.D. 1100.

During this time, often referred to as the *Old English Period*, the English language changed rapidly. Two important events helped change the English language: the coming of the Christian missionaries and the Viking invasions.

In the eyes of the Roman Catholic Church, the Angles, Saxons, and Jutes were savages who worshiped false gods. In the sixth century the head of the Church, Pope Gregory, sent the man who later became St. Augustine and a small group of monks to England as missionaries. St. Augustine and his monks were so successful in converting the native tribes that 100 years later most of England was Christian.

Christianity had a great effect on the English language. St. Augustine and his monks opened schools where they taught Latin, the official language of the Roman Catholic Church. All religious services were in Latin. Soon many Latin words, most having to do with learning and religion, found their way into English. Words such as *altar, candle, temple, school,* and *master* came into English from the Latin during this time.

The second event that helped change the English language was the Viking invasions. During the ninth century the Vikings, an adventuresome people living in what are now Sweden, Denmark, and Norway, launched their much-feared warships and sailed to the coast of England. Though they came to conquer, they remained to settle in England. Over a period of many years, they contributed many words from their Scandinavian language to English, for example, *law, skin, sky, until, both, die.*

Exercise 2: Identifying Old English Words

When Latin and Scandinavian words first came into Old English, they had a different form from the words you know today. The word *bull,* for example, was written *bula* in Old English. Below is a list of words English speakers adopted from Latin and Scandinavian. Use a dictionary to find the Old English form of each word and write it on a sheet of paper numbered 1–10.

Example

a. Birth
   Old English form byrde

Words from Latin

1. discipline
2. priest
3. master
4. Sabbath
5. candle

Words from Scandinavian

6. seat
7. call
8. take
9. fellow
10. low

Middle English

The years A.D. 1100–A.D. 1500 are called the *Middle English Period,* and the language that was spoken and written during that time is called *Middle English.*

On the first morning of the year A.D. 1100, people did not suddenly begin speaking a different kind of English, but in the next 400 years English changed until it became more like the English we speak and write today.

In the year A.D. 1066 a group of people called *Normans* defeated the English king at the Battle of Hastings.

In the same year a Norman, William the Conqueror, was crowned king of England. Because the new rulers were from Normandy, a place in France, French soon replaced English as the most important language in the land. Most of the people still spoke a form of English, but the ruling class spoke French.

As a result, many French words became a part of English vocabulary.

These new words showed much about the life of the Normans and their new English subjects. The French were religious people, and many words concerning religion, such as *chaplain* and *incense,* became a part of English vocabulary. The French built castles and manor houses and gave the words *castle, tower,* and *palace* to English. The French words *prison, robber,* and *culprit* also came into English at this time. What do these words say about the relationship between the Normans and the English?

In the fourteenth century, Europe was struck a terrible blow. A deadly disease called the Black Death swept across Europe and Asia, killing as much as three-fourths of the entire population. One result of this disaster was that the poor and middle classes of England gained economic power, since they were needed to run the businesses and farms. Because these less educated people spoke only English, it was used for business and commerce and soon replaced French as the most used language in England.

Exercise 3: *Identifying Middle English Words*

The words in Column 1 are French words that came into English during the Middle English Period. Over the years these words changed to become the words you know today. In Column 2 on this page and the next is the Modern English form of each French word in Column 1. On a sheet of paper numbered 1–10, write the Modern English word that matches each French word in Column 1. Use a dictionary for help with this exercise.

Example

a. The French word *crier.* The Modern English word is *cry.*

Column 1	Column 2
1. disner	govern
2. riviere	tower
3. gouverner	frown
4. celle	rob
5. roche	dinner
6. tir	cream

7.	frognier		river
8.	chapelain		rock
9.	rober		chaplain
10.	craime		cell

Modern English

The years after 1500 are called the *Modern English Period*.

As it had since its beginnings, the English language continued to change during this period. One reason for change was the peaceful contact the English people had with people from other nations.

In the 1300s and 1400s England began trading with European nations such as Spain and Portugal and with Asia. Words from these cultures came flooding into English. For example, from Spanish and Portuguese, English borrowed the strange and wonderful words *canoe, hammock, barbecue,* and *maize.*

The English that a person from England speaks today is called *British English*. When the first English settlers came to North America, they brought with them an older form of British English. Over the years, however, this English became Americanized.

British English began its slow change into American English when the first settlers left the shores of England. Many of the sailors on the *Mayflower,* the ship that brought the Pilgrims to this country, were Dutch. Some linguists (scientists who study language) believe that the Pilgrims adopted their first new words from the seafaring vocabulary of these Dutch.

Most of England was divided into neat farms, cut through by gently running streams. Pilgrims who landed on American shores saw dense forests and vast ocean shorelines. They met for the first time native Americans of such nations as the Penobscot, Delaware, Massachusetts, and Cherokee. Everywhere the colonists looked, they saw unfamiliar animals and plants.

Since English did not have terms for these new encounters, the pilgrims and later settlers had to bring new words into their vocabularies. Many names, especially those for places, were borrowed from native American languages, names such as *Connecticut* ("place of the long river") and *Massachusetts* ("place of the great hills"). The new Americans also borrowed native American words such as *raccoon, moccasin, muskrat.* Sometimes, animals were named for the way they looked or sounded, and these words also became a part of the language: *lightning bug, hummingbird, bobwhite, rattlesnake, hedgehog.* What other animals can you think of that may have been named this way?

Exercise 4: *Inventing Words*

Imagine you are one of the first settlers on a faraway planet. Use your imagination to invent names for each of the following animals you might find there:

1. A huge, wormlike creature that slithers across the sand

2. A small, cup-shaped creature with suction feet that hangs upside down

3. A birdlike creature that makes howling noises and zooms through the air

4. A small, furry creature with red, white, and blue stripes

5. A scaly creature that moves in a zigzag fashion and has long, pointed ears

American English

No one can say exactly when British English became American English. Many people who came to North America wanted to keep the English language "pure." They did not like to see new American words coming into the language. Even the famous American Benjamin Franklin believed for a time that Americans should speak and write English as it was spoken and written in England.

Many forces helped to create American English. Since the voyage from America back to England was a long, dangerous one, the settlers were cut off from English life as they had known it. Therefore, their language was more influenced by other settlers and by their new experiences than by hearing and reading British English.

The settlers were not content for long to stay in the original thirteen colonies. Even during the Revolutionary War period, the settlers began to move across the Appalachian Mountains. From that time on, a stream of pioneers made their way across prairie and desert, beginning new settlements along the way.

As they traveled, these pioneers—English, Scottish-Irish, Swiss, German, and other nationalities—left their mark not only on the land, but also on the language. Their new experiences called for new words that came into common usage as these hardy Americans made their way westward. With every new word American English became more different from its British parent.

Exercise 5: Understanding Language

Each of the following words that came into common usage during the westward movement of the 1800s tells a story about the life of the people who used it. Read the list carefully. Then write several sentences describing what these words tell you about pioneer life. Use your imagination. You may consult your dictionary if you do not know the meanings of the words.

squatter	salt lick	wire grass
tomahawk	coon dog	slippery elm
Indian trail	bear meat	timber
deer trace	bobcat	log cabin
buffalo trace	copperhead	horse thief

A Living Language

English is a living language. As long as people speak and write it, the language will continue to change. Just as people develop and change, language does also.

One reason for continual change is new developments in science and industry. The development of the steamboat during the 1800s was responsible for the common use of words such as *river town, steamboat whistle, steamboat landing*, and *steamboat captain*. The railroad brought with it such words as *boxcar, depot, switch, baggage, baggage clerk*, and *all aboard*.

Radio and television have had a powerful effect on American English. Words such as *network, station break, commercial, soap opera, game show, situation comedy, sportscaster*, and *newscaster* come from broadcasting. More important, the announcers on radio and television, who are heard and admired by millions of people, helped the spread of Standard English. (You will learn more about Standard English on pages 539–540.)

As people become more sensitive to the needs of other people, American English changes. For example, during the past decade many people, concerned about the role of women in our society, have become concerned that American English does not always place women on an equal status with men. Firefighters and police officers have been called *firemen* and *policemen*, even though some of them are women. Although adult males do not want to be called *boys*, adult females are sometimes called *girls*. To explain that every person in a room brought a book, a speaker might say, "Everyone brought *his* book," even when both men and women are present. Many people have instead begun to use words such as *firefighter*, *police officer*, and *flight attendant* (instead of *steward* or *stewardess*). These people also call adult females *women*, and they do not use the word *his* to mean both males and females.

Exercise 6: *Identifying Sources of New Words*

Following is a list of developments in science and other areas that helped change American English. On a sheet of paper, make a list of words you think one of the developments was responsible for bringing into common usage. Your teacher may ask you about other ways in which the development helped change American English.

1. The automobile

2. The space program

3. Nuclear energy

4. The computer

5. Roller-skating

Dialects of American English

The first part of this chapter discussed American English and how it has developed, but you should not think that at any one time people in this country all speak alike. If you listen to your classmates, you can probably hear differences in their speech. Two people in the same class may even speak different *dialects*.

The word *dialect* means "a way of speaking shared by people in a region, community, or group."

The people who speak a dialect are called a *speech community*. The American English in one speech community is different from that in other speech communities. These differences may be in the way people pronounce words, in vocabulary, and in grammar.

A *regional dialect* is spoken by people who live in the same area.

Major regional dialect areas in the United States are the *Northern, Midland,* and *Southern.* Many who live in these areas do not have much of a regional dialect, however, for when people go to school or when they move from one place to another, they often lose some of their regional dialect.

The first English settlers came to this country from different parts of the British Isles. The regional dialect of settlers from southern England was different from that of settlers from the northern part. In southern England, for example, speakers often did not pronounce *r* when it came before consonants or at the end of a word; therefore, the words *far* and *farm* sounded as though they were spelled *fah* and *fahm.* In northern England, however, speakers made the *r* sound more distinct.

Many of the first settlers came from southern England to the East Coast, establishing themselves from Massachusetts to Georgia. Others came later from northern England and settled farther west. One reason for the regional dialects that exist in the United States today is that the new citizens brought their dialect differences with them and passed them from one generation to the next.

Exercise 7: Understanding Dialects

The selection on the next page, from the book *I Wish I Could Give My Son a Wild Raccoon,* is part of an interview with Stanley Hicks, who lives in Sugar Grove, North Carolina. In the selection Stanley Hicks uses the *Appalachian* dialect to describe part of his childhood. With your teacher and classmates, discuss some of the ways in which this regional dialect differs from your own (unless, of course, you too speak the Appalachian dialect).

And we used to play fox and goose. You've got two red foxes—you know, red grains of corn—and the rest of them is white. Play on a board like a checkerboard. And then the geese tries to hem these foxes up. Dad'd get 'em hemmed up and he'd say, "Que-e-e-e-e-e-e! Listen to her wheeze!" He'd say, "Watch her wiggle her tail, boys! She's a-dying!" It'd made us so cussed mad, you know. He was good on it. And then every time he'd jump one of our geese, he'd go "Quack!" Make like a goose a-hollering, you know.

And then we had another game we'd play to see who could jump the furtherest. And then we had stilts—go to the woods and make us a pair of stilts, and then we had a line marked off and we'd see who could walk in this line and not get out of it. It was a job, you know!

And we made wagons and snow sleds to ride in the snow with. I tried to make me a pair of snowshoes but they didn't work out. I didn't make 'em long enough. They tripped me and banged up my nose.[1]

Standard English

Standard English is another important dialect though it is not regional. It is used by people from all parts of the country. In the United States today Standard English is the most accepted dialect, which means it is the preferred dialect in most schools and businesses. This is the form of English used by radio and television announcers.

Standard English can be traced back to fourteenth-century London. In fourteenth-century England, London was both the largest and most important city. Many people throughout England admired the people from London and the way they spoke. When the London dialect was brought to the United States by early settlers, it was much admired and widely used by educated speakers. Although it rapidly became "Americanized," this "London English" was the early form of Standard English.

In the United States today, most schools and businesses prefer people to speak and write Standard English. This is the reason why it is important for you to learn the rules of the Standard English dialect.

[1] Excerpt from "I'm from Out of the Beech" from *I Wish I Could Give My Son a Wild Raccoon* by Eliot Wigginton. Copyright © 1976 by Reading Is Fundamental. Reprinted by permission of Doubleday & Company, Inc.

Exercise 8: Identifying Features of Standard English

With your teacher and classmates, look through some of the pages in the "Grammar and Usage" unit of the book. Point out three or four features of Standard English that are explained there.

Using Language

Though you might not be aware of it, you change your language more often than you change your clothes. You use one kind of language when you talk with your friends and a different kind when you talk with your principal and your teachers. The language you use to write a quick note to a parent is not the language you use to write a report in school. You have one kind of language for relaxed, informal times and another for more formal times.

One way that your language changes for the occasion is the words you choose.

For example, if you and your friends were talking about George Willig, the "human fly" who climbed the 1,350-foot World Trade Center building in New York City, you might say, "Wow! That took a lot of guts." If, however, you were giving a report about George Willig to your classmates, you would be more likely to say, "The climb took a great deal of courage."

You would probably not use the words *wow* and *guts* at more formal times because they are *slang*. Slang words are very informal, used most often among people who know one another well. Teenagers, military people, police officers, lawyers—all of these groups have their slang.

Slang words are like clothes. Most go out of style quickly, and you may not recognize ones that were popular a few years ago. A few slang words, however, stay around and become an accepted part of more formal speaking and writing. The word *movie*, for example, was once a slang word for *motion picture*. The word *flu* was once a slang word for *influenza*. Today, however, both words are widely accepted.

Exercise 9: Defining Slang Words

On a sheet of paper, write the meanings of the slang words and phrases on page 541. Use a dictionary to find the meanings you do not know.

1. Bawl out
2. Chicken
3. Big shot
4. Get a move on
5. Chicken feed
6. On to
7. Pull the wool over someone's eyes
8. On the blink
9. Hang out
10. On the take

25 Library Skills

Most libraries today have comfortable places to sit and read and desks where you can study. They may have films and records you can borrow. They often have record players, filmstrip projectors, and machines to read books and articles on special film. Books are only one of the many resources you will find in most modern libraries. The librarian is there to help you locate what you need.

In this chapter you will learn about the many ways a library can be useful and rewarding to you.

Libraries often have thousands of books and other materials. These materials must be arranged in some order so that they are easy to find. There must be a guide that people can use to locate the books.

In the first part of this chapter, you will learn how most libraries are arranged. You will also learn how to find books and other materials in your library.

Fiction

One way that libraries arrange books is to put them into two groups: *fiction* **and** *nonfiction*.

A book with imaginary characters and events is called *fiction*. Books about real characters and events are called *nonfiction*.

In most libraries fiction and nonfiction books are arranged in different ways and are kept in separate areas of the library.

Fiction books are arranged on the shelves in alphabetical order by the author's last name. Madeleine L'Engle's book *A Wrinkle in Time* comes before Wilson Rawls' book *Where the Red*

Fern Grows because Madeleine L'Engle's last name begins with *L* and Wilson Rawls' last name begins with *R*.

Many authors write more than one book. These books are first grouped together by the author's last name and then are arranged by the first major word in the title. (*A, an,* and *the* are not major words.) For example, Margot Benary-Isbert wrote *The Ark*; she also wrote *A Time to Love* and *The Wicked Enchantment*. These books will be arranged in the following order:

The Ark

A Time to Love

The Wicked Enchantment

Exercise 1: *Learning to Find Fiction*

The following is a list of people who write fiction. Number a sheet of paper 1–10 and list the authors' names in the order you would find them on library shelves.

1. Rudyard Kipling
2. E. B. White
3. P. L. Travers
4. Mary Norton
5. Jack London
6. Ursula LeGuin
7. Herman Melville
8. L. Frank Baum
9. Langston Hughes
10. Jane Austen

Nonfiction

Nonfiction means "the opposite of fiction—not imaginary." An example of a nonfiction book is *My Career as a Quarterback*, by George Plimpton. Most libraries use a system called the *Dewey decimal system* to arrange their nonfiction.

Melvil Dewey, an American librarian who wanted to make libraries easier to use, invented the system of arranging nonfiction books that is named after him. It is the system most school libraries use today.

The *Dewey decimal system* divides all nonfiction books into ten groups of subjects.

Each group of subjects is given a range of numbers. The chart on the next page tells you the ten subject groups in the Dewey decimal system and the numbers assigned to each one.

000–099	General Works	Reference works such as encyclopedias, periodicals, and book lists
100–199	Philosophy	Philosophy, psychology, conduct, and personality
200–299	Religion	Bibles, the Koran, and other religious texts; books on religion and mythology
300–399	Social Sciences	Economics, education, etiquette, fairy tales, folklore, legends, government, and law
400–499	Language	Dictionaries in English; dictionaries of different languages; books on grammar
500–599	Science	Animals, astronomy, biology, botany, chemistry, geology, general science, mathematics, anthropology, and physics
600–699	Technology	Agriculture, aviation, business, engineering, health, home economics, manual training, and television
700–799	The Arts	Painting, sculpture, photography, movies, recreation, and sports
800–899	Literature	History of literature, poetry, drama, essays, and criticism
900–999	History	History, geography, travel history, and collective biography

Exercise 2: Using the Dewey Decimal System

On the following page are ten nonfiction books you might find in your library. Use the preceding chart to find the Dewey decimal group and numbers for each book. Number a sheet of paper 1–10, and write the Dewey decimal group and number on the correct line. Read the example before beginning the exercise.

Example

Book	Name of Group	Numbers
The History of the Roman Empire	History	900–999

1. *Wings in Your Future: Aviation for Young People*
2. *Collected Poems of Gwendolyn Brooks*
3. *The Spanish-English Dictionary*
4. *Astronomy Data Book*
5. *A Short History of Mexico*
6. *Introduction to Child Psychology*
7. *Folklore of the American Land*
8. *Encyclopedia Americana*
9. *The Sports Immortals*
10. *The Complete Grimm's Fairy Tales*

Call Numbers

To make them easy to find, libraries divide nonfiction books into groups and give each book a special number all its own.

The special number each nonfiction book has is its *call number*.

Call numbers are printed on the spines and on an inside page of books. The diagram below shows the four parts of a call number.

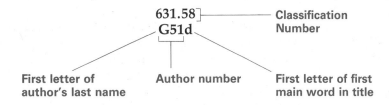

631.58 — Classification Number

G51d

First letter of author's last name

Author number

First letter of first main word in title

The *classification number* comes from the book's Dewey decimal group. Under that is the *author number*. The *author number* is made up of the first letter of the author's last name and a special number. Some books also have the first letter of the first major word in the title after the author number.

Biographies and Autobiographies

There are two exceptions to the rules of the Dewey decimal system: biographies and autobiographies. A *biography* is a book about the life of a real person. *Abe Lincoln Grows Up* by Carl Sandburg is an example of a biography. An *autobiography* is a writer's own life story. When Carl Sandburg wrote about his own life in *Prairie Town Boy,* he wrote an autobiography.

Biographies and autobiographies are in a separate section from other nonfiction books. These books are marked in a special way. Some libraries identify biographies and autobiographies with the letter *B*. Other libraries use the number *921*. The *B* or *921* is the first part of the call number for these books.

In their special section, biographies and autobiographies are arranged alphabetically according to the first letter of the last name of the person the book is about. An autobiography of Mahalia Jackson would come before a biography of Henry James. This letter makes up the second part of the call letter for these books.

Biography of Anne Morrow Lindbergh	$\frac{921}{L}$ or $\frac{B}{L}$
Autobiography of Jade Snow Wong	$\frac{921}{W}$ or $\frac{B}{W}$
Autobiography of Jesse Jackson	$\frac{921}{J}$ or $\frac{B}{J}$
Biography of John F. Kennedy	$\frac{921}{K}$ or $\frac{B}{K}$

Biographies written about the lives of several people are called *collective biographies*. All collective biographies are filed under the number *920* in the Dewey decimal system. Under the number *920* is the first letter of the last name of the author. Collective biographies cannot use the last name of the person the biography is about because they are about more than one person. Here is the call number for a book titled *Black Heroes of the American Revolution* by Burke Davis: 920.
                                           D

Exercise 3: *Identifying Call Numbers*

On the next page is a list of biographies, autobiographies, and collective biographies. Write the call number for each one. If it could begin with either *B* or *921*, write both call numbers.

Examples

Book and Author	**Call Number**
My World and Welcome to It by James Thurber	$\frac{B}{T}$ or $\frac{921}{T}$
Hunger Fighters by Paul de Kruif	$\frac{920}{K}$

1. *The Mets from Mobile: Cleon Jones & Tommie Agee* by A. S. Young

2. *General Custer and the Battle of the Little Big Horn: The Federal View* by John M. Carroll

3. *Lauren Bacall: By Myself* by Lauren Bacall

4. *Westward Adventure: The True Stories of Six Pioneers* by William O. Steele

5. *Cleopatra* by Ernie Bradford

6. *Bill Pickett: First Black Rodeo Star* by Sibyl Hancock

7. *Sports Star: Nadia Comaneci* by S. H. Burchard

8. *The Seventh Son* by W. E. B. du Bois

9. *Women of Power* by Mark Strage

10. *David Young: Chief of the Quileutes: An American Indian Today* by Ruth Kirk

Using the Card Catalogue

Every library, no matter what the size, has a guide for finding books called the *card catalogue*. Here are listed the books the library owns. The card catalogue looks like a large cabinet and has many drawers with letters for labels.

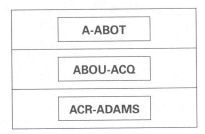

547

In each drawer is a series of cards arranged in alphabetical order. The first drawer shown above would have all the cards from *A* through *ABOT*. The second drawer would have cards from *ABOU* through *ACQ*. The third drawer would have the cards from *ACR* through *ADAMS* and so on.

The card catalogue has three basic kinds of cards: the *author card*, **the** *title card*, **and the** *subject card*.

The Author Card

The *author card* is the card to look for if you know the author, but not the title of the book. Author cards are arranged alphabetically, by the last name of the author.

On the first line of every author card is the name of the author, last name first. Below is the author card for the book *Famous Horses and Their People* by Edna Hoffman Evans.

636.1
E92

Evans, Edna Hoffman, 1913–

Famous horses and their people / Edna H. Evans. — Brat-
tleboro, Vt. : S. Greene Press, [1975]

viii, 168 p. : ill. ; 22 cm.

Bibliography: p. 165–168.
ISBN 0-8289-0231-3

1. Horses. 2. Statesmen—Biography. 3. Horsemen—Biography. I.
Title.

SF285.E93   636.1   74-31238
                                                                MARC

Library of Congress   74

The author's name is at the top of the card, with the last name first, followed by the author's first name and middle name or initial. Below the author's name is the book title. If the library has more than one book by an author, you will find a separate card for each book. These cards are arranged in alphabetical order by the first major word in the title of the book. (Remember that *a, an,* and *the* do not count as major words.) The call number is in the upper left-hand corner of the card.

The Title Card

Title cards are helpful when you know the name of a book, but not the author. The book title is on the first line of a title card. The following sample is a title card for the book *Famous Horses and Their People:*

```
636.1                  Famous horses and their people
E92
                    Evans, Edna Hoffman, 1913–

         Famous horses and their people / Edna H. Evans. — Brat-
      tleboro, Vt. : S. Greene Press, [1975]
         viii, 168 p. : ill. ; 22 cm.

         Bibliography: p. 165–168.
         ISBN 0-8289-0231-3


         1. Horses.  2. Statesmen—Biography.  3. Horsemen—Biography.  I.
      Title.

      SF285.E93                    636.1                   74-31238
                                                            MARC

         Library of Congress             74
```

Title cards are filed alphabetically by the first major word in the title. The author's name is under the title. The call number is in the upper left-hand corner.

The Subject Card

Subject cards help you find information about specific subjects. The first line of a subject card shows the general subject of the book. If you want to learn about the general subject *Horses,* for example, and do not know the names of any books about horses, the *subject card* tells you where to look. The sample card on the following page is the subject card for E.H. Evans' *Famous Horses and Their People.*

The author's name and the title of the book are listed below the subject. The call number is in the upper left-hand corner of the card.

Libraries usually include many subject cards under the same general subject heading. The list of titles below the subject card names some books that might be found under the subject *Moving Pictures:*

```
636.1                         HORSES
E92
                    Evans, Edna Hoffman, 1913–


        Famous horses and their people / Edna H. Evans. — Brat-
        tleboro, Vt. : S. Greene Press, [1975]
            viii, 168 p. : ill. ; 22 cm.
            Bibliography: p. 165–168.
            ISBN 0-8289-0231-3



        1. Horses.  2. Statesmen—Biography.  3. Horsemen—Biography.  I.
        Title.
        SF285.E93                       636.1                   74-31238
                                                                  MARC

        Library of Congress              74
```

Moving Pictures—History

Hollywood Rajah by Bosley Crowther

How to Read a Film by James Monaco

The History of World Cinema by David Robinson

The card catalogue sometimes files author cards, title cards, and subject cards together in alphabetical order. Larger libraries often have separate files for authors, titles, and subjects. For each book in the library, you will find at least three cards. You may find more than three cards if the book is about more than one subject.

Exercise 4: Understanding the Card Catalogue

The following labels are those of five catalogue drawers you might find in your library:

| Aab–Dun | Duo–Jow | Jox–Pin | Pio–Vy | Waa–Z |

Divide a sheet of paper into five columns. Make the heading for each column a drawer label.

Arrange the following list of authors' names, book titles, and subjects in alphabetical order as they would appear in the card catalogue.

Example

Authors, Titles, Subjects

Wildlife
Bruce Catton
Jane Addams of Hull House
Art
Rose Wilder
The Three Wishes: A Collection of Puerto Rican Folktales
My Darling, My Hamburger

Correct Placement

Aab–Dun	Duo–Jow	Jox–Pin	Pio-Vy	Waa–Z
Art	*Jane Addams of Hull House*	*My Darling, My Hamburger*	*The Three Wishes: A Collection of Puerto Rican Folktales*	Wilder, Rose
Catton, Bruce				Wildlife

1. *Alice in Wonderland*
2. Eskimo legends
3. *The Little Prince*
4. Hans Christian Andersen
5. Marjorie K. Rawlings
6. *The King's Drum and Other African Stories*
7. Yoshiko Ushida
8. Eve Merriam
9. Microbe hunters
10. *History of the Revolutionary War*

Guide Cards

Guide cards make the card catalogue easy to use. Guide cards divide the drawer into sections and show the letters of the alphabet in each section. Guide cards stick up farther than other cards so they are easy to find. They may also be a different color. On the next page are some sample guide cards from the card catalogue:

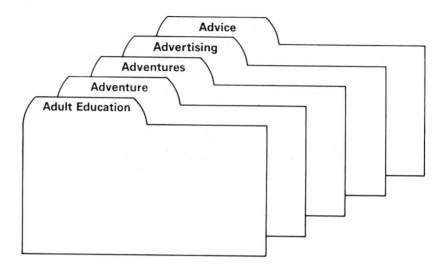

Exercise 5: *Using the Card Catalogue*

Below is a list of authors and subjects you might find in your card catalogue. Copy this list on a sheet of paper and take it with you to the library. Look up each author and subject in the card catalogue. After each name write down the books by that author or the books about that subject in your library's card catalogue. If you do not find any, write *None* in that space. (Numbers 1–5 may be both authors and subjects.)

1. Roberto Clemente
2. e. e. cummings
3. Anne Frank
4. Lorraine Hansberry
5. George Bernard Shaw

6. Nuclear Energy
7. Horses
8. Race Cars
9. Magic
10. History of China

Finding the Book on the Shelves

When you walk into a library, you can orient yourself by looking for the fiction section, the biography and autobiography section, and the nonfiction section.

To find a book of fiction, biography, or autobiography, look in the card catalogue to see if your library has the book. Then locate shelves where these books are kept. Remember that *fiction* books are arranged in alphabetical order by the last name of the author. Biographies and autobiographies are arranged by the last name of the person the book is about.

For example, one of Paul Zindel's books is titled *The Pigman*. To find this book, look along the fiction shelves for books with the letter Z on their spines. Once you have found the Z's, you will pass authors with names such as *Zane, Zarr,* and *Zeke* until you come to *Zindel*. All of the Paul Zindel books your library has will be filed there in alphabetical order by title. For example, you may find *Confessions of a Teenage Baboon; My Darling, My Hamburger;* and *Pardon Me, You're Stepping on My Eyeball.*

To find a nonfiction book on the shelves, first look up the book in the card catalogue. Write down its call number. Suppose you want to find *Project Apollo: Man to the Moon* by Thomas Alexander. The title card in the card catalogue tells you the call number for this book is 629.25.

A27p

The 629.25 is the book's Dewey decimal subject number. Locate the shelf for books with call numbers starting with 629. Move along that shelf until you come to 629.25. The next step is to look at the author number: A27. Author numbers are put in alphabetical order, so the A's will be first. Continue to look along the shelf until you come to the A27 books. You will pass author numbers such as A4, A16, and A21. The last step is to match up the small letter on the right. This small letter stands for the first letter in the first major word of title: *p* for *Project*. No two call numbers in a library are exactly alike. When you have found the final matching letter of the call number, you have found your book.

Exercise 6: *Ordering Call Numbers*

On the next page is a list of call numbers for nonfiction books. Number a sheet of paper 1–10. List the call numbers in the order you would find them on the library shelves. Read the example before you proceed.

Example

Call Numbers	Correct Order
a. 778.69 B14g	778.59 C13f
b. 778.59 C13f	778.69 B14g
c. 778.69 B14h	778.69 B14h

1. 926
   H24p

2. 204.7
   T16r

3. 338.7
   H46t

4. 559
   A11q

5. 500
   H96t

6. 338.7
   H46c

7. 926.7
   R29j

8. 600
   I42r

9. 204.6
   S21n

10. 559
    A11r

The Reference Area

One of the best places to look for any kind of information in a library is the *reference area*. The reference area is often a separate room or section of the library. Some libraries have special reference librarians to help you find what you need. In the reference area you will find such materials as dictionaries, encyclopedias, almanacs, newspapers and periodicals, and special reference books.

Sometimes you will need to use the reference area for a school report. Other times you may want to find out something on your own. In this section you will learn how.

Periodicals

A *periodical* is a magazine or journal that is published at regular intervals, such as once a week or once a month.

In the reference area you will usually find new issues of periodicals on display. Old issues are bound together like books and put on the shelves. Libraries usually post lists of all the periodicals they carry.

Suppose you want to learn more about Count Dracula. Perhaps you have read a magazine article about him, but cannot remember the magazine. How do you find the article? Every library has a guide to finding information in periodicals.

The guide for information in periodicals is the *Readers' Guide to Periodical Literature*.

Some libraries have a short version of the *Readers' Guide*, the *Abridged Readers' Guide*. Others carry the standard *Readers' Guide* of many volumes. Each has the same style and format.

The *Readers' Guide* is like a card catalogue for magazine articles. It has information about articles published in newspapers and magazines of general interest. Published in paperback volumes twenty-two times a year, the *Readers' Guide* also appears in yearly hardcover volumes. The information is arranged alphabetically by subject and by author. When you know the name of the author, look in the *Readers' Guide* under the author's last name. When you do not know the author's name, look under the general subject heading. The following sample entry is the *Readers' Guide* entry for the subject *Dracula*.[1]

> DRACULA, Prince of Wallachia. See Vlad II. Dracul, Prince of
>   Wallachia

The above entry is called a *cross-reference*, because it *refers* you to another entry to find information about the legendary Dracula. "See Vlad II" means look under *Vlad II*.
The following entry is the *Readers' Guide* entry you will find under *Vlad II*:

> VLAD II, Dracul, Prince of Wallachia
>   Is Dracula really dead? il, Time 109:60 My 23 '77
>   Dracula lives! D. Ansen. il Newsweek 90:74-5 + O 31 '77
> VLAD II, Tepes. See Vlad II, Dracul, Prince of Wallachia

The two articles listed under *Vlad II* are "Is Dracula Really Dead?" and "Dracula Lives!"

In the front of the *Readers' Guide*, you will find a key to reading abbreviations and magazine titles. With this key you learn to read entries such as the following:

> VLAD II, Dracul, Prince of Wallachia
>   Is Dracula really dead? il Time 109:60 My 23 '77

The above entry is an illustrated article titled "Is Dracula Really Dead?" You can find the article on page 60 of Volume 109 (May 23, 1977) of *Time* magazine.

No author is listed for the article above, but the article at the top of the next page has an author:

> Dracula lives! D. Ansen. il Newsweek 90:74-5 + O 31 '77

The above article is titled "Dracula Lives!" and is written by D. Ansen. You can find this article on pages 74–75 of Volume 90 (October 31, 1977) of *Newsweek* magazine.

---

[1]*Readers' Guide to Periodical Literature* Copyright © 1977, 1978 by The H. W. Wilson Company. Material reproduced by permission of the publisher.

Exercise 7: Understanding the Readers' Guide

The following columns are from the *Readers' Guide to Periodical Literature.*[1] Copy three of the entries on a piece of paper. Then look in the front of your library's *Readers' Guide* to find the abbreviation key. Use this key to find the meanings of abbreviations in the three entries you selected. Write a few sentences for each of your entries. Put in complete words for the abbreviations.

TELEVISION programs

See also
Television critics and criticism

Black programs
TV. B. Allen. il Essence 9:18 Ap; 10:18 J1; 20-1 O '79

Childrens programs
Station identification; excerpt. D. Bowie. Sat Eve Post 251:54-5 + N '79
Superheroes, antiheroes, and the heroism void in children's TV. E. M. Berckman. Chr Cent 96:704-7 J1 4; Discussion. 96:1064-5 O 31 '79

Reviews—Single works
Captain Kangaroo
    People il 12:107-8 + N 5 '79
Hot hero sandwich
    America 141:322 N 24 '79
Mister Rogers' neighborhood
    Chr Cent il 96:1268-9 D 19 '79
3-2-1- contact. il Time 115:79 Ja 21 '80
Uncle Floyd show
    N Y 13:74 Ja 21 '80

Conversation programs
Talk of television. H. F. Waters and others. il pors Newsweek 94:76-9 + O 29 '79

Cookery programs
TV's newest star chef, Burt Wolf, cooks by his own rules of thumb. H. Shapiro. il pors People 12:77 + N 12 '79

Dance programs
BBC-TV series highlights the history of dance: Fonteyn's Magic. J. Gruen. il pors Dance Mag 53:52-7 O '79
Dance in America: choreography moves from stage to television studio. C. L. Jenner. il Theatre Crafts 13:22-3 + O '79
Ralph Holmes: lighting and art director for Dance in America. P. MacKay. il Theatre Crafts 13:24-7 + O '79
Two rehearsals; Baryshnikov on Broadway. New Yorker 55:26-7 Ja 14 '80

Educational programs
See also
Television programs—Weather programs

Financial programs
Free to choose; M. Friedman's series. H. Anderson. il por Newsweek 95:57-8 Ja 14 '80

Game shows
Game shows—TV's glittering gold mine. T. Buckley. il N Y Times Mag p50 + N 18 '79

Humorous programs
In memoriam; this year's sitcoms. M. Kitman. New Leader 62:25-6 O 8 '79
Rhoda and Lou and Mary and Alex; television comedy writer J. L. Brooks. il por Time 114:97 O 22 '79

Finding Periodicals in the Library

From the *Readers' Guide* entries, write down the magazine, volume number, page, and the date, since it is easy to forget these on your way to the periodical shelves. Next, make sure that your library carries the magazine you want. If no list of magazines is posted, ask your librarian.

Most libraries file periodicals in alphabetical order. The issues are listed with the most recent ones first, and you may see the most up-to-date magazines still out on display.

Exercise 8: Using the Readers' Guide

Make a list of five subjects you would like to know more about. Use the *Readers' Guide* to find articles on at least three of your subjects. For each subject make a list that includes the following items:

a. The name of the article
b. The name of the author of the article
c. The full title of the periodical where the article may be found
d. The date of the periodical
e. The volume number of the periodical
f. The page numbers on which the article appears in the periodical

26 Reference Works

Using the Dictionary

When Noah Webster was a young man, American colonists were fighting the Revolutionary War. A devoted patriot, Noah Webster served in the war and dedicated himself to helping his new country.

In 1825, after twenty-five years of work, Noah Webster published a book that was to help shape the American language. This book, *An American Dictionary of the English Language*, was two volumes long and defined seventy thousand words. One of the important features of the dictionary was that it included *Americanisms*. These are words such as *applesauce, bullfrog, chowder, hickory*, and *skunk* that came into the language after the colonists arrived from England. For this attempt to show how language was actually used, the scholar was criticized by people who believed that the English language should remain "pure," just as it had come from England.

In time Noah Webster's feelings about language were accepted by the makers of dictionaries around the world. He believed in a living, spoken language that grows as people grow or as a new nation grows. His dream was to see the United States founded on a united language, and he helped to make the dream a reality.

Looking Up a Word in the Dictionary

You can easily find a word in the dictionary if you remember three important points:

1. All words are listed in alphabetical order

Sometimes, alphabetical order is simple: *ant* comes before *cat*, and *beach* comes before *dress*. When you are looking for words starting with the same letter, finding the word may be more difficult. Then it is important to read carefully and look at each letter in the word. For example, *bloom* comes before *blossom; brilliance* comes before *brilliant;* and *buggy* comes before *bugle*. Alphabetized words are printed in **boldface,** as the following example shows:

as·trol·o·gy

---

2. Two *guide words* are printed at the top of each page.

Guide words are the first and last words on that page. For example, if the guide words at the top of the page are *Zambezi* and *Zend*, all of the other words on that page, such as *zany, zap,* and *zebra*, come between the two guide words in alphabetical order.

---

3. Words are divided into sections.

There is an *A* section, a *B* section, a *C* Section, and so on. To find a word in the dictionary, first turn to the section for the first letter of your word. As you turn the pages, look at the guide words at the top of the page. Then when you come to the right set, look down the page until you find your word.

Sometimes, you may have trouble finding a word because you do not know how to spell it. When this happens, sound out the word and listen for sounds that could be spelled more than one way. A *k* sound, for example, may be spelled *k*, or it could be spelled *c* or *ck*, as in *padlock.* An *s* sound may be spelled *s*, *sc*, or *ss* as in *something scientific*, and *assignment* respectively. Note also the *gn* spelling in *assignment* for the *n* sound. Also, look for letters that might be doubled such as the *n* in *connection* or the *m* and *t* in *committee.* Chapter 23 of this textbook gives rules for spelling easily confused words such as *mischief* and *receive.* If you cannot find the word you need after using this resource, ask your teacher for help.

Exercise 1: Understanding Guide Words

In the two sets of words on the next page, Set 1 consists of pairs of guide words you might find in any dictionary. Set 2 consists of words to be listed in alphabetical order between the guide words on the page. Divide a clean sheet of paper into three columns and label each column with a set of guide words. Then write the words in Set 2 under the correct guide words on your paper. An example is provided for clarification.

Example

a. **renown**   **repeatable**
   rent
   repair
   repay
   repeal

Set 1

1. **weightless**   **we'll**
2. **wedgy**   **weight**
3. **weathered**   **Wedgewood**

Set 2

weatherly	weekday
weeper	welfare
well	weaver
weatherman	weekly
weed	weld
welcome	weird
weathering	weighty
wedlock	weeping willow
we'll	web

Reading Word Entries

Each word listed in alphabetical order in the dictionary is called a *main entry word*.

giant panda a large, black-and-white, bearlike mammal (*Ailuropoda melanoleuca*) of China and Tibet that feeds on bamboo shoots

GIANT PANDA
(4 ft. high at shoulder)

Words formed from other words, such as *liked* or *liking,* are listed under the word from which they are formed. *Liked* and *liking,* for example, will be found under *like.*

like² (līk) *vi.* liked, lik′ing [ME. *liken* < OE. *lician* (akin to Goth. *leikan*) < base of *lic*, body, form (see prec.): sense development: to be of like form—be like—be suited to—be pleasing to] 1. [Obs.] to please; be agreeable to: with the dative *[it likes me not]* 2. to be so inclined; choose *[leave whenever you like]* —*vt.* 1. to have a taste or fondness for; be pleased with; have a preference for; enjoy 2. to want or wish *[I would like to see him]* —*n.* *[pl.]* preferences, tastes, or affections —lik′er *n.*
-like (līk) [< LIKE¹] 1. *an adj.-forming suffix meaning* like, characteristic of, suitable for *[doglike, manlike, homelike]* 2. *an adv.-forming suffix meaning* in the manner of Words formed with *-like* are sometimes hyphenated, always if three *l's* fall together *[ball-like]*

Using Main Entry Words for Spelling

The main entry word tells you the correct spelling of the word. If a word is capitalized in the main entry, then it should always be written with a capital letter. The following main entry words show four such words in a row.

Ken·il·worth (ken′′l wurth′) urban district in Warwick-shire, England, near Coventry: pop. 16,000
Ken·nan (ken′ən), George F(rost) 1904– ; U.S. diplomat & historian
Ken·ne·bec (ken′ə bek′) [< Abnaki, lit., long-water place] river in W Me., flowing into the Atlantic: c. 150 mi.
Ken·ne·dy (ken′ə dē), Cape [after ff.] *former name* (1963–73) *of* Cape CANAVERAL

Using Main Entry Words to Learn Syllables

The main entry word shows how the word is divided into syllables.

In many dictionaries a raised dot shows the division between syllables. For example, the main entry word *microscope* looks like this: **mi·cro·scope.** From the main entry word you can tell that *microscope* has three syllables: *mi,cro,* and *scope.* Syllables help you to pronounce words correctly and show you where to divide a word at the end of a written line.

Words should be divided only between syllables.

Words of only one syllable cannot be divided at all. A hyphen (-) shows when a word of more than one syllable is divided at the end of a line.

Incorrect

Juana looked at the leaf through her new *mic-roscope*.

Correct

Juana looked at the leaf through her new *mi-croscope*.

Do not divide a word so that one letter is left by itself.

Many words have one-letter syllables: **e·lev·en.** Even when the dictionary shows a one-letter syllable, one letter should not be left on a line by itself.

Incorrect

The teacher counted *e-leven* absences due to the flu.

Correct

The teacher counted *elev-en* absences due to the flu.

Exercise 2: *Learning About Syllables*

Look up each of the following words in a dictionary. On a sheet of paper, copy each word as it appears in the dictionary, using raised dots to show how it is divided into syllables. Then draw a circle around each syllable that cannot be left alone on a written line.

Example

a. alive
    (a)·*live*

1. imaginary
2. popular
3. evil
4. military
5. aboard

6. necessary
7. latitude
8. hearty
9. unite
10. okra

The Main Entry

The *main entry* is the main entry word plus all the information the dictionary gives about it. This main entry is for the word *chariot:*

char·i·ot (char′ē ət) *n.* [ME. < OFr. *charriote* < *charrier* < VL. *csrricare:* see CHARGE] **1.** a horse-drawn, two-wheeled cart used in ancient times for war, racing, parades, etc. **2.** [Archaic] a light, four-wheeled carriage, used for pleasure or on some state occasions —*vt., vi.* to drive or ride in a chariot

CHARIOT

Using the Main Entry for Pronunciation

The pronunciation of a word is in parentheses after the main entry word. Here is the main entry word *radio* and its pronunciation: **ra·di·o** (rā′ dē ō′). To help you pronounce words, the dictionary uses a kind of code with three parts: *diacritical marks, simplified spelling,* and *accent marks.*

Diacritical Marks

Diacritical marks are marks placed over letters to show how sounds are pronounced.

You can learn about diacritical marks by looking at the pronunciation key in your dictionary. Many dictionaries have a short key at the bottom of every other page. The following key is from *Webster's New World Dictionary.*

fat, āpe, cär; ten, ē**ven; is, bī**te; gō, hôrn, tōōl, look; oil, out; up, fʉr; get; joy; yet; chin; she; thin, *th*en; zh, leisure; ŋ, ring; **ə** for *a* in *ago, e* in *agent, i* in *sanity, o* in *comply, u* in *focus;* ′ as in *able* (ā′b′l); Fr. bȧl; ë, Fr. coeur; ö, Fr. feu; Fr. mo*n*; ô, Fr. coq; **ü,** Fr. duc; ʁ, Fr. cri; H, G. ich; k**h,** G. doch. See inside front cover. ☆Americanism; ‡foreign; *hypothetical; <derived from

This key shows you how to pronounce the marked letters by using them in a word you already know. To use the key, look for a word with a letter and diacritical mark like the one in the word you want to pronounce. In the word *radio,* for example, the *a* and *o* both have the same diacritical mark. Both the *a* and *o* are long vowel sounds and are marked ā and ō. The key tells you that ā is pronounced like the *a* in *ape* and that the ō is pronounced like the *o* in the word *go.* This pronunciation key does not show a (ˇ) symbol for a short vowel sound. The short vowel sounds in this key are left blank.

Most dictionaries have a longer pronunciation key in the front before the word entries. Use the longer key to find more complete information about pronunciation.

The Schwa

In pronunciation keys you will find a letter that looks like an upside-down *e*. This symbol, called a *schwa*, is made like this: (ə). Dictionaries use the schwa to show vowels that have almost no sound. Because all vowels can have almost no sound in some words, here are examples of the schwa for each vowel:

ə	**a** in ago
	e in agent
	i in sanity
	o in comply
	u in focus
ər	perhaps, murder

When you find the (ə) sound in a word, you know that vowel has almost no sound when the word is pronounced.

Simplified Spelling

The *simplified spelling* of a word is a simple way of spelling the word to make it easy to pronounce.

Simplified spelling leaves out letters you do not pronounce. When you say the word *loaf,* for example, you do not pronounce the *a.* The simplified spelling of *loaf* in the dictionary looks like this: lōf. Simplified spelling also changes letters to ones that give the right sound. The plural of *loaf* is *loaves.* When you say *loaves,* you pronounce the letters *es* like a *z,* so the simplified spelling of *loaves* is written lōvz.

Accent Marks

An *accent mark* is different from a diacritical mark. It comes before or after a syllable instead of over a letter. The accent mark tells you what part of the word to stress when you speak.

If you say the word *elephant* to yourself, you will hear that you speak the first syllable more strongly than the next two. The syllable that you speak more strongly is known as the *accented syllable,* because you *accent* that syllable of the word with your voice.

Dictionaries differ in the way they show accent marks. Some show the accented syllable with a heavy straight mark *in front* of the syllable, like this: ('). Other dictionaries show the accent with a heavy slanted mark *after* the syllable, like this: ('). Depending on the dictionary you are using, the pronunciation of the word *elephant* could be written in either of two ways:

'el ə fənt *or* el' ə fənt

Both ways show that the first syllable is accented.

Some words need *two* accent marks to show the correct pronunciation. If you say the word *peppermint* to yourself, you can hear that both the first and last syllables are accented more than the middle one. When a word has two accented syllables, one of the two is spoken more strongly than the other. In the word *peppermint* the first syllable is stronger. The stronger syllable of the two is called the *primary accent.* The accent for the other syllable is called the *secondary accent.*

Dictionaries have different ways of showing primary and secondary accents. Some make a slanted heavy mark for the primary and a slanted light mark for the secondary accent, like this: pep' ər mint'. Other dictionaries show straight heavy marks above and below the letters, like this: 'pep ər ˌmint.

Exercise 3: Learning About Pronunciation

Look up the following words in the dictionary. On a sheet of paper, write each word as it appears in parentheses after the main entry word. Show the diacritical marks, the simplified spelling, and the accent marks.

Example

a. nation
    (nā' shən)

1. banana
2. toward
3. utensil
4. salmon
5. buffalo

6. perfect
7. demolition
8. gigantic
9. matador
10. punishment

Using the Main Entry for Definitions

The definition of a word takes the largest part of the main entry. Since many words have more than one meaning, dictionaries may list several meanings for one word. The following definition for the word *diary* is from *Webster's New World Dictionary:*

di·a·ry (dī′ə rē) *n., pl.* -ries [L. *diarium*, daily allowance (of food or pay): hence, record of this < *dies*, day: see DEITY] **1.** a daily written record, esp. of the writer's own experiences, thoughts, etc. **2.** a book for keeping such a record

When a word has more than one meaning, dictionaries number its definitions. Definition number 1 of the word *diary* is "a daily written record, especially of the writer's own experiences, thoughts, etc." Definition number 2 of *diary* is "a book for keeping such a record." From these definitions you learn that the word *diary* can mean either a special written record or a book to keep the record. When you look up a word, choose the definition that best fits the meaning of your sentence.

Abbreviations and Symbols

Dictionaries contain so much information that they must use abbreviations and symbols in their definitions to save space.

You probably know some of these abbreviations and symbols, such as *ft.* for *foot, U.S.* for *United States, &* for *and.* If you find an abbreviation or a symbol you do not know, turn to the list of abbreviations and symbols that is usually in the front of the dictionary. The following list gives twenty common abbreviations found in most dictionaries:

1. *adj.* adjective
2. *adv.* adverb
3. *cent.* century; centuries
4. *conj.* conjunction
5. *e.g.* for example
6. *esp.* especially
7. *ex.* example
8. *exc.* except
9. *i.e.* that is
10. *incl.* including
11. *n.* noun
12. *n. pl.* plural noun
13. *n. sing.* singular noun
14. *pl.* plural

15. *prep.* preposition

16. *pron.* pronoun

17. *pronun.* pronunciation

18. *pt.* past tense

19. *sp.* spelled; spelling

20. *specif.* specifically

Parts of Speech

Most of the words you use have more than one meaning. For example, the word *talk* can mean something that you do or something that you give. To help you find the exact meaning you are looking for, definitions are grouped by the parts of speech.

The parts of speech are *noun, pronoun, verb, adjective, adverb, preposition, conjunction,* and *interjection.* Abbreviations for these parts of speech always come before the definition of words. The following main entry is for a word that can be more than one part of speech:

land (land) *n.* [ME. < OE., akin to G. *land* < IE. base **lendh-*, unoccupied land, heath, steppe, whence Bret. *lann*, heath (whence Fr. *lande*, moor), W. *llan*, enclosure, yard] **1.** the solid part of the earth's surface not covered by water **2.** a specific part of the earth's surface **3.** *a)* a country, region, etc. *[a distant land*, one's native *land]* *b)* the inhabitants of such an area; nation's people **4.** ground or soil in terms of its quality, location, etc. *[rich land*, high *land]* **5.** *a)* ground considered as property; estate *[to invest in land]* *b)* [*pl.*] specific holdings in land **6.** rural or farming regions as distinguished from urban regions *[to return to the land]* **7.** that part of a grooved surface which is not indented, as any of the ridges between the grooves in the bore of a rifle ☆**8.** the Lord: a euphemism *[for land's sake!]* **9.** *Econ.* natural resources —*vt.* [ME. *landen* < the *n.*, replacing OE. *lendan* < **landjan*] **1.** to put, or cause to go, on shore from a ship **2.** to bring into; cause to enter or end up in a particular place or condition *[a fight landed* him in jail*]* **3.** to set (an aircraft) down on land or water **4.** to draw successfully onto land or into a boat; catch *[to land a fish]* **5.** [Colloq.] to get, win, or secure *[to land a job]* **6.** [Colloq.] to deliver (a blow) —*vi.* **1.** to leave a ship and go on shore; disembark **2.** to come to a port or to shore: said of a ship **3.** to arrive at a specified place; end up **4.** to alight or come to rest, as after a flight, jump, or fall

The word *land* can be used as either a noun or a verb. The dictionary gives nineteen separate definitions for this word. *Land* as a noun is listed in the first nine definitions. *Land* as a transitive verb (*vt.*) is listed in the second group of six definitions, and *land* as an intransitive verb (*vi*) is listed in the third group of four definitions.

To decide which definition is right for your purpose, you must know how the word is used in a sentence.

Many city dwellers are going back to the *land.*

In the sentence above, *land* is a noun. You will find its meaning in the first group of nine definitions. Read through the definitions in this group. Then reread the sentence itself: *Many people unhappy with life in the city are going back to the land.* The word *land* in this sentence is used with the words *going back*. The sentence also talks about the *city*. *Going back* means *return*, so you can guess that the correct definition is number 6 because it talks about returning and about urban areas. After definition number 6 the dictionary gives an example by using it in a phrase. The phrase in brackets reads: *to return to the land.* The meaning of *land* in this phrase is like the meaning in your sentence, so you know that the definition you have chosen is correct.

Exercise 4: *Locating Correct Definitions*

In the following ten sentences, each *italicized* word has more than one definition. Look up each word in a dictionary and decide which definition best fits the meaning of the sentence. Write the correct definition for each word on a sheet of paper numbered 1–10.

Example

a.   From the cliffs we saw enormous waves *lashing* the rocks.

Lashing = striking with great force

1. Ricky *baited* his older sister until she lost her temper.

2. The *stop* on the tape recorder wouldn't work.

3. Doctors in the past would *bleed* patients to make them well.

4. Anita called the airlines to find the cost of a *round* trip ticket.

5. The prime minister announced his intention to *step down*.

6. The small ship *listed* in the high winds.

7. Raul wouldn't tell us his grandmother's *pet* name for him.

8. Detectives *dragged* the river for evidence.

9. It was the third *down* and the team was in trouble.

10. The kitten *washed* itself carefully.

Synonyms

Synonyms are words that have almost the same meaning.

Dictionaries list synonyms for many words as the last part of the main entry. (The abbreviation for *synonym* is *syn*.) The following main entry has a long list of synonyms:

bright (brīt) *adj.* [ME. < OE. *bryht*, earlier *beorht* < IE. base **bhereg-*, to gleam, white, whence Goth. *bairhts*, E. BIRCH] **1.** shining with light that is radiated or reflected; full of light **2.** clear or brilliant in color or sound; vivid or intense **3.** lively; vivacious; cheerful *[a bright smile]* **4.** mentally quick; smart, clever, witty, etc. **5.** *a)* full of happiness or hope *[a bright outlook on life]* *b)* favorable; auspicious **6.** glorious or splendid; illustrious —*adv.* in a bright manner —*n.* [Poet.] brightness; splendor —**bright'-ly** *adv.*
SYN.—**bright**, the most general term here, implies the giving forth or reflecting of light, or a being filled with light *[a bright day, star, shield, etc.]*; **radiant** emphasizes the actual or apparent emission of rays of light; **shining** implies a steady, continuous brightness *[the shining sun]*; **brilliant** implies intense or flashing brightness *[brilliant sunlight, diamonds, etc.]*; **luminous** is applied to objects that are full of light or give off reflected or phosphorescent light; **lustrous** is applied to objects whose surfaces gleam by reflected light and emphasizes gloss or sheen *[lustrous silk]* See also INTELLIGENT —*ANT.* **dull, dim, dark**

A synonym never means exactly the same thing as the word itself.

Each synonym listed under *bright* is a little different from the others, and the dictionary gives information about the differences. For example, *shining* is defined as "continuous brightness," but *brilliant* is "intense or flashing brightness." Often the dictionary gives examples of synonyms used in a phrase, such as "the shining sun." When you choose a synonym, make sure that it is as close as possible to the meaning you want. For more information about synonyms, see Chapter 23.

Famous Places and People in the Dictionary

Many famous places, both real and imaginary, can be found in the dictionary. The dictionary can also tell you when a famous person lived and why the person was famous. For example, suppose you want to know whether or not King Arthur was a real person and when he was supposed to have lived. The following information is listed in the dictionary under *Arthur*:

Ar·thur (är'thər) [ML. *Arthurus*] **1.** a masculine name: dim. *Art;* equiv. It. *Arturo* **2.** a legendary king of Britain who led the knights of the Round Table: such a king is supposed to have lived in the 6th cent. **3. Chester Alan,** 1830–86; 21st president of the U.S. (1881–85) —**Ar·thu·ri·an** (är thoor'ē ən) *adj.*

This definition tells you that King Arthur is *legendary,* meaning that he is a character in many stories that cannot be factually verified. The definition also tells you that a real King Arthur is supposed to have lived during the sixth century.

Exercise 5 *Using the Dictionary*

Select five of the following famous people and places and look them up in the dictionary. On a sheet of paper, write what you learn about each one.

Example

Lawrence of Arabia

The name for Thomas Edward Lawrence—born in 1888 and died in 1935—a British adventurer and writer.

1. Utopia
2. Camelot
3. Casablanca
4. Stonehenge
5. Taj Mahal

6. Bluebeard
7. Paul Bunyan
8. Tolkien
9. Napoleon
10. Robinson Crusoe

Other Reference Works

Encyclopedias

Encyclopedias are reference books with general information about many subjects.

Some encyclopedias come in one volume. *The Concise Columbia Encyclopedia* is an example of this kind. Other encyclopedias have several volumes. The information found in encyclopedias is always arranged in alphabetical order by subjects, by names of people, and by names of places. Each volume of an encyclopedia is labeled with a number and a letter or words. The letters indicate the range of subjects in that volume.

There are two ways to find information you need in an encyclopedia:

1. Look for your subject in the volume with the letter that matches it. For example, look in the *R* volume of the encyclopedia to learn about Eleanor Roosevelt.

2. Look in the *index.*

An *index* is an alphabetical list of all the subjects in the encyclopedia. Because this list is very long, the index is usually found in a separate volume. The index is important because it lists *all* the articles on your subject, not just those under your subject's main entry.

Suppose you want to learn about black holes. You look in the *B* volume under *Black Hole* and learn that a black hole is a special area of outer space from which scientists believe that no light or matter of any kind can escape. If you check the index, you will find that information on black holes is listed under *Gravity* as well as *Black Hole.* Looking in the *G* volume for *Gravity*, you read about the stars that make black holes. You learn that stars take billions of years to die sometimes, and when they do they are called "white dwarf stars." Finally, some collapse in a few seconds, while some keep on collapsing because of gravity inside them. The second ones become "black holes."

Another important volume to check in addition to the index is the *yearbook.* Every encyclopedia has a yearbook to keep its information up-to-date. You will find a yearbook for each year after the encyclopedia was published.

Exercise 6: *Using the Encyclopedia*

On the following page you will find a list of subjects numbered 1-5 that you can explore with an encyclopedia. Choose the subject that interests you most, then look up the subject in the index of an encyclopedia. On a sheet of paper, list the name of each article on your subject that you find in the index. Then look up your subject under one of the listings in the encyclopedia. Write down three things you learn about your subject.

1. Rockets
2. The Taj Mahal
3. George Washington Carver
4. Archaeology
5. Money

Almanacs and Atlases

An *almanac* is a book of facts and figures about many different subjects.

An almanac gives information about people in history and famous people who are alive today. It also gives statistics about the world. In an almanac you can learn where to find the deepest place in the ocean and which airport is the busiest in the world. You can find out about climates, nations, and even disasters. Almanacs have up-to-date information on all their subjects because they are published every year. Unlike most encyclopedias, an almanac comes in one volume.

Almanacs arrange their information by subjects. To find what you are looking for, use the table of contents. Suppose you want to know how many home runs Hank Aaron hit in his career. In the table of contents under *Sports*, you will find where to look.

An *atlas* is a reference book of maps.

You would look in an atlas to find where the island of Bali is located or to find where the place you live is in relation to your state capital. An atlas also gives data about the cities, countries, and continents shown on its maps—data that includes information about population, natural resources, and industry.

There are world atlases that have maps of the whole world, and there are atlases for individual countries. You will also find special historical atlases that can show you how countries have changed.

Special Reference Books

Most libraries have what are known as *special reference books*. These include dictionaries like the *Dictionary of American Biography*, the *Dictionary of Computers, The Rhyming Dictionary, Roget's Thesaurus* (a dictionary of synonyms), and even a *Dictionary of Misinformation*.

Libraries also carry special encyclopedias. Check to see if your library has any of these titles: *The Encyclopedia of Baseball, The Encyclopedia of Animal Care, The Encyclopedia of Science Fiction and Fantasy, The New Space Encyclopedia,* and *The Encyclopedia of World Stamps*.

Some of these special reference books come in many volumes. One of these is the *Who's Who,* which gives biographical information about famous people and groups. Many libraries also have special books about people: *Who's Who in Science, Who's Who in Music, Who's Who in American Women,* and so on.

Exercise 7: Using Reference Works

The following is a list of ten subjects you can explore using the special reference books listed in the preceding section. On a sheet of paper, write which reference book you would use to find information on each subject.

1. Stamps of South Africa

2. Hank Aaron

3. *Star Trek*

4. Sarah Caldwell, the conductor

5. Computer games

6. Gerbils

7. The Beatles

8. A rhyme for *orange*

9. Space colonies

10. Will Rogers, the American humorist

27 Speaking and Listening Skills

Think about the many directions you hear daily. These are the "how to" messages that instruct you to do something. Your parent teaches you to answer the phone, "Hello. This is the Rodriguez residence. Ramon speaking." Your friend shares a sure-fire, three-step method for calming upset parents. These "how to" messages are aimed just at you. They are your way of learning new ideas.

You also give directions. For example, you tell the person cutting your hair how to cut it. Your little brother observes the "No Trespassing" sign on your bedroom door because you have clearly explained to him what will happen if he does not.

When you give directions, you are actually giving a speech. You have a purpose: to share information. You also have a topic: the directions. And you have an audience: the people who will respond to your directions. Whether you are "giving a talk" or "just talking," you must deal with *purpose*, *topic*, and *audience* effectively. This chapter will help you do so. You will begin by preparing a short speech.

Preparing a Short Speech

In order to prepare a short speech, you must first select an appropriate subject. You can then focus your speech and organize your material in the way that best develops your ideas.

Selecting a Subject

Most people do not have problems in "just talking" to friends with whom they share interests and topics for conversation. When these same people are asked to talk in front of an audience, however, their minds often go blank. "What can I talk about?" they ask.

Some useful guidelines will help you discover topics that you know about and that will interest your audience.

Pick Out a Subject That Interests You

Some speeches are uninteresting because the speaker is not really interested in the subject. To avoid this problem, choose a subject from your own experience or something that you have always wanted to know about. For example, you may be fascinated by puppetry but know little about it. A speech about this subject will give you a chance to learn about it.

Consider Your Audience's Interests

Almost any subject can be made interesting if the speaker thinks about the audience. What are the audience's interests? Ask yourself what your classmates would like to know or would find amusing about a subject. Then approach your subject from that point of view.

Exercise 1: Selecting a Subject

Divide a sheet of paper into the following three columns:

Labels	**Subjects**	**Personal Experiences**

Next, list all of the nouns, adjectives, and adverbs you can think of that describe you. Write those words in the Labels column. Under the Subjects heading, list any interesting subjects that relate to the labels. Finally, describe in a phrase any personal experience you have had involving each label. The Subjects and Personal Experiences columns are possible speech subjects as the example shows.

Labels	**Subjects**	**Personal Experiences**
1. Runner	The famous Olympic runner Carl Lewis	My first race
2. Female	Drafting of females into the military	Being the only female in a family of five children
3. Daring	*Guiness Book of World Records*— Most daring feats	Being dared to eat worms

Focusing Your Speech

Finding a subject is the first step in preparing a speech. Next, you must focus your speech. You do this by gathering information about your subject, by deciding the purpose of your speech, and by limiting your subject.

Taking Inventory

Finding out what you know and do not know about a topic is called *taking inventory*. If you have selected a personal experience for a subject, then you obviously know a great deal. If you have selected a subject such as *Plants have feelings*, however, you may think that you know very little, though actually you may know more than you realize.

Begin taking inventory by recalling bits and pieces of information you may have heard or seen. You can do this by yourself or with a group of people in a brainstorming session. Maybe you observe Leroy, a television character, singing to his plants in a situation comedy's opening scene. You also remember hearing someone say that plants should be given showers periodically. The lady down the street always talks about "sunning her plants" as if they were people.

These bits and pieces should help you to ask yourself questions about your subject such as the following:

What does singing do for a plant?

Do plants "talk" to their owners?

Do plants feel sad, happy, anxious like humans do?

Can plants "read" people's minds?

Can plants hear people talk?

How can you determine if plants have feelings?

Who started this idea in the first place?

You can also ask yourself the six basic questions about your subject: *who? what? why? when? where? how?* More information on the six basic questions is included in Chapter 1.

Exercise 2: *Taking Inventory*

By yourself or in a small group, brainstorm about one of the subjects following. Make a list of all of the bits and pieces of information you gather. Make a second list of inventory questions about the subject, using the six basic questions.

Body language	Air bags
Shoplifting	Sugarless gum
Amazon ants	Eye makeup
Acupuncture	Manners
Abbott and Costello	Cable TV
Dreams	Life in the year 2000

Deciding the Purpose of Your Speech

The second step of focusing your subject is deciding on the purpose of your speech. Do you want your listeners just to sit back and enjoy? Do you want them to change their beliefs about an idea? Maybe you want your listeners to learn something new. The purpose determines what information you will use and how you will present it. For example, if you want to talk about a serious topic such as cancer or fire prevention, you will probably not want the tone of your speech to be humorous.

Limiting Your Subject

Suppose you took a trip to Washington, D.C., with your family. While you were there, you stayed with friends and saw many sights: the White House, the Lincoln Memorial, the Capitol, and the Library of Congress. You also ate at a famous Japanese restaurant, went for a boat ride on the Potomac, saw a movie, and played sandlot baseball. In your social studies class your teacher asks you to talk for five minutes about your experience. Where do you begin? It is not possible to discuss a week's activities in five minutes, so you must limit your subject and talk about only certain parts of your trip. Because details make a speech interesting, it is better to cover a smaller amount of information in detail than to talk generally about a large subject. When you narrow your subject, you develop a speech *topic*.

Exercise 3: Developing a Topic

The following subjects are too broad for an interesting speech:

Music

Television

Sports

For *one* of the subjects on page 577, state three speech *topics*, each with a different purpose: one *to inform* (sharing new information with your audience); one *to persuade* (trying to get listeners to agree with you about an idea); and one *to entertain* (telling listeners ideas just for enjoyment).

The following example shows how to do this activity with the subject *Schools:*

To inform: To inform my audience about the use of television in the classroom

To persuade: To persuade my audience why it is important to finish school

To entertain: To entertain my audience with an insider's view of life in the back row

Organizing Your Material

Pretend for a minute that you have selected an interesting speech subject: *poltergeists,* which are noisy and mischievous ghosts. With the help of friends, family, and your local library, you have taken inventory. You have also decided that your purpose will be to inform your audience. And finally, you have limited the subject to defining poltergeists, describing what they do, and telling how to deal with them.

Too often, a beginning speaker stops preparing at this point and jumps into the middle of the speech instead of introducing the subject to the audience. Also, instead of concluding the talk, he or she just drops the subject. The result is that the speech does not have the effect the speaker had intended; the audience seems confused, unable to get the point.

You can avoid the risk of drowning in a speech by organizing a plan of action before you begin. Plan a beginning, a middle, and an end for what you say: an *introduction*, a *body*, and a *conclusion.*

Developing the Introduction

As you begin your speech, you must do two things. First, you must capture your audience's attention as you introduce your topic. Second, you prepare your audience for the rest of your speech. You can prepare an introduction in several different ways. For your first speech consider one of four different beginnings:

1. *Quotation.* Quoting what someone else has said is a good way to begin a speech. The following sample introduction shows how to use a quotation this way:

   A German observer once said that the world is not only stranger than we imagine, but that it is also stranger than we *can* imagine. You can tell this statement is true when you think about the strange world of poltergeists. *Poltergeist* is a German word for "noisy ghost." What these ghosts are, what they do, and what people must do to deal with them is quite interesting.

2. *Illustration.* Telling a vivid story is a second way to develop a good introduction:

   The Finleys were very happy about moving into the old house on Bellingham Road. With three bedrooms, it was their dream house. When they moved in, however, the dream became a nightmare. Pictures they put up turned 90 degrees on the wall. At night the children heard scratching under their beds and had their covers pulled off them. From time to time, the family could smell a funny, chemical odor. Furniture moved about and lightbulbs broke without warning. These unusual events are easily explained if you believe in *poltergeists.*

3. *Statement of topic.* Going directly to the point and defining your topic is the third way to start a speech:

   Everyone knows what ghosts are, but not everyone knows what *poltergeists* are. Actually a poltergeist is a mischievous, noisy ghost who can be found in anyone's house, that is, if you believe in ghosts. To understand this "ghost," let's take a closer look at what poltergeists are, what they do, and how to deal with them.

4. *Background information.* The final way for you to introduce your topic is by giving background information:

   The word *poltergeist* comes from German folklore. It means a noisy, mischievous spirit which likes to knock, bump, and throw objects. Poltergeists have been reported since A.D. 355. They also have many characteristics that I would like to explore in this speech.

Exercise 4: Developing an Introduction

Select a speech topic you have already used in this chapter or develop a new one. Use one of the preceding methods to form an introduction. Deliver just the introduction before your classmates. Keep this introduction for later use.

Developing the Body

In the body—the middle part of your speech—you give details about your topic. It is this segment that takes the most time. In the poltergeist speech, you would spend time giving information about what poltergeists are, what they do, and how to handle them.

In the body of a personal experience speech, you can develop your ideas as if you were planning a television show. Set the scene for your audience by introducing the characters, the time, and the place. Build the plot by explaining what happens to these characters. End this episode by explaining to your audience how the events affect the characters.

For an informative speech, you should break the subject down into its smaller units and explain each unit to your listeners. For example, you may want to inform your audience about the three branches of federal government, so in the body you give details about the judicial, the legislative, and the congressional branches. In this type of speech, you do not set scenes and develop action. In all speeches, however, you should include enough details and vivid examples to make the information come alive for your audience.

Exercise 5: Developing the Body

Select a speech topic based on a personal experience. Think of your experience as a half-hour television show. On a sheet of paper, answer the following questions about your story:

1. What is the time of the story?

2. What is the place of the story?

3. Who are the characters?

4. What are they like?

5. What happened in the story?

6. What events take place first, second, third, and so on?

7. How does each major character react to the events?

8. What is the point of the story?

9. What makes the story interesting?

10. How did the story make you feel?

Exercise 6: Developing the Body

Select one of the following topics. On a sheet of paper list the small units you would develop in the body of an informative speech.

1. Favorite hobbies
2. Types of magazines
3. Famous baseball teams
4. Types of Italian food
5. Types of school classes
6. Pet peeves
7. Uses for a coat hanger
8. Famous American heroes

Developing the Conclusion

The ending of your speech is like the final note of a song, letting listeners know that the speech or song is finished. Forgetting the final note leaves a listener hanging.

Like the introduction, the conclusion of a speech should be well planned. A speaker has to decide how to summarize the material and how to end the speech without just blurting out "That's all, folks!" The easiest way to do this is to return to your introduction and remind your listeners of your main ideas.

1. *Quotation.* Do not repeat the quotation word for word, but use its meaning to help you end your speech:

> There is no doubt that many people believe in poltergeists. These people study the behavior of poltergeists and write about their findings. I've tried to share some of those findings with you by explaining what poltergeists are, what they do, and how to deal with them. Now it's up to you to decide whether or not there are things in this world stranger than you can imagine.

2. *Illustration.* Reminding your listener of your illustration is a good way of tying up the loose ends of speech:

> After this speech you still may not believe in poltergeists. But the Finleys on Bellingham Road have no doubts. The tilted pictures, the strange smells, the moving furniture, and the broken light bulbs were enough to convince them.

3. *Statement of topic.* Restating the main point is the third way to end your speech:

> As I said in the beginning, poltergeists are those mischievous, noisy ghosts who can be found in anyone's home. Since you know a little bit more about what they

are, what they do, and how to deal with them, don't be afraid if you go home tonight and hear strange noises. At least you'll know what's causing them.

4. *Background information.* Retelling the background information you used in the introduction is the final way to end a speech:

The Germans invented the word "poltergeists," but they did not limit the activities of these noisy, mischievous ghosts to just Germany. These spirits, which date back to A.D. 355, are still with us today and will probably continue with a future of their own, that is, if you and I believe in them.

Exercise 7: *Developing a Conclusion*

For this activity use the introduction you prepared for Exercise 4 as a guide to prepare a conclusion on the same topic. In front of your classmates, deliver the introduction again. Then deliver the conclusion.

Delivering a Short Speech

When you write a composition, you let the words speak for you on paper. A speech, however, is quite different. How you give a speech is as important a part of your message as what you have to say.

Voice

What you do with your voice is one part of your message. You must speak loudly enough to be heard, and you cannot let your words fade out and die at the end of the sentences. Yet you cannot be so loud that your listeners think you are shouting at them. When you give your speech, have someone in the back row give you a signal if your voice is too loud or too soft.

A tired sounding or monotonous voice can ruin a speech. *Animation* means "bringing to life," as in *animated* cartoons. Sometimes a speaker's voice needs animation—life and liveliness. When you speak with friends, your voice is probably animated. Try to carry over that same voice quality in your speech.

Finally, ask yourself if your speaking voice is clear and distinct. Do you talk so quickly that sounds blend together? If a listener does not watch your lips, can he or she understand your words? Do you move your lips enough to let the words come out as they should sound, or do you sound as though your mouth is full of marbles?

Exercise 8: Animating Your Voice

Read the following sentences in the first column as if you were speaking to just one other person. Read the sentences in the second column loudly enough to be heard in an ordinary room and the sentences in the third column loudly enough to be heard in a large classroom. Some of the sentences are statements, some are questions, and some are exclamations. Your voice will have to show these meanings.

To One Person	To Six People	To Thirty People
Hush, baby, don't cry.	Be quiet now, all of you!	Don't anybody make any noise.
Do you see my book anywhere?	I think I've lost my book.	Did anybody here see the book I lost?
I think I'll do some housework.	Who messed up this room so badly?	Everybody is to clean his room today.
I'll help you work the problem, if you like.	Why don't we all do our math together right now?	Now class, this is how you work the problem.
I'd like to go swimming.	Does anybody want to go swimming?	Everybody in the pool!
Ann, isn't that chest like the one in your hall?	That chest is one of the prettiest things they've auctioned.	I bid fifteen dollars!
Have you planted any tulip bulbs yet?	I love tulips, don't you?	October is the time to plant tulips.[1]

[1]Hilda B. Fisher: *Improving Voice and Articulation,* 2nd edition, p. 118. Copyright © 1975 by Houghton Mifflin Company. Used by permission.

Exercise 9: Speaking Distinctly

Try saying some of the following tongue twisters quickly but clearly:

1. Rubber baby buggy bumpers beat no baby bumpers at all.

2. Theophilus Thistle, the thistle thruster, thrust three thousand thistles into the thick of his thumb.

3. He sawed six slick, slender, slim, sleek saplings.

4. A black back bath brush.

5. Imagine an imaginary menagerie manager imagining managing an imaginary menagerie.

6. Thomas Tattertoot took taut twine to tie ten twigs in two tall trees.

7. Mr. Shott and Mr. Nott agreed to fight a duel. Nott was shot and Shott was not, so it is better to be Shott than Nott. Shott shot the shot that shot Nott. If the shot that Shott shot which shot Nott had shot Shott and not Nott, Shott instead of Nott would have been shot and Nott would not.

Body Language

Your voice is one part of your message. The second part is what you do with body language.

Body language **is what you say with facial expression, gestures, posture, and eye contact.**

Too often, speakers think that they must smile in a speech, so they force a smile; that they must gesture, so they awkwardly raise an arm and point at the audience; and that they must look at their listeners, so they stare right through them.

As you may well guess, none of these unnatural attempts at body language will help your message. Natural, effective body language comes from the attempt to share an interesting topic with listeners.

Let your face show that you are interested. A blank expression will tell your listeners that you really do not care about what you are saying. If your face is deadpan when you tell of an exciting experience, your listeners will believe your facial expression before they believe your words.

The same is true of gestures and posture. If your gestures are mechanical and robot-like, they lose their effectiveness. If your posture is stiff or artificial, you will send a message you may not want to send. Try to relax. No one is asking you to be anything more than yourself in a speech. Stand up straight, but otherwise forget about putting movement into your speech. Do only what comes naturally.

An important part of body language is eye contact. Sometimes stage fright overcomes a speaker, and he or she forgets to look at the audience but stares off into space or hunches over notes. Looking at your audience helps in two ways. First, it lets you know whether your listeners understand what you say. By seeing how they respond, you can decide if you need to speed up, slow down, talk more loudly or softly, or explain an idea again. More importantly, looking at your listeners makes them feel that you are interested in them.

The only way to make your voice and body language natural is to practice the speech. The more comfortable you are with your speech, the more relaxed you will be when you deliver it in front of a group. The more relaxed you are, the more natural your voice and body will be. Practice will help to make the speech a conversation between one speaker and many listeners.

Exercise 10: Preparing a Speech

The following paragraphs describe three different speech assignments. Choose one of them and prepare a three- to five-minute speech to give to your classmates.

Option 1

Choose a personal experience topic you have already used in this chapter or make up a new one. Decide what you want to say about your experience. Tell your "story" as though it were the basis for a television show. Introduce the characters and set the scene. Build the plot. Explain how you and other people in your story react to the events.

Option 2

Create a fictional personal experience: your visit to another planet or what it is like to win an Olympic gold medal, for example. After planning what you want to say, tell this experience to your classmates.

Option 3

Choose a topic for an informative speech. Use pictures, diagrams, and props to help you remember what you want to say and to give your classmates something to view. For example, for the topic *puppetry,* bring in some puppets, show some pictures of different puppets, or use a diagram explaining the different types and uses of puppets.

Listening to a Short Speech

Scientists in the United States have been sending messages into outer space for several years, but they are still waiting for listeners to reply.

A speaker is often like these scientists. The listeners are somewhere in outer space, and the speaker does not know if the message has been received, let alone understood.

It takes two to make a speech work: a speaker who is prepared to talk and a listener who is prepared to hear. If the two are to communicate, the listener cannot be in "outer space." Following some simple suggestions can help you do your part as a listener.

Resist Distractions

A good listener will resist distractions and listen only to the speaker.

Anything that keeps you from hearing a speaker is a distraction —something that is happening in the room or within you. For example, you may pay attention to your classmate who is tapping a pencil against the desk. Or, you may be thinking about the compliment your teacher just gave you. In either case, you are tuning out the speaker.

Listen for Specifics

One way to focus your attention is to listen for specifics: identifying the information in a speech and observing how it is given. As you listen to a speech, ask the following questions about it:

What is the purpose of the speech?

What is the speaker's main idea?

What are the major points in the speech?

How does the speaker start the speech?

How does the speech end?

What examples does the speaker use?

What new words does the speaker use?

What facts does the speaker present?

What opinions does the speaker give?

Does the speaker use humor?

Is the topic a good choice for this audience?

Do the body language and voice support the meaning of the words?

If you can answer these questions, then you have listened for specifics.

Think While You Listen

Another way to focus on the speaker is to think while you listen. Since you can think faster than a person can speak, silently repeat the speaker's ideas. You may also want to take brief notes. You can jot down the answers to the questions you have asked to help you get the specifics.

React to What You Hear

You must let the speaker know what you think about the speech. This reaction is called *feedback*. It keeps you involved, and it lets the speaker know if the audience understands the speech. If you understand, nod your head. If you are confused, show that confusion by wrinkling your brow. Give feedback by using body language.

Exercise 11: Checking Your Listening

Choose a speech given by a classmate. Write your own short quiz about the information in the speech. Give the quiz to two of your classmates. Check your answers with the speaker.

Glossary of Terms

Accent The stress or emphasis placed on one syllable of a word to make that syllable sound louder than other syllables

Action words Words that tell what people and animals do

Adjectives Words that modify nouns and pronouns

Adverbs Words that modify verbs, adjectives, or other adverbs

Adverb connectors Adverbs used to connect sentences and to show that special relationships exist between the sentences

Apostrophe A punctuation mark (') used to show omission of letters and to show the possessive form of nouns

Autobiography A true story about the writer's life

Ballad An early story-poem

Biography A book about the life of a real person

Body That part of a composition that develops the topic

Brainstorm To let one's thoughts roam freely over a subject

Business letter Letter written to apply for a job, to place an order, to ask for information, or for other business reasons

Capitalization To write with an initial capital, or entirely in capitals

Coherent paragraph A paragraph in which the relationship between sentences is clear

Colon A punctuation mark (:) used to separate elements within a sentence or to call attention to a word, phrase, or list that follows it

Comma A punctuation mark (,) used to separate words or groups of words within a sentence

Composition A group of related paragraphs

Compound sentence A sentence that consists of two or more simple sentences joined by a conjunction

Compound subject of a sentence Two or more connected subjects that have the same verb

Conclusion A final paragraph that brings a composition to a close

Conjunctions Words that join words or groups of words

Connectors Words that join sentences and add meaning to them

Consonants Letters of the English alphabet other than the vowels

Context of a word The other words that surround a given word; a word's setting

Details Pieces of information used to describe something or to make a point about a topic

Dialogue A conversation between two or more people

Dictionary A book containing words listed in alphabetical order, with their pronunciations, meanings, and other information

Directions The how-to messages that instruct one to do something

Exclamation point A mark of punctuation (!) used after a sentence that shows excitement or a strong command

Fiction Stories or books with imaginary characters and events

Form A document with blanks for requested information

Formal outline A plan for writing a report, organizing material according to main and supporting ideas

Focusing a speech Gathering information about the subject, deciding the purpose of the speech, and limiting the subject

Friendly letter An informal letter to a friend, relative, or pen pal

Hyphen A punctuation mark (-) used to link two or more complete words in compound words or to link the syllables in a divided word

Incident A little story, usually about people, sometimes used to develop a paragraph

Informal outline A plan for arranging details

Instructions Step-by-step directions

Interjections Words that show a strong or sudden feeling

Introduction That part of a composition that names the topic and says something interesting about it

Letter to the editor A letter expressing one's opinion in a school or community newspaper

Main entry word Each word listed in a dictionary

Main idea of a paragraph The idea that holds the paragraph together

Meter The regular pattern of sounds in a poem

589

Modifiers Words that limit or describe other words

Nonfiction Books about real characters and events

Noun The name of a person, place, thing, or idea

Paragraph A group of sentences that develop or explain an idea or topic

Pen pal A friend made through letters

Period A punctuation mark (.) used after a declarative sentence or an abbreviation

Periodical A magazine or journal that is published at regular intervals

Point of view A way of looking at someone or something

Postcard A card the post office accepts without an envelope and for less postage than a regular letter

Predicate of a sentence That part of a sentence that says something about the subject of the sentence

Prefix A group of letters added to the beginning of a word to expand the root word's meaning

Prepositions Words that show the relationship between a noun and a pronoun and some other word in the sentence

Pronouns Words that take the place of nouns or other pronouns

Proofreading Checking for errors in capitalization, spelling, punctuation, and grammar

Question mark A punctuation mark (?) used after a sentence that asks a question

Quotation marks Marks of punctuation (" ") used to enclose or set off words that belong together

Regional dialect A way of speaking shared by people in a certain part of the country

Report A composition giving information about a subject

Revise To make changes in a piece of writing for the purpose of improving it

Rhyme The repetition of end sounds

Rhythm Sounds repeated in a regular pattern

Run-on sentence Two or more sentences separated by a comma or not separated by any punctuation

Salutation Greeting

Semicolon A mark of punctuation (;) stronger than a comma, but weaker than a period

Sense details Details about the five senses: sight, hearing, touch, taste, and smell

Sentence A group of words that express a complete thought

Sentence fragment A separated part of a sentence that does not express a complete thought

Simple sentence A sentence that has only one subject and one verb

Six basic questions The information-gathering questions: *who? what? where? when? why?* and *how?*

Slang Very informal words used most often among people who know one another well

Social letters A letter to extend or to respond to an invitation or to thank someone for a gift or for hospitality

Standard English The dialect of English most accepted by schools and businesses

Subject of a sentence A word (or words) that identifies the person, place, thing, or idea that is being spoken about in the sentence

Subordinators Connecting words that join sentences that are not of equal importance

Suffix A group of letters added to the end of a word to expand the root word's meaning

Supporting idea An idea that tells something about the main idea

Syllable One unit of language, spoken in one breath, that contains a vowel sound

Synonyms Words that have almost the same meaning

Tall tales Stories that are exaggerated and humorous

Tense The time expressed by a verb

Topic A limited subject

Topic sentence A sentence that gives the main idea or topic of a paragraph

Transition words Words that show relationships between sentences

Unified paragraph A paragraph in which each sentence explains or develops the topic

Verb A word that shows action or state of being

Vivid details Details that help readers see, feel, hear, taste, or smell what is described

Vowel sounds *a, e, i, o, u* and sometimes *y*

Writer's Notebook A record of a writer's thoughts and feelings

Index of Authors
and Titles

Index

Like, using to make connections, 176

Linking verbs, 312–313
  bad following, 391–392
  good following, 393–394
  predicate adjectives following, 456
  predicate noun or pronoun following, 456

Listening
  for directions, 574
  to speech, 586–587

Logical order, 79–84
  in composition, 103

-ly, adverbs formed with, 384–385, 399–400

M

Magazines, finding information in, 554–555

Main entry
  definition, 560
  using for pronunciation, 563–565
  using for definitions, 566
  using for synonyms, 569

Main entry words
  using to learn syllables, 561–562
  using for spelling, 561

Main headings for report, 133–135

Main idea
  for report, 105–107, 134–135

Manners, 214

Masculine pronouns, 293–294

Mental action, verbs showing, 311

"Mental bridges," 174–177

Messages
  writing, 116–119

Meter in poetry, 178–180

Middle English, 532–533

Mild interjections, 438, 440, 476–477

Modern English, 534–535

Modifiers
  adjectives as, 348
  adverbs as, 376, 391
  definition, 112
  demonstrative pronouns as, 290
  -ing forms as, 144–145
  inserting, 112–113
  possessives as, 237
  prepositional phrases, 411–412

More and *most*, using
  with adjectives, 364–366
  with adverbs, 381–382, 387

N

Names
  abbreviations, 502
  capitalizing, 498, 500–503
  geographical, 476
  of pets, capitalizing, 500
  of political parties, 502
  of products, 503
  regional, 502

Negative adverbs, 378–381, 398–399

Negatives, double, avoiding, 398–399

Neuter pronouns, 293–294

Nonfiction
  definition, 542
  finding in library, 543–547

Normans, 532

Not, use of, 379–380

Note cards, 130

Notes
  taking for report, 130
  taking while listening to speech, 587

Nouns, 258–281
  of address, 476–477
  adjectives modifying, 348–356
  collective, 337
  common, 259, 351–353
  compound, plurals, 308–310, 269–271
  definition, 258–259
  determiners before, 261
  features of, 261–263
  formed with suffixes, 262
  grouping by classes, 259–261
  plurals, 261–262, 264–271, 486
  possessive forms, 271–272, 485
  predicate, 456
  proper, 259, 273–279, 498
  singular, 261–262, 486–487
  use of, 264–281

O

Object
  direct, 455
  indirect, 461
  of preposition, 407
  of preposition, compound, 410–411

Object forms of pronouns, 293, 414–415

Old English, 531

Of, using correctly, 418

Off, using correctly, 418

Omission, showing, 471

On, using correctly, 418

On, onto, 416

Opinions, writing to explain, 124–126

Order
  alphabetical, 558–559
  chronological, 81–83
  logical, 79–84
  spatial, 83–85
  steps in a process, 80

use in reporting other people's ideas and information, 130

uses of, 491–492

Quotations in speech, 579, 581

R

Reacting to what you hear, 587

Readers' Guide to Periodical Literature, 554–55

Real, really, 395

Reference area, library, 554–557

Reference books, 558–573

almanacs and atlases, 572

encyclopedias, 570–572

Readers' Guide, 554–555

special, 573

Regional dialect, 538–539

Regional names, capitalizing, 502

Reports

coherent, 138

formal outline for, 134–135

gathering information for, 129

main headings for, 134–135

main and supporting ideas, 134–135

organizing information for, 131–133

revising, 141

topic, deciding on, 127

unified, 138

writing, 126–138

Resources for writing, 542–573

Revising, 18–22

checklist for, 22, 87, 111, 141, 163

composition, 111

definition, 18

paragraphs, 87

report, 141

Rhyme, 172–173

Rhythm

in poetry, 178–180

Rise, raise, 342–344

Root words, 513–514

prefixes added to, 513–516, 525

suffixes added to, 513–516, 525–529

Run-on sentences, avoiding, 463–465

S

Salutation

of business letters, 228–229

of social letters, 214, 217

Scandinavian words in English, 531–532

Schwa, 564

Second person pronouns, 285

Secondary accent, 565

-self or *-selves* with personal pronouns, 286

Semicolon

as sentence connector, 64–65, 465, 433

uses of, 480–481

Sense details, using in writing, 34–37, 48–50, 180–182

Sentence combining. *See* Sentence variety.

Sentence fragment, 444

avoiding, 462–463

Sentence outline, 105

Sentence variety

inserting sentences, 112–115, 142–145, 164–169, 195–199, 209–213, 237–241, 252–256

joining sentences, 25–29, 42–47, 64–69, 88–93

Sentences, 444–468

adding in a series, 88–91

capitalizing first word, 498

compound, 453–454

compound subjects, 451–452

conjunctions joining, 453

coordinating conjunctions joining, 429

declarative, 445

definition, 444

end marks with, 471–473

exclamatory, 446

imperative, 445

inserting. *See* Sentence variety.

interrogative, 446

interrupting elements, 476–478

joining. *See* Sentence variety.

patterns, 454–461

predicate, 447, 448–450

run-on, avoiding, 463–465

separated by period, 470

simple, 453–454

subject, 447

topic, 74–75

unequal in meaning, joining, 91–93

Setting

in stories, 185–187

Sexism in language, 537

Shall, 328

Shall have/will have, forming future perfect tense, 328

Sight details, using, 34

Signature

of business letters, 228–229

of social letters, 214, 217

Simple predicate, 449

Simple sentences, 453–454

Simple subject, 447

Simple tenses, 315–317

of irregular verbs, 324–327

progressive form, 317, 329

using, 320–322

Simplified spelling, 564

Singular

antecedents and pronouns, agreement, 297–301

of demonstrative pronouns, 289

T

Taking inventory, 576
Taking notes
  for report, 130
  while listening to speech, 587
Talk. *See* Speech.
Tall tale, 189–192
Taste details, using, 35
Tenses of verb
  future, 315–317, 321–322, 327, 329
  future perfect, 315–317, 323–324, 328, 330
  of irregular verbs, 324–328
  past, 315–317, 321–322, 324–327, 329
  past perfect, 315–317, 323–324, 327, 330
  perfect, 315–317, 322–324
  present, 315–317, 320–322, 324–326, 329
  present perfect, 315–317, 322–324, 327, 330
  simple, 315–317, 320–322
Thank-you letter
  information in, 219
There beginning sentence, subject/verb agreement with, 335
Thesaurus, 573
Thesis sentence, 106, 128
Thinking while listening, 587
Third person pronouns, 285
Thoughts
  sharing with readers, 59–61
  writing about, 59–61
Time, expressions of, colon in, 482
Title card, 549
Titles
  abbreviations, capitalizing, 500
  capitalizing, 499–500
  italicized, 488

of persons, in business letters, 229
of persons, capitalizing, 499–500
of persons, period after, 473
quotation marks enclosing, 491–492
underlining, 488–491
To, using correctly, 418
Topic
  distinguishing from subject, 98–99
  of paragraph, 70
  for report, deciding on, 127
  for speech, 574–578
  of speech, stating, 579, 581–582
  for writing, developing, 98–103
Topic outline, 105, 135
Topic sentence, 74–75
Touch details, using, 34
Transition words, 85, 122

U

Underlining, 488–491
Understood subject, 450–451
Unified composition, 107
Unified report, 138
Unity, meaning of, 79, 107

V

Verb phrases, 316
  compound, 452
  not modifying, 379–380
Verbs, 310–347
  action, 311–312
  adverbs modifying, 376
  agreement with subject, 331–332, 333–338
  compound, 452
  definition, 310–311
  features of, 315–320

formed with suffixes, 318
grouping by classes, 311–314
helping, 311, 313–314
irregular, 324–328
linking, 311–313
often confused, 338–344
plural, 318, 331–338
principal parts, 315, 324–326
progressive form, 317, 329–331
singular, 318
tenses, 315–317, 320–328
well modifying, 393–394
Vikings, 531
Vocabulary, 508–520
  special, 519–520
Voice, speaking, 582–584
Vowels, definition, 521

W

Well, good, 393–394
Will, 328
Words
  action, 55–56
  borrowed, 531–535
  choosing the best, 516–518
  compound, 260
  context, 509–512
  dividing at end of line, 483
  entries in dictionary, 558–561
  guide, 559
  hyphenated, 483–484
  interrupting, 476–477
  looking up in dictionary, 558–560
  main entry, 560–566
  meanings, 510–512
  new, making, 513–515
  often confused, 522
  parts of speech, 567–568
  rhyming, 172–173
  rhythm of, 178–180

root, 513–514
in series, comma separating,
    433, 475
showing family relationship,
    498
sounds of, 171–174
special vocabulary, 519–520
structure, 513–516
synonyms, 517–518, 569
transition, 85, 122
Writer's Notebook
    definition, 30
    as source of details, 31–37
    as source of ideas, 30
    as source of writing subjects,
        37, 96–97
    using to record experiences,
        31–34
    writing for readers, 30, 37
Writing
    about action, 55–58
    bibliography, 138–140
    business letters, 214, 227–236
    composition, 94–110
    dialogue, 187–189
    directions, 120–121
    developing a topic for, 98–103
    discovering subjects for, 37,
        96–97
    about events, 59–63
    to explain an opinion, 124–126
    explanations, 116
    about feelings, 37–40
    finding ideas for, 6–10, 96–97
    formal outline, 134–135
    friendly letters, 200–213
    gathering information for,
        11–15
    about ideas, 116–145
    letters, 200–208
    messages, 116–119
    paragraphs, 70–87
    about people, 51–55
    persuasively, 146–163
    about places, 48–50

point of view in, 16–18, 99,
    103
poems, 170–185
postcards, 206–207
process of. *See* Writing proc-
    ess.
about a process, 121–122
purpose, 13–16
reports, 126–141
resources for, 542–573
revising, 18–22, 87, 111, 141,
    163
social letters, 214–227
stories, 59–63, 185–194
about thoughts, 59–61
using details, 31–37, 48–55,
    202–203
with variety, 25–26
Writing process, 2–29
    prewriting, 4, 5, 6–18, 100–101
    postwriting, 4, 6, 18–24
    writing, 4, 5, 30–41, 48–63,
        70–87, 94–111, 116–141,
        146–163, 170–194, 200–208,
        214–236, 242–251

Y

Yearbook for encyclopedias, 571
You, understood, 450–451

Skills Index

Writing

About Ideas

directions, 120–121
messages, 116–119
opinions, 124–126
step-by-step instructions, 121–124

Compositions

definition and features, 94–96
developing topics. 98–100
discovering subjects, 96–98
gathering information, 100–101
introduction, body, conclusion, 106–110
organizing, outlining, 103–106
planning, 102–103

Forms

bicycle registration, 244–246
emergency health cards, 246–248
orders, 242–244

Friendly Letters

letters to a pen pal, 204–205
postcards, 206–207
readers, 200–203

From Experience

writing about action, 55–58
writing about events, 59–62
writing about people, 51–55
writing about places, 48–50

Paragraphs

coherent paragraphs, 79–85
definition and features, 70–73
developing the main idea, 73–74

developing with incidents, 76–77
topic sentence, 74–75

Poems and Stories

description in poems, 180–182
dialogue in stories, 187–189
metaphor and simile, 174–177
rhyme, 171–173
rhythm, 178–180
tall tales, 189–192

Prewriting Techniques

asking questions, 11–16
brainstorming, 6–8
changing points of view, 16–18
making connections, 8–9
using personal experience, 9–11

Reports

making formal outlines, 134–135
gathering information, 129
organizing information, 131–133
purposes and topics, 126–127

Social and Business Letters

form, 214–217, 227–232
invitations, 224–226
order letters, 235–236
proofreading, 221, 234
responses to invitations, 226–227
thank-you letters, 219–220

Writer's Notebook

writing about feelings, 37–39
recording experiences, 31–34
using sense details, 34–37

Grammar and Usage

Adjectives

comparative forms, 362–369
definition, features, and classes, 348–362
forming with suffixes, 369–370

Adverbs

definition, features, and classes, 376–387
forming, 399–400
using, 387–391

Conjunctions

definition and classes, 426–432
replacing with punctuation, 432–434
using too many, 435–436

Interjections

understanding, 438–440
using, 440–441

Nouns

definition, features, and classes, 258–263
capitalizing, 273–276
forming plurals, 264–271
forming possessives, 271–272

Prepositions

definition and types, 406–408
troublesome, 415–417
using, with object forms of pronouns, 414–415

Pronouns

agreement problems, 297–303

Checklist for Proofreading

1. Each sentence begins with a capital letter.

2. Each sentence ends with a period, question mark, or exclamation point.

3. Each word is spelled correctly.

4. All proper nouns and adjectives are capitalized.

5. Word endings such as *-s, -ing,* and *-ed* are not omitted.

6. A singular verb is used with each singular subject and a plural verb with each plural subject.

7. The standard form of pronouns is used.

8. The paper is neat.

Checklist for Revision

1. Does my writing have a clear focus?

2. Do I need to add more details?

3. Is my writing organized in a way that makes sense?

4. Are there any unnecessary parts I should leave out?

5. Is my writing style appropriate for my purpose and audience?

6. Are my sentences clear and complete?

7. Could I improve my choice of words?

Acknowledgments

Design and Production, Ligature, Inc.

Photo Credits 213, Animals Animals/Miriam Austerman; 16, ©
BEELDHECHT, Amsterdam/VAGA, New York. Collection Haags
Gemeentemuseum—The Hague, 1981; 49, Culver Pictures Inc.; 442, 443,
John L. Dengler, 1972 Scholastic/Kodak Photography Awards; 52, 84, 102,
105, 232, 257, 437, 469, Gregg Eisman; 196, Steven E. Gross; 30, 70, 94,
113, 116, 122, 131, 132, 136, 146, 148, 152, 156, 161, 170, 176, 185, 200,
214, 215, 220, 229, 236, 242, 246, Thomas Hooke Photography; 36, V. Lee
Hunter; 71, 101, Brent Jones; 14, Karsh, Ottawa, Courtesy of Woodfin
Camp; 71, Steven Kiecker; 1, 2, 3, 5, 12, 18, 26, 33, 35, 39, 44, 46, 47, 51, 55,
58, 62, 63, 66, 69, 72, 77, 89, 98, 109, 115, 119, 126, 128, 140, 151, 154,
157, 163, 165, 171, 172, 186, 189, 194, 199, 201, 202, 205, 206, 215, 223,
224, 237, 239, 241, 243, 249, 250, 253, 255, 281, 309, 347, 375, 425, 468,
Jean-Claude Lejeune; 29, 48, 49, 61, 65, 139, 160, 166, 171, 180, 182, 197,
218, 497, Vito Palmisano; 6, 31, 43, 74, 81, 90, 97, 147, 157, 168, 177, 254,
281, 374, 497, Bruce Powell; 117, D. Shigley; 82, Frank Siteman, The Marilyn
Gartman Agency; 10, 54, 78, 143, 174, 186, 193, 405, 506, 507, Arthur
Tress; 95, UPI; 95, 117, Jim Whitmer; 153, Lee Youngblood.